Year by Year & Day by Day with
the Minnesota Twins Since 1961

❖❖❖

Twins JOURNAL

❖❖❖

JOHN SNYDER

Copyright © 2010 by John Snyder

All rights reserved. No portion of this book may be reproduced in any fashion, print, facsimile, or electronic, or by any method yet to be developed, without express permission of the copyright holder.

For further information, contact the publisher at:

Clerisy Press
PO Box 8874
Cincinnati, OH 45208-0874

www.clerisypress.com

Library of Congress Cataloging-in-Publication Data

Snyder, John, 1951-
    Twins journal : year by year & day by day with the Minnesota Twins since 1961 /
      by John Snyder.
      p. cm.
    ISBN-13: 978-1-57860-380-0
    ISBN-10: 1-57860-380-3
    1. Minnesota Twins (Baseball team)--History. I. Title.

GV875.M55S69 2010
796.332'6409776579--dc22

2010002804

Distributed by Publishers Group West
Edited by Jack Heffron
Cover designed by Steven Sullivan and Scott McGrew
Interior designed by Mary Barnes Clark

Cover photo by AP Photo/Elise Amendola

Back cover photos of Rod Carew and Kirby Puckett courtesy of the *St. Paul Pioneer Press*.
    Back cover photo of Justin Morneau courtesy of WikiCommons.

St. Paul Pioneer *Press:* 20, 28, 34, 47, 49, 68, 74, 84, 104, 170, 188, 198, 220, 231, 248,
    256, 279

Topps: 50, 57, 77, 120, 129, 140, 148, 244, 261

WikiCommons: 286, 297, 303, 317, 327, 332, 340

About the Author

John Snyder has a master's degree in history from the University of Cincinnati and a passion for baseball. He has authored fifteen books on baseball, soccer, hockey, tennis, football, basketball, and travel and lives in Cincinnati.

❖ ❖ ❖

Acknowledgments

This book is part of a series that takes a look at Major League Baseball teams. The first was *Redleg Journal: Year by Year and Day by Day with the Cincinnati Reds Since 1866*, the winner of the 2001 Baseball Research Award issued by *The Sporting News* and SABR. That work was followed by *Cubs Journal: Year by Year and Day by Day with the Chicago Cubs Since 1876*, *Red Sox Journal: Year by Year and Day by Day with the Boston Red Sox Since 1901*, *Cardinals Journal: Year by Year and Day by Day with the St. Louis Cardinals since 1882*, *Indians Journal: Year by Year and Day by Day with the Cleveland Indians Since 1901*, *Dodgers Journal: Year by Year and Day by Day with the Brooklyn and Los Angeles Dodgers Since 1884*, *White Sox Journal: Year by Year and Day by Day with the Chicago White Sox Since 1901*, and *Angels Journal: Year by Year and Day by Day with the California Angels Since 1961*. Each of these books is filled with little-known items that have never been published in book form.

Greg Rhodes was my co-author on *Redleg Journal*, in addition to publishing the book under his company's name Road West Publishing. While Greg did not actively participate in the books about the Cubs, Red Sox, Cardinals, Indians, Dodgers, White Sox, Twins, or Angels he deserves considerable credit for the success of these books because they benefited from many of the creative concepts he initiated in *Redleg Journal*.

The idea for turning *Redleg Journal* into a series of books goes to Richard Hunt, president and publisher of Emmis Books and its successor company Clerisy Press, and editorial director Jeff Heffron.

Very special thanks to the *St. Paul Pioneer Press*—especially Thom Fladung, Debra Nygren, and Neal Lambert—for their support of *Twins Journal* through sending many wonderful photos.

And finally, although they should be first, thanks to my wife, Judy, and sons Derek and Kevin, whose encouragement and support helped me through another book.

Contents

Minnesota Twins Day by Day

Introduction: When Does Time Begin?. 6

1961–1969 10

1970–1979 81

1980–1989. 145

1990–1999. 207

2000–2009 270

❖ ❖ ❖

m Day by Day

When Does Time Begin?
Senators, Millers, Saints and Twins

The Twins have played in Minnesota since the start of the 1961 season, but the franchise dates to 1901. For 60 seasons it was located in Washington and was known as the Senators. From 1902 through 1960, the Twin Cities had two teams, the Minneapolis Millers and the St. Paul Saints, in the American Association, which was one of the top minor leagues in baseball. Minneapolis and St. Paul were also entities in the circuit that would eventually become the American League.

The creation of the American League is due to the vision, energy and perseverance of Cincinnati sportswriter Ban Johnson. The league had its genesis in November 1893 when a new minor league called the Western League was formed with franchises in Grand Rapids, Sioux City (Iowa), Minneapolis, Milwaukee, Kansas City, Toledo, Indianapolis and Detroit. St. Paul joined the league, replacing Sioux City, in 1895. The St. Paul club was owned by Charlie Comiskey, who later owned the Chicago White Sox from 1900 until his death in 1932. Johnson headed the Western League as president, treasurer and secretary.

At the time, the National League was baseball's only major league. It had prior competition from the American Association, which existed from 1882 through 1891, the Union Association in 1884, and the Players League, which lasted only the 1890 season. The National League from 1892 through 1899 was a 12-team organization with clubs in Baltimore, Boston, Brooklyn, Chicago, Cincinnati, Cleveland, Louisville, New York, Philadelphia, Pittsburgh, St. Louis and Washington.

Like many monopolies, the National League had grown arrogant during the 1890s. Tight controls on the players were common, including a maximum salary of $2,400. Competitive balance was almost non-existent. Meanwhile, Johnson's Western League had grown stronger each year as the top circuit in the minor leagues. Johnson wanted to jettison the smaller cities in the organization, place clubs in the larger Eastern and Midwestern metropolises, and create a second major league.

The National League reduced its roster from 12 to eight in March 1900 by dropping clubs in Baltimore, Cleveland, Louisville and Washington. This gave Johnson the room to achieve his aspirations. Within days after the contraction of the National League, Johnson changed the name of his organization to the American League. Teams in Grand Rapids, St. Paul and Toledo were replaced by new ones in Chicago, Cleveland and Buffalo. Many players were without jobs because of the reduction of four clubs in the National League and cast their lot with the American League.

Although the American League in 1900 was still confined to the Midwest and Great Lakes area and was still considered a minor league, Johnson had plans to expand to the Eastern Seaboard. Shortly after the 1900 season ended, Johnson announced plans for his American League to become a second major league to compete with the Nationals. The franchises in Minneapolis, Kansas City, Buffalo, and Indianapolis were eliminated in favor of those in the larger Eastern cities of Baltimore, Boston, Philadelphia and Washington. Johnson wrote a letter in late-October to NL president Nick Young seeking peace and an arrangement in which each league would respect the contracts of the other, which would prevent player raids and escalating salaries. The National League immediately rejected the plan. The league had vanquished all previous opposition and had no doubt that the American League would soon follow into oblivion.

Johnson retaliated by announcing that his new American League would attempt to sign the top players away from the NL. They certainly found a receptive audience. Players were not only saddled with a maximum salary of $2,400, they had to pay for their uniforms and other basic amenities.

Peace was brokered in January 1903, when the two leagues agreed to refrain from raiding one another's rosters. In addition, the Milwaukee franchise in the American League moved to St. Louis in 1902 and the Baltimore club was transferred to New York, where it would soon be nicknamed the Yankees.

The new Washington Senators club of the American League was usually at or near the bottom of the standings. From 1901 through 1911, the Senators never finished higher than sixth in an eight-team league. The team bottomed out in 1904 with a record of 38–113. About the only bright spot during the decade was the arrival of pitcher Walter Johnson in 1907. Through 1927, Johnson would win 417 games for the club, the second highest figure in major league history.

Meanwhile, professional baseball was re-established in the Twin Cities with the creation of the American Association in 1902 as a minor league circuit in the largest Midwestern cities not already a part of the National and American Leagues. There were franchises in Minneapolis, St. Paul, Columbus, Indianapolis, Kansas City, Louisville, Milwaukee and Toledo. With the exception of two seasons (1914–15) when the Toledo club moved to Cleveland, the league fielded teams in those eight cities every season through 1951.

The Minneapolis club, nicknamed the Millers, played at Nicollet Park on Nicollet Avenue at 31st Street. The Saints operated out of Lexington Park on Lexington Parkway at University Avenue. The Saints won the American Association pennant in 1902 and 1903. Minneapolis finished first in 1910, 1911, 1912 and 1915. The two clubs quickly formed an intense rivalry that began during the 1890s when both cities fielded teams in the Western League.

The Washington Senators franchise began to improve after the 1911 season beginning with the arrival of Clark Griffith as owner and manager. The Griffith family would continue to own the Senators and Twins until 1984. Griffith was one of the top pitchers in baseball during the 1890s and early 1900s, with a career record of 237–146. He played for the Chicago Cubs from 1893 through 1900. When the American League began luring players away from the National League, Griffith was one of those who jumped. In 1901, he not only managed the Chicago White Sox to the American League pennant he won 24 games on the mound. He was also the first manager of the New York Yankees, then called the Highlanders, in 1903, a job he held until 1908. Griffith then managed the Cincinnati Reds from 1909 through 1911.

The Senators finished in seventh place with a record of 64–90 in 1911. In his first season, Griffith took them to second place with a 91–61 mark in 1912. Another second-place finish followed in 1913, but Washington fell to third in 1914, fourth in 1915 and seventh in 1916. Griffith stepped down as manager following the 1920 season but remained the club president. The ballpark in Washington was named Griffith Stadium in his honor.

Back in the Twin Cities, the St. Paul Saints won American Association pennants in 1919, 1920, 1922 and 1924. The 1920 club had a record of 115–49.

In a surprising move, the Senators hired 27-year-old second baseman Bucky Harris as player-manager in 1924. In his first season at the helm, Harris won Washington's first American League pennant, then beat the New York Giants in a thrilling seven-game World Series. The players on the team included Walter Johnson, who was 23–7 at the age of 36, and future Hall of Fame outfielders Goose Goslin and Sam Rice. The Senators won the AL title again in 1925. After winning three of the first four games in the World Series against the Pittsburgh Pirates, the Senators lost three in a row. The 1924 world championship would prove to be the last one for the franchise until the Twins won it all in 1987.

Harris was fired as manager of the Senators following the 1928 season, and Johnson managed the club from 1929 though 1932. Johnson's clubs won 94 games in 1930, 92 in 1931 and 93 in 1932, but he was fired because he couldn't win the pennant. Griffith turned again to another young infielder as player-manager by hiring 26-year-old shortstop Joe Cronin. In his first season in 1933, Cronin won the AL championship with a record of 99–53 but lost the World Series to the Giants in five games. After the season ended, Cronin married Griffith's adopted daughter, Mildred Robertson. But after a seventh place finish in 1934 with a record of 66–86, Cronin was sold to the Red Sox for $225,000. Over the remainder of the 1930s, the Senators posted only one winning season, an 82–71 ledger in 1936, under Harris, who returned for a second term as manager that lasted from 1935 through 1942.

The 1933 season was an historic one in Minneapolis as outfielder Joe Hauser clouted 69 home runs. A left-handed hitter, Hauser was helped immensely by the cozy dimensions of Nicollet Park, which featured a 280-foot right-field foul line. The wall in the right power alley was a chummy 328 feet. Of his 69 home runs, Hauser hit 50 at the Minneapolis ballpark. Hauser was also on the club in 1932 and 1935 when the Millers won the American Association pennant. The Saints captured the AA title in 1931 and 1938.

Changes took place in the minor leagues during the 1930s when major league clubs began establishing farm systems. Until then, minor league clubs operated independently and sold players to the majors. In 1935, the Millers became a farm club of the Indians and the Saints were aligned with the White Sox. In 1937, the Millers switched ties from the Indians to the Red Sox. In 1938, Ted Williams played for the Millers and hit .366 with 43 homers and 142 RBIs. He was promoted to the Red Sox in 1939.

The Senators continued to field losing clubs throughout most of the 1940s. It was only in the final war year of 1945 that the club competed for a pennant. Under Ossie Bluege, Washington finished second, only 1 1/2 games behind the Tigers. By 1949, the Senators sank to last place with a record of 50–104 and crowds at Griffith Stadium dwindled.

There were no American Association pennants flying over Minneapolis during the 1940s. In 1946, the franchise became a farm club of the New York Giants, an arrangement that lasted until 1957. In 1951, Minneapolis fans had the privilege of watching Willie Mays for a brief time. He hit .477 in 35 games for the Millers before being called up by the Giants. Minneapolis won the AA pennant in 1955. The Millers were a farm club of the Red Sox from 1958 through 1960. The 1960 club included Carl Yastrzemski, who would replace Williams as the Red Sox left fielder a year later. Yastrzemski batted .339 for the Millers.

The Saints became a farm club of the Dodgers in 1946. In 1948, St. Paul finished third but won a four-team postseason playoff. Roy Campanella played 35 games for the Saints that year on his way to the big leagues. He was the first African-American player in the American Association. In 1949, the Saints won the regular-season pennant but lost in the playoffs. The Saints were affiliated with the Dodgers until 1960.

Bucky Harris started his third stint as manager of the Senators in 1950. The club improved to 78–76 in 1952 and 76–78 in 1953 but went into a rapid decline. Harris was fired after a 66–88 season in 1954. Under Chuck Dressen, Washington was 53–101 in 1955 and drew only 425,238 fans into Griffith Stadium.

Clark Griffith died at the age of 87 on October 27, 1955. Control of the club passed to Calvin Griffith, his nephew and adopted son who was 45. Clark adopted Calvin, the son of his wife's brother, at the age of 11 after Calvin's father passed away.

Calvin took over the Senators at a time of enormous change in baseball. In 1953, the Boston Braves moved to Milwaukee. It was the first shift of a major league franchise from one city to another since 1903. The Braves were a tremendous success in Wisconsin. After drawing just 281,278 fans in Boston in 1952, the club attracted 1,826,397 in 1953 in Milwaukee. Many in Minnesota adopted the Braves and traveled hundreds of miles to witness major league baseball. In 1954, the St. Louis Browns moved to Baltimore and were renamed the Orioles. In 1955, the Philadelphia Athletics moved to Kansas City.

The Twin Cities wanted a major league franchise of their own and in order to attract a team, Minneapolis and St. Paul joined forces to build Metropolitan Stadium in suburban Bloomington. It opened on April 24, 1956, with a capacity of 18,200 as the home of the Minneapolis Millers. A year later, the Saints abandoned Lexington Park and opened Midway Stadium at 1000 North Snelling Avenue in St. Paul.

Griffith wanted to move the Senators out of Washington, and in 1956 targeted Minneapolis-St.Paul, Los Angeles, San Francisco and Louisville as possibilities. But fellow American League owners were hesitant to allow the Senators out of Washington for fear that Congress would retaliate by passing legislation adverse to baseball. In addition, Griffith's minority stockholders, who held 40 percent of the franchise, threatened legal action if he should move. The federal government also promised the Senators a new stadium.

The New York Giants appeared to be the logical choice for a move to the Twin Cities. Attendance was declining at the Polo Grounds, which was built in 1911, and club owner Horace Stoneham was frustrated over the refusal of New York officials to build him a new stadium. Brooklyn Dodgers owners Walter O'Malley had similar problems at aging Ebbets Field and desired a move to Los Angeles after city and state politicians rebuffed his desire to build a new ballpark in downtown Brooklyn. O'Malley persuaded Stoneham to follow him to California. After the end of the 1957 season, the Dodgers moved to Los Angeles and the Giants to San Francisco.

This left New York without a National League club for the first time since 1882. New York attorney William Shea headed a committee to attempt to convince the NL to move another team to New York, or to expand to ten clubs with New York as one of the two new franchises. Shea's efforts failed.

Shea responded by establishing the Continental League in May 1959 with the idea of making it a third major league. Branch Rickey was named as president. Franchises in the Continental League were to be located in Atlanta, Buffalo, Dallas-Fort Worth, Denver, Houston, New York, Minneapolis-St. Paul and Toronto. The Minneapolis-St. Paul franchise was to be headed by Wheelcock Whitney, a Minneapolis businessman. In addition, Whitney spearheaded the creation of the Minnesota Vikings, which began play in 1961.

Our story begins with the establishment of the NFL's Minnesota Vikings, baseball's first expansion and the move of the franchise from Washington to Minnesota.

The 1960s

THE STATE OF THE TWINS

The franchise moved from Washington to Minnesota following the 1960 season. As the Washington Senators, the club hadn't finished higher than fifth in the eight-team American League since 1945. The Twins landed in seventh in a ten-team circuit in 1961, then leaped to second in 1962. The club was successful throughout most of the 1960s, with the high point coming in 1965 with an American League pennant. After a shift to two divisions in 1969, Minnesota captured the first Western Division title. Counting the 1960 season in Washington, the franchise was 862–747 during the decade, a winning percentage of .536, which ranked fourth in the American League, behind the Orioles, Tigers and Yankees. AL champions outside of Minnesota were the Yankees (1960, 1961, 1962, 1963 and 1964), Orioles (1966 and 1969), Red Sox (1967) and Tigers (1968).

THE BEST TEAM

The 1965 Twins still rank as the club with the most regular-season wins since the move to Minnesota with a record of 102–60. The Twins lost to the Los Angeles Dodgers in seven games in the World Series.

THE WORST TEAM

The first Minnesota edition in 1961 finished with a record of 70–90.

THE BEST MOMENT

The best moment was the clinching of the American League pennant on September 26, 1965.

THE WORST MOMENT

The Twins had a one-game lead with two games left on the 1967 schedule. All that was necessary to win the American League pennant was one win over the Red Sox in one of those two final contests at Fenway Park. The Twins lost both of them.

THE ALL-DECADE TEAM • YEARS W/TWINS

Earl Battey, c	1961–67
Harmon Killebrew, 1b	1961–74
Rod Carew, 2b	1967–78
Rich Rollins, 3b	1961–68
Zoilo Versalles, ss	1961–67
Bob Allison, lf	1961–70
Cesar Tovar, cf	1965–72
Tony Oliva, rf	1962–76
Jim Kaat, p	1961–73
Jim Perry, p	1963–72
Camilo Pascual, p	1961–66
Dave Boswell, p	1964–70

In determining the 1960s All-Decade Team, only the years the franchise was located in Minnesota was taken into consideration. Killebrew and Carew are in the Hall of Fame. Other top players with the Twins during the 1960s included center fielder Jimmie Hall (1963–66), first baseman Don Mincher (1961–66), center fielder Ted Uhlaender (1965–69) and relief pitcher Al Worthington (1964–69).

THE DECADE LEADERS (1961–69)

Batting Avg:	Tony Oliva	.308
On-Base Pct:	Harmon Killebrew	.388
Slugging Pct:	Harmon Killebrew	.547
Home Runs:	Harmon Killebrew	364
RBI:	Harmon Killebrew	923
Runs:	Harmon Killebrew	780
Stolen Bases:	Cesar Tovar	117
Wins:	Jim Kaat	141
Strikeouts:	Jim Kaat	1,410
ERA:	Jim Perry	2.88
Saves:	Al Worthington	88

THE HOME FIELD

Metropolitan Stadium opened in suburban Bloomington on April 24, 1956, as the home of the Minneapolis Millers. The unpretentious ballpark originally held 18,200 with a triple-decked grandstand that extended from first base to third and was expanded to 22,000 by 1960. It was built on a 161-acre tract, which previously had been a cornfield, with the idea of attracting a pro football or major league baseball franchise to the area. It was built in Bloomington because of the intense rivalry between Minneapolis and St. Paul. The ballpark was about the same distance (seven to eight miles) from the downtowns of both cities. When the National Football League granted the Twin Cities a franchise in January 1960, plans were put in place to increase the capacity of the Met to 40,000 before the Vikings played their first game in September 1961. The Washington Senators moved to Minnesota in October 1960 and were renamed the Twins. By Opening Day in April 1961, the stadium held 30,000. By 1969, capacity was 45,000. Because of the numerous expansions over the years and seats arranged to accommodate both baseball and football, the stadium looked like an erector set, with a patchwork combination of single, double and triple decks. The exterior was a strange blend of colored brick panels and corrugated metal, giving the ballpark a bizarre charm, as if it had been built without much thought or planning. Nestled between the triple-decked grandstand and the left field foul pole were bleachers with a single deck, which was added in 1961. In the lower half were chairs. In the upper half were wooden planks. Behind the left field fence were temporary bleachers. In 1965, double-decked stands that followed one of the sidelines for football were constructed. Small single-decked bleachers were behind the right field barrier. There was a huge scoreboard in right-center. The original field dimensions were 330 feet down each foul line and 412 feet to center field. Fans immediately embraced the Twins. While in Washington, the franchise hadn't finished in the top half of the AL in attendance since 1943 and hadn't done so in a peacetime season since 1933. The Twins finished in the top half of the league in attendance every season from 1961 through 1971, and led the circuit in 1963 and 1965. The club not only drew fans from Minnesota, but from Wisconsin, Iowa, North Dakota, South Dakota and Montana as well.

THE GAME YOU WISHED YOU HAD SEEN

The Twins won game six of the 1965 World Series on October 13 by a 5–1 score over the Dodgers with Mudcat Grant hitting a three-run homer and pitching a complete game.

THE WAY THE GAME WAS PLAYED

Baseball was played in new cities and ballparks during the 1960s with franchise shifts and expansion from 16 teams to 24. American League baseball was played for the first time in Minnesota, Southern California, Oakland and Seattle. The expansion of the strike zone in 1963 brought a decline in offense during the 1960s until the owners lowered the mound for the 1969 season. The league ERA dipped to 2.98 in 1968, the only time it has been lower than 3.000 since 1919.

THE MANAGEMENT

Calvin Griffith owned the Senators and Twins franchise from 1955 through 1984. There were no general managers during the 1960s, as Griffith also made trades and oversaw the day-to-day operation of the club. Field managers during the Minnesota years were Cookie Lavagetto (1961), Sam Mele (1961–67), Cal Ermer (1967–68) and Billy Martin (1969).

THE BEST PLAYER MOVE

The best player move was the signing of Rod Carew out of high school in 1964. The best trade brought Cesar Tovar from the Reds in exchange for Gerry Arrigo in December 1964.

THE WORST PLAYER MOVE

The worst player move was the failure to protect Reggie Smith following the 1963 season. He was drafted by the Red Sox. The worst trade occurred on December 10, 1969, when the Twins sent Graig Nettles, Bob Miller, Dean Chance and Ted Uhlaender to the Indians for Stan Williams and Luis Tiant.

1960

January 28 — Dallas and Minneapolis-St. Paul receive National Football League franchises when the organization expands to 14 teams. Twelve teams were fielded by the NFL in 1959 with two clubs in Chicago and others in Baltimore, Cleveland, Detroit, Green Bay, Los Angeles, New York, Philadelphia, Pittsburgh, San Francisco and Washington. Dallas was to begin play in 1960 with Minneapolis-St. Paul following in 1961. In addition, the Chicago Cardinals moved to St. Louis before the start of the 1960 season.

In July 1959, Minnesota businessmen Bill Boyer, H. P. Skoglund and Max Winter decided the join the fledging American Football League, which was to begin play in 1960 with eight teams. The other seven were to be located in Boston, Buffalo, Dallas, Denver, Houston, Los Angeles and New York. Boyer, Skoglund and Winter had second thoughts, however, and opted to join the NFL. Oakland was later tabbed to fill the eighth spot in the AFL line-up. The new team in the Twin Cities was named the Vikings.

April 27 — Three months after gaining a professional sports franchise, Minnesota loses one when the Minneapolis Lakers move to Los Angeles. Led by George Mikan, the Lakers were the dominant team in the early years of the NBA, winning five league titles in 1949, 1950, 1952, 1953 and 1954. In 1959–60, the NBA fielded eight teams in Boston, Cincinnati, Detroit, New York, Minneapolis, Philadelphia, St. Louis and Syracuse.

In 1959, there were 42 teams in Major League Baseball, the National Football League, the National Basketball Association and the National Hockey League. By 1969, there were 74 franchises in the four organizations. The Twins Cities would gain another major sports franchise in 1967 when the Minnesota North Stars were created as part of the NHL's first expansion. In 2009, there were 122 clubs in MLB, the NFL, the NBA and the NHL.

August 2 — At an historic meeting in Chicago's Conrad-Hilton Hotel, a four-man expansion committee of the American and National Leagues votes unanimously to expand by admitting four new clubs into the major leagues. The additions would increase each league from eight teams to ten. Eight teams had existed in each league since 1901. The committee sought to complete the expansion by 1962 at the latest. The committee also recommended the admission of four members of the Continental League into the established major leagues. The Continental League was formed in July 1959 with designs to become a third major league. It was the brainchild of New York City attorney William Shea. Branch Rickey was league president. Franchises were to be located in New York, Atlanta, Buffalo, Dallas-Fort Worth, Denver, Houston, Minneapolis-St.Paul and Toronto. The proposed Minneapolis-St. Paul club was to be owned by Wheelcock Whitney, Jr. With the decision to expand, those involved with the Continental League decided to disband the operation. The Twin Cities were a leading candidate for one of the four new clubs.

In 1960, there were American League teams in Baltimore, Boston, Chicago, Cleveland, Detroit, Kansas City, New York and Washington. National League clubs were located in Chicago, Cincinnati, Los Angeles, Milwaukee, Philadelphia, Pittsburgh, St. Louis and San Francisco.

OCTOBER 17   The National League votes with "unanimous enthusiasm" to expand to ten teams with the addition of franchise in New York and Houston. The two new teams would begin play in 1962.

OCTOBER 26   The American League votes to allow Washington Senators owner Calvin Griffith to move to Minneapolis-St. Paul and to expand the league from eight teams to ten with the addition of a new franchise Washington and another in Los Angeles. The two new clubs would begin play in 1961 and schedules were increased from 154 games to 162. The news was completely unexpected. Even Baseball Commissioner Ford Frick was surprised by the announcement and was unprepared for comment when approached by reporters.

The move ended a nearly half-century association with the Griffith family in Washington. Calvin's uncle Clark Griffith came to Washington as manager in 1912 and became club president in 1920. The new Minneapolis-St. Paul team was to play at Metropolitan Stadium in the suburb of Bloomington. Built in 1956, it had a capacity of 22,000. Since 1956, it had been used by the Minneapolis Millers of the American Association. Plans were underway to expand the facility to 30,000 by the start of the 1961 baseball season and to 40,000 by the beginning of the 1961 football campaign. In luring Griffith, the Metropolitan Sports Committee of Minneapolis-St. Paul guaranteed the club an attendance of close to a million per season over a five-year period and the concessions at the stadium but not the parking fees. Griffith's Washington Senators drew 743,404 in 1960. Although it was increase over the 1959 figure of 615,372 in 1959 and 475,288 in 1958, it ranked last among the eight AL teams. The Senators were last in attendance in the AL every year from 1955 through 1960. Besides the attendance guarantee in Minneapolis-St. Paul, Griffith revealed he had received five propositions for radio and television rights from local media outlets averaging close to $500,000 each. In Washington, he said, the club had collected only $180,000 for broadcasting rights in 1960. The Senators that season finished in fifth place with a record of 73–81 and had posted only one winning season since 1945—a 78–76 mark in 1952. The 73–81 mark in 1960 was a dramatic improvement over seasons 53–101 in 1955, 59–95 in 1956, 55–99 in 1957, 61–93 in 1958 and 63–91 in 1959. The organization possessed a bevy of young, rising stars led by Harmon Killebrew, Jim Kaat, Bob Allison, Earl Battey, Camilo Pascaul, Zoilo Versalles, Pedro Ramos, Jack Kralick, Don Mincher, Rich Rollins and Bernie Allen. The manager was Cookie Lavagetto, who had guided the Senators since 1957. Lavagetto was 48 years old on Opening Day in 1961. As a player, he was named to four consecutive All-Star teams as a third baseman with the Brooklyn Dodgers from 1938 through 1941 before missing four seasons due to military service during World War II. Cookie's last two seasons as a player were with the Dodgers in 1946 and 1947. His most famous moment in baseball came at Ebbets Field in Brooklyn in the final year of his big league career. With two out in the bottom of the ninth inning of game three in the 1947 World Series, Lavagetto stepped to the plate as a pinch-hitter with two runners on base, the Yankees leading the Dodgers 2–1. New York pitcher Bill Bevens had walked ten batters, but had a no-hitter in progress. Lavagetto lashed a two-run, walk-off double to score both runners and lift the Dodgers to an improbable 3–2 victory.

NOVEMBER 26   Three weeks after John Kennedy defeats Richard Nixon in the Presidential election, Calvin Griffith announces that the new baseball team in Minneapolis-St. Paul would be known as the Minnesota Twins. Griffith had considered calling the club the Twin Cities Twins.

> *One of Griffith's tasks was to unite the cities of Minneapolis and St. Paul behind his new team. The cities had maintained a heated rivalry between the Minneapolis Millers and the St. Paul Saints of the American Association since 1902. Griffith had to consolidate fan support from both cities without favoring or alienating either. With that goal in mind, the Twins were the first team in baseball to be named after a state rather than a city. The team logo featured two identical baseball players shaking hands across a river (symbolizing the Mississippi which separates Minneapolis and St. Paul) with an outline of the state of Minnesota in the background. Rather than place an "M" on the team cap, which may be construed by some St. Paul loyalists as representing Minneapolis, the hats had an interlocking "T" and "C" for the Twin Cities. The uniforms had "Twins" written across the front in blue and outlined in red. The home jerseys were pin-striped. The color scheme and design was nearly identical to the uniforms of the 1960 Washington Senators.*

DECEMBER 14   The Twins lose seven players in the expansion draft. The new Washington Senators selected Rudy Hernandez, Hector Maestri, Johnny Schaive and Hal Woodeshick. The Los Angeles Angels chose Julio Becquer, Tex Clevenger and Faye Throneberry. Of the seven, only Woodeshick enjoyed any significant success following that expansion draft, working as a reliever with Houston and St. Louis during the mid-1960s.

The Legacy of the Senators

The following is a list of the 25 best players on the Washington Senators from 1901 through 1960. Only the years a player spent in Washington were taken into consideration.

Player	Position	Years in Washington
Walter Johnson	P	1907–27
Sam Rice	OF	1915–33
Joe Judge	1B	1915–32
Clyde Milan	OF	1907–22
Mickey Vernon	1B	1939–48, 1950–55
Goose Goslin	OF	1922–30, 1933
Eddie Yost	3B	1944, 1946–58
Buddy Myer	2B	1925–27, 1930–41
Ossie Bluege	3B	1922–39
Buddy Lewis	3B-OF	1935–41, 1945–49
Joe Cronin	SS	1928–34
Cecil Travis	SS	1933–41, 1945–47
Joe Kuhel	1B	1930–37, 1944–46
Firpo Marberry	P	1923–32, 1936
Eddie Foster	3B	1912–19
George Case	OF	1937–45, 1947
Muddy Ruel	C	1923–30
Stan Spence	OF	1942–44, 1946–57
Dutch Leonard	P	1938–46
Roy Sievers	OF	1954–59
Heinie Manush	OF	1930–35
George McBride	SS	1908–20
Sammy West	OF	1927–32, 1938–41
Howie Shanks	OF-3B	1912–22
Tom Zachary	P	1919–25, 1927–28

Johnson was one of the five original Hall of Famers elected in 1936. The others were Ty Cobb, Babe Ruth, Christy Mathewson and Honus Wagner. Rice, Goslin, Cronin and Manush are also in the Hall of Fame. A combined list of the top 25 players who performed for either the Senators or Twins, or both, would still include Johnson, Rice, Judge, Milan, Vernon, Goslin, Yost, Myer, Bluege, Lewis, Cronin and Travis. The 13 Twins to round out the all-time franchise top 25 would be Harmon Killebrew, Rod Carew, Kirby Puckett, Tony Oliva, Kent Hrbek, Bob Allison, Jim Kaat, Bert Blyleven, Joe Mauer, Earl Battey, Bert Blyleven, Jim Kaat, Johan Santana and Brad Radke. Killebrew, Carew and Puckett are in the Hall of Fame. The "starting line-up" of a combined Senators and Twins squad would be Johnson (P), Mauer (C), Vernon (1B), Carew (2B), Killebrew (3B), Cronin (SS), Rice (OF), Puckett (OF), Milan (OF) and Oliva (DH).

1961

Season in a Sentence
The Twins inaugurate major league baseball in Minnesota by winning eight of their first ten games, but a streak of 20 losses in 22 games in May and June sends the club into a downward spiral.

Finish • Won • Lost • Pct • GB
Seventh   70   90   .438   38.0

Manager
Cookie Lavagetto (23–36) and Sam Mele (47–54)

Stats   Twins • AL • Rank
Batting Avg:	.250	.256	7
On-Base Pct:	.324	.329	8
Slugging Pct2:	.397	.395	5
Home Runs:	167		4
Stolen Bases:	47		6
ERA:	4.28	4.02	7
Errors:	174		8
Runs Scored:	707		7
Runs Allowed:	778		7

Starting Line-up
Earl Battey, c
Harmon Killebrew, 1b
Billy Martin, 2b
Bill Tuttle, 3b
Zoilo Versalles, ss
Jim Lemon, lf
Lenny Green, cf
Bob Allison, rf

Pitchers
Camilo Pascaul, sp
Pedro Ramos, sp
Jack Kralick, sp
Jim Kaat, sp
Ray Moore, rp
Don Lee, rp

Attendance
1,256,723 (third in AL)

Club Leaders
Batting Avg:	Earl Battey	.302
On-Base Pct:	Harmon Killebrew	.405
Slugging Pct:	Harmon Killebrew	.606
Home Runs:	Harmon Killebrew	46
RBI:	Harmon Killebrew	122
Runs:	Harmon Killebrew	94
Stolen Bases:	Lenny Green	17
Wins:	Camilo Pascaul	15
Strikeouts:	Camilo Pascaul	221
ERA:	Camilo Pascaul	3.46
Saves:	Ray Moore	14

FEBRUARY 21   The Twins first training camp begins in Orlando, Florida. The Washington Senators trained in Orlando from 1936 through 1942 and again from 1946 through 1960. The Senators trained in College Park, Maryland, on the campus of the University of Maryland from 1943 through 1945 because of World War II travel restrictions. The Twins continued to use Orlando as their spring training headquarters until 1990. During the more than 50 years that the Senators and Twins trained there, Orlando grew from a small town of 30,000 to a major metropolis. The ballpark in Orlando

was named Tinker Field, in honor of Hall of Fame shortstop Joe Tinker, who played in four World Series with the Cubs in 1906, 1907, 1908 and 1910. He is best known as a member of the famed Tinker-to-Evers-to-Chance infield. Tinker retired to Orlando and was a prominent citizen in the community. He died in 1948. The original Tinker Field was torn down in 1963 and replaced by a new facility.

MARCH 11 — The Twins play their first exhibition game and lose 4–1 to the Tigers in Orlando. Paul Giel was the starting pitcher. Zoilo Versalles was the first batter.

Giel had strong roots in Minnesota. He was born in Winona and was a two-time All-American as a quarterback with the University of Minnesota football team in 1952 and 1953. Giel opted to play baseball professionally and spent six seasons in the majors with four clubs in 1954 and 1955 and again from 1958 through 1961. He pitched in 12 regular season games with the Twins in 1961 with a 1–0 record but a 9.78 ERA in 19$^{2}/_{3}$ innings. Giel was the Director of Athletics at the University of Minnesota from 1971 through 1989. He was elected to the College Football Hall of Fame in 1975.

APRIL 11 — The first regular season game in Twins history results in a 6–0 victory over the Yankees in New York. The game was scoreless for six innings in a duel between Pedro Ramos of the Twins and Yankees ace Whitey Ford. Bob Allison led off the seventh with a home run to snap the deadlock. Before the inning was over, Ramos drove in two runs with a single. Reno Bertoia added a two-run homer in the eighth. Ramos pitched a complete-game three-hitter and retired the last 13 batters to face him.

The Opening Day line-up was Zoilo Versalles (ss), Lenny Green (cf), Harmon Killebrew (1b), Jim Lemon (lf), Bob Allison (rf), Earl Battey (c), Reno Bertoia (3b), Billy Gardner (2b) and Pedro Ramos (p).

APRIL 14 — Camilo Pascaul strikes out 12 batters during a 3–2 victory over the Orioles in Baltimore.

A native of Cuba, Pascaul made his major league debut at 20 with the Senators in 1954, the first of 18 seasons in the majors. After struggling early in his career on some terrible teams in Washington, Pascaul developed a devastating curveball and blossomed in 1959 with a 17–10 record. That season he was named to the All-Star team, an honor he would receive again in 1960, 1961, 1962 and 1964. With the Twins in 1961, Pascaul was 15–16 with a 3.46 ERA and a league-leading 221 strikeouts in 252$^{1}/_{3}$ innings. He led the AL in strikeouts again in 1962 and 1963 and topped the circuit in complete games in 1959, 1962 and 1963. Pascaul won 20 games for the Twins in 1962 and 21 more in 1963. Overall, he had a record of 88–57 during the years the franchise was located in Minnesota. Among Twins pitchers, Pascaul ranks third in shutouts (18), fourth in complete games (72) and fifth in strikeouts (994). On the all-time franchise leader lists, counting the Washington years, he is fourth in wins (145), third in losses (141), second in shutouts (31), fourth in games started (331), seventh in complete games (119), fourth in innings (2,465), second in walks (909) and third in strikeouts (1,885).

APRIL 16 — On the day of the unsuccessful Bay of Pigs invasion of Cuba, the Twins sweep the Orioles 10–5 and 6–4 during a double-header at Memorial Stadium in Baltimore.

1960s

The Twins scored six runs in the first inning of the opener. Baltimore starter Chuck Estrada fell behind 4–0 four batters into the game. Estrada walked Zoilo Versalles, Lenny Green and Don Mincher, then gave up a homer to Bob Allison. The blast by Allison was the first grand slam in Twins history. Before the inning was over, Versalles and Green walked again. Allison hit a three-run homer off Dick Hall in the sixth to finish the game with seven runs batted in. In the second tilt, Versalles hit a two-run homer in the 11th inning for the win. It was the first extra-inning homer by a Twin. It was also the first extra inning game and the first double-header in Twins history.

The Twins broadcasters in 1961 were Bob Wolff, Halsey Hall and Ray Scott. The trio did all 162 games on WCCO radio and 49 contests, 44 of them on the road, over WTCN-TV. Wolff was the announcer for the Senators from 1947 through 1960. He was the first broadcaster to do the play-by-play in the World Series, NFL championship game, NBA finals and Stanley Cup finals. Among the games he called were Don Larsen's perfect game in the 1956 World Series and the 1958 NFL championship overtime classic between the Baltimore Colts and New York Giants. He spent only one season in Minnesota. Scott was the lead announcer for four Super Bowls, including the first two in 1967 and 1968. He announced Twins games until 1966. Hall worked for three Twin Cities newspapers in addition to his broadcasting duties. He originated "Holy Cow!" as a home run call on WCCO long before Harry Caray used it.

APRIL 19   A crowd of 3,000 fans greet the Twins at the airport following their arrival from the season-opening road trip through New York, Baltimore and Boston.

APRIL 20   The Twins play to capacity crowds in a testimonial breakfast in St. Paul and a luncheon in Minneapolis. Attending both events were Minnesota Governor Elmer Anderson, St. Paul Mayor George Vavoulis and Minneapolis Mayor P. K. Peterson. Baseball Commissioner Ford Frick was present at the luncheon. Later, the Twins players, coaches and manager Cookie Lavagetto toured through both cities in a two-hour motorcade in top-down convertibles.

APRIL 21   The Twins play at home for the first time and lose 5–3 to the Senators before 24,606 at Metropolitan Stadium. The somewhat disappointing crowd was about 6,000 shy of capacity. The temperature was in the low 60s. Washington broke the 3–3 tie with two runs in the ninth. Don Mincher and Lenny Green homered for the Twins. Camilo Pascual was the Minnesota starting pitcher. The first batter in Metropolitan Stadium history was Marty Keough, who singled. Senators first baseman Dale Long hit the first home run later in the opening inning.

The day before the opener, hundreds of workers swarmed around the ballpark bolting down seats, laying decorative brick, checking electrical circuits and removing assorted debris. There were several glitches. The Senators players wandered around outside for five minutes trying to get directions to the proper gate. The American flag only went halfway up the flagpole and refused to budge. It remained at half-mast throughout the game. Calvin Griffith was denied access to the press box because he lacked the proper credentials. And, there were no line-up cards available. Managers Cookie Lavagetto of the Twins and Mickey Vernon of the Senators had to scribble their batting orders on scraps of paper.

The Original Twins

The following is a list of the 28 players, manager and four coaches who were on the Opening Day roster in 1961. An asterisk indicates that individual was a member of the 1960 Washington Senators.

Pitchers
- Fred Bruckbauer
- Paul Giel
- *Jim Kaat
- *Jack Kralick
- *Don Lee
- *Ray Moore
- *Camilo Pascual
- Bill Pleis
- *Pedro Ramos
- *Ted Sadowski
- Lee Stange
- *Chuck Stobbs

Catchers
- *Earl Battey
- Ron Henry
- *Hal Naragon

Infielders
- *Reno Bertoia
- *Billy Consolo
- *Billy Gardner
- *Harmon Killebrew
- *Don Mincher
- *Jose Valdivielso
- *Zoilo Versalles

Outfielders
- *Bob Allison
- *Don Dobbek
- *Lenny Green
- *Jim Lemon
- *Elmer Valo
- *Pete Whisenant

Manager
- *Cookie Lavagetto

Coaches
- Floyd Baker
- Ed Lopat
- Clyde McCullough
- *Sam Mele

APRIL 23 — Jack Kralick pitches and bats the Twins to a 1–0 win over the Senators at Metropolitan Stadium. He not only hurled the shutout in a complete game but drove in the lone run of the contest with a single in the fifth inning. The hit followed a two-out double by Billy Gardner.

Governor Elmer Anderson threw out the ceremonial first pitch prior to the first game on April 21. Before the second game on April 22, St. Paul Mayor George Vavoulis did the honors. Minneapolis Mayor P. K. Peterson threw out the first pitch on April 23.

APRIL 24 — The Twins score three runs in the ninth inning and four in the tenth to defeat the Athletics 10–6 in Kansas City. The final two runs in the ninth scored after two were out. Earl Battey drove in three runs in the tenth with a double, and then crossed the plate on a single from Reno Bertoia.

APRIL 25 — The Athletics rout the Twins 20–2 in Kansas City. Seven pitchers absorbed the pounding.

Fred Bruckbauer, a 22-year-old native of New Ulm, Minnesota, was one of the Twins pitchers. Making his big league debut, Bruckbauer faced four batters in the fourth inning and allowed two doubles, a single and a walk. He never pitched in the majors again.

APRIL 27   The Twins participate in the first American League game ever played in Los Angeles and defeat the Angels 4–2.

The Angels played their first season as an expansion team at Wrigley Field. The facility was used by the Los Angeles Angels of the Pacific Coast League from 1925 through 1957. The minor league Angels were owned by the Wrigley family, which also owned the Chicago Cubs from 1919 through 1981. The Angels shared Dodger Stadium with the Dodgers from 1962 through 1965 before moving to Anaheim in 1966.

MAY 9   Four days after Alan Shepard becomes the first American in space, Orioles first baseman Jim Gentile ties a major league record with two grand slams in a 13–5 win over the Twins at Metropolitan Stadium. He cleared the bases with home runs off Pedro Ramos in the first inning and Paul Giel in the second. Gentile later added a sacrifice fly in the eighth to finish the game with nine RBIs.

Even the batboys in 1961 were twins. They were 15-year-old Peter and Richard King, who were selected from among 74 sets of Twins who turned up for tryouts several months earlier in a blinding snowstorm.

MAY 12   Pedro Ramos and Angels hurler Eli Grba homer off of each other in the fifth inning of a 5–4 Twins win at Metropolitan Stadium. Grba put the Angels ahead 3–2 with a homer in the top of the fifth. Ramos led off the bottom half of the inning and tied the contest with a homer off Grba. It was the first home run by a Twins pitcher. Ramos broke the 3–3 deadlock by driving in two more runs with a single in the sixth.

MAY 13   Bob Allison homers twice and drives in five runs during a 13–6 victory over the Angels at Metropolitan Stadium.

Allison batted only .245 in 1961 but belted 29 homers and drove in 105 runs. It was one of five seasons in which he hit at least 29 home runs. Allison spent his entire career with one franchise, playing for the original Senators and the Twins from 1958 through 1970, and was an All-Star in 1959, 1963 and 1964. About two decades after his career ended, Allison contracted amyotrophic lateral sclerosis (Lou Gehrig's disease) and died in 1995 at the age of 60. Among Twins players, Allison ranks fourth in home runs (211) and third in walks (641). On the all-time franchise leader board, counting the Washington years, Allison's 256 career home runs ranks third.

MAY 19   Dan Dobbek hits a grand slam off Ed Rakow in the third inning of an 11–1 triumph over the Athletics at Municipal Stadium. Dobbek later added a solo homer against Don Larsen in the seventh.

MAY 21   The Twins are shut out in both ends of a double-header, losing 9–0 and 2–0 to the Indians at Metropolitan Stadium. Minnesota also collected only five hits during the two games. The Cleveland pitchers were Wynn Hawkins and Mudcat Grant.

Twin Cities baseball fans pack the airport for the arrival of the players on their new team.

MAY 25   The Twins take a thrilling 7–6 decision from the Tigers in 11 innings at Metropolitan Stadium. Detroit scored five times in the first inning, but the Twins chipped away at the lead and tied the contest 5–5 with a run in the ninth on a two-out single by Reno Bertoia. The Tigers scored in the top of the tenth, but the Twins knotted the game again on a two-out, one-base hit from Hal Naragon. The winning run crossed the plate on a walk-off single by Jim Lemon.

> *The win ended a five-game losing streak and evened the club's record at 19–19. The Twins lost their next 13 contests.*

MAY 26   The Twins play in Washington for the first time and lose 4–3 to the Senators at Griffith Stadium.

JUNE 1   The Twins trade Billy Consolo to the Braves for Billy Martin. On the same day, the Twins swapped Reno Bertoia and Paul Giel to the Athletics for Bill Tuttle. Giel pitched one game for the A's and retired. The Twins were forced to make a cash settlement with the Athletics because of Giel's retirement.

> *From the time he made his major league debut with the Yankees in 1950 until he died on Christmas Day in 1989, Martin was a controversial figure. He played in five World Series with the Yankees before being traded to the Athletics in June 1957 after he was involved in a fight in a New York nightclub. From 1957 through 1961, Martin played for seven different clubs. When he arrived in Minnesota, he was battling a lawsuit filed by Cubs pitcher Jim Brewer, who was asking for over $1 million in damages. While playing for the Reds in August 1960, Martin punched Brewer during a game at Wrigley Field. (The case was*

later settled out of court). Billy hit .246 in 108 games as a second baseman for the Twins in 1961, his last major league season as a player. He remained in the organization for the remainder of the decade as a scout (1962–64), coach (1965–68), minor league manager (1968) and as manager of the Twins (1969). The 1969 season was his first as a manager at the big league level. Despite winning the AL West title, Martin was fired at the end of the season, a situation which would be repeated often during the 1970s and 1980s.

JUNE 8   The Twins break a 13-game losing streak by defeating the Orioles 3–1 in Baltimore.

JUNE 12   Harmon Killebrew collects five hits, including a home run, in six at-bats, but the Twins lose 10–8 to the Red Sox in Boston.

A native of Payette, Idaho, Killebrew made his major league debut with the Senators at the age of 18 in 1954. Through his first five seasons in the majors, Harmon hit only .224 with 11 homers in 254 at-bats. In 1959, his prodigious slugging was on display for the first time as he led the AL in home runs with 42. In the Twins first season in Minnesota, Killebrew homered 46 times with 122 RBIs and a career-high .288 batting average. He would lead the league again in homers in 1962 (with 48), 1963 (45), 1964 (49), 1967 (44) and 1969 (49). Killebrew spent 21 of his 22 seasons in the majors with the original Senators and the Twins. He finished his career in 1975 with 573 home runs, which at the time, ranked fifth behind Hank Aaron, Babe Ruth, Willie Mays and Frank Robinson. Killebrew never received the respect due the other four players, however, because of a career batting average of .256 and his below-average defense. He wasn't even a first ballot Hall of Famer, waiting until the fourth year of his eligibility in 1984 for enshrinement at Cooperstown. But Killebrew possessed the ability to get on base, ranking in the top ten in base on balls 13 seasons during his career, including league-leading figures in 1966, 1967, 1969 and 1971. He was also in the top ten in on-base percentage nine times, and ranked first in 1969. Combining the franchise's Washington and Minnesota years, Killebrew ranks first in home runs (559), first in RBIs (1,540), first in walks (1,505), first in slugging percentage (.514), first in games played (2,329), second in at-bats (7.835), second in runs (1,258), and sixth in hits (2,024). Among Twins, Harmon is the all-time record holder in home runs (475), games (1,939), RBIs (1,325), walks (1,321) and slugging percentage (.518) and is second in at-bats (6,593) and runs (1,047) and fifth in hits (1,713).

JUNE 14   Camilo Pascaul is the losing pitcher in an unusual 9–2 defeat at the hands of the Athletics at Metropolitan Stadium. Through seven innings, he pitched shutout ball while allowing just two hits and striking out 13. But in the eighth, Pascaul was charged with four runs before being relieved.

On the same day, the Twins traded Billy Gardner to the Yankees for Danny McDevitt.

JUNE 18   Camilo Pascaul and Bob Allison fight in the dugout in the fifth inning of a 10–7 loss to the White Sox in the second game of a double-header at Comiskey Park. Chicago also won the opener 4–3.

JUNE 20   Batting for Chuck Stobbs, Julio Becquer leads off the ninth with a home run that beats the Orioles 5–4 at Metropolitan Stadium. It was both the first pinch-hit and first walk-off homer in Twins history. Becquer also hit the second walk-off homer in club history (see July 4, 1961).

JUNE 23   Harmon Killebrew drives in all four runs of a 4–0 win over the Yankees at Metropolitan Stadium with a homer, double and single. It was part of a six-game stretch from June 20 through June 25 in which he hit six homers, drove in 15 runs, and collected 13 hits in 24 at-bats.

> *On the same day, the Twins fired Cookie Lavagetto as manager and replaced him with 39-year-old Sam Mele, who had been a coach with the Senators and Twins since 1959. He spent ten years in the majors as an outfielder with six clubs from 1947 through 1956. In 1965, Mele guided the Twins to their first American League pennant. He continued as the club's manager until June 1967. Lavagetto never managed another big-league club.*

JUNE 27   Bob Allison breaks a scoreless tie with a grand slam off Gene Conley in the sixth inning, leading to a 6–3 victory over the Red Sox in the second game of a double-header at Metropolitan Stadium. The Twins also won the opener 6–5.

JUNE 30   The Twins break a 1–1 tie with a seven-run fourth inning and defeat the Athletics 8–2 in Kansas City.

JULY 1   Harmon Killebrew collects four hits and drives in five runs, including a grand slam off Bill Kunkel in the ninth inning, to lead the Twins to a 9–3 triumph over the Athletics in Kansas City.

JULY 3   Bob Allison hits a grand slam off Turk Lown in the seventh inning of a 7–6 victory over the White Sox at Metropolitan Stadium. It was Allison's third slam of the season and came after a 48-minute delay because of rain and hail in the top of the seventh.

JULY 4   Batting for Bill Tuttle, Julio Becquer hits a walk-off grand slam off Warren Hacker to down the White Sox 6–4 in the first game of a double-header at Metropolitan Stadium. In the second tilt, Harmon Killebrew hit the only inside-the-park homer of his career. It was a three-run blast to deep center field in the eighth inning of a 4–2 win.

> *Zoilo Versalles left the club for ten days in July because he said he was lonely for his wife and family in Cuba. Versalles returned to the club when his 18-year-old wife safely arrived in the United States.*

JULY 11   Pinch-hitting for Dick Donovan in the sixth inning of the All-Star Game at Candlestick Park in San Francisco, Harmon Killebrew homers off Mike McCormick of the Giants. The National League won 5–4 in ten innings in the first of two All-Star Games in 1961. There were two Midsummer Classics played each season from 1959 through 1962.

JULY 13   Third baseman Ted Lepcio hits a grand slam off Mudcat Grant in the first inning of a 9–6 win over the Indians in Cleveland.

JULY 16   Lenny Green collects five hits, including a triple and a double, in six at-bats during a 12–5 win over the Indians in the second game of a double-header at Municipal Stadium. Cleveland won the opener 7–5.

1960s

JULY 19 — Camilo Pascaul strikes out 15 batters during a 6–0 win over the Angels in the first game of a double-header in Los Angeles. The Angels won the second contest 2–1.

JULY 21 — In the ninth inning, Jose Valdivielso scores from second base on a 30-foot walk-off single by Lenny Green to provide the winning run of a 4–3 victory over the Indians at Metropolitan Stadium. Green's dribbler stopped along the first base line, and after pitcher Joe Schaffernoth fell trying to field it, Valdivielso kept running and crossed the plate. Making his first start since June 5, Don Lee pitched 7²/³ hitless innings before allowing three runs and five hits in the eighth and ninth, which tied the score 3–3.

JULY 23 — The Twins wallop the Indians 10–0 at Metropolitan Stadium. Pedro Ramos pitched the shutout.

> *Playing for both the Senators and Twins, Ramos led the AL in losses four years in a row, posting records of 14–18 in 1958, 13–19 in 1959, 11–18 in 1960 and 11–20 in 1961. He is the only pitcher in Twins history to lose 20 times in a season.*

JULY 28 — Bob Allison hits two-run homers in the first and ninth inning to drive in all four Twins runs during a 4–3 win over the Tigers in Detroit.

JULY 31 — Relieving in the seventh inning of the second of two All-Star Games played in 1961, Camilo Pascaul pitches three shutout innings, allowing no hits and a walk while striking out four. The contest at Fenway Park was called after nine innings by rain with the score tied 1–1.

AUGUST 11 — Earl Battey hits solo homers in the second and seventh innings, both off Paul Foytack, to provide the only Twins runs in a 2–1 win over the Tigers at Metropolitan Stadium.

> *One of the top catchers of the 1960s, Battey played in the All-Star Game as a Twin in 1962, 1963, 1965 and 1966. He also won three Gold Gloves. In 1961, Battey hit .302 with 17 home runs.*

AUGUST 13 — On the day in which the construction of the Berlin Wall commences, Bill Tuttle hits a grand slam off Phil Regan in the fourth inning of a 13–5 win over the Tigers at Metropolitan Stadium.

> *Tuttle played for the Twins from 1961 through 1963 at the end of a 12-year career. In nearly every one of his baseball cards, a large wad of chewing tobacco was evident in his cheek. In 1993, Tuttle was diagnosed with oral cancer, and died in 1998. During the last years of his life, Tuttle's face was disfigured because of surgery to remove the cancer, and traveled the country as a public speaker warning players of the dangers of chewing tobacco.*

AUGUST 20 — Pitchers Jack Kralick and Art Schroll both hit home runs during a 9–7 win over the Angels in Los Angeles. Kralick homered in the third inning and Schroll in the eighth. Lenny Green belted two home runs, the first one leading off the top of the first inning. It was the first lead-off homer in Twins history.

> *The homer by Schroll was the only one of his major league career, which included 33 at-bats in four seasons.*

AUGUST 23	Camilo Pascaul pitches a two-hitter to defeat the White Sox 4–0 at Comiskey Park. The only Chicago hits were singles by Al Smith in the second inning and Sherm Lollar with two out in the ninth.
SEPTEMBER 10	First baseman Julio Becquer pitches 1⅓ innings of a 13–1 loss to the Athletics in the first game of a double-header in Kansas City. The Twins won game two 7–0. Harmon Killebrew homered in both ends of the twin bill to give him home runs in four consecutive games.
SEPTEMBER 11	Camilo Pascaul stars with his arm and his bat during a 5–2 triumph over the Angels at Metropolitan Stadium. He struck out 13 batters and collected three hits, including a double, in three at-bats.
SEPTEMBER 15	The Twins score three runs with two out in the ninth inning to defeat the Indians 3–2 in Cleveland. The runs were driven in on singles by Bob Allison and Earl Battey and a double from Jim Lemon.
SEPTEMBER 17	The Vikings play their first regular season game and stun the Chicago Bears 37–13 at Metropolitan Stadium.

> *It wasn't the first regular season NFL game at the Met. The Chicago Cardinals played two "home" games in Bloomington in 1959. The Cardinals lost to the Philadelphia Eagles 28–24 on October 25 and fell New York Giants by a 30–20 score on November 22. Cardinals owner Bill Bidwell considered moving his club to Minnesota before deciding to relocate to St. Louis. The team moved from St. Louis to Phoenix in 1988 and is now known as the Arizona Cardinals.*

SEPTEMBER 23	Camilo Pascaul pitches a two-hitter to defeat the Senators 10–0 at Metropolitan Stadium. The only Washington hits were a single by Bud Zipfel in the second inning and a double from Bob Johnson with two out in the ninth.
SEPTEMBER 24	Dick Donovan of the Senators pitches a one-hitter to defeat the Twins 4–1 at Metropolitan Stadium. The only Minnesota hit was a home run by Joe Altobelli just inside the right field foul pole in the seventh inning.
SEPTEMBER 27	Al Schroll pitches no-hit ball through eight innings before closing out a 10–4 victory over the Indians at Metropolitan Stadium. Schroll allowed a single, two walks and a triple prior to recording the final three outs.
NOVEMBER 27	The Twins draft Jim Merritt from the Dodgers organization.

1962

Season in a Sentence
After a disappointing seventh place finish in 1961, the Twins chase the Yankees all year before landing in second place.

Finish • Won • Lost • Pct • GB
Second   91   71   .562   5.0

Manager
Sam Mele

Stats   Twins • AL • Rank
Batting Avg: .260   .255   3
On-Base Pct: .337   .325   1
Slugging Pct: .412   .394   2
Home Runs: 185   3
Stolen Bases: 33   10
ERA: 3.89   3.97   6
Errors: 129   3
Runs Scored: 798   3
Runs Allowed: 713   6

Starting Line-up
Earl Battey, c
Vic Power, 1b
Bernie Allen, 2b
Rich Rollins, 3b
Zoilo Versalles, ss
Harmon Killebrew, lf
Lenny Green, cf
Bob Allison, rf

Pitchers
Camilo Pascaul, sp
Jim Kaat, sp
Jack Kralick, sp
Ray Moore, rp
Lee Stange, rp
Dick Stigman, rp-sp
Joe Bonikowski, rp-sp

Attendance
1,433,116 (second in AL)

Club Leaders
Batting Avg: Rich Rollins   .298
On-Base Pct: Rich Rollins   .374
Slugging Pct: Harmon Killebrew   .545
Home Runs: Harmon Killebrew   48
RBI: Harmon Killebrew   126
Runs: Bob Allison   102
Stolen Bases: Bob Allison   8
                Lenny Green   8
Wins: Camilo Pascaul   20
Strikeouts: Camilo Pascaul   206
ERA: Jim Kaat   3.14
Saves: Ray Moore   9

APRIL 1   Six weeks after John Glenn becomes the first American to orbit the earth, the Twins trade Pedro Ramos to the Indians for Vic Power and Dick Stigman.

Flamboyant and controversial, Power was the Twins starting first baseman in 1962 and 1963. The best fielding first baseman of the period, Power played in the All-Star Game with the Athletics in 1955 and 1956 and as an Indian in 1959 and 1960. By the time he arrived in Minnesota, he was 34 years old, and his career was winding down. He posted on-base and slugging percentages below the league average while with the club.

APRIL 10   The Twins open the season with a 4–2 loss to the Athletics in Kansas City. Jack Kralick was the starting and losing pitcher.

The 1962 season was the first of 45 in which Herb Carneal graced the Twins broadcasting booth. A native of Richmond, Virginia, he first broadcast games for the Philadelphia Phillies and Philadelphia Athletics in 1954, then worked for the Baltimore Orioles from 1957 through 1961, and the Minnesota Vikings from 1961 through 1964. With his laid-back demeanor, Carneal was adored by Twins fans. By 2002, he semi-retired and worked about half of the club's home games. Carneal died of heart failure on April 1, 2007, at the age of 83. That season, the Twins wore commemorative patches on their uniforms in his honor.

APRIL 13	A six-inch snowfall postpones the Twins scheduled home opener against the Angels. A crowd of about 25,000 was expected.
APRIL 14	The Twins drop the home opener 12–5 to the Angels before 8,363 at Metropolitan Stadium. The temperature was 33 degrees. Lenny Green, Zoilo Versalles and Rich Rollins hit home runs in the losing cause.

> *Rollins was a 24-year-old rookie in 1962, and after a sizzling first half he was named the starting third baseman in the All-Star Game. He finished the season with a .298 average, 16 homers and 96 RBIs. After batting .307 in 1963, Rollins rapidly declined. He played for the Twins until 1968 and his big league career ended in 1970.*

APRIL 15	At 18 years, six months and 25 years of age, pitcher Jim Manning becomes the youngest player in Twins history when he hurls three shutout innings (the sixth through the eighth) during a 6–3 loss to the Angels at Metropolitan Stadium.

> *Manning made his debut after only 12 unimpressive games in the minors with Wythville in the Appalachian League in 1961. He was 2–2 with a 4.40 ERA. His big league career lasted only five games; he had a 5.14 ERA in seven innings, which included one start. His career started and ended when he was only 18. His last game was on May 2. He returned to the minors, where he posted a record of 28–45 at the Class A and Class AA levels before being released in 1966. The youngest position player in Twins history is catcher Paul Ratliff at 19 years, two months and 22 days on April 14, 1963. Ratliff played ten games in 1963, before spending six full seasons in the minors. He didn't play in a single big league game from September 1963 until April 1970. Ratliff appeared in 135 games for the Twins in 1970 and 1971, and the Brewers in 1971 and 1972. The last teenager to play for the Twins was 19-year-old pitcher Rich Garces in 1990.*

APRIL 20	The Twins play at Dodger Stadium for the first time and defeat the Los Angeles Angels 9–7 in ten innings.
APRIL 28	Don Mincher comes off the bench to hit two homers, but the Twins lose 8–7 to the Indians in Cleveland. Mincher pinch-hit for Vic Power in the third inning and homered. Facing Frank Funk in the seventh, Mincher walloped a grand slam that tied the score 7–7. Power left the game because of a pulled leg muscle.

> *Mincher hit 90 home runs and compiled a .244 batting average in 1,511 at-bats with the Twins from 1961 through 1966. A first baseman, he often found himself stuck on the bench behind Harmon Killebrew, Power and Bob Allison.*

APRIL 29	The Twins hit six solo home runs during a 7–3 win over the Indians in the second game of a double-header in Cleveland. Johnny Goryl homered twice, with Lenny Green, Bill Tuttle, Don Mincher and Zoilo Versalles adding the remainder. The Indians won the opener 8–4 with nary a home run.

> *The two homers and two RBIs by Goryl were his only ones during the 1962 season. His previous major league home run was three years to the day earlier on April 29, 1959, while playing for the Cubs. He batted only 26 times in 37 games in 1962 and was used primarily as a pinch-hitter and pinch-runner. The April 29*

contest was his first starting assignment in the majors since June 19, 1959, and one of only two starts he made in 1962. The other one was on June 28.

MAY 3 — Don Mincher belts a grand slam off Milt Pappas in the first inning of an 8–4 win over the Orioles at Metropolitan Stadium. It was Mincher's second grand slam in a span of six days.

MAY 4 — Rich Rollins hits a two-out, two-run, walk-off homer in the ninth inning to defeat the Tigers 4–2 at Metropolitan Stadium.

MAY 6 — Bernie Allen hits a three-run, walk-off homer in the ninth inning to defeat the Tigers 10–7 at Metropolitan Stadium.

Allen was the starting quarterback for Purdue University's football team in 1959 and 1960. He hit .269 with 12 homers in 1962 as a 23-year-old rookie second baseman for the Twins. Unfortunately, it proved to be his best season in the majors. By 1964, Allen was a utility infielder, a role he played for the remainder of his career, which lasted until 1973. He was a Twin until 1966 when he was traded to the Senators.

MAY 10 — Lenny Green and Bernie Allen lead off the first inning with back-to-back homers off Jim Perry, but the Twins lose 9–4 to the Indians at Metropolitan Stadium.

By the end of May, manager Sam Mele settled on a batting order of Lenny Green (cf), Vic Power (1b), Rich Rollins (3b), Harmon Killebrew (lf), Bob Allison (rf), Earl Battey (c), Bernie Allen (2b) and Zoilo Versalles (ss) preceding the pitcher. Mele used the batting order a remarkable 70 times over the last 129 games of the season. The eight players started as a group 92 times in 1962 and 15 more in 1963.

MAY 13 — Vic Power hits a grand slam off Dan Pfister in the seventh inning of a 10–3 win over the Athletics at Metropolitan Stadium.

MAY 21 — The Twins play at D. C. Stadium in Washington for the first time and defeat the Senators 5–3.

D. C. Stadium was renamed RFK Stadium in 1968. It served as the home of the Senators from 1962 through 1971 and the Nationals from 2005 through 2007.

MAY 30 — Vic Power hits a walk-off homer in the 11th inning to defeat the Yankees 5–4 in the second game of a double-header at Metropolitan Stadium. The Yanks won the opener 10–1.

JUNE 26 — Camilo Pascaul strikes out 12 batters and pitches a shutout to lead the Twins to a 5–0 win over the Yankees at Metropolitan Stadium. Rich Rollins collected two homers and two singles and drove in four runs in five at-bats.

JULY 14 — The Twins sign Frank Sullivan as a free agent following his release by the Phillies.

JULY 18 — The Twins wallop two grand slams, score 11 runs in the first inning and rout the Indians 14–3 at Metropolitan Stadium. The Twins scored six runs off Cleveland starter Barry Latman before a batter was retired, four of them on a slam by Bob Allison. Latman was relieved by Jim Perry after Earl Battey followed Allison's blast with another homer. Perry allowed five more runs. After Vic Power drove in the seventh run with his second single of the inning, Harmon Killebrew hit another Minnesota grand slam. Rich Rollins contributed an RBI-single and a walk to the rally and Bill Tuttle walked twice. Killebrew added a solo homer off Perry in the third inning.

Killebrew had a tremendous six-game streak from July 12 through July 18 in which he hit six homers and drove in 20 runs. He batted only .243 in 1962, but led the AL in home runs (48) and RBIs (126). Allison batted .266 with 29 homers and 102 RBIs. He also scored 102 runs.

JULY 20   Earl Battey hits a two-run, walk-off homer in the tenth inning to defeat the Orioles 7–5 at Metropolitan Stadium.

AUGUST 1   On the day before his 23rd birthday, Jim Kaat is the star of an 11-inning, 3–1 victory over the Orioles in Baltimore. He not only pitched a complete game with 12 strikeouts, but broke the 1–1 tie with an RBI-triple off Robin Roberts.

Team owner Cal Griffith was thrilled to be in a new city, a fresh start for an up-and-coming franchise.

Rushed to the majors too soon, Kaat entered the 1962 season with a 10–24 career record. He responded with an 18–14 record and a 3.14 ERA in 269 innings. Kaat pitched for the Senators in 1959 and 1960 and for the Twins from 1961 through 1973 at the start of a career that spanned 25 seasons. He closed his stay in the majors as a 44 year old in 1983 with a record of 283–237. Among those eligible for the Hall of Fame who have yet to be enshrined, only Tommy John (288) and Bert Blyleven (287) have more career wins. An all-around athlete, Kaat also hit 16 career home runs and won 14 consecutive Gold Gloves. Among Twins pitchers, Kaat ranks first in wins (189), losses (152), games started (422), innings (2,959 1/3) and walks (694), and is second to Blyleven in complete games (133), shutouts (23) and strikeouts (1,824). Kaat is also third in games pitched (468) and third in ERA (3.28) among pitchers with at least 1,000 innings.

AUGUST 3   Facing Jim Bunning in the fourth inning, Harmon Killebrew hits a home run over the left field roof at Tiger Stadium. He was the first of four players in the history of the ballpark to clear the double-decked stands in left.

August 5	The Twins erupt for six runs in the 11th inning and defeat the Tigers 8–3 in the first game of a double-header at Tiger Stadium. Detroit won the second tilt 5–2 with Jackie Collum starting for the second day in a row.
	Collum also started the August 4 contest against the Tigers in Detroit, won by the Twins 4–3. On both occasions, he lasted only 1 2/3 innings. They proved to be the last two starts of his career, which began in 1951. As a Twin, Collum pitched 15 2/3 innings and had an ERA of 11.15.
August 8	Ed Charles of the Athletics steals home with two out in the ninth inning to provide the winning run of a 4–3 win over the Twins in Kansas City. The victims of the steal were pitcher Ray Moore and catcher Jerry Zimmerman.
August 9	The Twins break a 9–9 tie with three runs in the ninth inning and outlast the Athletics 12–10 in Kansas City.
August 10	Jim Kaat pitches a complete game but loses 1–0 in 11 innings to the Angels in Los Angeles.
August 13	Harmon Killebrew drives in five runs with three singles and a double to lead the Twins to a 6–4 triumph over the Yankees at Metropolitan Stadium.
August 20	The Twins trade Jackie Collum and Georges Maranda to the Indians for Ruben Gomez.
August 26	Jack Kralick pitches a no-hitter and beats the Athletics 1–0 before 23,224 on a Sunday afternoon at Metropolitan Stadium. He entered the ninth inning with a perfect game in progress. Wayne Causey led off the ninth by grounding out to second baseman Bernie Allen. George Alusik worked the count to 3–2, fouled off a pitch, and then took an offering well wide of the plate for a walk. He proved to be the only Kansas City base runner of the contest. Kralick closed out the no-hitter by retiring Billy Consolo and Bobby Del Greco, both on foul pop-ups to Power. Kralick threw 97 pitches and struck out three. The no-hitter was preserved by right fielder Bob Allison, who leaped above the fence to rob Ed Charles of a home run in the fourth inning.
	The no-hitter was the first in Twins history and the first for the franchise since Billy Burke pitched one for the Senators in 1931.
August 28	Zoilo Versalles drives in both runs of a 2–0 win over the White Sox with a two-run single off Early Wynn in the fifth inning. Jim Kaat pitched the shutout.
	Versalles was the Twins starting shortstop from 1961 through 1967, played in two All-Star Games, and won the AL MVP award in 1965. Despite standing only five-foot-ten and weighing 160 pounds, Versalles had considerable power and reached double digits in home runs four consecutive seasons beginning in 1962, with a high of 20 in 1964. He also led the AL in triples in 1963, 1964 and 1965.
September 8	The Twins defeat the Tigers 9–2 in Detroit to pull within three games of the first-place Yankees.

The next day, the Twins began a four-game losing streak to end any hopes of capturing the AL pennant. They ended the year five games behind the Yanks.

SEPTEMBER 14 The Twins clobber the Indians 11–1 at Metropolitan Stadium. Tony Oliva drove in three runs in his first big league start.

SEPTEMBER 15 The Twins defeat the Indians by ten runs for the second day in a row with a 12–2 decision at Metropolitan Stadium. Harmon Killebrew hit two homers and drove in five runs despite the fact that he didn't start or finish the game. He entered the contest in the second inning after Tony Oliva was injured, and he was replaced by Bill Tuttle in the eighth.

SEPTEMBER 16 Camilo Pascaul strikes out 12 batters and collects three hits, including a double, in four at-bats while leading the Twins to a 4–3 victory over the Indians at Metropolitan Stadium.

SEPTEMBER 19 The Twins score seven runs in the sixth inning and defeat the Tigers 12–5 at Metropolitan Stadium. Vic Power hit a grand slam off Bob Humphreys.

SEPTEMBER 23 Harmon Killebrew homers for the fourth game in a row, but the Twins lose 5–1 to the Indians in Cleveland.

SEPTEMBER 30 On the last day of the season, Camilo Pascaul earns his 20th victory with a 1–0 decision over the Orioles at Metropolitan Stadium. The lone run of the contest crossed the plate on a single by Harmon Killebrew in the first inning. It was one of only two Minnesota hits. Pascaul allowed just three base hits.

Pascaul finished the season with a 20–11 record and a 3.32 ERA and a league-leading 206 strikeouts in 257 2/3 innings.

NOVEMBER 26 A month after nerves are frazzled worldwide by the Cuban Missile Crisis, the Twins draft Rich Reese from the Tigers organization. On the same day, the Red Sox drafted Joe Foy from the Twins.

1963

Season in a Sentence

The Twins lose 20 of their first 31 games and finish a distant third, despite clubbing 225 homers and scoring more runs than any team in the league.

Finish • Won • Lost • Pct • GB

Third   91   70   .565   13.0

Manager

Sam Mele

Stats   Twins • AL • Rank

Batting Avg:	.255	.247	1
On-Base Pct:	.322	.312	2
Slugging Pct:	.430	.380	1
Home Runs:	225		1
Stolen Bases:	32		9
ERA:	3.28	3.63	3
Errors:	144		8
Runs Scored:	767		1
Runs Allowed:	602		3

Starting Line-up

Earl Battey, c
Vic Power, 1b
Bernie Allen, 2b
Rich Rollins, 3b
Zoilo Versalles, ss
Harmon Killebrew, lf
Jimmie Hall, cf
Bob Allison, rf
Lenny Green, cf
Don Mincher, 1b

Pitchers

Camilo Pascaul, sp
Dick Stigman, sp
Lee Stange, sp-rp
Jim Kaat, sp
Jim Perry, sp
Bill Dailey, rp

Attendance

1,406,652

Club Leaders

Batting Avg:	Rich Rollins	.307
On-Base Pct:	Bob Allison	.378
Slugging Pct:	Harmon Killebrew	.555
Home Runs:	Harmon Killebrew	45
RBI:	Harmon Killebrew	96
Runs:	Bob Allison	99
Stolen Bases:	Lenny Green	11
Wins:	Camilo Pascaul	21
Strikeouts:	Camilo Pascaul	202
ERA:	Camilo Pascaul	2.46
Saves:	Bill Dailey	21

January 30 The Twins effort to end the segregated housing of players during spring training fails. For several years, white and black players stayed at separate facilities while the club trained in Orlando. The white players were housed at the Cherry Plaza Hotel and the black athletes at the Sadler Hotel. A club statement said the Twins had intensified efforts to end the segregation but the Cherry Plaza had "so far refused to change its policy." The club said that the hotel was the only one in the area that had "adequate facilities in number and quality of rooms and in eating facilities." (See March 3, 1964.)

April 8 The Twins purchase Bill Dailey from the Indians.

> *The Twins expected little from Dailey, but at the age of 28, he emerged as the Twins closer with a 6–3 record, 21 saves and a 1.99 ERA in 66 games and 108²/₃ innings. After 1963, he turned back into a pumpkin. The 1964 campaign was Dailey's last in the majors, and he had an 8.22 earned run average in 15¹/₃ innings.*

April 9 The Twins open the season with a 5–4 loss to the Indians before 22,091 at Metropolitan Stadium. Lenny Green and Vic Power homered. Camilo Pascaul was the starting and losing pitcher.

The Twins drew 1,406,652 fans in 1963 to lead the AL in attendance. The club was third in the majors, trailing only the Dodgers and Giants.

APRIL 16   The Twins take a thrilling 11–10 decision from the Angels in 13 innings at Metropolitan Stadium. The Twins trailed 7–5 with two out in the ninth and no one on base when Jimmie Hall doubled and Bob Allison homered. The Angels scored twice in the 11th, but Minnesota came back with two in their half. Bernie Allen tripled in a run and crossed the plate on Jim Lemon's pinch-single. Los Angeles scored again in the top of the 13th, but the Twins countered with two tallies for the victory. Bernie Allen singled in the tying run. The winning tally was recorded on a bases-loaded walk by Eli Grba to George Banks. There were 17 pitchers used by the two teams during the contest, nine of them by the Angels.

Hall scored four runs in the game, his first major league start. A 25-year-old rookie outfielder, Hall began the season on the bench but took the starting centerfield job away from Lenny Green. Hall finished the season with a .260 batting average and 33 homers. He was part of a powerful outfield trio in 1963. Harmon Killebrew batted .258 with 45 home runs. Bob Allison contributed a .271 average, 35 home runs and a league-leading 99 runs scored. Altogether, the Twins hit 225 home runs in 1963. It was the second-highest figure in major league history at the time, surpassed only by the 240 collected by the 1961 Yankees. Other sluggers were Earl Battey (26 homers), Don Mincher (17 in 225 at-bats), Rich Rollins (16), Vic Power (ten) and Zoilo Versalles (ten). It would be 1996, when the Orioles smacked 257 home runs, before any major league team hit as many as the 1963 Twins. The Twins added 221 more home runs in 1964, which was the third-highest total in big league history well into the 1990s. The 1963 and 1964 figures still rank first and second in club history. The next time any team hit at least 221 homers in back-to-back seasons was 1996 and 1997 by the Mariners and Rockies.

MAY 2   The Twins trade Jack Kralick to the Indians for Jim Perry.

The older brother (by three years) of Gaylord Perry, Jim was a spot starter and long relief man for the Twins for several seasons. In 1969, he suddenly developed as the club's number one starter while in his mid-thirties. Perry had a 20–6 record in 1969 and a 24–12 mark in 1970. Perry ranks first in ERA among Twins pitchers with at least 1,000 innings with a mark of 3.15. He is also third in wins (128), fourth in losses (90), third in innings (1,883 1/3), third in walks (541), fourth in strikeouts (1,025), fourth in games started (249), fourth in shutouts (17) and fifth in complete games (61).

MAY 4   The Twins sell Jim Lemon to the Phillies.

MAY 10   At Metropolitan Stadium, third baseman Jay Ward drives in both runs in a 2–0 victory over the Athletics with a two-run double in the second inning. Camilo Pascual pitched the shutout.

The double came in Ward's seventh big league at-bat and accounted for his first hit and first two RBIs. He didn't collect another hit in the majors until September 15, 1964, and failed to drive in another run until October 2, 1964. Ward finished his brief career with a .163 batting average and four runs batted in over 49 at-bats.

MAY 11   Ted Bowsfield of the Athletics enters the ninth inning with a no-hitter before allowing singles to Vic Power and Bob Allison and closing out a 5–1 win over the Twins at Metropolitan Stadium.

> *The Twins bottomed out with an 11–20 record on May 15. By June 28, the club was 42–32 and only 1½ games out of first. But the Yankees were too much for the rest of the American league in 1963, and the Twins couldn't keep pace. At the end of the year, Minnesota was 91–70 and in third place, 13 games out.*

MAY 16   The Twins purchase Wally Post from the Reds.

MAY 17   Bob Allison hits three consecutive homers and drives in six runs during an 11–4 triumph over the Indians in Cleveland. Allison hit home runs off Mudcat Grant in the fifth inning, Jerry Walker in the seventh, and Ron Nischwitz in the ninth. Harmon Killebrew and Zoilo Versalles also homered for the Twins.

> *Allison was the first Twins player to connect for three home runs in a game.*

MAY 18   Wally Post homers in his first game with the Twins, helping his new club to an 8–1 victory over the Indians in Cleveland.

MAY 19   Lenny Green hits a two-run homer with two-out in the ninth inning to lift the Twins to a 7–6 win over the Indians in the second game of a double-header at Municipal Stadium. Cleveland won the opener 6–4.

MAY 20   The Twins score seven runs in the third inning and beat the Red Sox 8–2 in Boston.

MAY 24   Jimmie Hall hits a two-run, walk-off homer in the ninth inning to down the White Sox 8–6 at Metropolitan Stadium. Chicago tied the score 6–6 in the top of the ninth on a two-out, three-run homer from Ron Hansen. Hall entered the game at the start of the ninth as a defensive replacement for Harmon Killebrew. Killebrew hit a grand slam in the fifth off Ray Herbert.

MAY 25   Camilo Pascaul pitches a two-hitter to defeat the White Sox 6–0 at Metropolitan Stadium. The only Chicago hits were a double by Pete Ward in the third inning and a single from Floyd Robinson in the ninth.

MAY 28   Bob Allison hits a three-run, walk-off homer in the ninth inning to defeat the Senators 6–3 at Metropolitan Stadium. Washington tied the score with three runs in the top of the ninth. It was the Twins eighth win in a row.

MAY 29   Dick Stigman pitches a two-hitter to defeat the Senators 10–1 at Metropolitan Stadium. The only Washington hits were a triple by Minnie Minoso in the first inning and a double from Eddie Brinkman in the third. Vic Power hit a grand slam in the fifth off Jim Coates.

MAY 30   The Twins run their winning streak to ten games with a 3–2 decision over the Senators at Metropolitan Stadium. Camilo Pascaul not only pitched a complete game, but drove in the winning run with a walk-off sacrifice fly in the ninth inning.

JUNE 1 Zoilo Versalles collects three doubles and a single in five at-bats during a 7–1 victory over the Tigers at Metropolitan Stadium.

JUNE 14 The Twins purchase Mike Fornieles from the Red Sox.

JUNE 18 The Twins sign Vic Wertz as a free agent.

JUNE 21 Harmon Killebrew homers for the fourth game in a row to help the Twins to a 5–2 win over the Orioles in the first game of a double-header at Metropolitan Stadium. Baltimore won the second tilt 10–2.

JUNE 25 Harmon Killebrew homers off Jim Bunning in the third inning for the lone run of a 1–0 victory over the Tigers at Metropolitan Stadium. It was one of only two Minnesota hits. Lee Stange pitched the shutout.

Harmon Killebrew powered the Twins through their early years in the Twin Cities, becoming one of the most feared hitters in the American League.

1960s

JUNE 27 — The Twins break a 4–4 tie with six runs in the sixth inning and defeat the Tigers 10–6 at Metropolitan Stadium. Both benches emptied in the fifth when Vic Power and Detroit pitcher Phil Regan tangled at first base. Power was ejected by the umpires.

JUNE 28 — The Twins sweep the Senators 10–6 and 11–4 during a double-header in Washington. Harmon Killebrew collected six hits, including two doubles and a homer, in ten at-bats.

JULY 2 — The Twins extend their winning streak to eight games with a 7–4 decision over the Tigers in Detroit.

Jimmie Hall homered in four consecutive games from June 30 through July 4. He homered in four straight games again from July 31 through August 4.

JULY 9 — In the All-Star Game at Municipal Stadium in Cleveland, Earl Battey drives in a run with a single in the third inning, but the American League loses 5–3.

JULY 14 — Don Mincher hits a grand slam off Barry Latman in the first inning of an 8–2 win over the Indians in the second game of a double-header at Metropolitan Stadium. The Twins also won the opener 5–3.

Through July 13, Mincher had only one hit in 22 at-bats on the season for an average of .045. Then from July 14 through July 24, he hit eight homers in ten games along with a total of 19 hits in 39 at-bats.

JULY 15 — The Twins trounce the Indians 13–1 at Metropolitan Stadium.

JULY 24 — The Twins sweep the Indians 9–0 and 5–0 in a double-header in Cleveland. Dick Stigman and Jim Kaat pitched the shutouts. In the second tilt, the Twins scored all five of their runs in the ninth inning, the last three on a home run by Kaat. He also struck out 11 batters.

AUGUST 14 — The Twins outlast the Orioles 2–1 in 13 innings at Metropolitan Stadium. The winning run scored on a double by Vic Power and a single from Bernie Allen. Jim Perry (seven innings), Gary Roggenburk (two innings) and Bill Dailey (four innings) combined on a six-hitter.

AUGUST 15 — The Twins lambaste the Orioles 13–3 at Metropolitan Stadium.

AUGUST 21 — The Twins score eight runs in the fourth inning and four in the fifth to defeat the Tigers 12–1 in Detroit.

AUGUST 24 — Jimmie Hall homers off Dick Hall in the eighth inning for the lone run of a 1–0 victory over the Orioles in Baltimore. Lee Stange pitched the shutout.

The Twins were 13–26 in one-run games in 1963.

AUGUST 29 — The day after Martin Luther King, Jr.'s "I Have a Dream" speech at the Lincoln Memorial, the Twins hit 12 home runs in a double-header and sweep the Senators 14–2 and 10–1 in Washington. There were 20 Minnesota hits in the opener, including a club record eight homers. Vic Power and Harmon Killebrew each homered twice with Rich Rollins, Jimmie Hall, Bob Allison and Bernie Allen adding the rest. Allen, Hall, Killebrew and Zoilo Versalles hit home runs in game two.

SEPTEMBER 18   Camilo Pascaul pitches a two-hitter to defeat the Tigers 10–0 at Metropolitan Stadium. Rocky Colavito collected both Detroit hits with a single in the second inning and a double in the seventh.

SEPTEMBER 21   Harmon Killebrew hits three homers and drives in five runs to lead the Twins to a 13–4 triumph over the Red Sox in the first game of a double-header in Boston. Killebrew homered off Bill Monbouquette in the first inning, Pete Smith in the fifth, and Arnold Earley in the eighth. Harmon homered again in the second tilt against Gene Conley in the sixth inning, giving him four on the day, but the Twins lost 11–2.

SEPTEMBER 22   Camilo Pascaul records his 20th victory of the season with a 6–1 decision over the Red Sox in Boston.

Pascaul finished the season with a record of 21–9 and an ERA of 2.46. He also led the AL in strikeouts for the third year in a row with 202 in 248 1/3 innings.

DECEMBER 2   Ten days after the assassination of President John Kennedy, the Red Sox draft Reggie Smith and the White Sox draft Rudy May from the Twins organization.

The Twins made a huge mistake in failing to protect Smith and May. Smith was a particularly tough loss. He played 17 seasons in the majors and appeared in seven All-Star Games and four World Series.

1964

Season in a Sentence
The Twins smack 221 home runs, at the time the third highest figure in major league history, and lead the AL in runs scored, but end the year with a losing record.

Finish • Won • Lost • Pct • GB
Sixth (tie) 79 83 .488 20.0

Manager
Sam Mele

Stats   Twins • AL • Rank
Batting Avg: .252 .247 4
On-Base Pct: .319 .315 2
Slugging Pct: .427 .382 1
Home Runs: 221   1
Stolen Bases: 46   8
ERA: 3.58 3.63 5
Errors: 145   9
Runs Scored: 737   1
Runs Allowed: 678   5

Starting Line-up
Earl Battey, c
Bob Allison, 1b-cf
Bernie Allen, 2b
Rich Rollins, 3b
Zoilo Versalles, ss
Harmon Killebrew, lf
Jimmie Hall, cf
Tony Oliva, rf
Don Mincher, 1b

Pitchers
Jim Kaat, sp
Camilo Pascaul, sp
Dick Stigman, sp
Mudcat Grant, sp
Al Worthington, rp
Bill Pleis, rp
Jim Perry, rp
Gerry Arrigo, rp
Jim Roland, sp-rp

Attendance
1,207,514 (third in AL)

Club Leaders
Batting Avg:	Tony Oliva	.323
On-Base Pct:	Bob Allison	.404
Slugging Pct:	Tony Oliva	.557
Home Runs:	Harmon Killebrew	49
RBI:	Harmon Killebrew	111
Runs:	Tony Oliva	109
Stolen Bases:	Zoilo Versalles	14
Wins:	Jim Kaat	17
Strikeouts:	Camilo Pascaul	213
ERA:	Mudcat Grant	2.82
Saves:	Al Worthington	14

March 3 — Four weeks after the Beatles make their historic first appearance on the Ed Sullivan Show, the Twins move to an integrated motel in Orlando after being pressured by civil rights groups to end segregated housing practices during spring training. In the past, white players stayed at the Cherry Plaza Hotel and black players at the Sadler Motel. The entire club moved to the Downtowner Inn, which accepted blacks. At the time, the Twins were the only team in baseball to permit segregated housing during training camp. Members of the Congress for Racial Equality had threatened to picket the Twins' home opener.

April 14 — Trailing 6–3 after four innings, the Twins rally for a 7–6, Opening Day win over the Indians at Municipal Stadium. Earl Battey hit a three-run homer in the fourth that gave the Twins a 3–2 lead before Cleveland scored four times in the bottom half off Camilo Pascaul and Gerry Arrigo. Jimmie Hall drove in two runs with a two-out, two-run double in the fifth. Rich Rollins drove in the tying and winning runs with a two-run single with two out in the sixth. Jim Roland pitched four hitless innings of relief. Mudcat Grant was the Indians starting pitcher. He would be a member of the Twins two months later.

APRIL 18	Tony Oliva leads off the tenth inning with a home run before the Twins add an insurance run to defeat the Senators 8–6 in Washington.

> *Oliva had one of the greatest rookie seasons in history in 1964 by leading the AL in batting average (.323), runs (109), hits (217) and doubles (43) in addition to hitting 32 homers and driving in 94 runs. Born Pedro Oliva in Cuba, he was signed by the Twins at the age of 22 in 1961. He entered the United States on his brother Tony's passport, and was known as Tony from that day forward. In 1961 at the Twins farm club in Wytheville, Virginia, Oliva hit .410 with 81 RBIs in 64 games. He was probably ready for the majors by 1963, but couldn't find a spot in the Twins crowded outfield of Harmon Killebrew, Jimmie Hall and Bob Allison. Oliva proved he was more than ready by collecting 58 hits in his first 136 big league at-bats for an average of .426. He made the All-Star team in each of his first eight full seasons in the majors. During that span, Oliva won three batting titles and led the AL in hits five times, doubles in four, and slugging percentage and runs once each. But a knee injury limited Oliva to ten games in 1972, and he was never the same player. In January 1973, the American League passed the designated hitter rule, which prolonged his career. He played in 471 games from 1973 through 1976 as a DH and pinch-hitter without appearing in a single contest defensively.*

APRIL 28	Jimmie Hall homers in the ninth inning to tie the score 8–8, then delivers a walk-off single in the tenth to down the Indians 9–8 at Metropolitan Stadium. The Twins led 7–2 before allowing Cleveland to score four runs in the seventh and two in the ninth to take an 8–7 lead.
MAY 1	Earl Battey drives in six runs with a grand slam off Moe Drabowsky in the sixth inning and a two-run single off Tom Strudivant in the eighth to lead the Twins to a 10–5 victory over the Athletics in Kansas City.

> *Battey hit .272 with 12 home runs in 1964.*

MAY 2	The Twins hit four consecutive home runs in the 11th inning to defeat the Athletics 7–3 in Kansas City. Facing Dan Pfister, Tony Oliva, Bob Allison and Jimmie Hall each homered to lead off the inning. Vern Hanrahan relieved Pfister and yielded a home run to Harmon Killebrew. Earlier in the contest, Oliva hit a home run in the third inning and Killebrew cleared the wall with a drive in the ninth.

> *The Twins were the third of six teams with four consecutive home runs. The others are the 1961 Milwaukee Braves, the 1963 Indians, the 2006 Dodgers, the 2007 Red Sox and the 2008 White Sox.*

MAY 4	Bob Allison hits two homers and drives in all five Twins runs, but the club loses 10–5 to the White Sox in Chicago.
MAY 7	Tony Oliva collects two homers and two singles and drives in six runs during a 9–1 win over the Angels at Metropolitan Stadium. Four of his half-dozen RBIs came on a grand slam off Jack Spring in the sixth inning. Oliva added a solo homer facing Paul Foytack in the eighth.
MAY 9	Trailing 7–1, the Twins rally with two runs in the fourth inning, three in the sixth and four in the seventh to defeat the Athletics 10–8 at Metropolitan Stadium.

Bob Allison put Minnesota ahead with a three-run double in the seventh. Gerry Arrigo struck out seven batters during a four-inning relief appearance. A day earlier, Arrigo was relieved in the second inning of a start against the A's, which the Twins lost 6–5 in ten innings.

MAY 12   The Twins rout the White Sox 11–1 at Metropolitan Stadium.

MAY 14   The Twins outslug the White Sox 15–7 at Metropolitan Stadium. Rich Rollins led the offense with a homer, two doubles, and five RBIs.

MAY 15   Camilo Pascaul pitches the Twins to a 1–0 win over the Red Sox in Boston. Bernie Allen drove in the lone run with a double in the eighth.

In four games from May 12 through May 15, the Twins run totals were 11, 1, 15 and 1.

MAY 19   The Twins erupt for five runs in the 13th inning and defeat the Yankees 7–2 in New York. Jimmie Hall capped the rally with a three-run homer.

In seven games from May 14 through May 20, Harmon Killebrew hit seven homers and drove in 14 runs.

MAY 22   With two out in the ninth inning and a 5–4 lead over the Orioles in Baltimore, Gerry Arrigo allows a home run to Sam Bowens. Bill Fischer relieved Arrigo and surrendered a walk-off homer to John Orsino for a 6–5 loss. Fischer never threw another pitch in the majors, ending a career that began in 1956.

MAY 29   Jim Roland pitches a two-hitter to defeat the Red Sox 3–2 at Metropolitan Stadium. The only Boston hits were a home run by Dick Stuart and a single from Lu Clinton, both in the second inning.

The victory evened Roland's won-lost record at 2–2. Over the remainder of the season, he was 0–4 with a 5.74 ERA in 42 1/3 innings. His victory on May 29, 1964 was his last in the majors until June 14, 1968.

JUNE 2   The Twins collect a club record four triples during a 6–2 win over the Yankees at Metropolitan Stadium. The triples were delivered by Earl Battey, Don Mincher, Bob Allison and Johnny Goryl. The Twins had only one double during the game.

JUNE 9   The Tigers clobber the Twins 16–1 in Detroit.

JUNE 11   As part of a three-team trade, the Twins send Vic Power and Lenny Green to the Angels and receive Frank Kostro from the Angels and Jerry Kindall from the Indians.

Kindall spent nine years in the majors, but hit just .213 in 742 games and 2,057 at-bats. No one with at least 2,000 at-bats since 1920 has a lower batting average. In 187 games and 470 at-bats with the Twins in 1964 and 1965, Kindall's batting average was .183. He later became coach of the University of Arizona baseball team and led the school to an NCAA championship in 1976, 1980, and 1986. Power, at 36, was near the end of his career, and with the emergence of Olivia, the Twins moved Bob Allison from the outfield to first base. Lenny Green, at 31, could not find playing time in the outfield and was expendable. Frank Kostro remained a utility player for the team.

JUNE 14 — The Twins hit eight home runs during a 6–5 and 9–2 sweep of the Senators during a double-header in Washington. In the first game, Harmon Killebrew homered twice with Bob Allison and Zoilo Versalles adding the others. During the second tilt, the home runs were delivered by Killebrew, Allison, Jimmie Hall and Jim Kaat.

JUNE 15 — The Twins trade Lee Stange and George Banks to the Indians for Mudcat Grant.

The Twins made a tremendous short-term deal in acquiring Grant, who was 28 and had a 67–63 lifetime record at the time of the trade. The Florida-born Grant earned his unusual nickname from a minor league teammate, who mistakenly believed that Grant was from Mississippi, which is sometimes known as the "Mudcat State." He went 11–9 over the remainder of the 1964 season, and then won the undying affection of Twins fans during the pennant-winning season of 1965. Grant was 21–7 with a 3.30 ERA and a league-leading six shutouts. He also won two World Series games. After dropping to 13–13 in 1966 and 5–6 in 1967, he was traded to the Dodgers.

JUNE 16 — In his first start with the Twins, Frank Kostro collects a home run, double and single in four at-bats, but the Twins lose 5–3 to the Indians in Cleveland.

JUNE 24 — Dick Stigman strikes out 12 batters during a 3–2 win over the Indians in the second game of a double-header against the Indians at Metropolitan Stadium. Cleveland won the opener 12–3.

JUNE 26 — Gerry Arrigo pitches a one-hitter to defeat the White Sox 2–0 in the first game of a double-header at Metropolitan Stadium. He had a no-hitter in progress until Mike Hershberger led off the ninth inning with a single. Arrigo retired the final three batters to close out the victory. Chicago won game two by a 9–4 score.

On the same day, the Twins purchased Al Worthington from the Reds. Worthington broke into the majors in 1953 with the New York Giants by pitching shutouts in his first two major league starts, but spent most of his career as a reliever. When acquired by the Twins, Worthington was 35 years old, had a lifetime record of 38–52 in the majors, and was pitching for the Reds' Class AAA affiliate in San Diego in the Pacific Coast League. Nonetheless, he starred as the club's closer for many years. In his first 37 1/3 innings with the Twins, Worthington didn't allow an earned run while surrendering 21 hits and striking out 34. From 1964 through 1968, he posted a 2.34 earned run average in 281 games and 412 1/3 innings and saved 85 games along with a record of 33–30.

JUNE 24 — The Twins sign Rod Carew as an amateur free agent shortly after his graduation from George Washington High School in New York City. He didn't play baseball on the high school team, however. Instead, Carew played sandlot ball for the Bronx Cavaliers, where he was discovered by Twins scout Monroe Katz. Carew reported to the Twins minor league team in Melbourne, Florida, and made his major league debut in 1967.

JUNE 28 — Playing in his first major league game since 1962, second baseman Jim Snyder drives in three runs during a 9–3 victory over the White Sox at Metropolitan Stadium.

Harmon Killebrew homered in five consecutive games from June 24 through June 28.

June 29   The Twins purchase Johnny Klippstein from the Phillies.

Over a 15-day span in June 1965, the Twins acquired three pitchers who were brilliant during the 1965 pennant-winning season. Mudcat Grant and Al Worthington preceded Klippstein, who was 36 when obtained by the club. In 1964 and 1965, Klippstein was 9–7 with a 2.14 ERA in 89 games and 122 innings.

July 1   The Twins break a scoreless tie with seven runs in the fourth inning and rout the Red Sox 14–3 in Boston. Bob Allison drove in six runs with a home run and two doubles.

July 2   The Twins out-slug the Red Sox 15–9 in Boston. The Twins scored five runs in the first inning and led 12–2 at the end of the sixth.

July 3   After scoring 29 runs in back-to-back games at Fenway Park, the Twins squeak past the Yankees 1–0 in ten innings in New York. The lone run scored on a triple by Don Mincher and a sacrifice fly from Jim Snyder. Dick Stigman pitched a complete-game shutout.

Snyder finished his career with a .140 batting average in 41 games and 86 at-bats.

July 7   In the All-Star Game at Shea Stadium in New York, Harmon Killebrew collects three hits and drives in a run in four at-bats, but the AL loses 7–6. The NL scored four runs in the ninth, the last three on a walk-off homer by Johnny Callison, for the victory.

July 9   Bob Allison and Don Mincher hit back-to-back homers off Jose Santiago in the sixth inning for the only two runs of a 2–1 win over the Athletics in Kansas City.

The Twins had a record of 46–37 on July 11, and then lost 22 of their next 29 games. The club scored 737 runs to lead the AL in runs for the second year in a row. The team also hit 221 home runs to become the first team in major league history to belt at least 200 homers in consecutive seasons (see April 16, 1963). The home run leaders in 1964 were Harmon Killebrew (49), Tony Oliva (32), Bob Allison (32), Jimmie Hall (25), Don Mincher (23), Zoilo Versalles (20), Rich Rollins (12) and Earl Battey (12).

July 15   Mudcat Grant allows 13 hits and walks a batter, but manages to beat the Senators 6–0 at Metropolitan Stadium. Grant helped himself defensively by starting two of the three double plays turned by the Twins. Washington left 12 runners on base.

July 23   Making his major league debut, Athletics shortstop Bert Campaneris hits two homers off Jim Kaat in an 11-inning, 4–3 Kansas City win at Metropolitan Stadium. The first homer came in the first inning on the first pitch thrown to Campaneris. The second blow was struck in the seventh.

July 31   Harmon Killebrew hits a two-out, two-run, walk-off homer in the ninth inning to defeat the Yankees 4–3 at Metropolitan Stadium.

Killebrew finished the year with a .270 average, 49 homers, 111 RBIs and 95 runs scored.

AUGUST 4 — The Twins use five homers to power past the Red Sox 12–4 at Metropolitan Stadium. The home runs were struck by Rich Rollins, Harmon Killebrew, Tony Oliva, Bob Allison and Earl Battey.

Allison hit .287 with 32 homers in 1964.

AUGUST 16 — The Twins scored six runs in the seventh inning of a 13–2 rout of the Indians at Metropolitan Stadium.

AUGUST 23 — With the Twins trailing 5–1 to the Tigers in the eighth inning in Detroit, Don Mincher hits a grand slam off Fred Gladding to tie the score. Tony Oliva drove in a run with a single in the ninth for a 6–5 win.

Mincher hit only .237 in 1964, but collected 23 home runs in 287 at-bats. Four of his home runs were as a pinch-hitter.

SEPTEMBER 1 — Harmon Killebrew hits solo homers off Steve Barber in the fourth and sixth innings for the only two runs of a 2–1 win over the Orioles at Metropolitan Stadium.

SEPTEMBER 2 — Milt Pappas of the Orioles pitches a one-hitter to defeat the Twins 2–0 at Metropolitan Stadium. Zoilo Versalles broke up the no-hit bid with a single with two out in the eighth inning.

SEPTEMBER 4 — The Twins score in six of eight turns at bat and trounce the Red Sox 14–3 at Metropolitan Stadium.

SEPTEMBER 5 — The Twins score eight runs in the third inning and defeat the Red Sox 10–4 at Metropolitan Stadium.

SEPTEMBER 6 — The Twins collect only one hit off Bill Monbouquette but defeat the Red Sox 2–1 at Metropolitan Stadium. In the sixth inning, Rich Rollins reached on a two-out error, and Zoilo Versalles followed with a two-run homer. It was the second time in five days in which Versalles delivered the only Minnesota base hit.

Versalles hit .259 with 20 home runs in 1964.

SEPTEMBER 18 — Making his major league debut in a start at the age of 19, Dave Boswell allows a home run to Felix Mantilla of the Red Sox leading off the first inning and exits after allowing three runs in three innings. The Twins lost 7–6 in Boston.

The Twins fielded the youngest team in the major leagues in 1962, 1963 and 1964.

OCTOBER 1 — Four days after the release of the Warren Commission report, which states that Lee Harvey Oswald was the lone assassin in the death of President John Kennedy, Camilo Pascual pitches 12 innings and strikes out 14 batters, but the Twins lose 5–4 to the Athletics at Metropolitan Stadium.

Pascaul struck out 213 batters in 267⅓ innings in 1964 while posting a 15–12 record and a 3.30 ERA. He fell four strikeouts shy of leading the AL in the category for the fourth consecutive season.

OCTOBER 2   Harmon Killebrew hits his 49th home run of the season during a 5–4 win over the Angels at Metropolitan Stadium. Killebrew had eight more plate appearances before the end of the season but failed in his attempt to connect for number 50.

The Twins were 28–38 in one-run games in 1964, after going 13–26 in 1963.

DECEMBER 4   A month after Lyndon Johnson defeats Barry Goldwater in the Presidential election, the Twins trade Gerry Arrigo to the Reds for Cesar Tovar.

Tovar was 24 at the time of the trade and had yet to play in a major league game. The deal proved to be one of the best in club history, as he wound up playing eight years for the Twins at the start of a 12-year career. Tovar excelled with his versatility, which was on display when he played all nine positions in a game on September 22, 1968. Tovar played in at least 200 games at five different positions (all three outfield spots, third base and second base) and another 75 at shortstop as a major leaguer. He was also an offensive force and led the AL in hits, triples and doubles during his career.

1965

Season in a Sentence
Behind a much more balanced offensive attack and improved pitching, the Twins win a club record 102 games and win the AL pennant before losing the World Series to the Dodgers.

Finish • Won • Lost • Pct • GB
First   102   60   .630   +7.0

World Series
The Twins lost four games to three to the Los Angeles Dodgers.

Manager
Sam Mele

Stats   Twins • AL • Rank
Batting Avg: .254   .242   1
On-Base Pct: .323   .311   2
Slugging Pct: .399   .369   2
Home Runs: 150   4
Stolen Bases: 92   4
ERA: 3.14   3.46   3
Errors: 172   10
Runs Scored: 774   1
Runs Allowed: 600   3

Starting Line-up
Earl Battey, c
Harmon Killebrew, 1b-3b
Jerry Kindall, 2b
Rich Rollins, 3b
Zoilo Versalles, ss
Bob Allison, lf
Jimmie Hall, cf
Tony Oliva, rf
Don Mincher, 1b
Sandy Valdespino, lf

Pitchers
Mudcat Grant, sp
Jim Kaat, sp
Jim Perry, sp-rp
Camilo Pascaul, sp
Jim Merritt, sp-rp
Al Worthington, rp
Johnny Klippstein, rp
Bill Pleis, rp
Dave Boswell, rp-sp

Attendance
1,463,258 (first in AL)

Club Leaders
Batting Avg: Tony Oliva   .321
On-Base Pct: Tony Oliva   .378
Slugging Pct: Tony Oliva   .501
Home Runs: Harmon Killebrew 25
RBI: Tony Oliva   98
Runs: Zoilo Versalles 126
Stolen Bases: Zoilo Versalles   27
Wins: Mudcat Grant   21
Strikeouts: Jim Kaat   154
ERA: Jim Perry   2.63
Saves: Al Worthington   21

APRIL 12   The Twins edge the Yankees 5–4 in 11 innings before an Opening Day crowd of 15,388 at Metropolitan Stadium. The gametime temperature was 44 degrees with an 18 mile-per-hour wind. Stranded by the rising floodwaters of the Mississippi River, Jim Kaat, Rich Rollins, Bill Bethea and Dick Stigman were brought to the ballpark by helicopter. They were picked up from an elementary school in suburban Burnsville. Players slipped on the soggy field throughout the game, and the Yanks made five errors. The Twins led 4–0 after four innings, with the help of a two-run single from Kaat, but the Yanks rallied to tie the score. Playing third base in his first major league game, Cesar Tovar dropped a pop-up with two out in the ninth to allow the Yankees to tie the game 4–4. Tovar redeemed himself by driving in the winning run with a single. He entered the game in the fourth following an injury to Rich Rollins.

A week before the game, Metropolitan Stadium was covered by five inches of snow. Rain and melting snow caused rivers to rise, turning the entire state into a disaster area. Twelve people died in Minnesota because of the floods.

1960s

Due to a pair of postponements, the Twins opened the season by playing their first three games against three different teams. The April 12 opener was followed by contests facing the Tigers on April 15 and the Indians on April 17.

April 27 The Twins score seven runs in the first inning and clobber the Indians 11–1 in Cleveland. Camilo Pascaul capped the rally with a grand slam off Stan Williams. The Twins pitcher later drove in another run with a single. Not only did Pascaul drive in five runs, but he allowed only two hits, a double by Dick Howser leading off the first and a single by Cam Carreon with two out in the eighth. From the first inning through the eighth, Pascaul retired 21 batters in a row.

The grand slam by Pascaul is the only one by a pitcher in the history of the franchise since the move to Minnesota in 1961. It was the second of his career. Pascaul also hit a slam for the Senators in 1960.

May 7 The Twins make seven errors during a 13–5 loss to the White Sox at Metropolitan Stadium. There were two errors each by shortstop Zoilo Versalles and third baseman Rich Rollins, and one each from second baseman Jerry Kindall, catcher Earl Battey and first baseman Harmon Killebrew.

A day earlier, tornadoes ripped through the northern and western suburbs of Minneapolis, killing 13.

May 15 Jerry Kindall drives in both runs of a 2–0 win over the Athletics in Kansas City with a single in the third inning and a homer in the fifth. Dave Boswell (7⅓ innings) and Mel Nelson (1⅔ innings) combined on the shutout.

May 25 The Twins collect 20 hits and trounce the Red Sox 17–5 in Boston.

June 8 Camilo Pascaul runs his record to 8–0 with a 6–2 win over the Indians at Metropolitan Stadium. Bothered by a back injury, Pascaul won only one more game the rest of the season, however, and finished with a 9–3 record and a 3.35 ERA.

On the same day, the first amateur draft takes place, and the Twins selected shortstop Eddie Leon from in the first round. Leon didn't sign with the Twins, and attended the University of Arizona instead. Second rounder Del Unser opted to remain in college at Mississippi State rather than sign with the Twins. Leon was drafted by the Indians in 1967, and had an eight-year career with a .236 batting average. Unser was picked by the Senators in 1966, and enjoyed a 15-year stay in the majors as an outfielder. Future major leaguers drafted and signed by the Twins in 1965 were Graig Nettles (fourth round), Ron Keller (eighth round) and Bob Gebhard (44th round). Nettles was traded following the 1969 season before becoming a star.

June 11 The Twins win a pair of extra-inning games, both by 5–4 scores, to defeat the Tigers in a double-header in Detroit. The first tilt went ten innings with Jimmie Hall driving in the winning run with a sacrifice fly. In game two, Minnesota scored three times in the top of the 12th with the opposition countering with two in their half.

June 25 Trailing 3–2 with two out and no one on base in the ninth inning, the Twins rally to win 4–3 over the Tigers at Metropolitan Stadium. The rally consisted of walks to Harmon Killebrew and Don Mincher, a run-scoring single from Bernie Allen, an intentional walk to Rich Rollins, and a walk-off pinch-single from Joe Nossek.

JULY 3 — Don Mincher leads off the 11th inning with a home run to defeat the Athletics 3–2 in Kansas City.

JULY 5 — The Twins take over sole possession of first place with a 6–2 and 2–0 sweep of the Red Sox in a double-header at Metropolitan Stadium.

The Twins remained in first for the rest of the season. The club won the pennant with a different offensive philosophy than in previous years. The Twins led the AL in home runs (225) and runs (767) in 1963, yet finished in third place, 13 games out of first. In 1964, Minnesota topped the circuit in home runs (221) and runs (737) again, but ended up with a record of 79–83. In between the 1964 and 1965 seasons, the Twins moved the fences back, changing the distance to left field from 330 feet to 344 and in center field from 412 feet to 430. In 1965, the Twins hit only 150 home runs, but increased the run production to 774 to lead the AL for the third year in a row. A more aggressive approach on the bases was a major factor in the increase in runs scored in 1965 despite the drop in home runs. The Twins stole 92 bases that season after swiping just 32 in 1963 and 46 in 1964. Defense was a problem all year, however. The Twins led the majors in errors with 172. In addition, second base was a weak spot for the second year in a row. Twins' second basemen combined to hit just .206 with six home runs and 139 strikeouts. In 1964, the club's second basemen batted just .190.

JULY 10 — The Twins extend their winning streak to nine games with a 4–1 win over the Yankees in the first game of a double-header at Metropolitan Stadium. The streak ended with an 8–6 loss in the second tilt.

JULY 11 — Harmon Killebrew hits a two-run, walk-off homer in the ninth inning to defeat the Yankees 6–5 at Metropolitan Stadium.

Killebrew was limited to 113 games because of injuries in 1965. He hit .269 with 25 home runs.

JULY 13 — The All-Star Game is played at Metropolitan Stadium, and the National League wins 6–5. The NL took a 5–0 lead with three runs in the first inning and two in the second. Willie Mays slammed the second pitch of the game for a home run off Milt Pappas. Before the inning was over Joe Torre added a two-run home run. Mudcat Grant gave up the two second-inning tallies on a home run to Willie Stargell. The AL tied the game with a run in the fourth inning and four in the fifth. Dick McAuliffe started the fifth-inning rally with a home run, and Harmon Killebrew added a two-run homer off Jim Maloney, the fifth of the game by the two clubs. The NL won the game with a run in the seventh, driven in on an infield single by Ron Santo. Grant and Killebrew were two of six Twins to play in the contest. The others were Tony Oliva, Zoilo Versalles, Earl Battey and Jimmie Hall. Oliva hit a double in two at-bats.

Future Hall of Famers on the rosters of the two clubs were Hank Aaron, Ernie Banks, Roberto Clemente, Don Drysdale, Bob Gibson, Al Kaline, Harmon Killebrew, Sandy Koufax, Mickey Mantle, Willie Mays, Brooks Robinson,

Frank Robinson, Willie Stargell, Billy Williams and Carl Yastrzemski. Pete Rose was also a part of the NL squad.

JULY 15   The Twins score seven runs in the fourth inning on only three hits during an 11–2 win over the Athletics in the first game of a double-header at Metropolitan Stadium. With one out, three Kansas City pitchers combined to walk five Minnesota batters in a row, the last four of which were with the bases loaded. The five drawing the base on balls were Tony Oliva, Jimmie Hall, Harmon Killebrew, Don Mincher and Earl Battey. The A's won the second game 3–2.

Oliva was batting only .267 on July 4, but hit .379 the rest of the way to win his second straight batting title with an average of .321. He also hit 16 home runs, scored 107 runs, and drove in 98.

JULY 18   The usually mild-mannered Sam Mele battles with umpire Bill Valentine in the sixth inning of a 5–3 loss to the Angels in the first game of a double-header at Metropolitan Stadium. The Twins won the second game 5–4.

Mele stormed out of the dugout after Valentine called Jim Fregosi safe on a play at first base, and the two almost immediately became involved in a pushing and shoving match. Mele appeared to take a swing at Valentine during the altercation. The other umpires and several players pulled the two apart. American League President Joe Cronin was in attendance during the game and later suspended Mele for five games.

Tony Oliva smacks a hit in the World Series. Despite a .321 average in the regular season, Olivia hit just .192 in the series, as the Dodgers shut down Twins hitters.

JULY 21	Tony Oliva collects five hits, including a double, in six at-bats during an 8–6 win over the Red Sox in the first game of a double-header in Boston. The Twins also won the second game 11–8.
	The Twins had a record of 17–1 against the Red Sox in 1965, including a sweep of nine games at the Met.
JULY 22	Bob Allison hits two homers and drives in five runs during an 11–5 victory over the Red Sox in Boston.
JULY 25	Trailing 5–1, the Twins score four runs in the eighth inning and three in the ninth to defeat the Orioles 8–5 in Baltimore. In the eighth, Zoilo Versalles drove in a run with a single, followed by a three-run homer from Tony Oliva. In the ninth, Versalles broke the 5–5 tie with a two-run triple, and scored on a sacrifice fly by Oliva.
	During the last week of spring training, Sam Mele fined Versalles $300 for lackadaisical effort and refusing to follow an order during an April 5 exhibition game versus the Mets. The shortstop followed with an MVP season. Versalles led the AL in runs (126), doubles (45) and triples (12). He also batted .273 and smacked 19 homers along with 77 RBIs. Versalles was only 25 in 1965 and appeared to have a bright future, but tailed off badly after his stellar season. After hitting .249 in 1966, Zoilo slumped to .200 in 1967 and was traded to the Dodgers.
JULY 28	Tony Oliva collects five hits in five at-bats and steals two bases to lead the Twins to an 8–1 win over the Senators in Washington. It was the second time in eight days in which Oliva had five hits in a game.
JULY 31	In the 11th inning, Tony Oliva dashes home from second base with the winning run, which beats the Orioles 2–1 at Metropolitan Stadium. With one out, Oliva was on second and Harmon Killebrew on first when Joe Nossek grounded to third baseman Brooks Robinson, who threw to second baseman Jerry Adair for the force. Nossek beat the throw to first as Oliva rounded third and crossed the plate for the victory.
AUGUST 2	Jimmie Hall hits a walk-off homer in the ninth inning to defeat the Orioles 6–5 at Metropolitan Stadium. Jim Merritt, the Minnesota starting pitcher, was making his major league debut. He had a 5–2 lead with two out in the ninth and a runner on first base before allowing a single to Jerry Adair and a three-run homer to Dick Brown which tied the score 5–5.
AUGUST 4	The Twins score two times in the ninth inning for a 4–3 triumph over the Senators at Metropolitan Stadium. Jerry Kindall led off the inning with a home run. After a walk and a single, Jimmie Hall delivered a walk-off single.
AUGUST 8	Jim Perry pitches a two-hitter to defeat the Red Sox 8–0 at Metropolitan Stadium. Perry had a no-hitter in progress until Felix Mantilla doubled with two out in the seventh inning. Jim Gosger added another double with two out in the ninth.
AUGUST 14	In his first major league start, Andy Kosco plays right field, bats fourth, and hits a home run with three strikeouts in four plate appearances during a 3–1 loss to the Indians at Metropolitan Stadium.

1960s

Bob Allison steals second base in the 6th inning of Game 6 as Dodger Maury Wills checks the umpire's call. Allison scored a few minutes later on Jim Grant's home run. Allison homered earlier in the game.

AUGUST 21   The Beatles play a concert at Metropolitan Stadium. Ticket prices ranged from $2.50 to $5.50.

AUGUST 23   The Twins score a run in the ninth inning and another in the tenth to defeat the Yankees 4–3 at Metropolitan Stadium. Tony Oliva tied the score 3–3 with a two-out double. Jerry Kindall's walk-off single drove home the winning run.

AUGUST 27   Mudcat Grant pitches a two-hitter to defeat the Indians 7–0 at Metropolitan Stadium. The only Cleveland hits were singles by Pedro Gonzalez in the fourth inning and Fred Whitfield in the seventh.

The win gave the Twins an 83–47 record and a nine-game lead in the American League pennant race.

SEPTEMBER 5   Bob Allison strikes out five times in five plate appearances during a 5–4 loss to the Tigers at Metropolitan Stadium.

SEPTEMBER 8   The Twins win a key game over the second-place White Sox by a 3–2 score in Chicago. The victory increased the Twins lead to six games.

SEPTEMBER 12 Mudcat Grant wins his 20th game of the season with a 2–0 decision over the Red Sox in Boston.

SEPTEMBER 14   The Twins tie a major league record by drawing five intentional walks during a 4–3 win over the Athletics at Metropolitan Stadium. Tony Oliva drew two of the free passes, with Earl Battey, Don Mincher and Jerry Kindall getting the others.

Battey hit .297 with six homers in 1965.

SEPTEMBER 15   The Twins extend their lead in the American League pennant race to ten games by defeating the Athletics 7–5 at Metropolitan Stadium.

SEPTEMBER 20   A crowd of only 547 watches the Twins lose 8–2 to the Athletics at Metropolitan Stadium. The contest was played on a scheduled off day to make up a postponement of a game originally slated for September 16.

SEPTEMBER 25   Mudcat Grant pitches a one-hitter to defeat the Senators 5–0 in the first game of a double-header in Washington. The only hit off Grant was a double by Don Blasingame in the third inning.

SEPTEMBER 26   The Twins clinch the pennant with a 2–1 win over the Senators in Washington. Jim Kaat was the winning pitcher. It was his 17th victory in a season in which he went 18–11 and had an ERA of 2.83.

It was fitting that the Twins should clinch the pennant in Washington, since the club moved from there to Minnesota in October 1960. It was the first pennant in Minnesota and the first for the franchise since the Senators won the AL crown in 1933. Heading into the 1965 season, the Yankees had dominated the American League, winning 15 of 18 championships from 1947 through 1964. The only teams to break the streak were the 1948 Indians, the 1954 Indians and the 1959 White Sox. The Yanks finished sixth in 1965 and wouldn't return to the World Series again until 1976.

Jim Grant had a career year in 1965 and one of the best years of any pitcher in Twins history.

SEPTEMBER 29   The Twins win their 100th game of the season with a 3–2 decision over the Orioles in Boston.

1960s

The 1965 season remains the only one in which the Twins won at least 100 games during the regular season. The next best win total since the move to Minnesota was 98 in 1970. The Senators were 99–53 in 1933, which was the best record during the years the franchise was located in Washington.

SEPTEMBER 30 — Zoilo Versalles hits a grand slam off Milt Pappas in the fifth inning of a 7–6 win over the Orioles in Baltimore.

The Twins played the Los Angeles Dodgers in the World Series. Managed by Walter Alston, the Dodgers were 97–65 in 1965 and won the NL pennant by two games over the Giants. The Dodgers were gunning for their fourth world championship in 11 years, having won in 1955 in Brooklyn and 1959 and 1963 in Los Angeles.

OCTOBER 6 — The Twins open the World Series with an 8–2 win over the Dodgers before 47,797 at Metropolitan Stadium. Mudcat Grant and Don Drysdale were the starting pitchers. Sandy Koufax, who had a 26–8 record in 1965, sat out the game because of a Jewish holiday. In the second inning, both teams scored on solo homers, with Ron Fairly connecting for the Dodgers and Don Mincher for the Twins. Minnesota broke the game open with a six-run third, the first three on a home run by Zoilo Versalles. Frank Quilici, a rookie second baseman who batted .208 in 1965, collected two singles in the inning. Grant pitched a complete game.

Hubert Humphrey, Vice-President of the United States and a former mayor of Minneapolis, threw out the ceremonial first pitch. The Series was telecast over NBC with Vin Scully, voice of the Dodgers, and Ray Scott, the Twins' broadcaster, serving as announcers.

OCTOBER 7 — The Twins take a two games to none lead with a 5–1 victory before 48,700 at Metropolitan Stadium. The game was scoreless through 5½ innings in a duel between Jim Kaat and Sandy Koufax. Bob Allison helped keep the Dodgers off the scoreboard with a spectacular diving catch down the left field line in the fifth inning. The Twins scored twice in the sixth. Tony Oliva doubled in the first run and scored on a single from Harmon Killebrew. Jim Kaat drove in two runs with a single off Ron Perranoski in the eighth and pitched a complete game. The Twins not only had a 2–0 lead, but beat Don Drysdale and Koufax, who combined for a 49–20 record in 1965.

A steady rain began shortly after the opening game and continued through the night and almost to game time. The Twins ground crew employed helicopters and flame-throwers to help dry the field.

OCTOBER 9 — In game three, the Dodgers defeat the Twins 4–0 at Dodger Stadium. Claude Osteen pitched the complete game shutout. Camilo Pascual took the loss.

Earl Battey crashed into a railing pursuing a foul ball. For the remainder of the Series, he was handicapped by a severely bruised neck and jaw. The Twins catcher couldn't swing properly and his injured throat held his voice to a faint whisper.

OCTOBER 10   The Dodgers even the 1965 World Series by beating the Twins 7–2 at Dodger Stadium. Don Drysdale pitched a complete game and struck out 11. The Minnesota runs came on solo homers by Harmon Killebrew in the fourth inning and Tony Oliva in the sixth.

OCTOBER 11   The Dodgers lead three games to two after beating the Twins 7–0 at Dodger Stadium. Sandy Koufax pitched the complete game shutout and struck out ten. After winning the first two at home, the Twins were outscored 18–2 in the three games in Los Angeles.

OCTOBER 13   The Twins force a seventh game by beating the Dodgers 5–1 before 49,578 at Metropolitan Stadium. Bob Allison started the scoring with a two-run homer in the fourth. Taking the mound on two days' rest, Mudcat Grant not only pitched a complete game, but hit a three-run homer in the sixth.

The home team won each of the first six games. Even though the Series went to seven games, none of the first six contests were close. The smallest margin of victory was four runs.

OCTOBER 14   The Dodgers claim the world championship by beating the Twins 2–0 before 50,596 at Metropolitan Stadium. Jim Kaat and Sandy Koufax both pitched on two days' rest. Koufax was brilliant, pitching a complete-game three-hitter with ten strikeouts. It was his second consecutive shutout. Kaat shutout the Dodgers through three innings, but was relieved in the fourth after allowing a home run to Lou Johnson, a double to Ron Fairly and a single to Wes Parker to score the two Los Angeles runs.

During the Series, Koufax had an 0.38 ERA and 29 strikeouts in 24 innings.

1966

Season in a Sentence
The Twins follow their pennant-winning season by losing 43 of their first 78 games and finish a distant second to the Orioles.

Finish • Won • Lost • Pct • GB
Second   88   74   .549   9.0

Manager
Sam Mele

Stats   Twins • AL • Rank
Batting Avg:	.249	.240	3
On-Base Pct:	.314	.306	3
Slugging Pct:	.382	.369	3
Home Runs:	144		6
Stolen Bases:	67		4
ERA:	3.13	3.44	2
Errors:	139		5 (tie)
Runs Scored:	663		3
Runs Allowed:	581		2

Starting Line-up
Earl Battey, c
Don Mincher, 1b
Cesar Tovar, 2b
Harmon Killebrew, 3b
Zoilo Versalles, ss
Jimmie Hall, lf
Ted Uhlaender, cf
Tony Oliva, rf
Bernie Allen, 2b
Rich Rollins, 3b

Pitchers
Jim Kaat, sp
Mudcat Grant, sp
Dave Boswell, sp
Jim Perry, sp
Jim Merritt, sp-rp
Camilo Pascaul, sp
Al Worthington, rp

Attendance
1,259,374 (second in AL)

Club Leaders
Batting Avg:	Tony Oliva	.307
On-Base Pct:	Harmon Killebrew	.391
Slugging Pct:	Harmon Killebrew	.538
Home Runs:	Harmon Killebrew	39
RBI:	Harmon Killebrew	110
Runs:	Tony Oliva	99
Stolen Bases:	Cesar Tovar	16
Wins:	Jim Kaat	25
Strikeouts:	Jim Kaat	205
ERA:	Jim Perry	2.54
Saves:	Al Worthington	16

JANUARY 13   Three months after competing against each other in the World Series, Mudcat Grant and Dodgers shortstop Maury Wills begin a three-week engagement as entertainers at the Basin Street East nightclub in New York City. Grant was the lead singer in a rock 'n' roll band called "Mudcat and the Kittens." The Kittens were three female back-up singers. Wills sang folk tunes and spirituals.

JANUARY 26   Earl Battey is sentenced to five days in the Ramsey County workhouse in St. Paul for failing to pay income tax from 1961 through 1964.

MARCH 5   The Major League Players Association hires Marvin Miller to be the new executive director of the organization. Miller formally took office on July 1. Under Miller's leadership, the association would take actions that led to a revolution in player-owner relations, including free agency by 1976.

APRIL 6   The Twins trade Dick Stigman to the Red Sox for Russ Nixon and Chuck Schilling.

APRIL 12   The Twins open the season with a 2–1 win over the Athletics before 21,658 at Metropolitan Stadium. Sandy Valdespino drove in both Minnesota runs with a single in the third inning and a walk-off single in the ninth. The two singles accounted for half of the Twins hits off Catfish Hunter. Mudcat Grant pitched a six-hit complete game for the victory.

APRIL 13   Tony Oliva hits a three-run homer with two out in the eighth inning to lift the Twins to a 5–3 win over the Athletics at Metropolitan Stadium.

> *The April 13 contest was the first of four straight in which Oliva hit a home run. He batted .307 with 25 homers, 87 RBIs and 99 runs scored in 1966.*

APRIL 22   The Twins play in Anaheim for the first time, and lose 2–1 to the Angels.

> *The game against the Angels was part of a six-city road trip to Kansas City, Anaheim, Detroit, Baltimore, Washington and Chicago. A run of foul weather postponed five Twins games in a row—in Detroit on April 26, in Baltimore on April 27 and 28, and in Washington on April 29 and 30.*

MAY 6   Dave Boswell (six innings) and Al Worthington (three innings) combine to strike out 17 batters during a 5–4 win over the Red Sox at Metropolitan Stadium. Boswell fanned 12 hitters and Worthington five. Despite the strikeouts, the Twins needed a walk-off homer from Tony Oliva with two out in the ninth for the victory.

> *Oliva collected 11 hits in 15 at-bats over a four-game span from May 3 through May 7. Included in the 11 hits were three homers and two doubles.*

MAY 16   Cesar Tovar is hitless in three official at-bats, but drives in both runs of a 2–1 win over the Senators at Metropolitan Stadium. Tovar hit a sacrifice fly in the third inning and drew a bases loaded walk on four straight pitches from Casey Cox with two out in the ninth to end the game.

MAY 18   The Twins get six runs batted in from their first basemen during a 7–1 triumph over the White Sox at Metropolitan Stadium. Harmon Killebrew started the game at first and hit a two-run homer in the first inning. In the top of the fifth, Killebrew moved to third base, replacing Rich Rollins, and Don Mincher became the first baseman. Mincher drew a bases loaded walk in the bottom of the fifth and a three-run homer in the seventh.

MAY 21   Harmon Killebrew hits his 300th career homer during a 4–2 loss to the Yankees in New York. The milestone was struck off Bob Friend in the fourth inning.

MAY 28   Dave Boswell holds the Indians hitless for six innings, but winds up losing 2–1 in Cleveland. In the seventh, Boswell allowed a single to Rocky Colavito, hit Duke Sims with a pitch, and gave up a two-run double to Pedro Gonzalez.

MAY 29   The Twins sweep the Indians 5–1 and 1–0 during a double-header in Cleveland. Mudcat Grant pitched the shutout in the second game. Earl Battey drove in the lone run with a single off Luis Tiant in the eighth inning.

JUNE 7   In the first round of the amateur draft, the Twins select third baseman Bob Jones from Dawson, Georgia.

> *Jones never advanced past Class A ball. The only future big leaguers drafted and signed by the Twins in 1966 were Steve Braun in the tenth round and Buzz Stephen in the first round of the secondary phase, which consisted of previously drafted players who did not sign with their original club. The Twins also chose*

1960s

Steve Garvey in the third round, but he opted to attend college at Michigan State rather than sign with the Twins. Garvey was drafted by the Dodgers in 1968.

JUNE 9   The Twins tie a major league record by hitting five home runs in the seventh inning of a 9–4 win over the Athletics at Metropolitan Stadium. Kansas City scored all four of their runs in the first. The Twins countered with a run in the fifth and closed the gap to a run on a two-run homer by Harmon Killebrew in the seventh. Earl Battey led off the seventh with a walk from Catfish Hunter, and scored on a one-out, pinch-hit homer from Rich Rollins. Zoilo Versalles followed Rollins to the plate with another home run and Paul Lindblad relieved Hunter. Lindblad retired Sandy Valdespino on a ground out, and then surrendered three homers in a row to Tony Oliva, Don Mincher and Killebrew. The Twins just missed a sixth homer in the inning, and the fourth in succession, when Jimmie Hall's drive hit the fence two feet from the top for a double.

The Twins are one of five teams, and the only AL club, with five homers in an inning. The others are the 1939 New York Giants, 1949 Phillies, 1961 San Francisco Giants and the 2006 Brewers. The four NL occurrences all came against the Cincinnati Reds.

JUNE 13   Rich Rollins collects three doubles and a single in four at-bats during a 6–1 win over the Athletics in the second game of a double-header at Municipal Stadium. Kansas City won the opener 5–2.

JUNE 18   Jimmie Hall drives in five runs on two homers and a single during a 9–8 win over the White Sox at Metropolitan Stadium.

JUNE 28   After earning a save in a 4–0 win over the Indians at Metropolitan Stadium, Al Worthington smashes the fingers on his pitching hand when he catches them in the garage door at his home. He was out of action for three weeks.

The next day, the Twins started a seven-game losing streak to fall to 35–43 on the season. The club was 54–30 the rest of the way to jump from seventh place to second.

JULY 19   Jim Perry pitches a two-hitter to defeat the Senators 4–0 in the second game of a double-header in Washington. The only hits off Perry were singles by Frank Howard in the fourth inning and Don Blasingame in the game. The Twins also won the opener 5–4.

JULY 21   Jim Merritt strikes out 12 batters, including seven in a row, and pitches a three-hitter to defeat the Senators 1–0 in Washington. From the third through the fifth innings, Merritt fanned Ken Harrelson, Frank Howard, Don Lock, Paul Casanova, Ken Hamlin, Eddie Brinkman and Jim Hannan in succession. The lone run scored in the ninth when Don Mincher doubled, advanced to third on an error, and crossed the plate on a wild pitch.

JULY 30   Dave Boswell pitches a one-hitter to defeat the Orioles 7–0 at Metropolitan Stadium. Russ Snyder broke up Boswell's no-hit bid with a single leading off the seventh inning. Boswell fanned 11 and retired 18 batters in a row after walking lead-off batter Luis Aparicio in the first inning.

August 2	Facing Don McMahon, Jimmie Hall hits a two-out, walk-off grand slam in the ninth inning to defeat the Red Sox 7–3 at Metropolitan Stadium.
August 10	Solo homers by Rich Rollins in the sixth inning and Harmon Killebrew in the ninth accounts for the only runs of a 2–0 win over the Angels in Anaheim. Mudcat Grant pitched the shutout.

> *After posting a 21–7 record in 1965, Grant was 5–12 on July 7, 1966, before finishing the season at 13–13. Lack of run support was a culprit in the early season showing. Grant had an ERA of 3.28 while compiling the 5–12 record. His earned run average was 3.24 while winning eight of his last nine decisions.*

August 11	Al Worthington strikes out all three batters he faces in the ninth inning to close out a 4–3 win over the Angels in Anaheim.
August 17	Al Worthington strikes out all three batters he faces in the ninth inning to close out a 5–3 win over the Angels at Metropolitan Stadium.
August 18	The Twins turn the first triple play in club history in the second inning of a 6–2 win over the Angels at Metropolitan Stadium. With runners on first and second, Frank Malzone grounded to third baseman Rich Rollins, who stepped on third and threw to second baseman Cesar Tovar for out number two. Tovar relayed to first baseman Harmon Killebrew to complete the triple play.
August 20	Tony Oliva and Harmon Killebrew hit back-to-back homers in the tenth inning to defeat the Red Sox 4–2 in Boston.
August 27	Jim Kaat earns his 20th win of the season with a 1–0 decision over the White Sox in Chicago. The lone run scored in the second inning on a single by Ted Uhlaender.
September 3	Harmon Killebrew hits a grand slam off Dooley Womack in the seventh inning of a 6–1 triumph over the Yankees in the first game of a double-header at Metropolitan Stadium. The Yankees won the second contest 7–4.
September 6	The Twins score two runs in the ninth inning and one in the 12th to defeat the White Sox 4–3 at Metropolitan Stadium. Harmon Killebrew drove in the two ninth-inning tallies with a home run. In the 12th, Chicago reliever Hoyt Wilhelm retired the first two Minnesota batters, then walked two and yielded a run-scoring single to Rich Rollins.
September 11	Trailing 4–2, the Twins erupt for nine runs in the eighth inning and defeat the Orioles 11–6 at Metropolitan Stadium. The Twins collected ten hits, including three doubles and a homer, during the nine-run rally, and seven of the nine runs were recorded after two were out. The last eight batters reached base on four singles, two doubles and two walks, one of which was intentional. The inning ended when Ron Clark was thrown out at home trying to score from second base on a single. Harmon Killebrew contributed a home run and a single, Ted Uhlaender doubled and singled, and Tony Oliva singled twice.
September 16	The Twins score two runs in the ninth inning to beat the Yankees 2–1 in New York. Yankee pitcher Jim Bouton retired the first 22 batters to face him before Don Mincher singled with one out in the eighth. Bouton entered the ninth with a one-hit

shutout intact. Zoilo Versalles led off the inning with a double and Sandy Valdespino was hit by a pitch. Versalles scored when third baseman Mike Ferraro fielded Cesar Tovar's bunt and threw wildly past first base. Valdespino moved to third base on the play and crossed the plate on a double play.

SEPTEMBER 18   Bob Allison breaks a 2–2 tie in the tenth with a three-run homer, and the Twins go on to win 5–3 over the Yankees in New York.

SEPTEMBER 23   Don Mincher hits a grand slam off Denny McLain in the first inning to spark a 12–4 victory over the Tigers at Metropolitan Stadium.

SEPTEMBER 25   Jim Kaat earns his 25th victory of the season with a 1–0 decision over the Tigers at Metropolitan Stadium. Tony Oliva ended the game with a walk-off homer off Earl Wilson to start the ninth. Kaat also won his 20th game of 1966 in a 1–0 contest.

> *Prior to 1967, there was only one Cy Young Award issued to the best pitcher in baseball. Had the present system of two Cy Young Awards, one for each league, been in place in 1966 there is little doubt that Jim Kaat would have been the AL winner. Kaat had a 25–13 record and led the league in wins, innings (304 2/3), games started (41), complete games (19), and fewest walks allowed per nine innings (1.62). He also posted a 2.75 ERA and struck out 205 batters. The 25 wins is a Minnesota record and the most by any pitcher in franchise history since General Crowder won 26 for the Senators in 1932.*

Big Jim Kaat posted 25 victories in 1966 and is the Twins all-time leader in wins.

OCTOBER 2   In the last game of the season, the Twins edge the Orioles 1–0 in the second game of a double-header at Memorial Stadium. Jim Perry (7 2/3 innings) and Al Worthington (1 1/3 innings) combined on the shutout. Perry also drove in the lone run of the game with a single off Eddie Watt in the eighth inning. Baltimore won the opener 6–2.

> *There was a coaching shake-up after the season ended. Sam Mele claimed that coaches Johnny Sain and Hal Naragon were "disloyal" and "cutting him up" behind his back and both were fired. They quickly were hired by the Tigers. Sain was considered by many to be the top pitching coach in the game during the 1960s and 1970s.*

DECEMBER 2   The Twins trade Jimmie Hall, Don Mincher, and Pete Cimino to the Angels for Dean Chance and Jackie Hernandez.

The Twins made a huge gamble in trading for Chance. In 1964, as a 23-year-old, Chance won the Cy Young Award with the Angels with a 20–9 record, 11 shutouts, and a 1.65 ERA. He followed the tremendous season, however, by dropping to 15–10 in 1965 and 12–17 in 1966. Chance gave the Twins a couple of excellent seasons with a 20–14 mark in 1967 and 16–16 in 1968. On August 5, 1967, he pitched a rain-shortened, five-inning perfect game, then followed it 20 days later with a nine-inning no-hitter. In 1969, Chance developed arm trouble, which probably stemmed from overwork at a young age. Chance was 20-years-old at the start of the 1962 season, and from that year through 1967 he averaged 256 innings per season. He hurled 283 2/3 innings in 1967 and 292 in 1968. In 1969, he was 5–4 and was traded to the Indians during the following off-season.

DECEMBER 3   The Twins trade Camilo Pascaul and Bernie Allen to the Senators for Ron Kline.

1967

Season in a Sentence

In one of the greatest pennant races in major league history, the Twins need only one victory in their last two games to seal the AL pennant, but lose both to the Red Sox in Boston.

Finish • Won • Lost • Pct • GB

Second   91   71   .562   1.0
(tie)

Managers

Sam Mele (25–25) and Cal Ermer (66–46)

Stats   Twins • AL • Rank

Batting Avg:	.240	.236	3
On-Base Pct:	.305	.303	4
Slugging Pct:	.369	.351	4
Home Runs:	131		4
Stolen Bases:	55		5
ERA:	3.14	3.23	2
Errors:	132		5 (tie)
Runs Scored:	671		3
Runs Allowed:	590		4

Starting Line-up

Jerry Zimmerman, c
Harmon Killebrew, 1b
Rod Carew, 2b
Cesar Tovar, 3b-cf-2b
Zoilo Versalles, ss
Bob Allison, lf
Ted Uhlaender, cf
Tony Oliva, rf
Rich Rollins, 3b

Pitchers

Dean Chance, sp
Jim Kaat, sp
Jim Merritt, sp
Dave Boswell, sp
Mudcat Grant, sp-rp
Al Worthington, sp
Ron Kline, rp
Jim Perry, rp-sp

Attendance

1,483,547 (second in AL)

Club Leaders

Batting Avg:	Rod Carew	.292
On-Base Pct:	Harmon Killebrew	.408
Slugging Pct:	Harmon Killebrew	.558
Home Runs:	Harmon Killebrew	44
RBI:	Harmon Killebrew	113
Runs:	Harmon Killebrew	105
Stolen Bases:	Cesar Tovar	19
Wins:	Dean Chance	20
Strikeouts:	Dean Chance	220
ERA:	Jim Merritt	2.53
Saves:	Al Worthington	16

1960s

April 11 — Three months after the Green Bay Packers defeat the Kansas City Chiefs 35–10 in the first Super Bowl, the Twins open the season with a 6–3 loss to the Orioles in Baltimore. Jim Kaat was the starting pitcher and allowed four runs in the first inning. Rod Crew made his major league debut in the game. Starting at second base and batting sixth, Carew collected two singles in four at-bats.

> *Carew made the jump from Class A ball in 1966 to the majors in 1967 and won the AL Rookie of the Year Award by batting .292 with eight homers. He played for the Twins from 1967 through 1978 and the Angels from 1979 until 1985. Carew made the All-Star team in each of his first 18 seasons in the majors and batted over .300 15 years in a row beginning in 1970. He was born in Panama in 1945 while his mother was traveling on a train. Carew was named after Dr. Rodney Cline, the physician who delivered him. Cline was riding at the time on one of the train's segregated whites-only cars. Carew emigrated to the United States at the age of 16 and was spotted on the sandlots by Twins scout Herb Stein. He played second base for the Twins until 1975, then moved to first. While with the club, Carew won seven batting titles and led the AL four seasons in on-base percentage, three in hits, twice in triples, and once in runs. His best season was in 1977, when he batted .388 with 239 hits and won the AL MVP award. Carew ended his career with a .328 batting average and 3,053 hits. In Twins history, he ranks first in batting average (.334), second in on-base percentage (.393), first in triples (90), fifth in games (1,635), fourth in at-bats (6,235), second in hits (2,085), second in stolen bases (271), third in runs (950) and fourth in walks (613).*

April 14 — In the home opener, the Twins defeat the Tigers 5–3 before 21,347 at Metropolitan Stadium. Bob Allison and Zoilo Versalles both homered.

> *Merle Harmon replaced Ray Scott in the Twins broadcast booth in 1967 on both radio and TV. Harmon worked for the Twins until 1969.*

April 21 — Tony Oliva loses a home run by passing Cesar Tovar on the base paths during a 12–4 loss to the Tigers in Detroit. Oliva's drive cleared the wall, but Tovar inexplicably ran back to first to tag up. Oliva hit another ball over the fence in the ninth, this time with no one on base.

April 30 — The Twins lose 7–3 and 3–0 to the Senators in a double-header in Washington. The pair of defeats dropped Minnesota's won-lost record to 5–10.

May 2 — The Twins score six runs in the first inning and wallop the Yankees 13–4 at Metropolitan Stadium. The game-time temperature was 32 degrees, and fell to 29 by the ninth inning.

May 3 — The Twins score three runs in the ninth, two of them after two were out, to defeat the Yankees 4–3 at Metropolitan Stadium. Pinch-hitter Rich Reese drove in the winning run with a single.

May 8 — Rod Carew collects five hits, including a double, in five at-bats, but the Twins lose 7–4 to the Senators at Metropolitan Stadium.

May 9 — Rod Carew extends his streak of hits in consecutive at-bats to seven over two games during an 11–1 triumph over the Senators at Metropolitan Stadium.

MAY 11	Dean Chance pitches a one-hitter to defeat the Athletics 8–0 at Metropolitan Stadium. The only Kansas City hit was a single by Danny Cater in the fourth inning. Chance walked six and struck out eight.
MAY 16	Dean Chance pitches his second consecutive shutout to earn a 1–0 victory over the White Sox in Chicago. The lone run scored on back-to-back doubles by Bob Allison and Zoilo Versalles in the second inning. The win broke Chicago's ten-game winning streak.
	The following day, the Twins lost 5–4 to the White Sox at Comiskey Park to fall to ninth place, 7½ games out of first, with a 12–16 record.
MAY 24	White Sox first baseman Tommy McCraw hits three homers and drives in eight runs to lead his club to a 14–1 win over the Twins at Metropolitan Stadium.
MAY 30	Jim Merritt pitches a two-hitter to defeat the Yankees 3–0 in the second game of a double-header at Yankee Stadium. The only New York hits were a single by Horace Clarke leading off the first inning and a double from Charlie Smith in the seventh. Merritt struck out 11 without walking a batter. The Yanks won the opener 4–3.
JUNE 3	Harmon Killebrew hits a home run into the left-field stands at Metropolitan Stadium estimated to have traveled 520 feet in the fourth inning of an 8–6 victory over the Angels. The blow was struck off Lew Burdette.
	The seat where the long drive landed was later suspended from the ceiling at the Mall of America, which was built on the former site of Metropolitan Stadium.
JUNE 4	Bob Allison drives in Ted Uhlaender from third base on a squeeze bunt in the tenth inning for the winning run in an 8–7 win over the Angels at Metropolitan Stadium.
JUNE 6	In the first round of the amateur draft, the Twins select outfielder Steve Brye from St. Elizabeth High School in Oakland, California.
	Brye played for the Twins from 1970 through 1976, mostly as a pinch-hitter and spare outfielder, at the start of a nine-year career. While in the majors, he batted .258 with 30 home runs in 697 games. Other future big leaguers drafted and signed by the Twins in the regular phase of the 1967 draft were Dave Goltz (fifth round), Steve Luebber (13th round), Rick Dempsey (15th round) and John Obradovich (24th round). In the secondary phase, the Twins chose Dan Monzon (second round), Mike Sadek (fifth round) and Pete Hamm (ninth round).
JUNE 9	Sam Mele is fired as manager of the Twins and replaced by 43-year-old Cal Ermer.
	The club had a 25–25 record at the time of the switch. Mele had been manager since June 1961. Under his leadership, the Twins were 524–436 and won the AL pennant in 1965. Clark Griffith stated that Mele was relieved because "he had lost control of the players." Ermer was the manager at the team's Class AAA farm club in Denver. His major league playing career consisted of one game with the Senators in 1947. Cal's given name was Calvin Coolidge Ermer. He was born in Baltimore three months after Coolidge became President.

Ermer was appointed over coach Billy Martin, who was regarded by many to be Mele's successor. The Twins were still at the .500 level on June 24 with a 33–33 record, then went 58–38 the rest of the way to nearly reach the World Series. The turnaround coincided with Ermer's crackdown on discipline. Dave Boswell, Tony Oliva and Ted Uhlaender were fined $250 apiece for their roles in an altercation on the bus in late June. Mele never managed another team.

JUNE 10 — Tony Oliva hits a home run and a double and drives in six runs during an 8–1 triumph over the Orioles at Metropolitan Stadium.

Oliva hit .289 with 34 doubles and 17 home runs in 1967.

JUNE 11 — After losing 5–2 to the Orioles in the first game of a double-header at Metropolitan Stadium, the Twins take game two 10–7.

JUNE 12 — The Twins score eight runs in the third inning and defeat the Tigers 11–5 at Metropolitan Stadium. Jim Merritt, Cesar Tovar, Rod Carew, Harmon Killebrew and Tony Oliva connected for five consecutive singles off Mickey Lolich, and Rich Rollins hit a grand slam against Mike Marshall.

JUNE 13 — The Twins reach double figures in runs scored for the third game in a row, but lose 15–10 to the Tigers at Metropolitan Stadium. The Twins led 5–1 before Detroit exploded for ten runs in the top of the sixth. Minnesota scored five times in the bottom of the sixth, to make the score 11–10, but couldn't regain the lead.

Cesar Tovar was a team sparkplug all season. He played in every game and appeared in 70 contests at third base, 64 in center, 36 at second base, ten in left, nine at shortstop and six in right field. Tovar batted .267 with 98 runs scored and 173 hits.

JUNE 23 — Harmon Killebrew's home run off Joel Horlen in the seventh inning accounts for the only run of a 1–0 victory over the White Sox at Metropolitan Stadium. Dean Chance pitched the shutout.

Killebrew was runner-up to Carl Yastrzemski in the MVP balloting in 1967 with 44 homers, 113 RBIs, 105 runs, a league-leading 131 walks, and a .269 batting average. Killebrew and Yastrzemski tied for the AL lead in home runs.

JUNE 28 — Dave Boswell strikes out 13 during a 3–2 win over the Red Sox at Metropolitan Stadium.

JULY 5 — The Twins extend their winning streak to eight games with a 10–4 victory over the Yankees at Metropolitan Stadium.

The Twins drew 1,483,547 fans into the Met in 1967, which set a club record that stood until 1984.

JULY 11 — Dean Chance is the AL starter in the All-Star Game, won by the National League 2–1 in 15 innings at Anaheim Stadium. Chance allowed a run and two hits in three innings of work.

Chance finished the season with a 20–14 record, 220 strikeouts and a 2.72 ERA. He led the AL in innings (283 2/3) and complete games (18 in 39 starts).

JULY 15 — Trailing the Athletics 2–1, Harmon Killebrew and Tony Oliva lead off the ninth with back-to-back homers on consecutive pitches to lift the Twins to a 3–2 victory at Metropolitan Stadium. Both were struck off Jack Aker, who had just entered the game in relief.

JULY 16 — Rich Rollins hits a walk-off homer in the ninth inning to down the Angels 7–6 in the second game of a double-header at Metropolitan Stadium. The Twins also won the opener by a 5–1 score.

JULY 24 — A day after race riots begin in Detroit that would claim 43 lives, the Twins defeat the White Sox 2–1 in an exhibition game at County Stadium in Milwaukee. The contests drew a crowd of 51,144.

The Braves played in Milwaukee from 1953 through 1965 before moving to Atlanta. Milwaukee was without a major league team until 1970 when the Seattle Pilots moved there and were renamed the Brewers. The White Sox played nine "home" games in Milwaukee in 1968 and 11 more in 1969, including one each season against the Twins.

JULY 25 — The Twins and Yankees finish in a 1–1 tie when the game in New York is called after nine innings by rain. Both runs scored on solo homers by Harmon Killebrew in the first inning against Al Downing and Mickey Mantle with two out in the ninth off Jim Kaat.

Early the following morning, manager Cal Ermer fined eight players $250 each for violating curfew.

JULY 26 — The Twins and Yankees play a twi-night double-header at Yankee Stadium to make up the tie game the previous evening. The Yanks won the opener 6–1. The second tilt went 18 innings before the Twins emerged with a 3–2 victory. Neither team recorded a run from the seventh inning through the 17th. The winning tally scored when Rod Carew drew a two-out walk, stole second and advanced to third on the play following a wild throw by catcher Jake Gibbs, and then crossed the plate on a single by Rich Rollins. Jim Merritt started for the Twins and pitched 13 innings. The relievers were Ron Kline (two innings), Al Worthington (two innings) and Jim Roland (one inning). It was Roland's first save since 1964. Yankee reliever Bill Monbouquette entered the game in the eighth and pitched nine shutout innings. The contest lasted four hours and 24 minutes.

JULY 28 — The Twins score seven runs in the fourth inning and defeat the Red Sox 9–2 in Boston. There were eight hits in the inning, including two singles by Bob Allison.

Allison batted .258 with 24 homers in 1967.

JULY 29 — The Twins use five home runs to power past the Red Sox 10–3 in the second game of a double-header at Fenway Park. Bob Allison hit two homers with the others coming from Tony Oliva, Harmon Killebrew and Ted Uhlaender. Boston won the opener 6–3.

1960s

AUGUST 6 — Dean Chance retires all 15 batters he faces to earn a rain-shortened, five-inning perfect game, defeating the Red Sox 2–0 at Metropolitan Stadium. The contest was called with one out in the bottom of the fifth (see August 25, 1967).

> *Chance was one of the worst hitters in baseball history. Playing before the passage of the DH rule, Chance had 44 hits and 420 strikeouts in 662 at-bats for a batting average of .066. His slugging percentage was .069. As a Twin, Chance batted .048 in 189 at-bats.*

AUGUST 9 — The Twins lose a 20-inning marathon 9–7 to the Senators at Metropolitan Stadium. The game lasted five hours and 40 minutes. The Twins led 7–0 with Dave Boswell working on a shutout before Washington scored seven runs in the seventh inning. There was no scoring from the bottom of the seventh through the top of the 20th. Al Worthington entered the contest with one out in the eighth inning and pitched 8 2/3 innings and allowed just two hits and no runs. He faced 30 batters and struck out eight. For most of his time on the mound, Worthington was matched against Senators reliever Darold Knowles, who pitched ten innings of three-hit shutout ball from the eighth through the 17th. Knowles fanned ten. Jim Roland hurled three shutout innings until the Senators broke loose for two tallies in the 20th. Ken McMullen led off the inning with a home run to break the 7–7 tie. Sandy Valdespino replaced Bob Allison in left field in the fifth inning, and struck out in five consecutive plate appearances, four against Knowles.

AUGUST 15 — The Twins take first place for the first time in 1967 with a 3–2 win over the White Sox at Metropolitan Stadium.

> *At the end of the day, only 2 1/2 games separated the top five teams in the American League, with the Twins, White Sox, Tigers, Angels and Red Sox involved in one of the tightest pennants races in major league history. The Angels soon fell off the pace, but the other four teams battled for first place until the final week, with the Twins, Tigers and Red Sox still holding a chance to win on the final day of the regular season.*

AUGUST 18 — Rich Reese hits a two-run homer in the ninth inning to defeat the Yankees 4–3 in the second game of a double-header in New York. The Yanks won the opener 1–0.

AUGUST 19 — Dave Boswell pitches the Twins to a 1–0 win over the Yankees in New York.

AUGUST 25 — Dean Chance pitches a no-hitter to defeat the Indians 2–1 in the second game of a double-header at Municipal Stadium. Cleveland scored in the first inning. Chance started the contest by walking Lee Maye and Vic Davalillo. Maye went to third on an error by third baseman Cesar Tovar and crossed the plate on a wild pitch. The Twins scored single runs in the second and sixth innings off Sonny Siebert, who pitched a no-hitter in 1966. Chance had pitched a rain-shortened perfect game just 19 days earlier (see August 6, 1967). In the ninth, Chance retired Davalillo and Chuck Hinton on ground outs from second baseman Rod Carew to first baseman Harmon Killebrew, and closed out the contest by inducing Tony Horton to hit a grounder to Tovar. Chance walked five and struck out eight. His parents traveled from Wooster, Ohio, to see him pitch the no-hitter. The Twins also won the opener 6–5 in ten innings.

AUGUST 31	Pinch-hitting for Jerry Zimmerman, Rich Reese hits a two-run, walk-off homer to defeat the Orioles 10–9 at Metropolitan Stadium. Baltimore scored three runs in the top of the ninth to take a 9–8 lead.
SEPTEMBER 8	Tony Oliva collects eight hits in nine at-bats during a double-header against the Orioles in Baltimore. Oliva had three hits, including two doubles, in four at-bats in the opener, won by the Twins 7–2. He was five-for-five in the nightcap, a 7–4 defeat.

In six games from September 7 through September 11, Oliva had an astonishing 16 hits in 23 at-bats. Included were six doubles and a triple. He also walked six times to reach base in 22 of 29 plate appearances.

SEPTEMBER 11	Trailing 5–2, the Twins erupt for seven runs in the fourth inning and defeat the Senators 13–5 in Washington.
SEPTEMBER 14	Walter Bond, who played ten games for the Twins as an outfielder at the start of the 1967 season, dies of leukemia at the age of 29.
SEPTEMBER 16	The Twins suffer a setback by allowing four runs in the ninth inning to lose 5–4 to the White Sox in Chicago. The defeat dropped the Twins out of a tie for first place into second, one game back.
SEPTEMBER 18	Jim Kaat pitches a ten-inning complete game shutout and strikes out 12 to defeat the Athletics 2–0 in Kansas City. Both runs scored on a two-out single from Ted Uhlaender off Catfish Hunter.

At the end of the day, the Twins, Tigers and Red Sox were tied for first with records of 85–66. The White Sox were fourth, one-half game back at 85–67.

SEPTEMBER 19	Dave Boswell pitches a two-hitter to defeat the Athletics 7–2 at Municipal Stadium. The only hits off Boswell were a double by Jim Gosger in the second inning and a single from Bert Campaneris in the third. It was also the last time the Twins played the A's in Kansas City. The club moved to Oakland in 1968. The Royals filled the void in Kansas City as an expansion team in 1969. In a scheduling quirk, the Twins and Athletics played four consecutive games, meeting in Kansas City on September 18 and 19 and in Bloomington on September 20 and 21.
SEPTEMBER 20	Dean Chance strikes out 13 batters to defeat the Athletics 6–2 at Metropolitan Stadium.
SEPTEMBER 21	Jim Merritt pitches a two-hitter to defeat the Athletics 4–0 at Metropolitan Stadium. The only Kansas City hits were singles by Bert Campaneris leading off the first inning and John Donaldson in the fourth.
SEPTEMBER 24	Dean Chance earns his 20th win of the season with a 9–4 decision over the Yankees at Metropolitan Stadium.
SEPTEMBER 26	The Twins take a one-game lead in the pennant race with a 7–3 win over the Angels at Metropolitan Stadium.

At the end of play on Friday, September 29, the Twins were in first place with a record of 91–69. The Tigers and Red Sox were both one game back in a virtual tie for second. The Tigers were 89–69 and the Red Sox 90–70. The Twins closed the season with two games against the Sox in Boston on September 30 and October 1. The Tigers had back-to-back double-headers on those dates against the Angels in Detroit. For the Red Sox, it was a remarkable turnaround. In 1966, the club finished in ninth place and hadn't ended a season above .500 since 1958.

SEPTEMBER 30   The Red Sox defeat the Twins 6–4 at Fenway Park to move into a tie for first place. The crowd included Vice-President (and Twins fan) Hubert Humphrey. The Sox caught a break in the third when Jim Kaat pulled a tendon in his elbow and had to leave the game. Boston took a 3–2 lead with a run in the sixth, and then salted the game away with Carl Yastrzemski's three-run homer in the seventh. In Detroit, the Tigers split a double-header with the Angels, winning 5–0 and losing 8–6. In the second game, the Tigers led 6–2 in the eighth inning before allowing California to score six times.

At the end of the day, the Red Sox and Twins were tied at the top of the league at 91–70. The Tigers were 90–70. With one game remaining, the loser of the Twins-Red Sox game on October 1 would be eliminated from the pennant. The Tigers could force a tie for first place with the victor by sweeping the Angels in a double-header.

OCTOBER 1   The Twins blow a chance at the American League pennant by losing 5–3 to the Red Sox before a delirious crowd at Fenway Park. Among those at the ballpark were movie stars Cliff Robertson and Lee Remick, along with Joseph P. Kennedy and sons Bobby and Ted, and the governors of six states. Jim Lonborg started for the Red Sox and Dean Chance for the Twins. Lonborg had a career record of 0–6 against the Twins. Chance was 16–8 against the Sox, including four wins in 1967. After 5½ innings, Chance and the Twins led 2–0. But the Red Sox erupted for five runs in the bottom of the sixth, and the Twins were unable to mount a comeback against Lonborg, who pitched a complete game. The Tigers won the first game of their double-header against the Angels 6–4, but lost the second 8–5. The Red Sox lost the World Series in seven games to the Cardinals.

The Metropolitan Sports Center, located just north of Metropolitan Stadium, opened in the fall of 1967. It served as the home of the Minnesota North Stars of the National Hockey League (1967–93), the Minnesota Muskies of the American Basketball Association (1967–68) and the Minnesota Pipers of the ABA (1968–69). The arena was demolished in 1994 and the area where it once stood is now part of the Mall of America complex.

NOVEMBER 28   The Twins trade Mudcat Grant and Zoilo Versalles to the Dodgers for Johnny Roseboro, Ron Perranoski and Bob Miller.

Grant and Versalles were two of the best players on the 1965 pennant-winning team. Versalles was MVP that season and had there been an AL Cy Young Award in 1965, Grant would have been the hands-down winner. But both declined rapidly, and were extreme disappointments during the 1967 season in which the Twins missed the AL title by one game. Versalles continued his slide, and batted .208 over the remainder of his career, which ended in 1971. The Dodgers moved Grant to the bullpen, where he excelled for a few seasons. Perranoski was one of the top closers in baseball during the 1960s, and continued in that role for the Twins. He saved 31 games in 1969 and 34 in 1970. Miller also gave Minnesota a couple of good years of relief. Roseboro was acquired to shore up the catching position. Twins' catchers combined to hit just .190 with two home runs and a slugging percentage of .233 in 1967. Roseboro was the club's starting catcher for two seasons and made the All-Star team in 1969.

DECEMBER 3   The Twins trade Ron Kline to the Pirates for Bob Oliver.

1968

Season in a Sentence
The Twins win their first six games, but totter to a seventh-place finish and hire Billy Martin as manager.

Finish • Won • Lost • Pct • GB
Seventh   79   83   .488   24.0

Manager
Cal Ermer

Stats

Stats	Twins	AL	Rank
Batting Avg:	.237	.230	2
On-Base Pct:	.295	.297	5
Slugging Pct:	.350	.339	4
Home Runs:	105		6
Stolen Bases:	98		3
ERA:	2.89	2.98	6
Errors:	170		10
Runs Scored:	562		5
Runs Allowed:	546		7

Starting Line-up
Johnny Roseboro, c
Harmon Killebrew, 1b
Rod Carew, 2b
Cesar Tovar, 3b-cf
Ron Clark, ss-3b
Bob Allison, lf
Ted Uhlaender, cf
Tony Oliva, rf
Rich Reese, 1b
Frank Quilici, 2b-3b

Pitchers
Dean Chance, sp
Jim Kaat, sp
Jim Merritt, sp
Dave Boswell, sp
Jim Perry, sp
Al Worthington, rp
Ron Perranoski, rp
Bob Miller, sp

Attendance
1,143,257 (fourth in AL)

Club Leaders
Batting Avg:	Tony Oliva	.289
On-Base Pct:	Tony Oliva	.357
Slugging Pct:	Tony Oliva	.477
Home Runs:	Bob Allison	22
RBI:	Tony Oliva	68
Runs:	Cesar Tovar	89
Stolen Bases:	Cesar Tovar	35
Wins:	Dean Chance	16
Strikeouts:	Dean Chance	234
ERA:	Dean Chance	2.53
Saves:	Al Worthington	18

JANUARY 27   With the first overall pick in the secondary draft, the Twins select Eric Soderholm.

MARCH 2   Vice-President Hubert Humphrey visits the Twins training camp on Orlando and eats lunch with the players.

APRIL 8   The Twins opener against the Senators in Washington is postponed because of riots in the city following the assassination of Martin Luther King, Jr., which occurred on April 4.

APRIL 10   The Twins open the season with a 2–0 win over the Senators in Washington. Dean Chance pitched the shutout, allowing four hits. The runs scored on solo homers by Harmon Killebrew in the sixth inning and Bob Allison in the eighth, both off Camilo Pascaul.

1960s

Chance was 16–16 with a 2.53 ERA and 234 strikeouts in a league-leading 293 innings in 1968.

APRIL 17 — In the home opener, the Twins score seven runs in the eighth inning and defeat the Senators 13–1 before 22,926 at Metropolitan Stadium. Cesar Tovar, Harmon Killebrew and Jackie Hernandez hit home runs.

The Twins won their first six games in 1968, but by mid-June had fallen below the .500 mark and out of pennant contention.

APRIL 25 — Only four Twins reach base, but do so consecutively, to defeat the White Sox 3–2 at Metropolitan Stadium. Chicago pitcher Gary Peters retired the first eight batters he faced before walking Jim Perry with two out in the third. Cesar Tovar and Tony Oliva then hit RBI-doubles and Harmon Killebrew singled home the third Minnesota tally. Peters retired the next 16 batters in a succession. The Twins were out-hit 12–3 during the contest. The White Sox left 11 men on base, and the Twins only one.

The 1968 season has become known as "The Year of the Pitcher." The average game in the American and National Leagues featured only 6.82 runs. It was the lowest figure since 1908, when there were 6.77 runs per game in the majors.

APRIL 29 — Johnny Roseboro collects five hits, including a home run and a double during an 11–2 triumph over the Red Sox in Boston.

MAY 6 — The Twins play in Oakland for the first time and lose 2–1 to the Athletics.

MAY 8 — Catfish Hunter pitches a perfect game to give the Athletics a 4–0 win over the Twins in Oakland. He also drove in three of the four A's runs and struck out 11. In the ninth inning, Hunter retired Johnny Roseboro on a ground out from second baseman John Donaldson to first baseman Ray Webster, and then he fanned Bruce Look and pinch-hitter Rich Reese.

MAY 25 — Jim Kaat pitches the Twins to a 1–0 win over the Red Sox at Metropolitan Stadium. The lone run crossed the plate on a single by Rich Reese in the eighth inning.

MAY 26 — The Twins defeat the Red Sox 5–4 at Metropolitan Stadium with two home runs in the ninth off Sparky Lyle. Harmon Killebrew led off the inning with a home run. With two out, Ted Uhlaender delivered a walk-off blast.

MAY 28 — For the second time in the season, the Twins bunch all three of their runs and all three of their hits in one inning to win a game (see April 25, 1968). This time it was in the first inning of a 3–1 victory over the Indians at Metropolitan Stadium. The runs scored on a double by Johnny Roseboro, who batted in the lead-off spot, a single by Rod Carew, a walk to Harmon Killebrew, Tony Oliva's double and a sacrifice fly from Rich Reese.

On the same day, the American League announced that it would divide into two divisions in 1969 with expansion to 12 teams. There would be a best-of-five playoff between the two division leaders to determine the league champion. The Twins were placed in the West with California, Chicago, Kansas City, Oakland and Seattle. The Eastern Division was made up of Baltimore, Boston, Cleveland, Detroit, New York and Washington.

MAY 29	Dave Boswell pitches a shutout and drives in the lone run of a 1–0 win over the Indians at Metropolitan Stadium. In the fifth inning, Cesar Tovar scored from third base on Boswell's foul pop-up, which was caught by first baseman Tony Horton about 50 feet past first base.
JUNE 1	Dean Chance is two outs from a no-hitter but winds up losing 1–0 to the White Sox at Comiskey Park. With one out in the ninth inning, Bill Voss and Tommy McCraw hit back-to-back singles, neither of which left the infield. Dick Kenworthy drove in the winning run with a two-out single.
JUNE 2	Tony Oliva collects six hits, including two homers, in eight at-bats during a doubleheader against the White Sox in Chicago, but the Twins lose twice—3–2 and 4–3.
JUNE 6	On the day that Robert Kennedy dies from bullet wounds suffered the previous day in Los Angeles while campaigning for the Democratic Party nomination, a two-run homer by Tony Oliva in the second inning accounts for the only runs of a 2–0 win over the Yankees in New York. Dave Boswell ($6^{2}/_{3}$ innings) and Al Worthington ($2^{1}/_{3}$ innings) combined on the shutout.
	Oliva batted .289 with 18 home runs in 1969.
JUNE 7	In the first round of the amateur draft, the Twins select outfielder Alex Rowell from Luther College.

Harmon Killebrew, Bob Allison, and Tony Olivia pose in the dugout in 1968. The trio provided much of the offense for the Twins in the late 1960s.

Rowell never advanced past Class AA. Future major leaguers drafted and signed by the Twins in 1967 were Jim Nettles (fourth round), Jerry Terrell (18th round) and Danny Thompson (first round of the secondary phase).

JUNE 18 — The Twins take a thrilling 9–8 decision over the Senators at Metropolitan Stadium. The Twins led 4–0 before Washington scored six runs in the top of the eighth. Minnesota responded with three tallies in the bottom of the eighth for a 7–6 advantage, only to have the Senators score twice in the top of the ninth to pull ahead 8–7. The Twins rallied again with two in their half for the victory. Frank Quilici tripled in the first run and scored on a ground out by Cesar Tovar.

JUNE 23 — Ted Uhlaender collects five hits in five at-bats during a 6–3 win over the Yankees at Metropolitan Stadium.

JULY 3 — Luis Tiant strikes out 19 Twins batters during a ten-inning, 1–0 Indians victory in Cleveland. Jim Merritt allowed only two hits through the first nine innings before surrendering two hits in the tenth to lose the game.

JULY 9 — Harmon Killebrew suffers a torn hamstring during the All-Star Game, a 1–0 National League win at the Astrodome in Houston. The injury occurred when Killebrew, playing first base, did a split while taking a throw from shortstop Jim Fregosi. He didn't play again until September 1.

JULY 11 — Playing shortstop, Rick Renick homers in his first major league at-bat during a 5–4 win over the Tigers at Metropolitan Stadium. The blow was struck off Mickey Lolich in the second inning. The Twins needed a walk-off single from Rod Carew in the ninth to seal the victory. Renick played five seasons in the majors, all with the Twins. He hit .221 with 20 home runs in 553 at-bats.

JULY 13 — After the Tigers score in the top of the 14th off Jim Roland, the Twins rally with two in their half to win 7–6 at Metropolitan Stadium. The Twins loaded the bases with one out and tied the game 6–6 on a ground out by Rod Carew. Johnny Roseboro was issued an intentional walk to reload the bases. Pitcher Jim Roland was up next, but Cal Ermer had used all of his position players and had no one to pinch-hit. Roland drew a walk from Dennis Ribant to bring home the winning run.

JULY 20 — Dean Chance strikes out 12 batters in nine innings, but the Twins lose an 11-inning encounter to the Athletics 2–1 at Metropolitan Stadium.

JULY 21 — The Twins sweep the Athletics 7–5 and 10–0 in a double-header at Metropolitan Stadium. Bob Allison homered in the first game and collected a homer, triple and double in the second.

JULY 24 — The Twins collect 20 hits and wallop the Angels 12–1 at Metropolitan Stadium.

AUGUST 9 — Johnny Roseboro homers in the 11th inning to defeat the Yankees 4–3 in New York.

AUGUST 16 — Jim Kaat is the star of a 5–2 victory over the Orioles at Metropolitan Stadium. Kaat not only struck out 12 batters without walking anyone, he hit a three-run double in the second inning.

AUGUST 19	Dean Chance pitches the Twins to a 1–0 win over the Yankees at Metropolitan Stadium.
AUGUST 26	On the first day of the Democratic National Convention in Chicago, an event marred by violent confrontations between anti-war demonstrators and police before the nomination of Hubert Humphrey, the Twins bunch all four of their runs and five of their six hits in the seventh inning to win 4–2 over the Senators in Washington. The Senators won the second tilt 1–0 in 13 innings, as the two teams combined for only seven hits. Jim Perry started for the Twins and allowed only two hits in nine hits. Frank Bertainia was the Washington starter, and surrendered just two hits in 11 innings.
AUGUST 27	Dean Chance holds the Senators without a hit through seven innings but winds up losing 2–0 in the first game of a double-header in Washington. Mike Epstein broke up the no-hit bid by leading off the eighth with a single and scored on Bernie Allen's one-out homer. The Twins won the second game 7–1.
AUGUST 30	Trailing 4–1, the Twins score a run in the eighth inning, two in the ninth, and one in the 11th to defeat the White Sox 6–5 at Metropolitan Stadium. Cesar Tovar drove in the two ninth-inning runs with a two-out triple. In the 11th, Rick Renick doubled and crossed the plate on a single from Rich Reese.
	Tovar hit .272 with 89 runs, 167 hits, and 35 stolen bases in 1968.
SEPTEMBER 2	Jim Kaat strikes out 11 batters and pitches a three-hitter to defeat the Red Sox 5–1 at Metropolitan Stadium.
SEPTEMBER 7	Playing right field, Graig Nettles hits two solo homers to defeat the Tigers 2–1 in Detroit. Nettles homered in the sixth and ninth innings, both off Pat Dobson.
SEPTEMBER 8	Graig Nettles hits a three-run homer off Earl Wilson in the sixth inning to account for all of the Twins runs in a 3–1 triumph over the Tigers in Detroit.
SEPTEMBER 9	Following up his 19-strikeout performance on July 1, Luis Tiant fans 16 Twins in a 6–1 Indians win at Metropolitan Stadium. Graig Nettles homered in the first inning. It was the third day in a row in which he drove in all of the Twins runs, and each came on a solo home run.
	Nettles hit his first career home run on September 6. He hit five homers in four consecutive games from September 6 through September 9. The streak gave Nettles five homers in his first 22 big league at-bats.
SEPTEMBER 10	The Twins pull off a triple play during a 6–2 loss to the Indians at Metropolitan Stadium. With runners on first and second in the fifth inning, Tony Horton grounded to third baseman Rich Rollins, who stepped on third for the force-out and threw to Rod Carew at second for out number two. Carew relayed to first baseman Bob Allison to complete the triple play.
SEPTEMBER 16	Trailing 3–0, the Twins score three run in the eighth inning and one in the ninth to beat the Angels 4–3 at Metropolitan Stadium. Rick Renick's walk-off homer was the winning blow.

1960s

The Twins made 170 errors in 1968, 19 more than any other team in the American League.

SEPTEMBER 22 — Cesar Tovar plays all nine positions during a 2–1 win over the Athletics at Metropolitan Stadium. Tovar was the starting pitcher, and first faced Bert Campaneris, who was the only previous individual to play all nine positions in a game. Campaneris did so in 1965. Tovar retired Campaneris on a foul pop-up, struck out Reggie Jackson, walked Danny Cater, and set down Sal Bando on another pop-up into foul territory. Tovar was the catcher in the second inning, played first base in the third, second in the fourth, shortstop in the fifth, third base in the sixth, left field in the seventh, center in the eighth, and right in the ninth. Because of all of the maneuvering, the Twins tied major league records for most shortstops used in a game with four (Jackie Hernandez, Tovar, Ron Clark and Rod Carew), and most centerfielders with four (Ted Uhlaender, Tovar, Bob Allison and Graig Nettles).

The only other players besides Campaneris and Tovar to play all nine positions in a game are Scott Sheldon of the Rangers and Shane Halter of the Tigers, both in 2000.

SEPTEMBER 30 — Cal Ermer is dismissed as manager of the Twins. Calvin Griffith said that Ermer had allowed the players too much freedom off the field and had lost control of the team. Ermer never managed another big league team, but he served as a minor league manager in the system for 11 seasons during the 1970s and 1980s.

OCTOBER 11 — The Twins hire 40-year-old Billy Martin as manager.

Martin became part of the Twins organization in 1961 (see June 1, 1961). He was a player in 1961, a scout from 1962 through 1964, and a coach from 1965 through 1968. In May of 1968, the Twins sent Martin to Denver to manage the club's Class AAA team in the Pacific Coast League. Martin took over a club that was 8–22 and guided them to a 65–50 record the rest of the way. "With the type of season we had in 1968," said Calvin Griffith, "Billy Martin, with his inspirational winning attitude, will get our club on the right track." Martin did just that, leading the Twins to a 97–65 record and the Western Division title. He was the subject of controversy all year long, however. The low point was a fight with player Dave Boswell (see August 6, 1969). Despite the successful season, Martin was fired soon after it was over (see October 13, 1969).

OCTOBER 15 — In the expansion draft, the Twins lose Bob Oliver, Pat Kelly, Jackie Hernandez and Jerry Cram to the Kansas City Royals and Buzz Stephen and Rich Rollins to the Seattle Pilots.

NOVEMBER 21 — Two weeks after Richard Nixon defeats Hubert Humphrey in the Presidential election, the Twins trade Jim Merritt to the Reds for Leo Cardenas.

This was the rare trade that helped both teams, as the Twins needed a shortstop and the Reds were desperately short of pitching. Cardenas was the Twins starting shortstop for three seasons and made the All-Star team in 1971. In Cincinnati, Merritt was 17–9 in 1969 and 20–12 in 1970 before developing arm trouble. He was 6–24 for the Reds and Rangers from 1971 through 1973.

1969

Season in a Sentence

Following a losing season in 1968, Billy Martin leads the Twins to the Western Division title in his first season as a major league manager, and then he is fired and replaced by mild-mannered Bill Rigney.

Finish • Won • Lost • Pct • GB

First   97   65   .599   +9.0

AL Championship Series

The Twins lost three games to none to the Baltimore Orioles.

Manager

Billy Martin

Stats   Twins • AL • Rank

Stat	Twins	AL	Rank
Batting Avg:	.268	.246	1
On-Base Pct:	.338	.321	2
Slugging Pct:	.408	.369	3
Home Runs:	163		4
Stolen Bases:	115		4
ERA:	3.24	3.62	3
Errors:	150		9
Runs Scored:	790		1
Runs Allowed:	618		4

Starting Line-up

Johnny Roseboro, c
Rich Reese, 1b
Rod Carew, 2b
Harmon Killebrew, 3b-1b
Leo Cardenas, ss
Graig Nettles, lf
Ted Uhlaender, cf
Tony Oliva, rf
Cesar Tovar, cf-2b

Pitchers

Jim Perry, sp
Dave Boswell, sp
Jim Kaat, sp
Tom Hall, sp-rp
Dean Chance, rp
Ron Perranoski, rp
Al Worthington, rp
Bob Miller, rp
Dick Woodson, rp

Attendance

1,349,328 (third in AL)

Club Leaders

Batting Avg:	Rod Carew	.332
On-Base Pct:	Harmon Killebrew	.427
Slugging Pct:	Harmon Killebrew	.584
Home Runs:	Harmon Killebrew	49
RBI:	Harmon Killebrew	140
Runs:	Harmon Killebrew	106
Stolen Bases:	Cesar Tovar	45
Wins:	Dave Boswell	20
	Jim Perry	20
Strikeouts:	Dave Boswell	190
ERA:	Jim Perry	2.82
Saves:	Ron Perranoski	31

APRIL 8   The Twins participate in the first game in Royals history and lose 4–3 in 12 innings at Municipal Stadium in Kansas City. Tom Hall was the Twins starter and went 5²/₃ innings, allowing three runs. It was only the fifth start in Hall's career. Joe Keough drove in the winning run with a single off Dick Woodson. Graig Nettles homered in the losing cause.

APRIL 9   The Twins lose 4–3 to the Royals in Kansas City for the second game in a row, this time in 17 innings. Jim Kaat started and pitched 11 innings. Lou Piniella drove in the winning run with a single off Bob Miller. Rod Carew stole home in the fifth inning.

The Twins started the season with four consecutive losses, and then won seven in a row to boost their record to 7–4.

1960s

APRIL 16 The Twins play in Seattle for the first time, and score three runs in the ninth inning to win 6–4 at Sicks Stadium. Tony Oliva drove in the tying run with a single and Rich Reese broke the deadlock with a two-run double.

> *The Pilots lasted only one season in Seattle. The franchise moved to Milwaukee in 1970 and was renamed the Brewers. The Mariners were created as an expansion team in 1977.*

APRIL 18 After starting the season on a four-city road trip to Kansas City, Anaheim, Oakland and Seattle, the Twins play their home opener and defeat the Angels 6–0 before 22,857 at Metropolitan Stadium. Tom Hall pitched a two-hitter. The only California hits were a triple by Jim Fregosi in the first inning and a single by Lou Johnson in the seventh.

APRIL 20 The Twins score five runs in the first inning to spark a 12–1 trouncing of the Angels at Metropolitan Stadium.

APRIL 26 The Twins rout the White Sox 12–1 in Chicago.

APRIL 27 Harmon Killebrew hits his 400th career home run in the first inning of a 4–3 win over the White Sox in Chicago. The milestone was struck off Gary Peters.

> *Killebrew had the best season of his career in 1969, winning the MVP award. He came to spring training still bothered by the hamstring injury suffered in the 1968 All-Star Game, and many feared his career might be over. Killebrew recovered to play in all 162 games in 1969, and he led the AL in home runs (49), RBIs (140), walks (145) and on-base percentage (.427). Killebrew also batted .276 and scored 106 runs.*

APRIL 28 The Twins play the Royals for the first time at home and win 4–0 at Metropolitan Stadium.

APRIL 30 The Twins pull off a triple steal during a 6–4 victory over the Pilots at Metropolitan Stadium. With one out in the fifth inning, Rod Carew stole home with Tony Oliva swiping third base and Harmon Killebrew second.

> *Carew stole home seven times in 1969, the second highest figure in major league history. Only Ty Cobb with eight in 1912 had more steals of home in a single season. Carew also won the first of his seven career batting titles by batting .332 in 1969. He played in only 123 games, however, because of military commitments as a soldier in the Army Reserve.*

MAY 4 The Twins extend their winning streak to eight games with a 4–3 decision over the White Sox at Metropolitan Stadium. In the second inning, Frank Quilici walked, took second and third on two wild pitches, then stole home. It was Quilici's first stolen base since 1965, and one of only three he recorded during a five-year big league career.

MAY 13 Rod Carew contributes two bunt singles and an inside-the-park homer to a 4–2 win over the Orioles at Metropolitan Stadium. The homer came with a man on base in the eighth and gave the Twins a 3–2 lead. Dave Boswell struck out 13 batters in $8^2/_3$ innings.

Rod Carew bedeviled American League pitchers—and catchers—in 1969 by stealing home seven times. He stole home 17 times in his career.

Boswell entered the season as a 24-year-old with a 44–35 record. He went 20–12 in 1969 accompanied by an earned run average of 3.70 and 190 strikeouts in 256⅔ innings. Boswell's season is unforgettable, not because of winning 20 games, but for fighting Billy Martin (see August 6, 1969). Plagued by arm trouble, Boswell was 3–7 with a 6.42 ERA in 1970 and was released by the Twins. He was 1–2 for the Orioles and Tigers in 1971, his last big league season.

May 15   Cesar Tovar breaks-up the no-hit bid of Dave McNally by stroking a single with one out in the ninth inning. Rod Carew followed Tovar to the plate and grounded into a double play to end a 5–0 loss to the Orioles at Metropolitan Stadium.

May 18   The Twins tie a major league record with two steals of home in one inning, but they prove to be the only two runs of an 8–2 loss to the Tigers at Metropolitan Stadium. Cesar Tovar led off the third inning with a single off Mickey Lolich and went to second on a balk. He then stole third. Rod Carew walked. With Harmon Killebrew at bat, Tovar stole home with Carew taking second on a double steal. Killebrew was still at bat when Carew proceeded to swipe third and then home. When Tovar batted in the fourth, Lolich hit him in the head with a pitch.

May 31   The Twins score seven runs in the second inning and defeat the Red Sox 10–4 in Boston.

1960s

JUNE 4 — The Twins pull off a triple steal in the eighth inning of a 4–2 victory over the Yankees at Metropolitan Stadium. With Leo Cardenas batting, Rod Carew stole home, Harmon Killebrew third base, and Johnny Roseboro second.

JUNE 5 — In the first round of the amateur draft, the Twins select outfielder Paul Powell from Arizona State University.

Powell was a bust, playing in only 30 big league games with a .167 batting average in 42 at-bats. The Twins struck gold in the third round, however, by choosing Bert Blyleven. The only other future major leaguer drafted and signed by the Twins was Jim Hughes in the 33rd round.

JUNE 7 — The Twins score seven runs in the fourth inning and wallop the Senators 10–1 at Metropolitan Stadium. Harmon Killebrew capped the rally with a three-run homer.

JUNE 11 — Joe Lahoud of the Red Sox hits three homers to lead his club to a 13–5 win over the Twins at Metropolitan Stadium.

JUNE 21 — The Twins erupt for 11 runs in the tenth inning and defeat the Athletics 14–4 in Oakland. The first eight batters in the inning reached base on singles by Ted Uhlaender and Rod Carew, a home run by Harmon Killebrew, a walk to Tony Oliva, Cesar Tovar's single, a walk to Frank Quilici, and singles by Leo Cardenas and Johnny Roseboro. Carew singled again in his second at-bat of the inning. The inning ended when Cardenas lined into a double play with the bases loaded.

JUNE 22 — Jim Perry's suicide squeeze bunt in the 13th inning scores Tony Oliva with the winning run for a 4–3 victory over the Athletics in the second game of a double-header in Oakland. Perry entered the game in the 12th as a reliever. The A's won the opener 7–3. Oliva collected six hits, including three doubles and a homer, in ten at-bats during the twin bill.

JUNE 29 — Tony Oliva collects eight consecutive hits during a double-header against the Royals in Kansas City. In the opener, Oliva collected three singles in four at-bats of a 7–2 loss. In the second tilt, he picked up five hits, including two homers and a double, in five at-bats and drove in five runs. One of his homers was estimated to have traveled 500 feet. The Twins won 12–2.

Oliva had a streak of 25 hits in 45 at-bats over ten games from June 21 to 29. Among the 25 hits were 11 doubles and five home runs. He finished the season with a .309 batting average, 24 homers, and 101 RBIs.

JULY 1 — After falling behind 5–0 in the third inning, the Twins score ten unanswered runs to defeat the White Sox 10–5 in Chicago. Rich Reese broke the 5–5 tie with a two-run homer in the fifth inning.

JULY 5 — Harmon Killebrew drives in six runs with two homers and a single in four at-bats to lead the Twins to a 13–1 thrashing of the Athletics at Metropolitan Stadium.

The victory put the Twins into first place in the AL West in the first season of divisional play. The club remained in first for the remainder of the season.

July 9	A controversial play highlights a 4–3 loss to the Royals at Metropolitan Stadium. In the second inning, Bob Oliver of the Royals attempted to steal second with Ellie Rodriguez at bat. Minnesota catcher Johnny Roseboro pushed Rodriguez' bat out of the way and his throw to second nailed Oliver. After huddling for eight minutes, the umpires declared Rodriguez out for interference and ordered Oliver back to first base. The rules, however, state that an out nullifies an interference call.
July 12	The Twins clobber the Pilots 11–1 at Metropolitan Stadium.
July 13	Trailing 4–0, the Twins score two runs in the eighth inning and three in the ninth to defeat the Pilots 5–4 in the second game of a double-header at Metropolitan Stadium. Charlie Manuel drove in the winning run with a single. The Twins also won the opener 5–2.
July 14	Trailing 3–2, the Twins score a run in the 12th inning and another in the 13th to defeat the White Sox 4–3 at Metropolitan Stadium. With two out and no one on base in the 12th, Rod Carew singled and scored on a double by Cesar Tovar. Leo Cardenas drove in the winning run with a single in the 13th.
	In his first season with the Twins, Cardenas batted .280 with ten home runs.
July 16	In the second inning of a 9–8 triumph over the White Sox in the first game of a double-header at Metropolitan Stadium, the Twins pull off their third triple steal of the season. Rod Carew stole home with Harmon Killebrew taking third base and Charlie Manuel second. Rich Reese homered twice and drove in five runs. The Twins completed the sweep with a 6–3 victory in the second tilt.
	The Twins also accomplished triple steals on April 30 and June 4. Carew stole home in all three. Killebrew was also on base on all three occasions. He came into the season with eight stolen bases from 1954 through 1968. Under the aggressive style of Billy Martin, Killebrew stole eight bases in ten attempts in 1969.
July 17	The Twins extend their winning streak to nine games with an 8–5 decision over the White Sox at Metropolitan Stadium. Jim Kaat, who won 16 Gold Gloves during his career, was the winning pitcher despite committing three errors.
July 19	The Twins and Pilots play 16 innings in Seattle before the contest is suspended by curfew with the score 7–7. American League rules stipulated that no inning could start after 1:00 a.m. The Twins led 6–0 before the Pilots scored two runs in the sixth inning, one in the eighth, and three in the ninth. Both teams scored in the 15th.
July 20	On the day Neil Armstrong becomes the first man to walk on the moon, the Twins and the Pilots complete their suspended game of the previous evening in Seattle, and the Twins score four times in the 18th inning to win 11–7. The tie-breaking run scored on a balk by John Gelnar with the bases loaded. Ted Uhlaender finished the game with four hits, including a homer, in seven at-bats, and drove in five runs. Jim Perry pitched the 17th and 18th innings of the suspended game, and retired all six batters he faced, then started the regularly scheduled contest, and hurled a nine-inning, complete game shutout to win 4–0. In all, he hurled 11 shutout innings during the Sunday afternoon, and was credited with two victories.

Perry was acquired by the Twins in a trade with the Indians in 1963, and through the end of the 1968 season, he was a spot starter and long reliever. He began the 1969 campaign in that role, but was plugged into the starting rotation in late May. Perry responded to the challenge winning 20 games for the first time in his career at the age of 34. He ended the year with a 20–6 record and a 2.82 ERA in 261 2/3 innings.

JULY 25   The Twins outlast the Indians 4–2 in 16 innings at Municipal Stadium. Cleveland tied the score 2–2 on a two-run homer by Duke Sims with one out in the ninth. Rod Carew broke the deadlock with a two-run double. Ron Perranoski pitched 5 2/3 innings of one-hit, shutout relief and struck out six.

The Twins won 21 of 26 games from June 29 through July 25.

JULY 29   The Twins score seven runs in the fifth inning and down the Tigers 11–5 at Metropolitan Stadium.

AUGUST 3   The Twins deal Dave McNally his first loss of the 1969 season with a 5–2 victory over the Orioles at Metropolitan Stadium. Rich Reese gave the Twins the lead with a grand slam in the seventh inning. McNally entered the game with a 15–0 record in 1969, and had a 17-game winning streak including two victories at the end of the 1968 campaign.

AUGUST 6   Dave Boswell is punched by Billy Martin following a 3–1 win over the Tigers in Detroit.

Martin was upset because Boswell failed to run the specified 18 laps in the outfield. Instead, Boswell ran only two laps and left the field, exchanging angry words with pitching coach Art Fowler. Later that evening, Martin and Boswell were in the same bar. Martin asked the pitcher to explain himself. Boswell said he preferred to talk about

Though he quickly wore out his welcome, fiery Billy Martin inspired the Twins to ninety-seven wins and an AL West championship in managerial debut.

it later. After Martin went to the other end of the bar and sat down, Boswell began shouting at him. Teammate Bob Allison tried to calm Boswell, leading him outside. Boswell was so angry he threw a punch at Allison. Martin went outside and was charged by Boswell, who hit him in the left temple. Martin retaliated and knocked Boswell unconscious with a flurry of blows to the chest and head. Though Boswell was larger and younger than Martin, he needed 20 stitches to close his wounds and clearly was beaten. Martin received seven stitches in his right hand, which was badly swollen. Allison had several teeth chipped and sustained a black eye. The next day, Boswell was sent home for disciplinarian reasons by Calvin Griffith. Boswell didn't pitch again until August 18, and then won eight of his last 11 decisions to finish the season with 20 wins.

AUGUST 10   Cesar Tovar breaks up the no-hit bid of an Orioles pitcher for the second time in 1969 (see May 15, 1969). Mike Cuellar carried a no-hitter and a 2–0 lead into the ninth in Baltimore when Tovar started the inning with a single. Cuellar retired the next three batters to close out the win.

AUGUST 13   Rich Reese collects four hits, including two home runs, in four at-bats to spark the Twins to a 5–2 win over the Yankees in New York.

AUGUST 22   Four days after the end of Woodstock, Tony Oliva clouts two homers and drives in five runs to lead the Twins to a 6–0 win over the Yankees at Metropolitan Stadium.

AUGUST 24   George Mitterwald's walk-off single in the ninth inning accounts for the lone run in a 1–0 win over the Yankees at Metropolitan Stadium. Tom Hall pitched the shutout.

A 7–3 loss to the Senators at the Met the following day cut the Twins' lead in the AL West in 1½ games. By September 9, the Twins opened their lead to 9½ games to all but seal the division title.

SEPTEMBER 4   Cesar Tovar breaks a 5–5 tie in the tenth inning with a grand slam off Lew Krausse, and the Twins topple the Athletics 10–5 in Oakland.

SEPTEMBER 6   The Twins outlast the Athletics 8–6 in 18 innings in Oakland. Cesar Tovar provided the winning margin with a two-run homer in the 18th. It was his second extra-inning homer in three days. There was no scoring from the sixth inning through the 15th. Both teams scored in the 16th with Tony Oliva delivering a home run in the top half. Jim Kaat entered the game in the eighth and pitched $9^{1}/_{3}$ innings of relief, allowing one run while striking out ten. Ron Perranoski earned the save by retiring the final two Oakland hitters. The A's used 25 players during the game.

SEPTEMBER 7   Harmon Killebrew drives in seven runs in the first two innings of a 16–4 trouncing of the Athletics in Oakland. Killebrew hit a three-run homer off Fred Talbot in the first inning, and a grand slam against Vida Blue in the second. With a big lead, Billy Martin pulled many of his starters, and Killebrew left the contest in the bottom of the fourth. Ted Uhlaender extended his hitting streak to 20 games.

SEPTEMBER 9   Trailing 7–4, Twins score seven runs in the sixth inning and defeat the Angels 11–7 in Anaheim. Rich Reese broke the 7–7 tie with a three-run triple.

SEPTEMBER 19	Dave Boswell strikes out 14 batters during a 2–1 win over the Pilots at Metropolitan Stadium.
SEPTEMBER 20	Jim Perry earns his 20th victory of the season with a 3–2 decision over the Pilots at Metropolitan Stadium.
SEPTEMBER 22	The Twins clinch the AL West title with a 4–3 win over the Royals in Kansas City.
SEPTEMBER 28	Dave Boswell earns his 20th victory of the season with a 5–2 decision over the Pilots in the first game of a double-header in Seattle. The Pilots won the second contest 4–1.

The Twins played the Baltimore Orioles in the first American League Championship Series. Managed by Earl Weaver, the Orioles were 109–53 in 1969. The series was a best-of-five affair. The Championship Series in both leagues went to seven games in 1985.

OCTOBER 4	The Twins open the Championship Series with a 4–3 loss to the Orioles in 12 innings at Memorial Stadium in Baltimore. Tony Oliva gave the Twins a 3–2 lead with a two-run homer in the seventh. Jim Perry was the starter and took the 3–2 advantage into the ninth before Boog Powell homered. In the 12th, Mark Belanger reached on an infield single off Ron Perranoski, moved to second on a sacrifice, took third on a ground out, and crossed the plate on a bunt from Paul Blair.

The fans failed to respond to the first Championship Series with sellout crowds. The two games in Baltimore drew 39,324 and 41,704 into Memorial Stadium, which had a capacity of 52,000. The third game at Metropolitan Stadium, played on a Monday afternoon, attracted 32,735, about 15,000 shy of a full house.

OCTOBER 5	The Twins lose to the Orioles again in extra frames, this time 1–0 in 11 innings. Dave Boswell and Dave McNally were the starters. Both were still on the mound in the 11th. Boog Powell led off the inning with a walk and advanced to second on a bunt. After Ron Perranoski relieved Boswell, pinch-hitter Curt Motton singled home the winning run. McNally allowed only three hits.

The series was telecast nationally by NBC. The announcers were Curt Gowdy and Tony Kubek in games one and two, and Jim Simpson and Sandy Koufax in game three.

OCTOBER 6	The Orioles complete the sweep of the Twins with an 11–2 win at Metropolitan Stadium. Starter Bob Miller was routed in the second inning.

In the World Series, the Orioles were upset in five games by the Mets.

OCTOBER 13	After winning 97 games and the division title in his first year as manager, Billy Martin is dismissed by Calvin Griffith. Martin squabbled with the front office all year over team policy and had a running feud with vice-president Howard Fox. Martin punched Fox in 1966 when Martin was a coach. The publicity over Martin's fight with Dave Boswell (see August 6, 1969) may have sealed his fate. Griffith said the firing was due to Martin's failure to carry out his instructions. "I still like him,"

said Griffith. "You know Billy can go into a crowd and charm the hell out of you. But he ignored me." Martin's popularity with the fans and subsequent departure created a public relations problem for the Twins' owner. The Twins drew 1,349,328 fans in 1969. That figure wouldn't be reached again until 1984.

Martin would continue to revive teams for the next 20 years, but ultimately fell out of favor with management and was fired. He managed the Tigers (1970–73) and Rangers (1973–75) before taking over as manager of the Yankees late in the 1975 season. As a result of his love-hate relationship with George Steinbrenner, Martin had five different stints as manager of the Yankees from 1975 through 1978 and again in 1979, 1983, 1985 and 1988. Martin also managed the Athletics from 1980 through 1982. He led the Yanks to World Series appearances in 1976 and 1977, with a win over the Dodgers in 1977. Martin died in an auto accident on Christmas Day in 1989.

OCTOBER 22   The Twins hire 51-year-old Bill Rigney as manager.

Rigney had an eight-year career as an infielder with the New York Giants from 1946 through 1953. He managed the Giants in both New York and San Francisco from 1955 through 1960. He took over as the first manager of the expansion Angels in 1961 and remained in the position until 1969. He led the Twins to 98 wins and another division title in 1970, but the team fell to fifth place in 1971 and Rigney was fired in June 1972.

DECEMBER 10   The Twins trade Dean Chance, Bob Miller, Ted Uhlaender and Graig Nettles to the Indians for Luis Tiant and Stan Williams.

Chance's arm was used up and Miller and Uhlaender weren't missed. Nettles was a great loss, however. At the time of the trade, he was 25 and had a .224 lifetime batting average with 12 homers in 304 major league at-bats. Moved by the Twins to the outfield, Nettles returned to his natural position of third base with the Indians. After three years in Cleveland, he was dealt to the Yankees. His 11 seasons in New York included five All-Star appearances and four World Series. Another All-Star Game and World Series would come during a three-year stint with the Padres. Nettles' career didn't end until 1988. He played in 2,700 games and hit 390 home runs. Williams gave the Twins one great season out of the bullpen, with a 10–1 record and a 1.99 ERA. The trade turned out to be one of the worst in club history because of the success of Nettles after leaving Minnesota. It might have been one of the best, had Tiant rejuvenated his career sooner. He was 21–9 in 1968 and 9–20 in 1969 for the Indians, then went 7–3 in an injury-plagued season for the Twins in 1970. The club released him near the end of spring training in 1971. Picked up by the Red Sox, he was 1–7 in Boston in 1971 before mounting an unexpected comeback. In five seasons beginning in 1972, Tiant had a record of 96–58 and became one of the most popular players in Red Sox history.

THE STATE OF THE TWINS

The Twins won the AL West in 1969 and repeated the feat in 1970. On both occasions, the club was swept by the Orioles in the Championship Series. The Twins fell to fifth place in 1971 and wallowed in mediocrity for most of the remainder of the 1970s. The only teams to make any serious run at a pennant were in 1976 (third place and five games behind) and 1979 (fourth place and six games out). Overall, the Twins were 812-794, a winning percentage of .506, which ranked sixth in the AL. American League pennant winners were the Orioles (1970, 1971 and 1979), Athletics (1972, 1973 and 1974), Red Sox (1975) and Yankees (1976, 1977 and 1978). AL West champs were the Twins (1970), A's (1971, 1972, 1973, 1974 and 1975), Royals (1976, 1977 and 1978) and Angels (1979).

THE BEST TEAM

The 1970 Twins were 98-64 and finished first in the AL West. The franchise hasn't won as many as 98 regular season games in a single season since then.

THE WORST TEAM

The 1978 edition under Gene Mauch was 73-89 and finished fourth.

THE BEST MOMENT

The Twins clinched the division title on September 23, 1970. Fans would wait until 1987 before the club reached the postseason again.

THE WORST MOMENT

Calvin Griffith put his foot squarely in his mouth in 1978 with some racist comments concerning the club's move from Washington to Minnesota 18 years earlier (see February 3, 1979).

THE ALL-DECADE TEAM • YEARS W/TWINS

Butch Wynegar, c	1976-82
Harmon Killebrew, 1b	1961-74
Rod Carew, 2b	1967-78
Steve Braun, 3b	1971-76
Roy Smalley, ss	1976-82; 1985-87
Larry Hisle, lf	1973-77
Cesar Tovar, cf	1965-72
Dan Ford, rf	1975-78
Tony Oliva, dh	1962-76
Bert Blyleven, p	1970-76; 1985-88
Dave Goltz, p	1972-79
Geoff Zahn, p	1977-80
Jim Kaat, p	1961-73

Killebrew, Carew, Kaat and Oliva were on the 1960s All-Decade Team. Killebrew and Carew are in the Hall of Fame. Blyleven, Kaat and Oliva deserve to be in Cooperstown, but have not yet been selected. Other significant players during the 1970s were shortstop Leo Cardenas (1969-71) and second baseman Ron Wilfong (1977-82).

THE DECADE LEADERS

Batting Avg:	Rod Carew	.345
On-Base Pct:	Rod Carew	.406
Slugging Pct:	Rod Carew	.460
Home Runs:	Harmon Killebrew	113
RBI:	Rod Carew	584
Runs:	Rod Carew	759
Stolen Bases:	Rod Carew	235
Wins:	Bert Blyleven	99
Strikeouts:	Bert Blyleven	1,402
ERA:	Bert Blyleven	2.80
Saves:	Mike Marshall	53

THE HOME FIELD

There were few changes to Metropolitan Stadium during the 1970s, and the ballpark was beginning to lose its charm. The Twins drew over 1,000,000 fans every year from the first season in Minnesota in 1961 through 1970, and finished in the top half of the American League in attendance every year from 1961 through 1971. With losing teams and dissatisfaction over the frugal fiscal policies of Calvin Griffith, the Twins were in the bottom half of the AL in attendance each year from 1972 through 1986, and landed dead last in 1974, 1975, 1976, 1980, 1981 and 1982. By the end of the decade, both the Twins and the Vikings were clamoring for a domed stadium in a downtown location, which came to fruition with the opening of the Metrodome in 1982.

THE GAME YOU WISHED YOU HAD SEEN

It was Rod Carew Day on June 26, 1977. Carew scored five runs and drove in six and Glenn Adams contributed eight RBIs to a 19–12 win over the White Sox.

THE WAY THE GAME WAS PLAYED

Speed and defense were more prominent during the 1970s than in any decade since the lively ball was introduced in 1920. Stolen bases per team in the American League rose from 72 in 1970 to 107 in 1979, while home runs declined from 146 in 1970 to 94 in 1976 before surging upward at the end of the decade. The designated hitter rule was introduced in the AL in 1973.

THE MANAGEMENT

Calvin Griffith ran the franchise in both Washington and Minnesota from 1955 through 1984 and also served as general manager. Griffith was very conservative in making trades and his lack of bold moves and penny-pinching practices contributed to the stagnation of the franchise during the 1970s and early 1980s. Field managers were Bill Rigney (1970–72), Frank Quilici (1972–75) and Gene Mauch (1976–80).

THE BEST PLAYER MOVE

The best trade brought Larry Hisle and John Cumberland from the Cardinals in exchange for Wayne Granger on November 29, 1972.

THE WORST PLAYER MOVE

The worst player move was the sale of Jim Kaat to the White Sox on August 15, 1973. The worst trade sent Rick Dempsey to the Yankees for Danny Walton on October 27, 1972.

1970

Season in a Sentence

In a near repeat of 1969, the Twins win 98 games under a new manager but again are swept by the Orioles in the playoffs.

Finish • Won • Lost • Pct • GB

First   98   64   .605   +9.0

AL Championship Series

The Twins lost to the Baltimore Orioles three games to none.

Manager

Bill Rigney

Stats

Stats	Twins	AL	Rank
Batting Avg:	.262	.250	1
On-Base Pct:	.324	.322	3
Slugging Pct:	.403	.379	2
Home Runs:	153		5
Stolen Bases:	57		8
ERA:	3.23	3.71	2
Errors:	123		3
Runs Scored:	744		3
Runs Allowed:	605		3

Starting Line-up

George Mitterwald, c
Rich Reese, 1b
Danny Thompson, 2b
Harmon Killebrew, 3b
Leo Cardenas, ss
Brant Alyea, lf
Cesar Tovar, cf
Tony Oliva, rf
Jim Holt, lf-cf
Rod Carew, 2b

Pitchers

Jim Perry, sp
Jim Kaat, sp
Bert Blyleven, sp
Luis Tiant, sp
Ron Perranoski, rp
Stan Williams, rp
Tom Hall, rp
Bill Zepp, rp

Attendance

1,262,887 (third in AL)

Club Leaders

Batting Avg:	Tony Oliva	.325
On-Base Pct:	Harmon Killebrew	.411
Slugging Pct:	Harmon Killebrew	.546
Home Runs:	Harmon Killebrew	41
RBI:	Harmon Killebrew	113
Runs:	Cesar Tovar	120
Stolen Bases:	Cesar Tovar	30
Wins:	Jim Perry	24
Strikeouts:	Tom Hall	184
ERA:	Jim Perry	3.04

MARCH 21 Two months after the Vikings lose the Super Bowl 23–7 to the Kansas City Chiefs, the Twins trade Joe Grzenda and Charlie Walters to the Senators for Brant Alyea.

APRIL 7 In his first game with the Twins, Brant Alyea collects four hits in four at-bats and drives in seven runs to lead the Twins to a 12–0 Opening Day win over the White Sox in Chicago. Batting fifth and playing left field, Alyea singled in his first two plate appearances, and then hit a pair of three-run homers. Jim Holt replaced Alyea in left field in the eighth. Holt singled in the ninth giving the Twins five hits from their left fielders. Tony Oliva scored three runs and Jim Perry pitched a complete game shutout.

Perry won the AL Cy Young Award in 1970 with a 24–12 record and a 3.04 ERA in 278^2/$_3$ innings over a league-leading 40 starts.

APRIL 11 The Twins win their home opener 8–2 over the Athletics before 21,658 at Metropolitan Stadium.

APRIL 15   In Anaheim, the Twins score all eight of their runs in the sixth inning of an 8–2 win over the Angels. Brant Alyea hit a grand slam off Andy Messersmith.

Alyea spent most of the season in a left field platoon with Jim Holt. In his first 11 games with the Twins, Alyea hit .429. hit four homers, and drove in 20 runs. Over 258 at-bats in 1970, he hit 16 homers with 61 RBIs and a .291 batting average. Alyea drove in seven runs in a game twice, on April 7 and September 7. From September 7 through September 13, he drove in at least one run in nine consecutive games. In 1971, however, he batted .177 with two home runs in 158 at-bats and was dealt to the Athletics.

Jim Perry stepped out of the shadows when he reached his mid-thirties, winning seventy-four games for the Twins from 1969 through 1972.

APRIL 18   The Twins score seven runs in the fourth inning and down the Athletics 11–5 in Oakland. Rick Renick hit a grand slam off Al Downing. Rod Carew delivered five hits in five at-bats.

APRIL 25   A bizarre play highlights a 4–3 win over the Tigers at Metropolitan Stadium. With two out in the seventh inning, Tigers pitcher Earl Wilson swung and missed at a two-strike pitch from Jim Kaat. Catcher Paul Ratliff, believing the inning was over, rolled the ball back to the mound and the Twins began to leave the field. Home plate umpire John Rice ruled that Ratliff had trapped the third strike, however, meaning that Wilson was not out. Wilson began circling the bases and reached third base before left fielder Brant Alyea retrieved the ball and threw to shortstop Leo Cardenas, who was standing by home plate. Wilson turned back toward third but was out in a rundown between Alyea and Cardenas. Wilson pulled a hamstring on the play and had to leave the game with the Tigers trailing 2–1. Harmon Killebrew ended the game with a walk-off single.

APRIL 29   Jim Kaat (8 2/3 innings) and Stan Williams (one-third of an inning) combine on a shutout to defeat the Indians 1–0 at Metropolitan Stadium.

MAY 3   Harmon Killebrew hits a two-run homer off Jim Palmer with one out in the ninth inning to defeat the Orioles 4–3 in Baltimore.

Killebrew homered in five consecutive games from May 3 through May 8.

1970s

MAY 5   The day after four students are killed by Ohio National Guardsmen at Kent State University, Tony Oliva drives in six runs with a run-scoring single, a two-run homer, and a bases-loaded triple to lead the Twins to an 8–5 win over the Tigers in Detroit.

Oliva and Cesar Tovar tied for the league lead in doubles with 36 in 1970. Tovar also scored 120 runs. Oliva batted .325 and hit 23 homers along with 107 RBIs and 204 hits.

MAY 16   The Twins play the Brewers in Milwaukee for the first time and win 11–7 at County Stadium.

The victory gave the Twins sole possession of first place. The club remained in first for the remainder of the season.

MAY 20   Rod Carew becomes the first Twin to hit for the cycle while leading the club to a 10–5 triumph over the Royals in Kansas City. Facing Bob Johnson, Carew hit a single in the first inning, a home run in the third and a double in the fifth, and then tripled against Al Fitzmorris in the eighth.

MAY 31   Harmon Killebrew hits a walk-off homer in the tenth inning to defeat the Yankees 7–6 at Metropolitan Stadium.

Killebrew hit .271 with 41 homers and 113 RBIs and drew 128 walks in 1970.

JUNE 4   In the first round of the amateur draft, the Twins select shortstop Bob Gorinski from Mt. Pleasant High School in Calumet, Pennsylvania.

Gorinski's career in the majors lasted 54 games in 1977 in which he hit .195. The only other future major leaguers drafted and signed by the Twins in 1970 were Mark Wiley (fourth round) and Steve Staggs (14th round).

JUNE 5   Bert Blyleven makes his major league debut, and pitches seven innings for a 2–1 win over the Senators in Washington. Blyleven gave up a home run to Lee Maye leading off the first inning, but he settled down and didn't allow another run.

Blyleven was only two months past his 19th birthday when he made his big league debut. He was born in the Netherlands and grew up in Garden Grove, California. He finished his rookie season with a 10–9 record and a 3.18 ERA in 164 1/3 innings. He lasted in the majors until 1992 and pitched for the Twins from 1970 through 1976 and again from 1985 through 1988. Overall, he had a career record of 287–250, with 3,701 strikeouts and 60 shutouts. There are 20 pitchers in major league history with 50 or more career shutouts, and every one of them is in the Hall of Fame except for Blyleven. From 1970 to the present, the only pitcher with more shutouts than Blyleven is Nolan Ryan, who had 61. (Roger Clemens is third with 46). Through 2009, Blyleven is also fifth in career strikeouts with 3,701, trailing only Ryan, Clemens, Randy Johnson and Steve Carlton. There are 11 pitchers with 2,850 or more strikeouts and are eligible for the Hall of Fame. Blyleven is the only one of the 11 not enshrined in Cooperstown. Among Twins pitchers, Blyleven ranks first in shutouts (29), first in complete games (141), first in strikeouts (2,035), second in walks (674), second in wins (149), second in defeats (138), second in games started (345), second in innings (2,566⅔), and second in earned run average (3.28). In 1996, he joined the Twins' broadcasting team.

JUNE 7 — Rich Reese hits a grand slam off Dick Bosman in the sixth inning of an 11-inning, 10–9 victory over the Senators in Washington. Reese's slam gave the Twins a 7–3 lead, but the Senators tied the score with two runs in the eighth inning and two more in the ninth. The Twins added three runs in the top of the 11th before surviving a two-run Washington rally in the bottom half.

JUNE 22 — Rod Carew injures his knee while colliding with Mike Hegan on a double play during a 4–3 win over the Brewers in Milwaukee.

Carew was hitting .376 at the time of the injury, which required surgery. With the exception of five plate appearances in four games in late September, Carew didn't play again in 1970.

JUNE 27 — Bert Blyleven pitches a two-hitter to defeat the White Sox 9–1 at Comiskey Park. The only Chicago hits were a single by Tom McCraw leading off the first inning and a homer from Bob Spence in the eighth.

Blyleven's given name is Rik Aalbert Blyleven.

JUNE 30 — With the Twins trailing 5–2, Rick Renick hits a pinch-hit grand slam off Bob Johnson in the sixth inning to spark an 8–5 win over the Royals at Metropolitan Stadium.

Cotton Nash played six games for the Twins in 1969 and four more in 1970. Before pursuing baseball, Nash was an All-American basketball player for the University of Kentucky and appeared in 45 games for the Los Angeles Lakers and San Francisco Warriors during the 1964–65 NBA season. He also played for the Kentucky Colonels of the American Basketball Association in 1967–68.

JULY 14 — Tony Oliva hits a double in the All-Star Game at Riverfront Stadium in Cincinnati, but the American League loses 5–4 in 12 innings. Pete Rose scored the winning run by barreling over catcher Ray Fosse.

JULY 22 — Jim Perry (7⅔ innings) and Ron Perranoski (1⅓ innings) combine on a two-hitter to down the Tigers 2–1 at Metropolitan Stadium. Don Wert collected both Detroit hits with a single in the sixth inning and a double in the eighth.

AUGUST 1 — The Twins explode for eight runs in the tenth inning and defeat the Tigers 12–4 in Detroit. Danny Thompson collected a double and a single in the inning, and Cesar Tovar singled twice.

AUGUST 4 — Bert Blyleven strikes out 12 batters during a 5–2 victory over the Brewers at Metropolitan Stadium.

AUGUST 6 — George Mitterwald's walk-off homer in the 14th inning beats the Angels 2–1 at Metropolitan Stadium.

1970s

August 7 — Jim Holt hits a walk-off homer in the 11th inning to defeat the Athletics 2–1 at Metropolitan Stadium. It was the second day in a row in which the Twins won with a home run in extra innings.

August 13 — Cesar Tovar's bunt single leading off the first inning is the only hit off Dick Bosman in a 1–0 loss to the Senators in Washington.

Tovar set a major league record by collecting his team's only hit on five different occasions. The others were against Barry Moore of the Senators in 1967, Dave McNally of the Orioles in 1969, Mike Cuellar of the Orioles, also in 1969, and Catfish Hunter of the Yankees in 1975. Tovar broke up Hunter's no-hitter while he was playing for the Texas Rangers.

August 18 — Pinch hitter Jim Holt hits a two-run, walk-off single with one out in the ninth inning to beat the Yankees 8–7 at Metropolitan Stadium.

August 25 — A 1–0 loss to the Red Sox at Metropolitan Stadium is interrupted by a bomb scare. In the fourth inning, the crowd of 17,697 had to evacuate. A caller informed police that the bomb would explode at 9:30 p.m. At 9:15 p.m., the crowd was told to calmly file out of the ballpark. Players from both teams moved into the center field area. Many spectators joined them. Most fans gathered in the parking lots surrounding the Met. After a search found nothing, play resumed at 9:58 p.m. A tracer on the call showed it had been made from a telephone booth in the first deck.

Public address announcer Bob Casey, who was known for his occasional verbal gaffes, told the crowd to "leave the stadium quickly and calmly, as we have gotten a call that there is going to be an explosion in ten minutes." There were also bomb threats that night to the Minneapolis Star-Tribune *Building and the Minneapolis Armory, both located downtown. Bombs exploded at the old Minneapolis Federal Building on August 17 and at a downtown St. Paul department store on August 22.*

September 1 — The Twins score six runs in the 11th inning to beat the Brewers 7–1 in Milwaukee. The rally was capped by a three-run homer from Harmon Killebrew. Killebrew also hit a three-run homer in the first inning of the opener, which the Twins won 4–0. Jim Perry pitched the shutout for his 20th win of the season.

The Twins had a nine-game lead on August 8 and then lost 17 of 26 to cut the margin to three games over the Angels by September 3. A streak of nine wins in ten games beginning on September 4 gave the Twins a comfortable 8½-game advantage.

September 7 — Brant Alyea drives in all seven runs of a 7–6 win over the Brewers in the first game of a double-header at Metropolitan Stadium. He hit a grand slam in the first inning and a three-run homer in the third, both off Lew Krausse. Alyea drove in two more runs in the second tilt, an 8–3 victory. Hal Haydel was the winning pitcher in his major league debut, pitching five innings of relief while allowing two runs. At the plate, Haydel doubled in his first big league at-bat, then homered in his second, both off Al Downing. Haydel finished the contest with those two hits in three at-bats.

Haydel didn't make another plate appearance until July 11, 1971, and didn't collect another hit until September 10, 1971. He pitched in 35 games in the majors, all in relief, and had a 6–2 record and a 4.04 ERA in 49 innings. As a batter, Haydel was three-for-six to finish his career with a .500 average.

SEPTEMBER 10   Tom Hall strikes out 11 batters and beats the Athletics 6–1 in the first game of a double-header at Metropolitan Stadium. The Twins completed the sweep with a 7–2 victory in the nightcap.

SEPTEMBER 15   Leo Cardenas hits a grand slam in the second inning of a 7–5 win over the Angels in the first game of a double-header at Metropolitan Stadium. Tom Hall struck out 12 batters in eight innings in the second contest, but the Twins lost 5–3.

Hall struck out 184 batters in 155 1/3 innings in 1970 at the age of 22. Making 11 starts and 41 relief appearances, he had an 11–6 record and a 2.52 ERA.

SEPTEMBER 16   Bert Blyleven strikes out the first six batters to face him and fans ten in 6 2/3 innings, but he gives up five runs and loses 5–1 to the Angels at Metropolitan Stadium.

SEPTEMBER 21   Vida Blue pitches a no-hitter for the Athletics to defeat the Twins 6–0 in Oakland. The only Minnesota base runner was Harmon Killebrew, who walked in the fourth inning. Cesar Tovar was the last batter for the Twins and fouled out to first baseman (and long-time Twin) Don Mincher. Blue was only 21 years old. The game was his sixth big league start, and second in 1970.

SEPTEMBER 22   The Twins clinch the pennant with a 5–3 win over the Athletics in Oakland.

SEPTEMBER 23   Tom Hall (7 2/3 innings) and Bill Zepp (1 1/3 innings) combine on a two-hitter to defeat the Athletics 7–4 in Oakland. Both hits were home runs off Hall, a solo shot by Bert Campaneris with two out in the seventh inning, and a three-run shot by Dave Duncan in the eighth.

SEPTEMBER 25   Jim Perry records the Twins second consecutive two-hitter and beats the Royals 1–0 in Kansas City. It was his 24th win of the season. Cookie Rojas collected both hits off Perry with singles in the sixth and eighth innings. Steve Brye drove in the lone run with a double in the fourth inning. It was his first extra base hit of his career.

SEPTEMBER 28   Tom Hall (eight innings) and Ron Perranoski (one inning) combine on a shutout to defeat the Royals 1–0 at Metropolitan Stadium. The lone run scored on a suicide squeeze bunt by Danny Thompson that scored Brant Alyea from third base.

SEPTEMBER 29   A day after winning 1–0, the Twins play 12 innings against the Royals and lose 14–13 at Metropolitan Stadium. Both teams had 20 hits. The Twins led 9–5 before Kansas City scored six times in the top of the ninth. Minnesota rebounded with two in their half on two-out, run-scoring singles from Leo Cardenas and Charlie Manuel. Both teams scored twice in the 11th, with Cardenas delivering a two-run single to tie the score 13–13. Pitcher Ted Abernathy drove in the winning run with a single in the 12th. Cardenas had a total of five hits in six at-bats. The two teams combined to use 49 players, 27 of them by the Twins.

1970s

The Twins played the Baltimore Orioles in the American League Championship Series for the second year in a row. The Orioles swept the Twins in 1969. After winning 109 games in 1969 before losing to the Mets in the World Series, Baltimore was 108–54 in 1970 under Earl Weaver. During the regular season, the Twins won seven of 12 meetings with the Orioles.

OCTOBER 3 — The Twins open the ALCS with a 10–6 loss to the Orioles before 26,847 at Metropolitan Stadium. Baltimore broke a 2–2 tie with seven runs in the fourth inning, six of them off Jim Perry. After four singles scored the first run, Orioles pitcher Mike Cuellar hit a wind-aided grand slam over the right field fence. Don Buford followed with another homer before Perry was relieved. Harmon Killebrew homered in the losing cause, and Tony Oliva had three hits, two of them doubles. Because of a strike by major league umpires, minor league umps were used. The regular arbiters returned in game two.

The series was telecast nationally by NBC. The announcers were Jim Simpson and Sandy Koufax in the first and second games, and Curt Gowdy and Tony Kubek in the third.

OCTOBER 4 — The Twins lose game two by an 11–3 score before 27,499 at Metropolitan Stadium. For the second game in a row, the Orioles scored seven runs in an inning, this time in the ninth. Harmon Killebrew and Tony Oliva homered in the losing cause. A controversial incident occurred in the eighth inning when Orioles manager Earl Weaver asked the umpires to check the hand of Ron Perranoski. Umpire Bill Haller ruled that Perranoski illegally had pine tar on his hand, and ordered the Twins pitcher to the clubhouse to wash his hands. Perranoski pitched a scoreless eighth but gave up five runs in the ninth.

Both crowds at the Met were about 20,000 shy of capacity. The games were played on Saturday and Sunday afternoons. Game three in Baltimore attracted 27,608. A four-game regular-season series between the Orioles and Twins at Metropolitan Stadium in July drew 132,860.

OCTOBER 5 — The Orioles complete the sweep of the Twins with a 6–1 win at Memorial Stadium in Baltimore. Jim Palmer pitched a complete game and struck out 12.

The Orioles outscored the Twins 27–10 in the three games. Baltimore went on to win the World Series in five games over the Cincinnati Reds.

OCTOBER 23 — Sherry Robertson, director of the Twins farm system, is killed in a single-car accident near Houghton, South Dakota, while traveling from Aberdeen, South Dakota, to Ashby, Minnesota, on a hunting trip. He had held the post of farm director in both Washington and Minnesota since 1958. Robertson was 51. He was also the younger brother (by eight years) of Twins owner Calvin Griffith. The two were nephews of Clark Griffith, who owned the Senators from 1912 until 1955. Calvin took Griffith's last name, while Sherry did not.

1971

Season in a Sentence
After winning the division title in 1969 and 1970, the Twins tumble to fifth place, the pitching staff implodes, and team draws fewer than one million fans for the first time since the move to Minnesota.

Finish • Won • Lost • Pct • GB
Fifth   74   86   .463   26.5

Manager
Bill Rigney

Stats

Stats	Twins	AL	Rank
Batting Avg:	.260	.247	2
On-Base Pct:	.324	.317	3
Slugging Pct:	.372	.364	5
Home Runs:	116		6
Stolen Bases:	66		8
ERA:	3.81	3.46	11
Errors:	118		6
Runs Scored:	654		5
Runs Allowed:	670		11

Starting Line-up
George Mitterwald, c
Harmon Killebrew, 1b-3b
Rod Carew, 2b
Steve Braun, 3b
Leo Cardenas, ss
Cesar Tovar, lf-rf
Jim Holt, cf
Tony Oliva, rf
Rich Reese, 1b

Pitchers
Jim Perry, sp
Bert Blyleven, sp
Jim Kaat, sp
Tom Hall, rp
Stan Williams, rp
Ray Corbin, rp

Attendance
940,858 (fifth in AL)

Club Leaders
Batting Avg:	Tony Oliva	.337
On-Base Pct:	Harmon Killebrew	.386
Slugging Pct:	Tony Oliva	.546
Home Runs:	Harmon Killebrew	28
RBI:	Harmon Killebrew	119
Runs:	Cesar Tovar	94
Stolen Bases:	Cesar Tovar	18
Wins:	Jim Perry	17
Strikeouts:	Bert Blyleven	224
ERA:	Bert Blyleven	2.81
Saves:	Tom Hall	9

MARCH 13   The Twins play an exhibition game against the Tokyo Giants in Orlando and win 6–3.

MARCH 31   The Twins release Luis Tiant and Dave Boswell.

The Twins released two former 20-game winners in one day. Tiant won 20 for the Indians in 1968. The Twins would come to regret letting Tiant go (see December 11, 1969) but Boswell, who suffered from shoulder problems was finished. Boswell captured 20 wins for the Twins in 1969, but fell to 3–7 in 1970 as a result of the sore shoulder. During his years in Minnesota, he fought Billy Martin, grappled with a fan in the Metropolitan Stadium parking lot, cut the tendon of his left pinkie finger while fishing, broke down Rod Carew's hotel room door in a rage, and needed 22 stitches in his right hand after hitting catcher Paul Ratliff in a motel hallway on the night of the Twins' division title clinching in 1970. In 1971, Boswell pitched first for the Detroit Tigers—managed by Billy Martin—and then for the Orioles, finishing the year with one win and two losses and a 4.66 ERA in 29 innings. Unable to recapture his early brilliance, his career ended.

APRIL 6	The Twins open the season with a 7–2 loss to the Brewers before 18,863 at Metropolitan Stadium. Jim Perry was the starting and losing pitcher.
	The Twins radio broadcasting team in 1971 consisted of Herb Carneal, Halsey Hall and Ray Christensen. The TV announcers were Hall, Frank Buetel and Bob Allison.
APRIL 10	Making his first major league start, center fielder Paul Powell homers in the eighth inning of a 5–3 victory over the White Sox in Chicago.
	The home run proved to be the only one of Powell's career. He had 42 at-bats over 31 games for the Twins in 1971 and the Dodgers in 1973 and 1975.
APRIL 11	Jim Kaat gives up 11 hits and walks a batter, but pitches a shutout to defeat the White Sox 6–0 in Chicago.
APRIL 13	The Twins and Royals tie an American League record by combining to hit seven batters with pitches during a 5–4 Kansas City win at Municipal Stadium. The offending pitchers for the Twins were Ron Perranoski, who plunked two hitters, and Stan Williams. The Royals hurlers were Tom Burgmeier, who hit a pair of batters, Ted Abernathy and Jim York. Six batters took first base after being thumped with pitches, led by Rich Reese who was hit twice.
APRIL 19	The Twins take a 9–0 lead after three innings, then hang on to defeat the Royals 9–8 at Metropolitan Stadium. Harmon Killebrew drove in six runs on a two-run single, a ground out, and a three-run homer.
	Killebrew batted .254 with 28 homers and a league-leading 119 RBIs in 1971, along with a league-leading 114 walks. Now thirty-five years old, he had the last great year of his career.
APRIL 24	The Twins score six runs in extra innings and out-last the Yankees 11–8 in 11 innings in New York. Both teams scored three runs in the tenth inning before Minnesota put the game away with three tallies in the 11th. The Yanks left 20 runners on base.
APRIL 25	Jim Kaat pitches a two-hitter to down the Yankees 8–0 in New York. The only hits off Kaat were singles by Horace Clarke in the third inning and Ron Woods in the eighth.
MAY 1	Jim Perry allows the first five batters to face him to reach base, then settles down for a 7–3 win over the Red Sox in Boston. Perry started the first inning by surrendering back-to-back homers to Luis Aparicio and Reggie Smith, and then loaded the bases on two walks and a single.
MAY 4	Trailing 5–4, the Twins achieve a 6–5 victory over the Yankees at Metropolitan Stadium on home runs by Rod Carew in the ninth inning and Jim Holt in the tenth. Both homers came with two out off Lindy McDaniel.
MAY 5	Leo Cardenas drives in all five runs of a 5–3 win over the Yankees at Metropolitan Stadium. Cardenas delivered a three-run homer in the second inning and run-scoring singles in the fourth and fifth.

MAY 7 — The Twins lead 5–2 with two out in the ninth inning, no one on base, and Bert Blyleven on the mound, but wind up losing 6–5 to the Senators at Metropolitan Stadium. Blyleven gave up a triple and single before yielding a three-run homer to Paul Casanova. The winning run was scored off reliever Ray Corbett on a single, a wild pitch and an error by rightfielder Tony Oliva.

MAY 12 — Bert Blyleven strikes out 11 batters and beats the Red Sox 1–0 at Metropolitan Stadium. The lone run scored in the fourth inning on a triple by Rod Carew and a single from Jim Holt.

MAY 17 — Bert Blyleven and Tom Hall combine to strike out 15 batters during a 3–2 win over the Angels in Anaheim. Blyleven struck out 12 batters in eight innings and Hall fanned all three batters he faced in the ninth.

MAY 19 — Tom Hall retires all 12 batters he faces and strikes out six while pitching the sixth, seventh, eighth and ninth innings of a 12–6 triumph over the Angels in Anaheim.

Over four relief appearances from May 17 through May 25, Hall allowed no runs and one hit in 10 2/3 innings while striking out 19 batters.

MAY 26 — Bert Blyleven strikes out 12 batters during a 4–1 win over the Brewers in Milwaukee.

Blyleven was 16–15 with a 2.81 ERA and 224 strikeouts in 278 2/3 innings in 1971.

MAY 29 — Trailing 7–0, the Twins score seven runs in the fifth inning, but wind up losing 11–8 to the Orioles at Metropolitan Stadium.

JUNE 4 — With the Twins trailing the Indians 4–2 in the sixth inning at Metropolitan Stadium, play is halted and fans are evacuated to spaces underneath the grandstand as tornadoes threaten the area. The game was not resumed.

JUNE 8 — In the first round of the amateur draft, the Twins select shortstop Dale Soderholm from Coral Park High School in Miami, Florida. He was the brother of Eric Soderholm, who played for the Twins from 1971 through 1975.

Dale Soderholm never made it past the Class AAA level. Future major leaguers drafted and signed by the Twins in 1972 were Dave Edwards (seventh round), Rob Wilfong (13th round), Chuck Baker (36th round) and Glenn Borgmann (first round of the secondary phase).

JUNE 12 — After trailing the Tigers 4–3 with two out and no one on base, the Twins score two runs off Mickey Lolich to win 5–4 in Detroit. The pair of runs came through a single by Danny Thompson, a walk to Steve Braun, and singles from Cesar Tovar and Rich Reese.

JUNE 14 — Three batters into the game against the Indians in Cleveland, the Twins score three runs on a single by Cesar Tovar, a walk to Rod Carew and a homer by Tony Oliva. The Twins were shut out the rest of the way but won 3–1.

1970s

June 17   After the White Sox score three runs in the top of the 11th inning, the Twins respond with four in their half to win 7–6 at Metropolitan Stadium. Tony Oliva drove in the first two tallies with a bases loaded single with one out. The contest was tied 6–6 on a sacrifice fly by Rich Reese. George Mitterwald's single drove in the winning run.

June 19   George Mitterwald delivers a walk-off single in extra innings for the second time in three days, this time in the tenth for a 2–1 victory over the White Sox at Metropolitan Stadium. Tony Oliva tied the score with a home run leading off the ninth.

June 22   Harmon Killebrew hits his 498th career homer during a 10–1 win over the Athletics at Metropolitan Stadium.

June 29   Tony Oliva injures his knee diving for a ball in the outfield during a 5–3 win over the Athletics on Oakland.

> *Oliva was hitting .375 at the time of the injury. He didn't start another game until July 18. He finished the season with a .337 average, good enough for his third career batting title but was never again the same player. He played only ten games in 1972 and was exclusively a designated hitter from 1973 through the end of his career in 1976.*

July 11   Trailing the Royals 5–4 in the first game of a double-header at Metropolitan Stadium, the Twins receive solo homers from George Mitterwald in the ninth inning and Jim Nettles in the tenth to win 6–5. The homer by Nettles was the first of his career. He hit another one in the second game, a 7–1 victory.

> *Jim Nettles played for the Twins from 1970 through 1972. His older brother Graig (by 2½ years) was a Twin from 1967 through 1969.*

July 13   Harmon Killebrew hits a two-run homer off Ferguson Jenkins in the sixth inning of the All-Star Game, played at Tiger Stadium in Detroit. The American League won 6–4.

July 15   Rico Petrocelli hits a three-run, walk-off homer off Stan Williams in the 13th inning to lift the Red Sox to a 3–0 win over the Twins in Boston. Jim Perry pitched ten shutout innings and allowed only three hits.

July 19   The Twins play the Senators in Washington for the last time and lose 5–3. The Senators moved to Arlington, Texas, at the end of the season and were renamed the Rangers.

July 20   The Yankees score five runs in the ninth inning to defeat the Twins 6–5 in New York.

July 25   Harmon Killebrew hits his 499th career homer during a 6–2 win over the Red Sox at Metropolitan Stadium. Killebrew had 69 at-bats and 92 plate appearances in between his 498th homer on June 22 and number 499 (see August 10, 1971).

July 27   Tony Oliva hits a two-run, walk-off homer in the ninth inning to defeat the Senators 4–2 at Metropolitan Stadium.

> *Oliva had nine consecutive multi-hit games from July 30 through August 7. During that span, he collected 20 hits in 37 at-bats.*

JULY 30 — After leading 9–1 at the end of the fifth inning, the Twins wind up losing 11–9 to the Yankees at Metropolitan Stadium. The Yanks scored twice in the ninth to snap a 9–9 tie.

On the same day, the Twins sold Ron Perranoski to the Tigers. Perranoski, who had come to Minnesota in a highly publicized trade involving star players, had given the Twins excellent work from the bullpen, but at the age of thirty-five was losing effectiveness. He would retire at the end of the 1973 season.

AUGUST 10 — Harmon Killebrew drives in all three Twins runs during a ten-inning, 4–3 loss to the Orioles at Metropolitan Stadium with his 500th and 501st career homers. He hit his 498th homer on June 22 and number 499 on July 25. Killebrew reached the 500-homer milestone with a solo homer off Mike Cuellar in the first inning, and then added a two-run shot against Cuellar in the sixth.

AUGUST 13 — Harmon Killebrew delivers a two-run, walk-off single in the ninth inning to defeat the Tigers 4–3 at Metropolitan Stadium.

One of the highlights of the season during the 1970s at Metropolitan Stadium was Campers Weekend. The idea was conceived by Early Wynn, who was a Twins coach in 1969 and an avid camper. The club invited fans in trailers, motor homes, camper trucks, converted buses and tents to stay in the parking lot for a weekend series for $3.00. Tickets to the games were extra, but there was no requirement that those camping out attend the games. In 1971, more than 10,000 people from 20 states and three Canadian provinces to advantage of the promotion. Campers were invited to ice skate at the adjacent Metropolitan Sports Complex. The schedule also included square dances, rock 'n' roll dances, "old fashioned" dances, movies outside the left-field wall, and folk singers. On Sunday, both Protestant and Catholic services were held in the stands. Free water and septic service was available, and ice and dairy products could be purchased from trucks. There were also amusement park rides and bicycle rentals.

AUGUST 20 — Trailing 5–0, the Twins score a run in the sixth inning, five in the eighth, and two in the ninth to defeat the Orioles 8–5 in Baltimore. Leo Cardenas put the Twins into the lead with a two-out, three-run homer in the eighth.

AUGUST 27 — Harmon Killebrew hits two homers and drives in five runs during an 8–4 win over the Indians in Cleveland.

AUGUST 31 — The Twins score two runs in the ninth inning and one in the tenth to defeat the White Sox 4–3 at Metropolitan Stadium. In the ninth, Steve Braun drove in a run with a triple and scored on a sacrifice fly by Jim Nettles. The game ended on a sacrifice fly from Harmon Killebrew.

SEPTEMBER 1 — The Twins trade Stan Williams to the Cardinals for Dan Ford and Fred Rico. Williams, at the age of thirty-four, was near the end of his career, though he pitched well for the Cardinals for the remainder of that season, his last full year in the majors. Ford, a young minor leaguer at the time, would reach the majors in 1975 and give the Twins four good seasons during an eleven-year, major league career. Rico, who played briefly for the Kansas City Royals in 1969, would never make it back to the majors.

1970s

SEPTEMBER 3 — Harmon Killebrew hits a grand slam off Mudcat Grant in the sixth inning of a 9–4 win over the Athletics in the first game of a double-header at Metropolitan Stadium. Eric Soderholm hit a home run in the second plate appearance of his major league debut. In the second tilt, the Twins won 2–1 on a pair of solo homers, both off Vida Blue. Jim Nettles delivered the first one in the second inning, and George Mitterwald belted a walk-off home run in the ninth.

Soderholm didn't hit his second career homer until May 12, 1972.

SEPTEMBER 13 — Steve Braun's homer off Tom Murphy in the fourth inning accounts for the lone run of a 1–0 win over the Angels in the second game of a double-header in Anaheim. Jim Kaat pitched the shutout. California won the opener 3–2.

SEPTEMBER 15 — The Twins win 1–0 for the second game in a row, defeating the Brewers at County Stadium. Entering the ninth, Milwaukee's Skip Lockwood was working on a one-hitter. With two out, he walked Harmon Killebrew and gave up a triple to Steve Braun for the game's only run. Bert Blyleven pitched the shutout.

SEPTEMBER 29 — Rick Renick's home run off Clyde Wright in the second inning accounts for the only run in a 1–0 triumph over the Angels at Metropolitan Stadium. Bert Blyleven pitched a ten-hit shutout.

OCTOBER 22 — The Twins trade Paul Powell to the Dodgers for Bobby Darwin.

A first-round pick (seventh overall) in the 1969 draft, Powell never achieved his potential, batting .167 in 47 plate appearances during a brief major league career. Darwin, who at the age of 28 had only minimal experience in the majors, turned in several productive years for the Twins.

NOVEMBER 29 — Brant Alyea is drafted by the Athletics.

NOVEMBER 30 — The Twins trade Leo Cardenas to the Angels for Dave LaRoche.

DECEMBER 3 — The Twins trade Tom Hall to the Reds for Wayne Granger.

Granger pitched 90 games and 144 2/3 innings for the Reds in 1969, led the NL in saves in 1970, and pitched 70 games and 100 innings in 1971. He pitched 63 games out of the Twins bullpen in 1972 before being traded to the Cardinals in the deal that brought Larry Hisle to Minnesota. If he had come along 20 years later, Hall might have been a star as a one-inning closer with a blazing fastball. He stood six-feet tall and weighed about 150 pounds, and the Twins didn't think he had the stamina to be a regular starting pitcher. In four seasons with the Twins, Hall was a long reliever and a spot starter. In 1970 and 1971, he struck out 321 batters in 285 innings and a 2.91 ERA in 22 starts and 78 relief appearances. The Reds used him in a similar role in 1972. Hall was 10–1 and had an ERA of 2.61 while fanning 134 in 124 1/3 innings in 47 games, seven of them starts. He was only 24 that season, but the Twins and Reds ruined a promising arm with the shuttle from the bullpen to the rotation, and he was seldom effective after 1972.

1972

Season in a Sentence
The Twins are 16–5 on May 14, but Bill Rigney is fired and replaced by Frank Quilici in July as the club drops out of contention.

Finish • Won • Lost • Pct • GB
Third   77   77   .500   15.5

Managers
Bill Rigney (36–34) and Frank Quilici (41–43)

Stats   Twins • AL • Rank
Batting Avg: .244   .239   4
On-Base Pct: .307   .306   4
Slugging Pct: .344   .343   7
Home Runs: 93   7
Stolen Bases: 53   10
ERA: 2.84   3.06   3
Errors: 159   11
Runs Scored: 537   7
Runs Allowed: 535   7

Starting Line-up
Glenn Borgmann, c
Harmon Killebrew, 1b
Rod Carew, 2b
Steve Braun, 3b
Danny Thompson, ss
Steve Brye, lf
Bobby Darwin, cf
Cesar Tovar, rf
Eric Soderholm, 3b
Jim Nettles, cf
Rich Reese, 1b

Pitchers
Bert Blyleven, sp
Dick Woodson, sp
Jim Perry, sp
Ray Corbin, sp
Jim Kaat, sp
Dave Goltz, sp
Wayne Granger, rp
Dave LaRoche, rp

Attendance
797,901 (seventh in AL)

Club Leaders
Batting Avg: Rod Carew   .318
On-Base Pct: Rod Carew   .369
Slugging Pct: Harmon Killebrew   .450
Home Runs: Harmon Killebrew   26
RBI: Harmon Killebrew   80
Runs: Cesar Tovar   86
Stolen Bases: Cesar Tovar   21
Wins: Bert Blyleven   17
Strikeouts: Bert Blyleven   228
Saves: Wayne Granger   19

APRIL 6   The Twins scheduled season opener against the Angels at Metropolitan Stadium is canceled by baseball's first player's strike. The Twins first eight games were eliminated by the labor action, which began on April 1 and ended on April 13.

During the walkout, Twins players shared homes and cars and practiced daily at St. Olaf College in Northfield, Minnesota.

APRIL 15   In the strike-delayed season opener, the Twins lose 4–3 in 11 innings to the Athletics in Oakland. The three Minnesota runs scored on solo homers by Danny Thompson, Harmon Killebrew and Bobby Darwin. It was also Killebrew's 2,000th career game. Bert Blyleven was the starting pitcher and went six innings.

The game was Darwin's debut with the Twins. He homered again in his second game with the club the following day, a 3–2 win over the A's in Oakland. After 12 games with the Twins, Darwin had six home runs, 19 RBIs, and a batting average of .432. By the end of the season, he had a .267 average and 22 homers. Darwin's travels to Minnesota were unique to say the least. He played in his first major league game as a 19-year-old pitcher with the Angels in 1962. He didn't play in his second big league game until 1969 with the Dodgers. He hooked up with the team in 1968 when club vice-president Al Campanis was involved in a collision, and Darwin showed up in his off-season job driving a tow truck. The Dodgers, at the suggestion of Tommy Lasorda, converted Darwin into an outfielder in 1970. He was acquired by the Twins in a trade in October 1971. Darwin started in the Minnesota outfield for three seasons beginning in 1972, and hit 65 homers, but also led the AL in strikeouts all three years. During that span, he struck out 409 times while drawing 121 walks.

APRIL 23   The Twins play their first home game of the season and defeat the Athletics 8–4 before 17,876 at Metropolitan Stadium. Bobby Darwin hit a home run.

The contest was the ninth home game on the original schedule. Games against the Angels on April 6, 8 and 9 and versus the White Sox on April 10, 11, 12 and 13 were canceled by the strike. The April 22 game facing the Athletics was postponed by rain.

APRIL 25   The Twins pound the Red Sox 12–0 at Metropolitan Stadium. Jim Perry pitched the shutout.

The Twins sported new uniforms in 1972. Along with every other club during the early 1970s, the club switched to lighter-weight, double-knit jerseys. Pinstripes were dropped for the home whites. The new pants for both the home and road uniforms incorporated a red, white and blue elastic waistband in place of the standard belt. Additional red, white and blue striping was added down the pants legs, on the sleeve ends, and around the collar. The script Twins was now red and outlined in blue. From 1961 through 1971, it had been the reverse. Further changes were introduced in 1973. The crown of the caps at home was changed from blue to scarlet and pullover shirts replaced the button-down variety. The shoes worn at home were also red. The gray road uniforms were now powder blue. This combination was retained until 1986.

APRIL 29   Harmon Killebrew drives in both runs of a 2–0 win over the Yankees in New York with a first-inning triple. Jim Kaat (six innings) and Dave LaRoche (three innings) combined on the shutout.

MAY 12   The game between the Twins and Brewers at Metropolitan Stadium is suspended because of curfew after 21 innings with the score tied 3–3. The Brewers tied the contest 3–3 with two runs in the seventh, and there was no scoring over the next 14 innings. Minnesota relievers Dave LaRoche, Wayne Granger, Ray Corbin, Bob Gebhard and Tom Norton shut out Milwaukee from the eighth through the 21st. The game was stopped because of an AL rule stipulating that no inning could start after 1:00 a.m. It was completed the following afternoon.

MAY 13   A day after playing 21 innings, the Twins and Brewers play 16 more on a Sunday afternoon at Metropolitan Stadium. First, the two clubs completed the suspended game of the night before, which was called after 21 innings with the score 3–3. Bert Blyleven started the 22nd inning and allowed a run on a single, a walk, and another single by Mike Ferraro to give Milwaukee a 4–3 advantage. Jim Lonborg pitched the bottom of the 22nd to earn his first save since 1966. The Twins left 23 runners on base. Rod Carew finished the contest with five hits, including two doubles, in seven at-bats. He also drew a pair intentional walks, two of five issued by Milwaukee pitchers. Bobby Darwin struck out five times. Blyleven and Lonborg also started the regular scheduled contest, and each allowed two runs in the first inning. Blyleven went nine innings and left with the score tied 3–3. The Brewers scored in the top of the 15th to take a 4–3 lead. The Twins were shut out in 12 straight innings from the third through the 14th, but came off the mat to score twice in the 15th to win 5–4. With two out and no one on base, Jim Nettles walked and Eric Soderholm hit a two-run, walk-off homer. It was Soderholm's second career homer. The first came on September 3, 1971, in his major league debut.

> *The Twins and Brewers played 37 innings in less than 24 hours. They set an American League record for most innings played by the same two clubs in consecutive games. The 22-inning game last five hours and 47 minutes. The 15-inning tilt went three hours and 36 minutes.*

MAY 14 — The Twins defeat the Brewers 4–2 at Metropolitan Stadium. The win gave Minnesota a 16–5 record and a 2½-game lead in the AL West, but the club dropped out of the top spot on May 21 and was ten games out of first by July 9.

MAY 19 — The Twins play the Rangers in Arlington for the first time and lose 2–1.

MAY 24 — The Twins defeat the Royals 1–0 in 12 innings in Kansas City. The lone run scored on a double by Danny Thompson and a single from Rod Carew. Jim Kaat (11 innings) and Wayne Granger (one inning) combined on the shutout. Dick Drago pitched a complete game for Kansas City.

MAY 27 — The Rangers score nine runs in the second inning and six in the third on the way to a 16–2 thrashing of the Twins at Metropolitan Stadium.

MAY 28 — Harmon Killebrew hits a grand slam off Bill Gogolewski in the third inning of a 7–2 win over the Rangers at Metropolitan Stadium.

JUNE 6 — The Twins outlast the Orioles 5–4 in 15 innings in Baltimore. Minnesota entered the ninth trailing 4–1, then scored three times off Jim Palmer to tie the contest. Eric Soderholm drove in the first two tallies with a home run. Danny Thompson's single brought the tying run across the plate. A single by Steve Brye drove home the winning run.

> *On the same day, the Twins selected pitcher Dick Ruthven from Fresno State University in the first round of the amateur draft. The club failed to sign Ruthven, who was chosen by the Phillies in the secondary draft in January 1973. His career included 123 wins and 127 losses from 1973 through 1986. Future major leaguers drafted and signed by the Twins in 1972 were Willie Norwood (third round), Doug Clarey (sixth round), Randy Bass (seventh round), Lyman Bostock (26th round) and Al Woods (second round of the secondary phase). Gary Ward was signed as an amateur free agent in August.*

JUNE 11 — The Nettles brothers both homer during a 5–3 win over the Indians at Municipal Stadium. Jim Nettles homered off Vince Colbert in the sixth. Big brother Graig hit a home run off Jim Kaat in the seventh. Kaat also hit a home run, the last by a Twin pitcher before the passage of the designated hitter rule.

1970s

Kaat hit 14 home runs for the Twins from 1961 through 1972. He later added two as a National Leaguer to give him 16 during his career.

JUNE 26 — Nine days after the break-in of Democratic Party National Committee headquarters at the Watergate complex in Washington, Eric Soderholm hits a grand slam off Eddie Fisher in the seventh inning of a 7–4 win over the Angels at Metropolitan Stadium.

JUNE 27 — Shoddy base running in the fourth inning contributes to a triple play and a 3–1 loss to the Angels at Metropolitan Stadium. With Harmon Killebrew on third base and Steve Braun on second, Jim Nettles hit a fly ball to Jim Spencer. Killebrew faked toward home and Spencer fired the ball to Ken McMullen at third base. McMullen spotted Braun off the bag at second, and threw to second baseman Sandy Alomar, who tagged Braun for the second out. Alomar then tossed the ball to shortstop Leo Cardenas, who tagged Killebrew standing off third to complete the triple play.

JULY 2 — Jim Kaat breaks his left (pitching) hand while sliding during a 6–1 win over the White Sox in the first game of a double-header at Comiskey Park. Chicago won the second tilt 2–1.

Kaat was 10–2 with a 2.06 ERA at the time of the injury. He didn't play again in 1972.

JULY 6 — Bill Rigney is fired as manager and replaced by 33-year-old Frank Quilici.

At the time of the switch, the Twins were 36–34 and had lost their previous four games while scoring only three runs. "The most important reason for making this change," explained Calvin Griffith at a press conference, "was that the players weren't reacting. Too many were nonchalant." Quilici was an infielder for the Twins in 1965 and again from 1967 through 1970, hitting .214 with five home runs in 682 at-bats and 405 games. He was a coach with the Twins at the time of his appointment as manager. Quilici was manager through the end of the 1975 season. After filling a variety of roles with the Athletics for several seasons, including as a radio broadcaster, Rigney managed the Giants in 1976.

JULY 9 — Rich Reese hits a pinch-hit, grand slam off Lindy McDaniel in the seventh inning of a 9–6 loss to the Yankees at Metropolitan Stadium. It was the third pinch-hit slam of Reese's career.

JULY 10 — Bobby Darwin hits a grand slam off Earl Stephenson in the first inning of an 8–1 triumph over the Brewers at Metropolitan Stadium.

JULY 13 — The Twins trounce the Red Sox 10–0 at Metropolitan Stadium. Ray Corbin pitched the shutout.

JULY 14 — The Twins score three runs in the ninth inning to defeat the Red Sox 7–6 at Metropolitan Stadium. After Jim Nettles reached on an error with out, Rich Reese, Cesar Tovar, Danny Thompson and Rod Carew hit four consecutive singles to tie the score 6–6. The winning run crossed the plate on a bases-loaded walk by Don Newhauser to Harmon Killebrew.

July 30	Harmon Killebrew's homer off Wilbur Wood in the sixth inning accounts for the only run of a 1–0 win over the White Sox at Metropolitan Stadium. Jim Perry (eight innings) and Wayne Granger (one inning) combined on the shutout.
	Killebrew batted .231 with 26 homers in 1972. It was the beginning of the decline of the team's greatest star.
July 31	Richie Allen hits two inside-the-park homers against the Twins to lead the White Sox to an 8–1 win at Metropolitan Stadium.
August 7	Jim Perry pitches a two-hitter to defeat the Rangers 4–0 at Metropolitan Stadium. The only Texas hits were back-to-back singles by Dick Billings and Ted Ford in the fifth inning.
August 30	The Twins score all seven of their runs in a 7–1 victory over the Orioles at Metropolitan Stadium in the seventh inning.
September 1	Rod Carew steals home with the winning run in the tenth inning for a 5–4 triumph over the Indians at Metropolitan Stadium. Bobby Darwin drove in the other four Minnesota runs with two homers and a double.
September 6	Phil Roof has a hand in both runs of a 2–0 win over the Rangers in Arlington. Roof doubled and scored in the third inning and contributed an RBI-single in the seventh. Dick Woodson pitched a two-hit shutout. The only Texas hits were singles by Jim Mason in the fifth inning and Tom Grieve in the seventh.
September 10	The Twins play at Municipal Stadium in Kansas City for the last time, and lose 3–1 to the Royals.
September 16	Harmon Killebrew drives in five runs to lead the Twins to an 11–1 walloping of the Royals at Metropolitan Stadium.
September 19	Cesar Tovar hits a two-run, walk-off homer in the ninth inning to defeat the Rangers 5–3 at Metropolitan Stadium.
September 22	A walk-off single by Rod Carew in the ninth inning accounts for the lone run of a 1–0 win over the Angels at Metropolitan Stadium. Bert Blyleven pitched the shutout.
	Carew won the batting title with a .318 average in 1972. Blyleven was 17–17 with a 2.72 ERA and 228 strikeouts in 287 1/3 innings. They were two bright spots in an otherwise lackluster season as the aging stars of the powerful teams in the 1960s began to fade.
September 27	The Twins allow only three runs in a double-header against the Athletics in Oakland, but lose 1–0 in 11 innings and 2–1 in ten innings.
October 4	In the last game of the season, the Twins clobber the White Sox 14–2 at Metropolitan Stadium.
	The Twins drew only 797,801 fans in 1972, about half of the 1,483,547 the club attracted in 1967.

1970s

OCTOBER 27 The Twins trade Rick Dempsey to the Yankees for Danny Walton.

Dempsey made his major league debut as a 20-year-old with the Twins in 1969 but played in only 41 games over four seasons with the club. The Twins made a poor decision in dealing Dempsey, who had a 24-year major league career. He played for the Orioles from 1977 through 1986, and was the starting catcher on the 1979 and 1983 World Series teams. In the 1983 Series, he was the MVP as the Orioles defeated the Phillies for the world championship. Dempsey also played for the 1988 world champion Dodgers. Walton played two seasons in Minnesota as an outfielder and batted an abysmal .176 in 159 at-bats over 79 games.

NOVEMBER 29 Four weeks after Richard Nixon defeats George McGovern in the Presidential election, the Twins trade Wayne Granger to the Cardinals for Larry Hisle and John Cumberland.

Hisle was 25 at the time of the trade and had struggled in the Phillies and Cardinals organizations. After playing in the majors from 1969 through 1971, he spent the entire 1972 season in the minors. He found a starting role with the Twins right away and spent five good years with the club. In 1977, he made the All-Star team and led the AL in runs batted in. Hisle didn't get along with Calvin Griffith, however, and signed with the Brewers as a free agent following the 1977 campaign. Granger was only 28 but his arm was about used up from overwork by the Reds and Twins. His unorthodox, submarine-style delivery may have added to the arm woes. After the trade, he bounced around with five clubs over four seasons before his career ended.

NOVEMBER 30 On a busy day, the Twins make three deals involving front-line players. Dave LaRoche was traded to the Cubs for Bill Hands, Joe Decker and Rob Maneely. Rich Reese was sold to the Tigers. Cesar Tovar was dealt to the Phillies for Ken Sanders, Joe Lis and Ken Reynolds.

La Roche had 11 seasons ahead of him as an effective reliever for four different clubs. Two of his sons (Adam and Andy) were teammates on the 2009 Pirates. Hands won 38 games for the Cubs in 1969 and 1970 but was on the downside of his career by the time he arrived in Minnesota. Decker was 23 at the time of the trade and had a 7–9 career record, but he won 16 games for the Twins in 1974. He explained his success by stating: "I try to tranquilize myself when I pitch. If I'm lethargic, I have better stuff." Decker pitched only 111 2/3 innings over three seasons after 1974, however, because of arm trouble. After batting .322 in 1969, Reese looked like a coming star. But his averages fell to .261 in 1970, .219 in 1971, .218 in 1971 and .144 in 125 at-bats and 81 games in 1973. He would play 22 more games with the Twins late in the 1973 season. Tovar was a fan favorite and gave the Twins eight solid seasons, but he was about through when traded to Philadelphia. None of the three players acquired for Tovar had an impact in Minnesota.

DECEMBER 10 The American League votes to adopt the designated hitter rule on a three-year experimental basis. Under the new rule, the designated hitter replaced the pitcher in the batting order unless otherwise noted before the game. The rule was adopted permanently by the AL in 1975, but to this day, the NL has declined to go along with the change.

1973

Season in a Sentence
In Frank Quilici's first full year as manager, the Twins stay in contention for a pennant until the end of July before finishing with a .500 record for the second year in a row.

Finish • Won • Lost • Pct • GB
Third   81   81   .500   13.0

Manager
Frank Quilici

Stats

Stats	Twins	AL	Rank
Batting Avg:	.270	.259	1
On-Base Pct:	.341	.328	2
Slugging Pct:	.393	.381	2
Home Runs:	120		7
Stolen Bases:	87		7
ERA:	3.77	3.82	6
Errors:	139		5 (tie)
Runs Scored:	738		4
Runs Allowed:	692		7

Starting Line-up
George Mitterwald, c
Joe Lis, 1b
Rod Carew, 2b
Steve Braun, 3b
Jerry Terrell, ss
Jim Holt, lf
Larry Hisle, cf-lf
Bobby Darwin, rf
Tony Oliva, dh
Danny Thompson, ss
Steve Brye, cf
Harmon Killebrew, 1b

Pitchers
Bert Blyleven, sp
Jim Kaat, sp
Joe Decker, sp
Dick Woodson, sp
Ray Corbin, rp
Bill Hands, rp-sp
Dave Goltz, rp

Attendance
907,499 (tenth in AL)

Club Leaders
Batting Avg:	Rod Carew	.350
On-Base Pct:	Rod Carew	.411
Slugging Pct:	Rod Carew	.471
Home Runs:	Bobby Darwin	18
RBI:	Tony Oliva	92
Runs:	Rod Carew	98
Stolen Bases:	Rod Carew	41
Wins:	Bert Blyleven	20
Strikeouts:	Bert Blyleven	258
ERA:	Bert Blyleven	2.52
Saves:	Ray Corbin	14

FEBRUARY 16 The Twins reveal that shortstop Danny Thompson is found to have chronic granulocytic leukemia. The illness was discovered during a routine physical examination. A spokesman for the club said the disease was discovered in an early stage and should not affect him for five years.

> Thompson continued to play with the ailment for four more seasons, appearing in 99 games for the Twins in 1973, 97 in 1974, 112 in 1975. "There's no use crying and sitting around," he said. "I've got a lot of spunk in me and I'm going to use it up." In 1976, he played 34 games for the Twins and 64 more with the Rangers following a midseason trade. Thompson died at the age of 29 at the Mayo Clinic in Rochester, Minnesota, on December 10, 1976.

MARCH 27 The Twins trade Jim Perry to the Tigers for Danny Fife and cash. On the same day, Ken Reynolds was dealt to the Brewers for Mike Ferraro.

> Perry was traded to shed payroll. He was 14–13 with the Tigers in 1973, and then he went 17–12 with the Indians in 1974 as a teammate of his brother Gaylord. Fife's big league career lasted just 14 games.

1970s

APRIL 6 — The Twins open the season with an 8–3 win over the Athletics in Oakland. It was the first regular season game for both clubs using the designated hitter rule. Tony Oliva was Minnesota's DH, and he it a three-run homer in the first inning. He thus became the first designated hitter to hit a home run in a regular season game. Playing in his first contest with the Twins, Larry Hisle had hits in his first four plate appearances, collecting a home run, a double, and two singles. Jim Holt also homered and Bert Blyleven pitched a complete game.

Ray Scott, who broadcast Twins games from 1961 through 1966, returned to announce the contests on television in 1973. He replaced Halsey Hall, who retired. Scott's second stint with the club lasted until 1975. On the radio in 1973 were Herb Carneal and Ray Christensen.

Bert Blyleven won twenty games in 1973, the only time he reached that pinnacle during a twenty-two-year career in which he won 287. He posted double-digit victory totals in every full season he pitched for the Twins.

APRIL 7 — In his second game with the Twins, Larry Hisle homers again to help the club to a 5–3 win over the Athletics in Oakland.

APRIL 13 — In the home opener, the Twins defeat the Athletics 8–4 before 13,080 at Metropolitan Stadium. Larry Hisle and Bobby Darwin hit home runs.

APRIL 17 — The Twins score eight runs in the seventh inning and defeat the Angels 10–5 at Metropolitan Stadium. Danny Walton hit a grand slam off Steve Barber as a pinch-hitter for designated hitter Tony Oliva.

MAY 11 — The Twins play at Royals Stadium in Kansas City for the first time and lose 6–2 to the Royals.

MAY 14 — Bobby Darwin breaks a 4–4 tie with a home run in the 11th inning and the Twins add an insurance run to defeat the Rangers 6–4 in Arlington.

MAY 19	Bert Blyleven strikes out 13 batters during an 8–3 win over the White Sox in Chicago.
MAY 24	Bert Blyleven pitches a one-hitter to defeat the Royals 2–0 at Metropolitan Stadium. The only Kansas City hit was a bunt single by Ed Kirkpatrick in the fifth inning.

> *Blyleven won 20 games for the only time in his 22-year major league career in 1973. He was 20–17 with 258 strikeouts and a 2.52 ERA. Blyleven also completed 25 of his 40 starts and pitched 325 innings. Nine of his victories were shutouts, a Minnesota club record. The only pitcher in franchise history with more than nine shutouts in a season was Walter Johnson, who had 11 for the Senators in 1913.*

MAY 29	Bobby Darwin's homer off Jim Slaton in the seventh inning accounts for the only run of a 1–0 victory over the Brewers at Metropolitan Stadium. Bert Blyleven pitched his second consecutive shutout.
JUNE 2	Joe Lis hits a walk-off homer in the tenth inning to down the Tigers 3–2 at Metropolitan Stadium.
JUNE 5	In the first round of the amateur draft, the Twins select pitcher Eddie Bane from Arizona State University.

> *The Twins wasted no time rushing Bane to the majors (see July 4, 1973). Other future major leaguers drafted and signed by the Twins in 1973 were Luis Gomez (seventh round) and Larry Wolfe (ninth round).*

JUNE 6	The Twins sweep the Indians 7–3 and 13–9 in a double-header in Cleveland. The opener went 15 innings. There was no scoring from the fourth inning through the 14th before the Twins erupted with four runs in the 15th. Relievers Ken Sanders and Ray Corbin each pitched four innings of shutout baseball. In the second tilt, the Twins scored six runs in the first inning and took a 9–0 lead in the fifth before hanging on for the win. Dave Goltz gave up eight runs and 13 hits in three innings of relief, but was credited with a save.
JUNE 8	Bert Blyleven pitches a two-hitter to defeat the Orioles 2–0 at Memorial Stadium. The only Orioles hits were singles by Tommy Davis in the fourth inning and Rich Coggins in the seventh.
JUNE 10	The Twins score seven runs in the third inning and beat the Orioles 11–4 in Baltimore.
JUNE 15	Bobby Darwin drives in seven runs with two homers and two singles during a 13–6 win over the Tigers in Detroit.
JUNE 21	A walk-off single by Joe Lis in the ninth inning accounts for the lone run of a 1–0 victory over the Angels at Metropolitan Stadium. Bert Blyleven pitched the shutout.
JUNE 26	Joe Decker strikes out 15 batters and pitches a four-hitter to defeat the White Sox 4–0 in Chicago. Decker had 14 strikeouts at the end of the seventh inning.
JUNE 27	David Clyde, the number one overall pick in the amateur draft, held just 22 days earlier, makes his major league debut at the age of 18 pitching for the Rangers

against the Twins in Arlington. Clyde gave up only one hit in five innings and struck out eight, but also walked seven and left the game with a 4–2 lead. Texas won the game 4–3.

Clyde's debut drew 35,698 fans, the largest crowd of the year at Arlington Stadium. His second start on July 2, attracted 33,010, the year's second largest crowd at the Texas ballpark. The average attendance figure at the Rangers home games that season was 8,470. The box office numbers gave Calvin Griffith ideas about rolling out Eddie Bane, who was the 11th overall choice in the same draft (see July 4, 1973).

June 29 Bobby Darwin's grand slam off Nolan Ryan in the eighth inning accounts for all four runs of a 4–0 win over the Angels in Anaheim. Bert Blyleven pitched the shutout.

With the changing times, many Twins players began growing mustaches and beards in 1973. The trend started the previous season when Oakland A's owner Charlie Finley ordered his players to grow mustaches as a publicity stunt. The 1972 A's were the first major leaguers with facial hair during the regular season since 1903. Among the 1973 Twins with mustaches were Steve Brye, Jim Strickland, Danny Walton, Larry Hisle and Dick Woodson.

July 1 Jim Kaat pitches a one-hitter to defeat the Angels 2–1 in Anaheim. The only California hit was a home run by Frank Robinson in the second inning. After Robinson's homer, Kaat retired 24 of the next 25 batters to face him, with the only base runner reaching on an error in the seventh inning.

July 2 The Twins defeat the Royals 5–2 in Kansas City to take first place.

The victory put the Twins four percentage points ahead of the second-place Athletics with a record of 41–33. The Twins lost 35 of their next 54 games, however, to slide out of contention.

July 3 Tony Oliva hits three home runs, but the Twins lose 7–6 to the Royals in Kansas City. All three were solo homers off Mark Littell in the first and sixth innings and Gene Garber in the ninth.

The contest was part of an unusual four-game series against the Royals. The two clubs met in Kansas City on July 2 and 3 and at the Met on July 4 and 5.

July 4 Eddie Bane, who was drafted in the first round by the Twins on June 5, makes his professional baseball debut before a crowd of 45,890 at Metropolitan Stadium. Heavily promoted as the historic debut of a great young phenom, the game was delayed for 15 minutes to allow the unusually large crowd time to get to their seats. Bane had pitched Arizona State to the College World Series and had set an NCAA record with 505 strikeouts to complement a record of 41–4. The Twins had high hopes for him-as a pitcher and a box-office draw. Facing the Royals, Bane allowed a run and three hits in seven innings and left the game with the Twins trailing 1–0. Kansas City scored four times in the ninth and won the game 5–4.

The crowd was the largest of the season at the Met. Bane's next start on July 8 attracted 27,425, the third biggest home crowd of 1973. He made four starts before being shuttled to the bullpen, where he pitched eight consecutive hitless innings over seven appearances in July and August. By the end of the season, Bane was 0–5 with a 4.92 ERA in 60 1/3 innings over 23 games, six of them starts. He spent the entire 1974 season in the minors and returned to the Twins in 1975 and 1976 but pitched sparingly. Bane was only 24 when he pitched his last big league game and ended his career with a 7–13 record and an earned run average of 4.66. If he had fulfilled his promise, the Twins might have enjoyed a good bit more success during the latter half of the decade. He's still active in baseball as a scouting director for the Angels.

JULY 15   The Twins edge the Indians 7–6 in ten innings at Metropolitan Stadium. The Twins trailed 5–3 in the eighth when George Mitterwald, Joe Lis and Jim Holt hit three consecutive homers off Gaylord Perry for a 6–5 lead. After Cleveland tied the score in the ninth, a sacrifice fly by Danny Thompson in the tenth brought home the winning run.

The Twins were an enigmatic team in 1973. They were 14–4 against the AL champ Oakland Athletics, 12–27 in one-run games, 37–44 at home, and 44–37 on the road.

JULY 26   A two-run, walk-off homer by George Mitterwald in the tenth inning beats the Athletics 7–5 in the second game of a double-header at Metropolitan Stadium. The Twins also won the opener 5–1.

JULY 27   George Mitterwald hits a three-run homer to spark a seven-run first inning and an 8–2 triumph over the Athletics at Metropolitan Stadium.

AUGUST 3   The Twins sell Ken Sanders to the Indians.

AUGUST 14   The Twins wallop the Tigers 12–1 at Metropolitan Stadium.

AUGUST 15   The Twins sell Jim Kaat to the White Sox.

At 34, Kaat was 11–12 with a 4.41 ERA in 1973 before being sold to the Sox. In Chicago, Kaat was reunited with pitching coach Johnny Sain, who held that role for the Twins in 1965 and 1966, two seasons in which Kaat had a combined record of 43–24. Taking Sain's suggestion, Kaat shortened his delivery and was 21–13 in 1974 and 20–14 in 1975. He remained in the majors until 1983.

AUGUST 17   The Twins score nine runs in the second inning and trounce the Indians 14–2 in Cleveland. Tony Oliva hit a grand slam off Dick Bosman, and Phil Roof added a three-run homer. The Twins collected ten hits in the inning, including two each by Steve Brye and Jerry Terrell.

On the same day, the Twins signed Rich Reese as a free agent following his release by the Tigers.

SEPTEMBER 3   Trailing 5–4, the Twins explode for seven runs in the ninth inning and beat the Royals 11–5 in Kansas City. Larry Hisle collected five hits, including a double, in five at-bats.

SEPTEMBER 14	Bert Blyleven strikes out 12 batters during a 6–0 win over the White Sox in Chicago.
SEPTEMBER 26	Bert Blyleven earns his 20th win of the season with a 4–1 decision over the Athletics in Oakland.
SEPTEMBER 27	During an 11-inning 5–4 Angels victory in Anaheim, Nolan Ryan strikes out 16 Twins to break the single-season strikeout record. He entered the contest with 367 strikeouts in 1973, 15 shy of the record of 382 set by Sandy Koufax with the Dodgers in 1965. Ryan had 15 strikeouts through the first eight innings to tie the mark. The 15th strikeout victim was Steve Brye, and on the pitch Ryan tore a muscle in his leg. Receiving treatment on the leg between innings by the Angels training and medical staff, Ryan failed to record a strikeout in the ninth or the tenth before fanning Rich Reese with two out in the 11th to surpass Koufax.

Rod Carew won the batting title with a .350 average in 1973, well ahead of second-place finisher Reggie Smith of the Red Sox, who batted .306. Carew also led the AL in hits (203) and triples (11) in addition to scoring 98 runs and swiping 41 bases.

OCTOBER 24	The Twins trade Ken Gill to the Royals for Tom Burgmeier.

The Twins pulled off a steal of a deal as Gill never played in a major league game while Burgmeier gave Minnesota four solid seasons out of the bullpen.

DECEMBER 6	The Twins trade George Mitterwald to the Cubs for Randy Hundley.

With the exception of 1971, when he was sidelined with injuries, Hundley had been the Cubs starting catcher since 1966. With the Twins, he played in only 32 games and batted .193. Mitterwald had been a solid if unexceptional catcher for the Twins and provided similar production for the Cubs.

1974

Season in a Sentence

After finishing with a .500 record in both 1972 and 1973, the Twins end up two games above .500 in 1974, but fans are unimpressed and the club winds up last in the AL in attendance.

Finish • Won • Lost • Pct • GB

Third   82   80   .506   8.0

Manager

Frank Quilici

Stats

Stats	Twins	AL	Rank
Batting Avg:	.272	.258	1
On-Base Pct:	.333	.323	2
Slugging Pct:	.378	.371	2
Home Runs:	111		7
Stolen Bases:	74		9
ERA:	3.64	3.62	6
Errors:	151		9
Runs Scored:	673		5
Runs Allowed:	669		8

Starting Line-up

Glenn Borgmann, c
Craig Kusick, 1b
Rod Carew, 2b
Eric Soderholm, 3b
Danny Thompson, ss
Larry Hisle, lf-cf
Steve Brye, cf
Bobby Darwin, rf
Tony Oliva, dh
Steve Braun, lf
Harmon Killebrew, dh-1b
Jerry Terrell, ss-3b-2b

Pitchers

Bert Blyleven, sp
Joe Decker, sp
Dave Goltz, sp
Vic Albury, sp-rp
Ray Corbin, sp-rp
Bill Campbell, rp
Tom Burgmeier, rp
Bill Hands, rp
Bill Butler, rp-sp

Attendance

662,401 (12th in AL)

Club Leaders

Batting Avg:	Rod Carew	.364
On-Base Pct:	Rod Carew	.433
Slugging Pct:	Larry Hisle	.465
Home Runs:	Bobby Darwin	25
RBI:	Bobby Darwin	94
Runs:	Rod Carew	86
Stolen Bases:	Rod Carew	38
Wins:	Bert Blyleven	17
Strikeouts:	Bert Blyleven	249
ERA:	Bert Blyleven	2.62
Saves:	Bill Campbell	19

APRIL 5 Three months after the Vikings lose the Super Bowl 24–7 to the Miami Dolphins, and two months after the kidnapping of Patty Hearst, the Twins defeat the Royals 6–4 in 11 innings on Opening Day in Kansas City. The 11th-inning runs were driven in by Rod Carew on a single and Larry Hisle with a sacrifice fly to deep center field that scored Sergio Ferrer from second base. Carew and Randy Hundley each collected three hits. The game was Hundley's first with the Twins. Bert Blyleven (nine innings) and Bill Campbell (two innings) were the Minnesota pitchers.

Sergio Ferrer's dash from second base on a sacrifice fly came in his first major league game. He was the Twins lead-off hitter and starting shortstop, and earlier in the contest hit a triple. Ferrer is one of the most obscure players ever to appear in a Twins Opening Day line-up. Over four big league seasons, two of which were spent in Minnesota, he appeared in only 125 games and had just 178 at-bats.

APRIL 6 In the second game of the season, the Royals clobber the Twins 23–6 in Kansas City. Bill Hands was the starting pitcher and allowed seven runs in the first inning. The Twins narrowed the gap to 10–6 in the fifth inning before the Royals scored 13 unanswered runs.

1970s

The Twins placed numbers on the fronts of their jerseys for the first time in 1974.

APRIL 9	In the first game after surrendering 23 runs, the Twins hold the White Sox to a single tally and win 3–1 before 10,409 at Metropolitan Stadium. Larry Hisle hit a home run.

The Twins drew 662,401 fans in 1974 to finish last in the American League in attendance.

APRIL 14	Bobby Darwin hits a grand slam in the seventh inning of an 8–0 triumph over the Royals at Metropolitan Stadium.
APRIL 20	Bert Blyleven strikes out 13 batters but the Twins lose 1–0 to the Rangers in Arlington. The lone run scored on a walk-off single by Jim Fregosi with two out in the ninth inning.
APRIL 23	Steve Braun's home run off Lerrin LaGrow leading off the tenth inning accounts for the lone run of a 1–0 win over the Tigers in Detroit. Dick Woodson (eight innings) and Bill Campbell (two innings) combined on the shutout.
MAY 4	The Twins rout the Tigers 10–0 at Metropolitan Stadium. Bert Blyleven pitched the shutout.

On the same day, the Twins sent Dick Woodson to the Yankees for Mike Pazik and cash.

MAY 18	The Twins score in seven of eight turns at bat and beat the Angels 10–4 at Metropolitan Stadium.
MAY 26	In the seventh inning of a 6–1 win over the Rangers, Bobby Darwin becomes only the second player to reach the upper deck of the left field stands at Metropolitan Stadium. Harmon Killebrew was the first. Darwin's long drive was estimated at 515 feet and was struck off Ferguson Jenkins.
MAY 29	A balk by Diego Segui in the 13th inning scores Rod Carew from third base with the winning run in a 5–4 decision over the Red Sox in Boston.
JUNE 5	In the first round of the amateur draft, the Twins choose shortstop Ted Shipley from Vanderbilt University.

Shipley peaked at Class AA. While the Twins wasted their first round pick, the second was a gem with the selection of Butch Wynegar. The rest of the picks fared little better than Shipley. The only other future major leaguers drafted and signed by the Twins in 1974 were Bud Bulling (14th round) and Jerry Garvin (first round of the secondary draft in January).

JUNE 7	The Twins play at Shea Stadium in New York for the first time and defeat the Yankees 3–2.

The Yankees played all of their home games at Shea in 1974 and 1975 while Yankee Stadium was being remodeled.

June 14	The Twins score seven runs in the third inning and down the Indians 8–2 in Cleveland. Eric Soderholm hit a grand slam off Ken Sanders.
June 17	Bobby Grich hits a home run off Vic Albury in the sixth inning to lift the Orioles to a 1–0 win over the Twins in Baltimore.
June 18	Bobby Grich hits three consecutive homers and drives in six runs to power the Orioles past the Twins 10–1 in Baltimore.

> *The Twins hit the low point of the season on June 23 with a record of 26–39. The club was 56–41 the rest of the way.*

June 28	Tony Oliva collects four hits, including two home runs, in four at-bats to lead the Twins past the White Sox 10–3 in Chicago.
July 4	The Twins score three runs in the ninth inning and Bert Blyleven pitches a one-hitter to defeat the Rangers 3–1 at Metropolitan Stadium. Blyleven allowed a home run to Toby Harrah in the third inning and headed into the bottom of the ninth trailing 1–0. Jim Holt tied the contest 1–1 with a sacrifice fly. Larry Hisle followed with a two-out, two-run, walk-off homer.

> *Hisle batted .286 with 19 home runs in 1974.*

July 13	Rod Carew's infield single in the 11th inning drives in the winning run of a 2–1 win over the Indians at Metropolitan Stadium.
July 14	Steve Braun hits a home run in the tenth inning to defeat the Indians 6–5 at Metropolitan Stadium. It was the second game in a row won on a walk-off hit in extra innings.
July 15	The Twins win with a walk-off hit for the third game in succession, this time in the ninth inning to down the Brewers 4–3 at Metropolitan Stadium. The winning tally scored on a double by Glenn Borgmann and a single from Steve Brye.
July 17	Bobby Darwin contributes two homers, a triple and a single in four at-bats to a 10–5 victory over the Brewers at Metropolitan Stadium.
July 21	The Twins score seven runs in the fourth inning and defeat the Tigers 10–7 in Detroit.
July 28	The Twins hit four home runs, but lose 12–9 to the Angels in the second game of a double-header in Anaheim. Bobby Darwin clouted two homers facing Frank Tanana and drove in six runs. The other two Minnesota home runs came from a pair of future Hall of Famers in a pinch-hit role off another Cooperstown inductee. Harmon Killebrew batted for Tony Oliva in the eighth and homered off Nolan Ryan, who was making a rare relief appearance. Hitting for Jerry Terrell, Carew homered against Ryan in the ninth. Ryan never pitched in relief again before his career ended 19 years later in 1993. The Twins won the opener 5–3.

> *Carew hit only three home runs in 1974 but led the AL in batting with a .364 average. He won the batting race by 48 points, easily outdistancing*

the .316 average compiled by Jorge Orta of the White Sox. It was Carew's fourth career batting title and third in a row. He also led the league in on-base percentage (.433) and hits (218).

AUGUST 8   On the day that Richard Nixon announces his resignation as President, effective the following day, the Twins outlast the Royals 3–2 in 14 innings in Kansas City. Harmon Killebrew tied the score 2–2 with a pinch-hit double with two out in the ninth inning. Tony Oliva drove in the winning run with a sacrifice fly. Bill Campbell was the winning pitcher with seven innings of relief.

The game was halted at the end of the first inning when Nixon's speech announcing his resignation was shown on the video board on the Royals Stadium scoreboard. Play resumed when the speech was concluded.

AUGUST 11   On Harmon Killebrew Day at Metropolitan Stadium, Killebrew drives in two runs to help the Twins to a 5–4 win over the Orioles before 27,363 at Metropolitan Stadium. It was the second-largest crowd at the ballpark in 1974. Among those at the Met were Minnesota Governor Wendell Anderson, Senators Hubert Humprhrey and Walter Mondale, and the mayors of Minneapolis, St. Paul and Bloomington.

AUGUST 14   The Twins edge the Indians 1–0 in Cleveland. Glenn Borgmann drove in the winning run with a sacrifice fly in the seventh inning. Joe Decker (eight innings) and Bill Campbell (one inning) combined on the shutout.

Campbell emerged as a relief standout in 1974 with an 8–7 record, 19 saves, and a 2.66 ERA in 63 games and 120 innings. He didn't pitch professionally until he was 22 after serving 12 months in Vietnam in both jungle combat zones and at a firebase north of Da Nang.

AUGUST 19   The Twins trade Jim Holt to the Athletics for Pat Bourque.

AUGUST 24   Larry Hisle hits a grand slam off Wayne Garland in the second inning of a 9–5 triumph over the Orioles in Baltimore.

AUGUST 30   Bert Blyleven strikes out 14 batters and beats the Red Sox 3–2 at Metropolitan Stadium. Rod Carew drove in the winning run in the ninth inning with a walk-off sacrifice fly.

SEPTEMBER 1   After falling behind 5–0, the Twins score a run in the fifth inning, another in the sixth, three in the seventh, and four in the ninth to defeat the Red Sox 9–6 at Metropolitan Stadium. The Twins were down 6–2 in the seventh when a run scored on a wild pitch and Steve Braun followed with a two-run double. In the ninth, Bobby Darwin tied the score 6–6 with an RBI-single. Pat Bourque won the game with a three-run, walk-off homer. Bourque entered the game as a pinch-hitter in the seventh. The homer was the only one he hit as a member of the Twins and was the last of the 12 he collected during his four-year major league career.

SEPTEMBER 8   On the day that President Gerald Ford pardons Richard Nixon for any crimes he may have committed, Phil Roof hits a grand slam off Steve Mingori in the sixth inning of an 8–4 win over the Royals in Kansas City.

September 9 — The Twins sell Bill Hands to the Rangers.

September 10 — The Twins take a thrilling 8–7 decision from the White Sox in 15 innings at Metropolitan Stadium after trailing three times in extra innings. Chicago scored three runs in the top of the ninth on a home run by Brian Downing to knot the contest at 4–4. The Sox scored in the top of the 11th, 13th and 14th innings, but each time the Twins rallied to tie. Craig Kusick homered in the 11th. Glenn Borgmann singled in a run in the 13th. With two out and no one on base in the 14th, Eric Soderholm singled and crossed the plate on a pinch-hit double by Tony Oliva. In the 15th, Rod Carew walked, stole second, and scored on a single by Larry Hisle.

September 11 — The Twins win in extra innings for the second game in a row when Harmon Killebrew hits a two-run, walk-off homer in the tenth to defeat the Athletics 5–3 at Metropolitan Stadium.

September 13 — The Twins emerge with a victory in extra innings for the third time in a span of four games against three different teams when Rod Carew hits a walk-off homer in the tenth to down the Royals 2–1 at Metropolitan Stadium.

September 21 — Bert Blyleven strikes out 12 batters to beat the Angels 8–1 at Metropolitan Stadium.

September 25 — Bert Blyleven pitches the Twins to a 1–0 victory over the Athletics in Oakland. Steve Brye drove in the winning run with a double in the fourth inning.

Blyleven was 17–17 with a 2.66 ERA and 249 strikeouts in 281 innings in 1974.

September 28 — Nolan Ryan pitches a no-hitter to beat the Twins 4–0 in Anaheim. Ryan walked eight, seven of them in the first five innings, and struck out 15. Eric Soderholm made the last out with a strikeout.

October 1 — Dave Goltz pitches a two-hitter to beat the Rangers 6–0 at Metropolitan Stadium. The only Texas hits were a single by Toby Harrah in the first inning and a triple from Pete Mackanin with two out in the ninth. Both played shortstop, with Mackanin replacing Harrah in the second. Goltz retired 21 batters in a row from the first through the eighth.

A native of Pelican Rapids, Minnesota, Goltz was drafted by the Twins in 1967. His ascent to the majors was delayed by a stint in Vietnam in 1968 and 1969. He played for the Twins from 1972 through 1979 before moving to the Dodgers as a free agent. He won 14 or more games for the club for five straight seasons beginning in 1975. Goltz's best season was 1977 when he was 20–11.
A notoriously slow starter, he had a lifetime record of 4–16 in April, but was 21–7 in May.

October 23 — The Twins trade Pat Bourque to the Athletics for Dan Ford and Dennis Myers.

The Twins pulled off an excellent deal, as Bourque never played in another big league game while Ford was a starting outfielder in Minnesota for four seasons.

1975

Season in a Sentence
After a losing season, Calvin Griffith fires Frank Quilici as manager and brings in Gene Mauch.

Finish • Won • Lost • Pct • GB
Fourth   76   83   .478   20.5

Manager
Frank Quilici

Stats   Twins • AL • Rank
Batting Avg:	.271	.258	2
On-Base Pct:	.339	.328	2
Slugging Pct:	.386	.379	6
Home Runs:	121		8
Stolen Bases:	81		9
ERA:	4.05	3.78	10
Errors:	170		8
Runs Scored:	724		3
Runs Allowed:	736		10

Starting Line-up
Glenn Borgmann, c
Johnny Briggs, 1b-lf
Rod Carew, 2b
Eric Soderholm, 3b
Danny Thompson, ss
Steve Braun, lf
Dan Ford, cf
Lyman Bostock, rf-cf
Tony Oliva, dh
Jerry Terrell, ss-2b
Larry Hisle, lf-cf
Steve Brye, rf

Pitchers
Bert Blyleven, sp
Jim Hughes, sp
Dave Goltz, sp
Ray Corbin, sp-rp
Tom Burgmeier, rp
Bill Campbell, rp
Vic Albury, rp-sp
Bill Butler, rp

Attendance
737,156 (12th in AL)

Club Leaders
Batting Avg:	Rod Carew	.359
On-Base Pct:	Rod Carew	.421
Slugging Pct:	Rod Carew	.497
Home Runs:	Dan Ford	15
RBI:	Rod Carew	80
Runs:	Rod Carew	89
Stolen Bases:	Rod Carew	35
Wins:	Jim Hughes	16
Strikeouts:	Bert Blyleven	233
ERA:	Bert Blyleven	3.00
Saves:	Tom Burgmeier	11

JANUARY 16   Four days after the Vikings lose 16–6 to the Pittsburgh Steelers in the Super Bowl, the Twins release Harmon Killebrew.

The two players on the Twins roster with the highest salaries in 1974 were Harmon Killebrew and Tony Oliva. Because of injuries and advanced age, both were designated hitters, and it was too expensive to keep them. Calvin Griffith offered Killebrew a contract for 1975 at a much-reduced figure, but he declined and asked for his release. Killebrew was the last player remaining from the original Twins team in 1961. He signed with the Royals and batted .222 with 13 homers in 121 games. The 1975 season was Killebrew's last in the majors.

APRIL 8   The Twins open the season with an 11–4 win over the Rangers in Arlington. The Twins scored three runs in the first inning and three more in the second off Ferguson Jenkins. Tony Oliva and Larry Hisle each walloped three-run homers. Danny Thompson had three hits and Lyman Bostock scored three runs in his major league debut. Bert Blyleven (6 2/3 innings) and Bill Campbell (2 1/3 innings) were the Minnesota pitchers.

About four hours before the start of the game, a helicopter used to dry the Arlington Stadium playing field crashed. The helicopter was whirling a few feet above the field when it suddenly dipped and hit the grass behind third base.

The pilot wasn't injured, but the accident left a gash in the field, which was repaired before the first pitch. A tractor was used to haul the helicopter off the field.

APRIL 15 — The Twins lose the home opener 7–3 to the Angels before 11,909 at Metropolitan Stadium. The temperature was 48 degrees.

The Twins drew 737,156 fans in 1975 to finish last in the AL in attendance for the second year in a row. The club's lease at Metropolitan Stadium expired at the end of the season, and Calvin Griffith signed only a one-year renewal, prompting rumors that the Twins might move out of Minnesota to Toronto, Seattle or New Orleans.

APRIL 20 — Bert Blyleven strikes out 12 batters in eight innings, but the Twins lose 4–1 to the Athletics in the first game of a double-header in Oakland. The A's also won the second tilt 5–1.

After winning 16 games in 1974, Joe Decker was on the disabled list with a virus from April 18 through June 6, and when he returned he couldn't find the plate. In 26 1/3 innings, he had an ERA of 8.54 and walked 36 batters while striking out only eight. From 1975 through the end of his career in 1977, Decker had a record of 3–11 with an earned run average of 5.80 and 101 walks in 111 2/3 innings.

MAY 3 — The Twins rout the Royals 14–5 at Metropolitan Stadium.

Calvin Griffith brought in the fences from 346 feet to 330 feet in left field and from 425 feet to 410 in center. Dwindling attendance figures were a motivation. "The fans liked us when we were the power club of the American League," said Griffith, "and we want them to like us again."

MAY 4 — The Twins retire Harmon Killebrew's number 3 in ceremonies prior to a 6–3 win over the Royals at Metropolitan Stadium. Playing designated hitter for Kansas City, Killebrew homered on the first pitch off Vic Albury in the first inning.

MAY 21 — After the Tigers score in the top of the 11th, Larry Hisle hits a two-run, walk-off homer in the bottom half for a 6–5 victory at Metropolitan Stadium.

MAY 23 — Trailing 1–0 with one out in the ninth inning, Tony Oliva, Larry Hisle, Eric Soderholm and Tom Kelly hit four consecutive singles to produce two runs and a 2–1 win over the Brewers in Milwaukee.

JUNE 5 — In the first round of the amateur draft, the Twins select shortstop Rick Sofield from Morristown High School in Morristown, New Jersey.

After being converted into an outfielder, Sofield played for the Twins from 1979 through 1981, and hit .243 with nine homers in 207 games. The only other future major leaguers drafted and signed by the Twins in 1975 were Dan Graham (fifth round) and Hosken Powell (first round of the secondary phase).

1970s

June 8 — The Twins beat the Red Sox 7–5 at Fenway Park in a contest in which ten runs cross the plate in the ninth inning. After eight innings, the score was 1–1. Minnesota plated six runs in the top of the ninth and Boston responded with four in their half.

June 9 — The Twins score four runs in the ninth inning and one in the 11th to defeat the Indians 11–10 in Cleveland. Danny Walton tied the score 10–10 with a two-out, pinch-hit homer in the ninth. Walton batted for catcher Phil Roof, who came into the contest after starting catcher Glenn Borgmann was lifted for another pinch-hitter in the eighth. Normally an outfielder, Walton became the third Minnesota catcher of the evening. Danny Thompson drove in the winning run with a single. Vic Albury pitched five hitless innings of relief.

The game was the second of only two in which Walton played as a catcher in 297 career games over nine seasons. The homer was his first since June 8, 1973. Walton never hit another big league home run.

June 10 — The Twins win in extra innings for the second night in a row, downing the Indians 5–3 in 12 innings in Cleveland. The 12th-inning runs scored on four walks and a single by Steve Brye.

June 14 — The Twins trade Bobby Darwin to the Brewers for Johnny Briggs.

June 16 — The Twins score three runs in the ninth inning to stun the Athletics 7–6 at Metropolitan Stadium. Steve Braun's led off the ninth with a homer. The other two tallies were produced with singles from Tom Kelly, Danny Walton, Dan Ford, an intentional walk to Rod Carew, and another single by Larry Hisle.

June 29 — The Twins lose an odd 9–7 decision to the Rangers in Arlington. Texas scored eight runs in the fourth inning and the Twins plated seven tallies in the sixth. Tony Oliva hit a pinch-hit grand slam off Jim Umbarger.

July 4 — Dan Ford hits two homers and a double and drives in five runs during an 8–0 triumph over the Rangers in the first game of a double-header at Metropolitan Stadium. Texas won the second tilt 4–2.

July 9 — The Twins score seven runs in the third inning to take a 7–1 lead, but wind up losing 9–8 to the Red Sox at Fenway Park. The Twins still had an 8–4 advantage before Boston scored three runs in the eighth and two in the ninth.

July 11 — The Twins thrash the Yankees 11–1 in the first game of a double-header in New York. The Yanks won the second contest 4–3.

July 12 — The Twins and Yankees play 14 innings to a 6–6 tie in New York before the contest is suspended because of the American League's curfew rule that stipulated no inning could start after 1:00 a.m. The Twins scored four runs in the top of the ninth to take a 6–3 lead. There were five straight singles during the rally from Dan Ford, Rod Carew, Johnny Briggs, Tony Oliva and Larry Hisle. Eric Soderholm pinch-ran for Oliva, who was playing DH. Soderholm moved to third base in the bottom of the ninth, which meant that the Twins lost the use of the designated hitter for the remainder of the contest. With a three-run lead in the ninth, it didn't appear that it would matter, but the Yanks scored three times to tie the contest. Relief pitchers

Vic Albury and Bill Campbell both batted in extra innings and struck out. It was the first time that a Minnesota pitcher batted in a game since 1972. The game was scheduled to be completed before the July 13 contest, but was rained out. It was completed later at Metropolitan Stadium on July 19.

JULY 15 At the All-Star Game at County Stadium in Milwaukee, Rod Carew catches the ceremonial first pitch from Secretary of State Henry Kissinger. Carew was selected for the honor because both he and Kissinger attended George Washington High School in New York City.

JULY 19 At Metropolitan Stadium, the Twins and Yankees complete their suspended game of July 12, and the Twins lose 8–7 in 16 innings. Although the game was in Minnesota, the Twins batted first because the contest started in New York. The Twins scored in the top of the 16th on an RBI-single by Tom Lundstedt, who was batting for Bill Campbell, but the Yankees rallied to score two in their half to win 8–7 with both runs coming after two were out. The Twins won the regularly scheduled contest 2–1.

When the game began on July 12, Lundstedt was in the minor leagues. He was eligible to play during the completion of the contest on July 19 because he was called up from Class AAA Charlotte in the interim. Lundstedt's 16th-inning RBI was the only one of his career, which spanned three seasons, 44 games, and 65 at-bats. His career batting average was .092.

JULY 25 The Twins score seven runs in the second inning to take a 10–0 lead and crush the Angels 12–1 in Anaheim.

AUGUST 3 The Twins sweep the White Sox 7–4 and 12–9 in a double-header at Metropolitan Stadium. The Twins scored eight runs in the third inning of the second tilt to take a 10–1 lead.

AUGUST 9 Dave Goltz outduels Mickey Lolich to beat the Tigers 1–0 in Detroit. Glenn Borgmann drove in the lone run with a single.

AUGUST 16 The Twins collect 20 hits and beat the Indians 9–1 at Metropolitan Stadium. Each of the nine starters garnered at least two hits. The nine were Lyman Bostock, Dan Ford, Rod Carew, Johnny Briggs, Tony Oliva, Eric Soderholm, Steve Braun, Jerry Terrell and Phil Roof.

A native of Waseca, Minnesota, Terrell played for the Twins from 1973 through 1977. While with the club, he played seven different defensive positions, plus designated hitter, appearing in 179 games at shortstop, 148 at third base, 124 at second, 36 as a DH, 18 at first, ten in right field, six in left and one in center. In 1979, he pitched in two games for the Royals, giving him appearances at every position but catcher during his eight-year big league career.

AUGUST 22 Third baseman Dave McKay hits a home run in his first major league plate appearance. It was struck off Vern Ruhle in the third inning of an 8–4 win over the Tigers at Metropolitan Stadium.

A native of Vancouver, British Columbia, McKay hit another homer three days later in career plate appearance number 14, but he didn't connect for his third home run until 1977 when he was playing for the Blue Jays. McKay finished his career with 21 home runs in 1,928 at-bats. Since 1986, McKay has been a coach with Tony LaRussa-managed clubs in both Oakland and St. Louis.

AUGUST 27   Bert Blyleven pitches an 11-inning shutout and strikes out 13 batters to defeat the Brewers 1–0 in Milwaukee. The lone run scored on a pinch-hit single by Tony Oliva. Craig Kusick tied a major league record when he was hit by a pitch three times in the game, each of them by Bill Travers.

SEPTEMBER 7   Steve Brye homers twice in two plate appearances during a 9–1 win over the White Sox in Chicago. Brye entered the fray as a pinch-hitter in the seventh and homered. He remained in the line-up as a left fielder, and homered again in the eighth.

SEPTEMBER 12   Rod Carew starts both ends of a double-header against the Athletics in Oakland as a first baseman. The Twins lost 11–4 and won 7–6.

Prior to September 12, 1975, Carew's only previous game as a first baseman was in 1970. After that day he played almost exclusively at first over the remainder of his career, which ended in 1985. Altogether, he played 1,184 games at first and 1,130 at second. During the 1975 season, he won his fourth consecutive batting title with an average of .359. He also led the AL in one-base percentage (.421) and collected 192 hits.

SEPTEMBER 15   The Twins outlast the Angels 7–6 in 12 innings at Metropolitan Stadium. California scored in the top of the tenth, but the Twins tied the contest in the bottom half on a two-out single from Johnny Briggs. Glenn Borgmann drove in the winning run with a walk-off double. Bert Blyleven struck out 12 batters in ten innings, but gave up six runs.

Blyleven was 15–10 with a 3.00 ERA and 233 strikeouts in $275^{2/3}$ innings in 1975.

SEPTEMBER 16   Craig Kusick hits a three-run, pinch-hit, walk-off homer with one out in the ninth inning to defeat the Angels 4–3 at Metropolitan Stadium.

SEPTEMBER 19   The Twins outhit the Angels 12–3 but lose 1–0 in Anaheim.

SEPTEMBER 28   The Twins dismiss Frank Quilici as manager. He was only 36 when fired and had been on the job since July 1972, guiding the club to a record of 280–287. Quilici remained with the club, teaming with Herb Carneal in the radio booth in 1976 and 1977. Quilici never managed another team.

NOVEMBER 24   The Twins name 50-year-old Gene Mauch as manager.

Mauch was an infielder in the majors for six clubs over parts of ten seasons from 1944 through 1957. He had previously managed in the Twin Cities with the minor league Minneapolis Millers in the American Association in 1958 and 1959. Mauch began his managerial career at the big league level with the Phillies in 1960. His 1961 club was 47–107 and suffered through a 21-game losing streak, but by 1964 Philadelphia was on the brink of an NL pennant with a $6^{1/2}$-game lead with only two weeks remaining. The Phils blew the opportunity, *however, and finished second to the Cardinals. The Phils fired Mauch in 1968. He then became the first manager of the expansion Montreal Expos in 1969 and held the job until the end of the 1975 season. None of his seven teams in Montreal had a winning record. Mauch had winning records with the Twins in his first two seasons and three of the first four before being fired in August 1980.*

DECEMBER 22 — The Twins trade Danny Walton to the Dodgers for Bob Randall.

DECEMBER 23 — A ruling by arbitrator Pete Seitz strikes down the reserve clause, which binds a player to one club in perpetuity.

The ruling brought about free agency in baseball. In an agreement completed between the players and owners in 1976, a player had the right to declare himself a free agent after six seasons in the majors. This would have a major impact on the Twins and many other smaller market clubs. In Minnesota, Calvin Griffith was unable, or unwilling, to pay high salaries to star players, and one after another left the Twins or was traded.

1976

Season in a Sentence
The Twins finish only five games out of first, but are never in serious contention for the pennant and wind up last in the league in attendance for the third year in a row.

Finish • Won • Lost • Pct • GB
Third   85   77   .525   5.0

Manager
Gene Mauch

Stats   Twins • AL • Rank
Batting Avg: .274   .256   1
On-Base Pct: .339   .320   1
Slugging Pct: .375   .361   3
Home Runs: 81   8
Stolen Bases: 146   5
ERA: 3.69   3.52   10
Errors: 172   12
Runs Scored: 743   1
Runs Allowed: 704   10

Starting Line-up
Butch Wynegar, c
Rod Carew, 1b
Bob Randall, 2b
Mike Cubbage, 3b
Roy Smalley, ss
Larry Hisle, lf
Lyman Bostock, cf
Dan Ford, rf
Steve Braun, dh
Craig Kusick, dh
Steve Brye, cf

Pitchers
Dave Goltz, sp
Jim Hughes, sp
Bill Singer, sp
Pete Redfern, sp
Bert Blyleven, sp
Bill Campbell, rp
Tom Burgmeier, rp
Steve Luebber, rp

Attendance
715,394 (12th in AL)

Club Leaders
Batting Avg: Rod Carew   .331
On-Base Pct: Rod Carew   .395
Slugging Pct: Rod Carew   .463
Home Runs: Dan Ford   20
RBI: Larry Hisle   96
Runs: Rod Carew   97
Stolen Bases: Rod Carew   49
Wins: Bill Campbell 17
Strikeouts: Dave Goltz   133
ERA: Bill Campbell 3.01
Saves: Bill Campbell 20

1970s

January 7 — With the first overall pick in the secondary phase of the amateur draft, the Twins select pitcher Pete Redfern from the University of Southern California.

After just four games in the minors, Redfern made his major league debut on May 15, 1976. He pitched seven seasons in the majors, all with the Twins, and had a record of 42–48. Redfern's career ended in 1983 when he was paralyzed in a diving accident. Others future major leaguers drafted and signed by the Twins in the January 1976 draft were Bob Veselic (also in the first round) and Kevin Stanfield (ninth round).

March 11 — The Twins sign Tony Oliva as a player-coach.

The 1976 season was Oliva's last as a player. He was a coach with the club from 1976 through 1978 and again from 1985 through 1991.

April 9 — The Twins open the season with a 2–1 loss to the Rangers in 11 innings in Arlington. Bert Blyleven was the Minnesota starting pitcher and went nine innings. The winning run scored on a single by Toby Harrah off Bill Campbell. Gaylord Perry hurled all 11 innings for Texas.

Among those in attendance was President Gerald Ford. He was in Arlington campaigning during the Presidential Primary in Texas in a race for the nomination against Ronald Reagan. Ford is the only sitting president ever to watch the Twins play in a regular-season game since the club moved to Minnesota. While the franchise was located in Washington, visits from presidents were common, particularly on Opening Day.

April 13 — In the home opener, the Twins lose 4–1 to the White Sox before 20,732 at Metropolitan Stadium.

A year after retiring as a player, Harmon Killebrew announced Twins games on television with Joe Boyle. On the radio in 1976 were Herb Carneal and Frank Quilici. Quilici managed the Twins from 1972 through 1975 and had a chance to second-guess his successor Gene Mauch. Killebrew lasted three seasons in the broadcast booth, while Quilici remained for two.

April 15 — In the first regular season game at remodeled Yankee Stadium, the Yankees defeat the Twins 11–4.

April 18 — The Twins score three runs in the ninth inning off Catfish Hunter to defeat the Yankees 5–4 in New York. Lyman Bostock tied the score with a two-run homer. Butch Wynegar followed with another homer to break the deadlock. It was the first major league home run for both Bostock and Wynegar. The blast by Bostock came in his 387th career at-bat. At 20 years, one month and four years of age, Wynegar also became the youngest player in Twins history to hit a home run.

Wynegar made the American League All-Star team as a 20-year-old rookie catcher in 1976 to become the youngest non-pitcher ever to appear in the Midsummer Classic. He ended the season with a .260 batting average and ten home runs. Wynegar followed with another All-Star berth in 1977, but never played in the game again during his 13-year career. He played for the

Twins until 1982 when he was traded to the Yankees. Bostock had 369 at-bats as a rookie with the Twins in 1975 and failed to hit a home run. He burst into stardom in 1976 with a .323 average in 128 games.

APRIL 24 — The Twins outlast the Orioles 2–1 in 14 innings at Metropolitan Stadium. Dan Ford drove in the winning run with a sacrifice fly. Bill Campbell pitched 5 1/3 innings of scoreless relief.

Campbell was 17–5 with 20 saves in 1976 while compiling a 3.01 ERA in 78 games and 167 2/3 innings. The wins total is the second highest by a reliever in major league history, exceeded only by Roy Face, who was 18–1 for the Pirates in 1959. Campbell turned the year into a lucrative contract as a free agent at the end of the season (see November 6, 1976).

A gifted athlete, Lyman Bostock appeared to be a budding superstar until his violent death in 1978 at the age of twenty-seven.

MAY 4 — Butch Wynegar and Dan Ford hit back-to-back homers in the tenth inning for a 5–3 lead, and the Twins go on to defeat the Tigers 5–4 in Detroit.

MAY 8 — The Twins score six runs in the second inning and wallop the Brewers 13–2 in Milwaukee.

MAY 12 — Starting pitcher Joe Decker allows ten runs in one official inning during a 17–5 loss to the Royals in Kansas City. Decker surrendered seven runs in the first inning and three more in the second before retiring a batter.

MAY 15 — The Twins sweep the Angels 5–2 and 15–5 during a double-header in Anaheim. Bert Blyleven fanned 12 batters in the opener. The Twins scored seven runs in the sixth inning of the second tilt. Dan Ford collected three hits in each game and drove in six runs in the nightcap.

MAY 17 — Steve Brye delivers a walk-off single in the 11th inning to down the Athletics 5–4 at Metropolitan Stadium.

MAY 18 — Dan Ford delivers a walk-off single in the 11th inning to defeat the Athletics 4–3 at Metropolitan Stadium. It was the second night in a row in which the Twins beat Oakland in 11 innings.

1970s

MAY 24 — Athletics shortstop Bert Campaneris steals five bases during a 12–7 win over the Twins in Oakland. With Don Baylor batting in the fifth inning, Minnesota pitcher Steve Luebber threw three consecutive wild pitches.

MAY 31 — Bert Blyleven flashes an obscene gesture toward fans during a 3–2 loss to the Angels at Metropolitan Stadium.

> *"I couldn't care less about the fans," said Blyleven afterward. "Maybe I should flip them every game and that would bring in more fans to the park. Maybe that fat bastard (Calvin) Griffith would have some money to pay us." Blyleven was traded the following day.*

JUNE 1 — The Twins send Bert Blyleven and Danny Thompson to the Rangers for Bill Singer, Roy Smalley, Mike Cubbage, Jim Gideon and $250,000.

> *All things considered, it was a good trade. Neither Blyleven nor Thompson had signed contracts and were due to become free agents at the end of the 1976 season. In exchange, the Twins received three starters plus a bundle of cash. Blyleven still had more than a decade of effective pitching ahead of him. He lasted in the majors until 1992 and pitched for five clubs, including a return engagement with the Twins from 1985 through 1988. After the 1976 trade, Blyleven won 188 more big league games to bring his final total to 287. Thompson would die of leukemia on December 10, 1976, (see February 16, 1973). Singer had 20-win seasons for the Dodgers in 1969 and Angels in 1973, but by the time he arrived in Minnesota his career was about over. After a 9–9 record with the Twins over the remainder of the 1976 season, Singer went to the Blue Jays in the expansion draft. Cubbage was the Twins starting third baseman for a couple of seasons while posting batting numbers around the league average. Smalley proved to be the best player taken by the Twins in the deal. He was the club's starting shortstop until early in the 1982 season when he was traded to the Yankees. Smalley was also a nephew of Gene Mauch. Smalley's father, also named Roy, was a teammate of Mauch's with the Cubs in 1948 and 1949. At that time, Mauch met the sister of the elder Smalley and the two eventually married.*

JUNE 4 — Larry Hisle hits a two-run homer off Mike Flanagan in the tenth inning to defeat the Orioles 8–6 in Baltimore. The home run completed the cycle for Hisle. Earlier, he double in the fourth inning and tripled in the fifth against Doyle Alexander and singled in the eighth facing Flanagan.

JUNE 6 — The Twins sweep the Orioles 3–2 and 11–6 in Baltimore. Steve Brye collected four hits and scored four runs in the second game.

JUNE 7 — Butch Wynegar hits into a triple play and homers in consecutive plate appearances during a 7–2 win over the Indians in Cleveland. Wynegar hit into the triple play in the fifth and connected for the home run in the eighth.

JUNE 8 — In the first round of the amateur draft, the Twins select third baseman Jamie Allen from Davis High School in Yakima, Washington.

Allen didn't sign with the Twins and instead attended Arizona State University. He was drafted by the Mariners in the second round in 1979, but played in only 86 games in the majors. Future major leaguers drafted and signed by the Twins in 1976 were Terry Felton (second round), John Castino (third round) and Mike Funderburk (16th round).

June 26   Rod Carew hits a grand slam off Paul Mitchell in the second inning of an 11–3 triumph over the Athletics in Oakland.

The Twins played 21 games in 20 days in June, including a rough stretch of travel. After a match-up against the Tigers at the Met on Sunday, June 20, the Twins flew to Anaheim to play the Angels on Monday and Tuesday, then returned to Minnesota to face the White Sox for a three-game, two-day series on Wednesday and Thursday. The Twins returned to California for a series versus the Athletics from Friday June 25 through Sunday June 27. Then it was back to Bloomington for games against the Royals on Monday, Tuesday and Wednesday.

June 29   Dave Goltz allows only three hits in ten innings, but loses 1–0 to the Royals at Metropolitan Stadium on an unearned run. Al Fitzmorris pitched all ten innings for Kansas City and surrendered just five hits.

July 3   Steve Braun has a hand in both runs of a 2–0 win over the Angels at Metropolitan Stadium. In the third inning, Braun drove in a run with a single, moved to second on a walk, and crossed the plate on a single from Rod Carew. Bill Singer pitched the shutout.

July 4   On the day of the nation's Bicentennial, the Twins spilt a double-header with the Angels at Metropolitan Stadium with a 5–3 loss and a 9–5 win. The second game was unusual as the Angels collected five runs on only two hits. Pete Redfern retired the first 16 batters to face him and entered the seventh inning with a no-hitter in progress and a 5–0 lead. Mario Guerrero collected the first California hit leading off the seventh and Redfern retired the next two hitters. He then walked the next two hitters and was replaced by Vic Albury. Albury walked in a run and was relieved by Bill Campbell. Campbell quickly surrendered a grand slam to Ron Jackson to tie the score 5–5. In the eighth, Rod Carew hit a grand slam off Sid Monge to lift the Twins to the 9–5 victory. It was Carew's second grand slam in a span of nine days.

July 7   Butch Wynegar hits a grand slam off Bill Castro in the eighth inning of an 8–2 win over the Brewers in Milwaukee.

The Twins hit the low point of the 1976 season on July 20 with a 41–48 record. The club was 44–29 the rest of the way.

July 24   Lyman Bostock not only hits for the cycle, he contributes a walk and a sacrifice fly in a 17–2 win over the White Sox in Chicago. He walked in the first inning off Jesse Jefferson and tripled in the second against Pete Vukovich. Facing Chris Knapp, Bostock homered in the fourth, hit a sacrifice fly in the sixth, and doubled in the eighth. He completed the cycle with a single off Blue Moon Odom in the ninth.

1970s

JULY 25   The Twins outslug the White Sox 13–8 in the first game of a double-header at Comiskey Park. The victory gave the Twins 30 runs in consecutive games. Chicago led 5–0 after three innings. Rod Carew put Minnesota into the lead with a three-run triple in the sixth. The White Sox won the second contest 7–4.

> *The Twins pulled off an unusual triple play in the first inning of the opener. The Chicago runners on base were Jim Spencer at first and Jorge Orta at second. Bill Stein popped up a bunt, which was caught by catcher Glenn Borgmann, who fired the ball to shortstop Luis Gomez. Gomez stepped on second to force Orta and tagged Spencer coming into the base.*

JULY 30   Trailing the Athletics 7–1 at Metropolitan Stadium, the Twins score five runs in the fifth inning and two in the eighth to win 8–7. Butch Wynegar hit a grand slam off Dick Bosman in the fifth. In the eighth, Steve Braun singled in the tying run and Larry Hisle broke the deadlock with a sacrifice fly.

AUGUST 1   Despite making five errors, the Twins take a thrilling 8–7 decision from the Athletics in 12 innings in the first game of a double-header at Metropolitan Stadium. The A's led 4–1 before the Twins scored a run in the eighth inning and two in the ninth. Craig Kusick made the score 4–2 with a home run in the eighth. The ninth-inning tallies were created with two walks, a single from Roy Smalley and a sacrifice fly by Larry Hisle. Oakland scored in the top of the tenth but the Twins came back to tie on the bottom half with Steve Braun driving in the run on a triple. The Athletics plated two runs in the 12th, and this time, the Twins countered with three runs in their half without a batter being retired for the victory. Singles by Mike Cubbage, Steve Brye and Steve Braun produced the first run. Rod Carew doubled to tie the score. After an intentional walk to Tony Oliva to load the bases, Roy Smalley drew a walk from Stan Bahnsen to force across the winning run. The Twins completed the sweep with a 6–2 triumph in the second contest.

AUGUST 2   The Twins extend their winning streak to eight games with a 3–0 decision over the Athletics at Metropolitan Stadium.

AUGUST 7   Steve Luebber (8 2/3 innings) and Bill Campbell (one-third of an inning) combine on a two-hitter to defeat the Rangers 3–1 in Arlington. Luebber retired the first 19 batters to face him before walking ex-Twin Danny Thompson with one out in the seventh, and entered the ninth with his no-hitter intact. Luebber started the ninth by inducing Gene Clines to ground out from second baseman Bob Randall to first baseman Rod Carew and by setting down Lenny Randle on a flyball to rightfielder Dan Ford. Luebber was now one out from a no-hitter, but surrendered a single on a 3–2 pitch to Roy Howell, who advanced to second on an error by centerfielder Lyman Bostock. Mike Hargrove brought Howell across the plate with another single and Campbell relieved Luebbers.

> *In his previous start five days earlier, Luebbers pitched what would prove to his only career shutout. He played for the Twins in 1971 and 1972 and returned in 1976 after three seasons in the minors. He later pitched for the Blue Jays in 1979 and the Orioles in 1981 and finished his career with a 6–10 record and a 4.62 ERA.*

AUGUST 11	Dan Ford drives in both runs of a 2–0 win over the Orioles in Baltimore. Ford hit a sacrifice fly in the second inning and singled in a run in the fourth. Bill Singer pitched the shutout.
AUGUST 21	The Twins score four runs in the tenth inning after two are out to defeat the Tigers 7–3 in Detroit. Dan Ford broke the 3–3 tie when he was hit by a Mark Fidrych pitch with the bases loaded.
AUGUST 22	The Twins win in extra innings for the second game in a row, defeating the Tigers 6–4 in 12 innings in Detroit. The two runs in the 12th scored on back-to-back doubles by Butch Wynegar and Lyman Bostock and a single from Mike Cubbage.
AUGUST 25	The Twins lose 5–4 to the Yankees in a 19-inning marathon in New York. The Yanks scored three runs in the fifth to tie the score. Neither team dented the plate from the sixth inning through the top of the 19th. Mickey Rivers drove in the winning run with a single. Bill Campbell pitched $5^{2}/_{3}$ innings of shutout relief. Tom Burgmeier entered the contest at the start of the 12th inning and held the Yankees scoreless until the 19th. The loss was the only one of the season for Burgmeier, who had an 8–1 record in 1976. Roy Smalley had 20 fielding chances (nine putouts and 11 assists) to set an American League record for shortstops.

> *In the 15th inning, Gene Mauch employed a five-man infield with no one out and runners on first and third. The ploy worked, as Carlos May grounded to second baseman Jerry Terrell, who threw out Thurman Munson trying to score from third.*

AUGUST 28	Three days and two games after losing in 19 innings, the Twins drop a 4–3 decision in 17 innings against the Indians at Municipal Stadium. Cleveland scored two runs in the ninth off Bill Singer to tie the score 3–3. The winning run crossed the plate in the 17th on a wild pitch by Jim Hughes. Bill Campbell pitched six innings of shutout relief from the ninth inning through the 14th.
AUGUST 30	After relieving Pete Redfern with one out in the first inning, Tom Burgmeier pitches $8^{2}/_{3}$ innings of relief and is the winning pitcher in a 10–3 decision over the Brewers at Metropolitan Stadium. Burgmeier allowed one run and three hits.

> *Paced by Bill Campbell (17–5) and Burgmeier (8–1), Twins relievers had a record of 33–9 and a 2.80 ERA in 1976. The starters were 52–68 with an earned run average of 4.16.*

AUGUST 31	Dave Goltz pitches a two-hitter to defeat the Brewers 4–0 in the first game of a double-header at Metropolitan Stadium. Goltz held Milwaukee hitless until Bill Sharp singled with one out in the seventh inning. Tim Johnson added another single in the eighth. The Brewers won the second tilt 6–3.
SEPTEMBER 1	The Twins score two runs in the ninth inning and one in the 12th to down the Brewers 3–2 at Metropolitan Stadium. Dan Ford drove in the first run in the ninth and crossed the plate on a two-out single from Roy Smalley. Rod Carew started the 12th inning rally with a single. He scored on a bunt from Lyman Bostock and a throwing error by Milwaukee catcher Darrell Porter.

1970s

SEPTEMBER 3	The Twins rout the White Sox 11–1 at Metropolitan Stadium.
SEPTEMBER 5	The Twins score ten runs in the fifth inning and wallop the White Sox 18–1 at Metropolitan Stadium. There were 22 Minnesota hits during the contest, nine of them in the fifth. Rod Carew singled twice during the ten-run rally, and Mike Cubbage contributed a triple and a single and drove in three runs. With one out, eight straight batters reached base on four singles, two doubles and two walks.

On September 4, in between the 11-run and 18-run outbursts, the Twins were shutout in a 4–0 defeat at the hands of the White Sox at Metropolitan Stadium.

SEPTEMBER 6	Craig Kusick delivers a walk-off home run with two out in the ninth inning to defeat the White Sox 3–2 at Metropolitan Stadium.
SEPTEMBER 7	The Twins edge the Rangers 1–0 in Arlington. The lone run scored in the third inning when Steve Brye doubled off Gaylord Perry and advanced on a bunt and a ground out. Pete Redfern (six innings) and Bill Campbell (three innings) combined on the shutout.
SEPTEMBER 9	Pinch-hitting for Bob Randall in the seventh inning, Rod Carew hits a grand slam off Steve Hargan to spark a 6–0 win over the Rangers in Arlington. It was Carew's third grand slam of the season.

Carew entered the 1976 season without a grand slam. He hit his first one on June 26 in his 1,239th career game. Carew finished his 19-year sojourn in the majors with five bases-loaded homers.

SEPTEMBER 10	The Twins crush the Royals 18–3 at Metropolitan Stadium. It was the second time in eight days that the Twins scored exactly 18 runs in a game. The club scored in each of the first seven innings with one in the first, one in the second, two in the third, six in the fourth, five in the fifth, two in the sixth and one in the seventh for an 18–0 lead. The three Kansas City runs crossed the plate in the eighth.

Combined with a rain-shortened seven inning, 3–1 win over the Rangers in Arlington on September 8 and the 6–0 triumph on September 9, the Twins scored 27 unanswered runs over three games.

SEPTEMBER 16	Dan Ford hits a pair of two-run homers in the fourth and sixth innings off Stan Bahnsen to account for all four runs of a 4–0 win over the Athletics in Oakland. Bill Singer pitched the shutout.
SEPTEMBER 21	The Twins score seven runs in the third inning and defeat the White Sox 13–6 in Chicago. Bob Randall delivered the key hit of the rally with a two-out, three-run double.
SEPTEMBER 23	Pete Redfern pitches a three-hitter to defeat the White Sox 3–0 in Chicago.
SEPTEMBER 25	Dave Goltz makes it two complete game shutouts in a row for Minnesota pitchers by hurling a two-hitter to defeat the Angels 6–0 at Metropolitan Stadium. The only California hits were singles by Dave Collins leading off the first inning and Mario Guerrero with two out in the ninth. Goltz walked four in between the two widely spaced hits.

The Twins led the league in runs scored in 1976, as the club had previously done in 1963, 1964, 1965 and 1969. The Minnesota clubs of the 1960s relied on power. In 1976, the Twins hit only 81 home runs to rank eighth in a 12-team league while stealing 146 bases. The 81 home runs are the fewest by a Twins team with the exception of the 1981 outfit, which had only 47 in a strike-shortened season. In 1977, the Twins scored 867 runs to top the AL again. That season the club increased their home run total to 123, but the figure ranked 11th in a 14-team league.

OCTOBER 3   In the final game of the season, tempers flare over the batting title during a 5–3 win over the Royals in Kansas City. Entering the contest, Rod Carew and Royals teammates George Brett and Hal McRae each had a shot at finishing first in the AL in batting average. McRae's average was .33078, closely followed by Brett (.33073) and Carew (.32945). Carew had two hits in four at-bats, but couldn't keep pace with Brett and McRae, each of whom had two hits in their first three at-bats. When the Royals came to bat in the ninth, Brett was hitting .33230 just behind McRae's .33270. Brett hit a fly ball to center, which was badly misplayed by Steve Brye. The ball bounced to the wall, and Brett circled the bases for an inside-the-park homer. McRae grounded out, and Brett won the title .33333 to .33207. McRae touched off a fracas with two obscene gestures toward the Twins' bench and by shouting angrily. McRae believed that Twins manager Gene Mauch had ordered Brye to misplay the drive by Brett. Mauch went onto the field, and both he and McRae had to be restrained by players and umpires. McRae charged that both Mauch and Brye were guilty of racism. A brief investigation by the American League was conducted, but the league office concluded that Brye was guilty of nothing more than human error. Brye said he was playing too deep and did not see the ball well.

Carew finished the year with a .331 average, nine homers and 49 stolen bases in 1976. Had he collected two more hits in 1976, he would have won seven straight batting titles from 1972 through 1978.

NOVEMBER 5   Three days after Jimmy Carter defeats Gerald Ford in the presidential election, the Twins lose Jerry Garvin, Al Woods, Bill Singer and Dave McKay to the Blue Jays and Steve Braun to the Mariners in the expansion draft.

NOVEMBER 6   Bill Campbell signs a contract with the Red Sox as a free agent.

Campbell was the first free agent to sign with any major league club after the system went into effect at the end of the 1976 season. After earning $22,000 in 1976, Campbell inked a five-year deal with Boston worth approximately $1,000,000. Campbell gave the Red Sox one great season in 1977, with a 13–9 record and 31 saves, but struggled over the remaining four years of his contract with arm troubles, likely due to his workload. From 1974 through 1977, Campbell pitched an average of 64 games and 137 innings per season. Over his last seven seasons in the majors, from 1981 until 1987, Campbell bounced around with six teams.

NOVEMBER 26   Eric Soderholm signs as a free agent with the White Sox.

Soderholm missed the entire 1976 season with a knee injury that required two operations. He hit a career-high 25 homers for the White Sox in 1977 and added 20 more in 1978.

1977

Season in a Sentence
Rod Carew pursues a .400 batting average while the Twins stay atop the AL West for 59 days before finishing a distant fourth.

Finish • Won • Lost • Pct • GB
Fourth   84   77   .522   17.5

Manager
Gene Mauch

Stats   Twins • AL • Rank
Batting Avg:	.282	.266	1
On-Base Pct:	.347	.330	1
Slugging Pct:	.417	.405	5
Home Runs:	123		11
Stolen Bases:	105		6
ERA:	4.36	4.06	12
Errors:	143		9
Runs Scored:	867		1
Runs Allowed:	776		12

Starting Line-up
Butch Wynegar, c
Rod Carew, 1b
Bob Randall, 2b
Mike Cubbage, 3b
Roy Smalley, ss
Larry Hisle, lf
Lyman Bostock, cf
Dan Ford, rf
Craig Kusick, dh
Glenn Adams, dh-rf
Rich Chiles, dh
Jerry Terrell, 3b

Pitchers
Dave Goltz, sp
Paul Thormasgard, sp
Geoff Zahn, sp
Pete Redfern, sp
Tom Johnson, rp
Tom Burgmeier, rp
Ron Schueler, rp

Attendance
1,162,727 (11th in AL)

Club Leaders
Batting Avg:	Rod Carew	.388
On-Base Pct:	Rod Carew	.449
Slugging Pct:	Rod Carew	.570
Home Runs:	Larry Hisle	28
RBI:	Larry Hisle	119
Runs:	Rod Carew	128
Stolen Bases:	Rod Carew	23
Wins:	Dave Goltz	20
Strikeouts:	Dave Goltz	186
ERA:	Dave Goltz	3.36
Saves:	Tom Johnson	15

MARCH 18   Two months after the Vikings lose the Super Bowl 32–14 to the Oakland Raiders, the Twins sign Geoff Zahn, most recently with the Cubs, as a free agent.

Zahn was a 31-year-old pitcher with a lifetime record of 6–13 when signed by the Twins. He won his first five decisions with the club and pitched in the Minnesota starting rotation for four seasons with 53 wins and 53 losses.

MARCH 21   The Twins sell Steve Brye to the Brewers.

APRIL 9   The Twins open the season with a 7–4 loss to the Athletics in Oakland. Dave Goltz was the starting pitcher and lasted 4 1/3 innings. In his Twins debut, reliever Ron Schueler took the loss by allowing a home run to Earl Williams in the sixth inning that broke a 4–4 tie.

One of the rare catchers to bat first in the line-up, Butch Wynegar was the Twins lead-off batter on Opening Day. Wynegar started 49 games during his career as the lead-off hitter.

APRIL 11   The Twins play the Mariners for the first time and win 12–3 at the Kingdome in Seattle. Jerry Terrell hit into three double plays during the contest.

APRIL 15   In the first home game of the season, the Twins lose 3–2 to the Athletics before 14,788 at Metropolitan Stadium. Rod Carew homered in the losing cause.

Carew was in the national spotlight all year in his quest to become baseball's first .400 hitter since Ted Williams batted .406 in 1941. After the third game of the season, Carew was over the .400 mark only from June 26 through July 10 but stayed within striking distance most of the summer before finishing with a .388 average to win his sixth batting title. The only other players since 1941 to hit .380 or better in a season are Williams (.388 in 1957), George Brett (.390 in 1980) and Tony Gwynn (.394 in the strike-shortened season of 1994). Carew's 239 hits in 1977 were the most by a major leaguer after Bill Terry's 254 in 1930 and the 240 collected by Wade Boggs in 1985. Carew also led the AL in 1977 in runs (128), triples (16) and on-base percentage (.449) in addition to 38 doubles, 14 homers, and 100 RBIs, and the Most Valuable Player Award.

APRIL 17   The Twins score seven runs in the second inning and rout the Athletics 10–2 at Metropolitan Stadium. The rally climaxed when Rod Carew brought home four runs on one play with a triple. Carew's drive came with two out and the bases loaded. After the three runners crossed the plate, Carew came home on an error by pitcher Mike Norris, who missed the cut-off throw.

APRIL 20   Three Minnesota pitchers combine to allow 15 hits and three walks, but the Twins prevail 3–2 over the Royals in Kansas City. The Twins turned five double plays.

APRIL 24   The Twins score seven runs in the fourth inning and defeat the Rangers 12–6 in Arlington. Larry Hisle capped the rally with a grand slam off Nelson Briles.

In his last year with the Twins (see November 17, 1977), Hisle batted .302 with 28 home runs and a league-leading 119 runs batted in.

APRIL 25   Pitchers Mike Pazik and Dan Carrithers are injured in a head-on collision. Carrithers was driving when the car collided with another driven by a 23-year-old woman near Bloomington. The woman was entering Interstate 494 in an exit lane as the players' car was coming off the freeway at 1:06 a.m. Pazik, who began the season in the starting rotation, suffered two broken legs and never played in another major league game. Carrithers, who was acquired by the Twins from the Expos only 19 days earlier, sustained a broken wrist and knee injury and returned to play in five games in August and September.

APRIL 26   The Twins play the Mariners for the first time at home and win 5–3 at Metropolitan Stadium.

APRIL 30   After being hit by a pitch in the second inning of a 7–2 win over the Tigers at Metropolitan Stadium, Rod Carew charges the mound and takes a few swings at Detroit pitcher Dave Roberts. Carew was ejected.

MAY 1   The Twins score four runs after two are out in the ninth to stun the Tigers 6–5 at Metropolitan Stadium. Larry Hisle drove in the first run with a single. Dan Ford was hit by a pitch, and Craig Kusick brought home both Hisle and Ford with a double to tie the score. Roy Smalley accounted for the winning tally with a walk-off single. Detroit took a 5–0 lead in the second inning before the Twins countered with runs in

	the sixth and seventh to set up the game-winning rally.
May 6	The Twins play the Blue Jays for the first time and win 7–2 at Exhibition Stadium in Toronto. It was also the first time the Twins played a regular season game outside of the United States.
May 8	Rod Carew collects two triples, a double and a single in five at-bats to lead the Twins to a 5–4 triumph over the Blue Jays in Toronto.
May 13	The Twins play the Blue Jays at home for the first time and win 4–3 in 11 innings at Metropolitan Stadium.
May 14	The Twins collect 20 hits and clobber the Blue Jays 13–3 at Metropolitan Stadium.
May 25	The Twins sweep the Red Sox 13–5 and 9–4 in a double-header against the Red Sox in Boston. The Twins had 24 hits in the opener. Batting in the lead-off spot, Larry Hisle walloped a grand slam off Tom Murphy in the seventh inning. Rod Carew collected five hits, including a double, in six at-bats. Playing center field in the second tilt, Lyman Bostock tied a major league record by recording 12 putouts. The only other outfielder to accomplish the feat in a nine-inning game was Earl Clark of the Boston Braves in 1929.

Rod Carew had one of the greatest seasons ever for a Twins hitter, reaching career highs in many categories and winning the AL MVP.

The sweep gave the Twins a 27–14 record and a 3½-game lead in the AL West. The club held first place continuously from April 30 through June 18.

May 29	A freak home run by Roy Smalley highlights a 3–2 win over the Orioles in Baltimore. In the second inning, left fielder Pat Kelly had Smalley's drive in his glove, but his arm hit the seven-foot high wire fence and the ball dropped on the other side for a home run.
June 1	The Twins score three runs in the ninth inning to down the Yankees 4–3 at Metropolitan Stadium. The rally started with three straight singles by Craig Kusick, Jerry Terrell and Butch Wynegar off Ron Guidry. Sparky Lyle relieved Guidry and recorded two outs before walking Roy Smalley and surrendering a two-run, walk-off single to Rod Carew.
June 6	The White Sox score four runs in the 12th inning to defeat the Twins 9–5 at Metropolitan Stadium.
June 7	The Twins edge the White Sox 6–5 in 11 innings at Metropolitan Stadium.

On the same day, the Twins selected outfielder Paul Croft from Morristown High School in Morristown, New Jersey, in the first round of the amateur draft.

Croft never played higher than Class AA ball. Future major leaguers drafted and signed by the Twins that year were Roger Erickson (third round), Darrell Jackson (ninth round) and Scott Ullger (18th round).

JUNE 8 — The Twins play in extra innings for the third game in a row and slip past the Royals 9–8 at Metropolitan Stadium. Glenn Borgmann tied the score 8–8 with a two-run homer with one out in the ninth. Larry Hisle led off the tenth with a walk-off homer.

JUNE 22 — In his first game as manager of the Rangers, Eddie Stanky beats the Twins 10–8 at Metropolitan Stadium.

Stanky had previously managed the Cardinals (1952–55) and White Sox (1966–68). At a press conference before the game, he enthusiastically told reporters of his "zest" for the game. The following morning, Stanky said he was "homesick" and left the club.

JUNE 23 — The Twins crush the Rangers 12–2 at Metropolitan Stadium.

JUNE 26 — On Rod Carew Day before 46,463 at Metropolitan Stadium, the Twins outlast the White Sox 19–12. Entering the ballpark, fans were given T-shirts with Carew's number 29 on them. In storybook fashion, Carew had one of the best games of his career with a home run, double and two singles in four at-bats, five runs scored, and six RBIs. The outburst gave Carew a season average of .403. It was the first time he was over the .400 mark since the third game of the season. Glenn Adams also starred by tying a club record with eight runs batted in. He doubled in two runs in the first inning and hit a grand slam in the second, both off Steve Stone. Adams later singled in a tally in the third and added a sacrifice fly in the seventh.

Playing mostly as a platoon outfielder and designated hitter, Adams hit .338 with six home runs and 49 RBIs in 269 at-bats in 1977.

JULY 10 — The Twins pummel the Mariners 15–0 at Metropolitan Stadium. Geoff Zahn pitched a three-hit, complete-game shutout.

JULY 24 — After winning the first game of a double-header against the Athletics at Metropolitan Stadium by a 5–3 score, the Twins take a thrilling 10–9 decision in 12 innings in the nightcap. The Twins trailed 8–5 heading into the ninth before scoring three times to send the game into extra innings. Bud Bulling drove in the first two ninth-inning runs with a single. Two more singles from Butch Wynegar and Roy Smalley produced another run. The A's scored in the top of the tenth, but Larry Hisle hit a two-run homer in the bottom half to tie the contest at 9–9. Lyman Bostock led off the Minnesota 12th with a walk-off home run for the victory.

The two-run single by Bulling in the ninth inning accounted for his first two major league RBIs. A catcher, he played in only 15 games for the Twins and hit .156.

JULY 25 — Dave Goltz pitches all 11 innings of a 2–1 win over the Athletics at Metropolitan Stadium and strikes out 14 batters. Larry Hisle drove in the winning run with a single.

July 26	Lyman Bostock contributes a triple, two doubles and a single in five at-bats, but the Twins lose 9–7 to the Mariners in Seattle.
July 27	Butch Wynegar hits a three-run double with two-out in the ninth inning to sink the Mariners 4–1 in Seattle.
July 30	The Twins defeat the Indians 4–3 in 14 innings in Cleveland. Roy Smalley snapped the 3–3 tie by leading off the 14th with a home run.
August 5	Trailing 7–1, the Twins explode for 11 runs in the fourth inning and beat the Indians 14–10 at Metropolitan Stadium. The 11 runs scored on only six hits, four of them for extra bases. Glenn Adams led off the big inning with a home run. Mike Cubbage drove in five runs during the rally with a single off Al Fitzmorris and a grand slam against Pat Dobson.
August 7	Mike Cubbage drives in five runs with a home run, a triple and a double during an 11–1 thrashing of the Indians at Metropolitan Stadium.
August 12	The Twins score seven runs in the second inning and five in the third to take a 12–3 lead, then hang on to defeat the Tigers 12–11 in Detroit. Rod Carew hit a grand slam in the third off Jim Crawford.
	The Twins scored 111 runs over 14 games from July 31 through August 15.
August 15	The Twins outslug the Orioles 13–9 in Baltimore. Craig Kusick, playing first base to give Rod Carew a rest, hit two homers and drove in five runs. One of the homers gave the Twins a 6–5 lead in the fifth inning. In the eighth, Carew pinch-hit for Kusick and singled in a run.
	The win put the Twins into first place with a 68–50 record. The club quickly fell out of pennant contention, however, by posting a 16–27 record the rest of the way.
August 23	Dave Goltz pitches a one-hitter to defeat the Red Sox 7–0 at Metropolitan Stadium. The only Boston hit was a single by Jim Rice in the fourth inning.
September 18	The Twins score seven runs in the eighth inning but it comes too late in a 10–8 loss to the Rangers in Arlington.
October 2	In the last game of the season, Dave Goltz earns victory number 20 with a 6–2 decision over the Brewers in Milwaukee.
	Goltz was 20–11 with a 3.36 ERA in 303 innings in 1977. He made 39 starts and completed 19 of them. Goltz wasn't the only Minnesota pitcher with a heavy workload that season. Reliever Tom Johnson, a native of St. Paul, pitched in 71 games and 146²/₃ innings. He had a 16–7 record, 15 saves and an earned run average of 3.13. Only 26 in 1977, Johnson's usage by Gene Mauch took a toll. After just 32²/₃ ineffective innings in 1978, Johnson never pitched in the majors again.
November 17	The Brewers sign Larry Hisle as a free agent.

Hisle signed a six-year deal worth $3,155,000, more than tenfold over what he earned with the Twins in 1977. It was made him the highest paid player in baseball for a brief period. Hisle hit 34 homers and drove in 115 runs for Milwaukee in 1978 and finished third in the MVP balloting. But he was injured early in the 1979 season and never fully recovered. From 1979 through the end of his career in 1982, Hisle had only 274 major league at-bats.

NOVEMBER 18   The Twins board of directors decides that Gene Mauch must fulfill his contract and manage the Twins in 1978. Mauch signed a three-year deal in November 1975. He was frustrated over Calvin Griffith's refusal to bid for free agents and the loss of players like Larry Hisle, Lyman Bostock and Tom Burgmeier to other clubs. Gene Autry, the principal owner of the Angels, had sought Mauch to manage his team.

NOVEMBER 21   The Angels sign Lyman Bostock as a free agent.

Bostock was only 26 and seemed poised for greatness after hitting .336 with 14 homers, 12 triples and 36 doubles and 104 runs scored in 1977. He fled the penurious Calvin Griffith to sign a multimillion-dollar deal with generous Angels owner Gene Autry. Bostock slumped badly early in the 1978 season, however, and refused to collect salary for the month of April. Autry turned down the gesture, but Bostock donated the money to charity. Eventually, he started hitting again and lifted his average to .296 in late-September when the Angels traveled to Chicago for a series against the White Sox. On September 23, Bostock went to visit an uncle in Gary, Indiana. His uncle was driving a car containing Bostock and two women he'd met only a few minutes earlier. Another vehicle pulled alongside, and the husband of one of the women fired shots at the car. One of the bullets struck Bostock, and he died three hours later.

1978

Season in a Sentence
Weakened by the loss of free agents during the previous off-season, the Twins win a meager 73 games.

Finish • Won • Lost • Pct • GB
Fourth   73   89   .451   19.0

Manager
Gene Mauch

Stats   Twins • AL • Rank
Batting Avg: .267   .261   4
On-Base Pct: .339   .326   1
Slugging Pct: .375 .385   10
Home Runs: 82   14
Stolen Bases: 99   5
ERA: 3.69 3.76   10
Errors: 146   9 (tie)
Runs Scored: 666   8
Runs Allowed: 678   9

Starting Line-up
Butch Wynegar, c
Rod Carew, 1b
Bob Randall, 2b
Mike Cubbage, 3b
Roy Smalley, ss
Willie Norwood, lf
Dan Ford, cf
Hosken Powell, rf
Glenn Adams, dh
Bombo Rivera, rf
Jose Morales, dh
Larry Wolfe, 3b
Rob Wilfong, 2b

Pitchers
Roger Erickson, sp
Geoff Zahn, sp
Dave Goltz, sp
Gary Serum, sp-rp
Darrell Jackson, sp
Mike Marshall, rp

Attendance
787,878 (13th in AL)

Club Leaders
Batting Avg: Rod Carew   .333
On-Base Pct: Rod Carew   .411
Slugging Pct: Rod Carew   .441
Home Runs: Roy Smalley   19
RBI: Dan Ford   82
Runs: Rod Carew   85
Stolen Bases: Rod Carew   27
Wins: Dave Goltz   15
Strikeouts: Roger Erickson 121
ERA: Dave Goltz   2.49
Saves: Mike Marshall 21

FEBRUARY 17   The Red Sox sign Tom Burgmeier as a free agent.

Burgmeier continued to pitch well in a relief role for many more years. He had earned run averages under 3.00 in six straight seasons with the Red Sox and Athletics beginning in 1979.

APRIL 5   On Opening Day, the Twins lose 3–2 to the Mariners in Seattle. Dave Goltz was the starting and losing pitcher.

The Twins opened the season with an unusual five-game series against the Mariners and faced the Seattle club nine times in the first 12 games including four at Metropolitan Stadium.

APRIL 13   Joe Rudi hits a walk-off homer in the 11th inning off Tom Johnson to lift the Angels to a 1–0 win over the Twins in Anaheim. By prior agreement, it was decided that no inning could start after 3:50 p.m. to allow the Twins sufficient time to catch a plane. Rudi's homer was struck at 3:55 p.m.

APRIL 14   In the first home game of the season, the Twins crush the Mariners 14–5 before 17,425 at Metropolitan Stadium. Craig Kusick drove in five runs.

APRIL 26   Dan Ford drives in seven runs, but the Twins lose 9–8 in 12 innings to the Athletics in Oakland. The Twins led 6–4 in the ninth before Mitchell Page hit a two-out, two-run homer off Greg Thayer to tie the score. In the 12th, Ford drove in two runs with a double, but the A's rebounded with three runs in their half off Tom Johnson before a batter was retired. The loss was the Twins ninth in a row and sent the season won-lost record to 6–14.

MAY 6   Trailing 5–1, the Twins score seven runs in the top of the ninth, then survive a two-run Orioles rally in the bottom half to win 8–7 in Baltimore. Rod Carew put the Twins into the lead with a three-run triple.

Carew won his seventh batting title in 1977 with a .333 average. He also led the AL in on-base percentage (.411) and collected 188 hits, ten of them triples.

MAY 7   Roy Smalley reaches base in all six plate appearances with a double and a club record five walks during a 15–9 triumph over the Orioles in Baltimore.

Smalley entered the season with 12 home runs in 1,347 career at-bats, but suddenly developed a power stroke. He hit a team-high 19 home runs in 1978 along with a .273 batting average.

MAY 15   Willie Norwood hits a three-run walk-off homer in the tenth inning to down the Orioles 9–6 at Metropolitan Stadium.

On the same day, the Twins signed Mike Marshall as a free agent. Marshall made his major league debut in 1967 with the Tigers and struggled for several years before developing into one of baseball's top relievers. At the start of the 1972 season, he was 29 and pitching for the Expos, his fourth big league club. Marshall had a major league record of 12–29. He also developed a reputation as an iconoclast because of his surly personality and his academic pursuits. In the off-season, Marshall attended classes at Michigan State University with designs on obtaining a doctorate in kinesiology, the study of the principles of mechanics and anatomy as they relate to human movement. In 1972, under Gene Mauch in Montreal, Marshall developed a screwball and became nearly unhittable. He collected 14 wins and 18 saves and had an ERA of 1.78. In 1973, Marshall pitched in 92 games and 179 innings and won 14 more games with 31 saves. After a trade to the Dodgers, he had an historic season in 1974. Marshall pitched in 104 games, a major league record which will likely never be broken, and accumulated 208$2/3$ innings, a record for relievers that will also stand the test of time. He finished the year with 15 wins, 21 saves, and a Cy Young Award. But injuries reduced his effectiveness, and he bounced from Los Angeles to Atlanta to Texas before being released by the Rangers in June 1977. He was retired when convinced by Mauch to return to baseball. It proved to be a great move as Marshall gave the Twins two brilliant seasons before physical ailments cropped up again. In 1978 and 1979 he combined for 20 wins, 53 saves and a 2.57 ERA. In 1979, Marshall set a club record by appearing in 90 games.

JUNE 3   Larry Wolfe hits two homers and drives in five runs during a 9–3 win over the Tigers in Detroit.

The homers were Wolfe's first two in the majors, and they came in his 86th and 87th career at-bats. He had 135 homerless at-bats before connecting for home run number three on September 3.

June 6 — In the first round of the amateur draft, the Twins select shortstop Lenny Faedo from Jefferson High School in Tampa, Florida.

Faedo was only 20 when he reached the majors in 1980, but his career lasted only five years. He hit .251 with five home runs in 179 games and 521 at-bats. There were two other future major leaguers drafted and signed by the Twins in 1978, and both had long, productive careers. In the second round of the January draft, the club chose Jesse Orosco, who played 25 years in the majors and set a record for games by a pitcher with 1,252. Orosco made his major league debut with the Mets, however, in 1979 following a trade (see December 5, 1978). In the 17th round, the Twins drafted Kent Hrbek from Kennedy High School in Bloomington. He became one of the most popular Twins players in the team's history.

June 13 — Willie Norwood scores both runs of a 2–0 victory over the Blue Jays in the first game of a double-header Toronto. Norwood crossed the plate after doubling in the first inning and singling in the third. Dave Goltz (eight innings) and Mike Marshall (one inning) combined on the shutout. The Twins completed the sweep with a 7–2 win in the second tilt.

Goltz was 15–10 with a 2.49 ERA in 1978. He missed about ten starts with three different injuries. Goltz bruised a rib in a fight against the Angels, burned an index finger on a backyard grill, and hurt his back after slipping on the mound in Anaheim.

June 25 — The Twins score seven runs in the fourth inning and defeat the White Sox 9–6 in a double-header in Chicago. Roy Smalley hit a grand slam off Jim Willoughby. The Twins also won the opener 8–5.

July 1 — The Twins clobber the White Sox 10–0 at Metropolitan Stadium. Dave Goltz pitched the shutout.

July 7 — Darrell Jackson pitches a three-hitter to beat the Athletics 1–0 in the second game of a double-header in Oakland. The Twins also won the opener 3–2.

The shutout came in Jackson's fourth big league start. It would prove to be the only one of his career, which ended in 1982 with a 20–27 record. Jackson was one of three Twins pitchers who were 22 years old or younger. The trio combined to start 75 games for the Twins in 1978. Jackson started 15. The other two were Roger Erickson (37) and Gary Serum (23). Erickson was 14–13 with a 3.96 ERA in 265$^{2}/_{3}$ innings in 1978. The workload at the age of 21 wrecked a promising arm, however. Over the rest of his career, which lasted until 1983, Erickson was 21–40.

July 8 — The Twins collect 23 hits and beat the Athletics 9–8 in 11 innings in Oakland. Minnesota took a 6–0 lead in the third inning, fell behind 7–6 in the fifth, and then knotted the score with a run in the eighth. Both teams plated a run in the tenth. Willie Norwood drove in the winning run with a single in the 11th.

July 9	The Twins extend their winning streak to eight games with a 7–0 decision over the Athletics in Oakland. Dave Goltz held the A's hitless until Mike Edwards singled with one out in the eighth inning and finished with a three-hitter.
	The July 9 victory came in the last game before the All-Star break and gave the club a 39–42 record. There were hopes of a winning record for the third year in a row, but the Twins lost their first nine games following the break.
July 11	At the All-Star Game in San Diego, Rod Carew hits two triples in his first two at-bats, the first leading off the first inning, and scores twice, but the American League loses 7–3. Carew is the only player to hit two triples in a single All-Star Game.
July 15	Rod Carew collects his 2,000th career hit during a 5–4 loss to the Red Sox in Boston. The milestone hit was a single off Bill Lee in the fifth inning.
July 27	Mike Cubbage hits for the cycle in four plate appearances during a 6–3 win over the Blue Jays at Metropolitan Stadium. Facing Jim Clancy, Cubbage hit a double in the second inning and a home run in the fourth. Against Jerry Garvin, Cubbage singled in the fifth and tripled in the seventh.
July 28	Willie Norwood hits a two-run homer in the tenth inning to beat the Yankees 7–5 in New York.
August 1	Roy Smalley collects four hits, two of them homers, in four at-bats, but the Twins lose 13–6 to the Mariners in Seattle.
August 8	The Twins score seven runs in the fourth inning and beat the Mariners 10–2 at Metropolitan Stadium. Mike Cubbage hit a grand slam off Mike Parrott.
August 17	Dan Ford's walk-off single in the tenth inning beats the Royals 6–5 at Metropolitan Stadium.
August 18	The Twins score two runs in the ninth inning and one in the tenth to defeat the Blue Jays 4–3 at Metropolitan Stadium. Rod Carew tied the score with a single in the ninth. Glenn Adams drove in the winning run with a walk-off double in the tenth. It was the second game in a row in which the Twins won in extra innings.
August 19	Gary Serum pitches a two-hitter to defeat the Blue Jays 5–0 at Metropolitan Stadium. The only Toronto hits were singles by Alan Ashby in the third inning and Al Woods in the fifth.
	The shutout was the only one of Serum's career. He made his major league debut at the age of 20 in 1977, but lasted only three years with a 10–12 record and a 4.72 ERA.
August 25	Substitute umpires are used during a 7–3 loss to the Blue Jays in Toronto. Regular umpires Terry Cooney, Al Clark, Bill Deegan and Bill Kunkel failed to arrive on time from Oakland because of travel delays. The substitutes were local amateur umpires Joe Sawchuk (home plate) and Alan Contant (first base), Blue Jays coach Don Leppert (second base) and Twins coach Jerry Zimmerman (third base).

1970s

SEPTEMBER 5   A base-running blunder by Dan Ford contributes to a 4–3 loss to the White Sox at Metropolitan Stadium. In the bottom of the seventh, the Twins trailed 4–0 with the bases loaded. Ford was on third base, Jose Morales on second and Larry Wolfe on first. Bombo Rivera lined a single to second, and Ford backpedaled toward home while waving Morales home. Ford stopped short of home plate and continued to urge on Morales, who passed Ford and slid across the plate. Morales was called out for passing Ford on the base path. An angry Gene Mauch immediately removed Ford from the line-up and replaced him with Hosken Powell. The Twins scored twice in the ninth, but lost 4–3.

SEPTEMBER 18   The Twins score seven runs in the fourth inning and defeat the Angels 10–4 at Metropolitan Stadium. Dan Ford contributed a single and a double to the rally, and Hosken Powell hit a pair of singles.

DECEMBER 4   The Twins trade Dan Ford to the Angels for Ron Jackson and Danny Goodwin.

Ford had five years ahead of him as a serviceable outfielder. A catcher, Goodwin is the only player in major league history to be the overall number one draft pick twice. He was chosen by the White Sox in 1971, but opted to attend Southern University instead. Goodwin was selected again by the Angels in 1975, but hit only .226 in 159 at-bats for California over three seasons before being traded to the Twins. He played three seasons in Minnesota, and batted .242 with eight homers in 425 at-bats. Jackson was the Twins starting first baseman for two seasons, largely because of a lack of better alternatives.

DECEMBER 8   The Twins trade Jesse Orosco and Greg Field to the Mets for Jerry Koosman.

Neither Orosco nor Field had played in the majors when traded by the Twins. Field never did play in a big league contest. Orosco, on the other hand, played 25 years in the majors and set a record for pitchers by appearing in 1,252 games. He was a Met from 1979 through 1987. Over the course of his career, Orosco played for nine clubs. The last of them was the Twins, playing eight games in 2003. A native of Appleton, Minnesota, Koosman pitched 12 seasons for the Mets. He was 21–10 in 1976 to raise his career record to 129–102. He then slipped to an 8–20 mark in 1977 and 3–15 in 1978, although his earned run averages in both losing seasons were around the league average. He threatened to retire if he wasn't traded to the Twins so that he could play near home. Although Koosman was 36 when he played his first game for the Twins, he enjoyed a revival in his home state, posting records of 20–13 in 1979 and 16–13 in 1980.

1979

Season in a Sentence
Without Rod Carew, the Twins win 22 of their first 30 games, and remain in contention for the pennant until September before finishing in fourth place.

Finish • Won • Lost • Pct • GB
Fourth 82 80 .506 6.0

Manager
Gene Mauch

Stats   Twins • AL • Rank
Batting Avg: .278   .270   5
On-Base Pct: .341   .334   5
Slugging Pct: .402   .408   11
Home Runs: 112   12
Stolen Bases: 66   12
ERA: 4.13   4.22   7
Errors: 134   6 (tie)
Runs Scored: 764   6
Runs Allowed: 725   6

Starting Line-up
Butch Wynegar, c
Ron Jackson, 1b
Rob Wilfong, 2b
John Castino, 3b
Roy Smalley, ss
Ken Landreaux, lf-cf
Willie Norwood, cf-rf
Hosken Powell, rf
Glenn Adams, dh-lf
Bombo Rivera, lf-rf
Mike Cubbage, 3b
Dave Edwards, lf-cf-rf

Pitchers
Jerry Koosman, sp
Dave Goltz, sp
Geoff Zahn, sp
Paul Hartzell, sp
Roger Erickson, sp
Mike Marshall, rp
Pete Redfern, rp

Attendance
1,070,521 (11th in AL)

Club Leaders
Batting Avg: Ken Landreaux   .305
On-Base Pct: Butch Wynegar   .363
Slugging Pct: Ken Landreaux   .450
Home Runs: Roy Smalley   24
RBI: Roy Smalley   95
Runs: Roy Smalley   94
Stolen Bases: Rob Wilfong   11
Wins: Jerry Koosman   20
Strikeouts: Jerry Koosman   157
ERA: Jerry Koosman   3.38
Saves: Mike Marshall   32

FEBRUARY 3   The Twins trade Rod Carew to the Angels for Ken Landreaux, Dave Engle, Paul Hartzell and Brad Havens.

At the time of the trade, Carew had won seven of the previous eight AL batting titles and was an All-Star in each of his 12 big league seasons. He wanted to remain in Minnesota but had a long-standing feud with Calvin Griffith over the Twins owner's frugality. The final break came late in 1978 when Griffith made some racist comments to a Lions Club meeting in Waseca, Minnesota. There, he spoke off-the-cuff about why he moved the club from Washington in 1960. "I'll tell you why I came to Minnesota," said Griffith. "It was when we found out you had only 15,000 blacks here. Blacks don't go to ballgames, but they'll fill up a rassling ring and put up such a chant it'll scare you to death. We came here because you've got good hardworking white people here." Griffith was demonized in the press and Carew said he no longer wanted to be a part of Griffith's "plantation." Carew had one year remaining on his contract, and Griffith decided to trade him rather than risk losing him at the end of the season to free agency without any compensation. As a player with at least ten years in the majors and five with the Twins, Carew had the right to reject any trade. To complicate matters further, Commissioner Bowie Kuhn stipulated that Carew had to agree to a contract with his new club before the transaction could be completed and that the Twins couldn't receive any cash in the deal. Griffith worked out a trade with the Giants, but Carew refused to go to San Francisco, preferring to stay in the American League. When initial negotiations with the Angels broke down, the Yankees stepped into the picture. Griffith worked out another trade with George Steinbrenner, but Carew balked at going to New York. Finally, a deal with the Angels was worked out. Carew played in California for seven seasons, hit over .300 in his first five seasons with the Angels, and appeared in six more All-Star Games. Landreaux started for two seasons with the Twins and four more with the Dodgers, but his offensive production was a little below average for major league outfielders. He did have one shining moment in Minnesota with a club record 31-game hitting streak in 1980. None of the other three players acquired for Carew had a positive impact on the Twins future.

APRIL 6   Nine days after the nuclear disaster at Three Mile Island in Pennsylvania, the Twins defeat the Athletics 5–3 in the season opener in Oakland. Three runs in the sixth inning gave Minnesota a 3–1 advantage. Dave Goltz pitched 8 1/3 innings for the win.

The Twins radio announcers in 1979 were Herb Carneal and Joe McConnell. On TV were Bob Kurtz and Larry Coleman.

APRIL 7   A two-out, two-run double by Butch Wynegar in the 12th inning beats the Athletics 3–1 in Oakland. Roger Erickson (nine innings) and Mike Marshall (three innings) combined on a five-hitter.

The Twins won their first four games and were 7–2 on a season-opening trip to Oakland, Anaheim and Seattle.

APRIL 15   The Twins collect 20 hits and rout the Mariners 18–6 in Seattle. It was a team effort, as 11 different players scored a run, 12 garnered hits, and ten drove in at least one run.

APRIL 17   The Twins lose the first home game of the season 6–0 to the Angels before 37,529 at Metropolitan Stadium. Nolan Ryan pitched the shutout.

APRIL 18   Rod Carew torments his former club with four hits, including two doubles, in four at-bats to lead the Angels to an 11–6 win over the Twins at Metropolitan Stadium.

APRIL 30   The Twins sign Ken Brett as a free agent.

The older brother of future Hall of Famer George Brett, Ken played only nine games for the Twins before being released. The Twins were the eighth of ten teams for which Ken played during his 14-year major league career. After his playing days were over, Brett did a Miller Lite commercial in which he had trouble determining which city he was in.

MAY 8   The Twins collect a team-record 12 extra base hits during a 16–6 fight-filled thrashing of the Blue Jays in Toronto. The even dozen extra base hits were two home runs by Craig Kusick, two homers from Roy Smalley, a home run and a double by Ken Landreaux, John Castino's triple, a pair of doubles by Bombo Rivera and doubles from Willie Norwood and Bob Randall. Landreaux's homer was inside-the-park. He also had two singles and drove in five runs. In addition to his two home runs, Smalley also delivered two singles, scored four runs, and drove in four. Both benches emptied three times during the eventful contest. Minnesota first baseman Ron Jackson was hit by a pitch from Mike Willis in the sixth and was thrown out when he charged the mound. In the seventh, the dugouts and bullpen were cleared again when Toronto's Balor Moore threw a pitch past Smalley's head. Following Landreaux's homer, Moore hit Castino, and this time a number of punches were thrown, resulting in the ejection of Moore, Castino and Blue Jays outfielder Otto Velez.

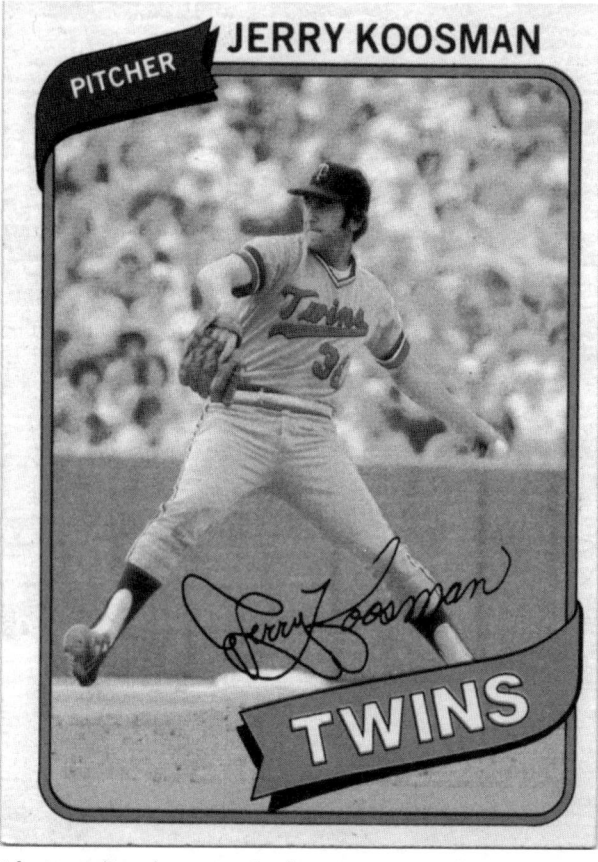

After two dismal seasons, fan favorite Jerry Koosman came home to Minnesota at the age of thirty-six and won twenty games in 1979. He followed his comeback season with sixteen more victories in 1980.

Smalley had a batting average of .372 with 15 homers and 62 RBIs on July 4 after playing in 78 games. He then hit only .178 over the final 84 games, and finished the year with a .271 average, 24 homers and 95 runs batted in. Smalley appeared in all 162 games, and was the starting shortstop in 160 of them.

MAY 12   The Twins score all four of their runs in the sixth inning to defeat the Indians 4–0 at Metropolitan Stadium. Jerry Koosman (eight innings) and Mike Marshall (one inning) combined on the shutout.

The victory gave the Twins a 22–8 record and a 4½-game lead in the AL West. The Twins fell out of the top spot on May 27, but remained in contention for the pennant until mid-September.

MAY 15   John Castino's first major league homer is an inside-the-park shot off Sparky Lyle in the seventh inning of a 9–8 loss to the Rangers at Metropolitan Stadium.

Castino hit .285 with five homers as a rookie in 1979. He shared the Rookie of the Year Award with Blue Jays shortstop Alfredo Griffin. Each received seven votes of the 28 cast. In all, six players picked up votes by the baseball writers polled. The tie led to a change in the voting procedures. Beginning in 1980, the writers voted for three players, with the first choice garnering five points, the second choice three, and the third entry one. Castino was a regular in the Twins infield for five years and switched from third base to second in 1982 after the arrival of Gary Gaetti. But Castino underwent back surgery after playing in just eight games in 1984. The back problem ended his career at the age of 29.

May 17   In his first season with the Twins, Jerry Koosman extends his record to 7–0 with a 7–6 victory over the Royals in Kansas City.

Koosman finished the season with a 20–13 record and a 3.38 ERA in 263²/₃ innings.

May 18   The Twins score four runs after two are out in the tenth inning to defeat the Royals 10–6 in Kansas City. The first two tallies crossed the plate on back-to-back, bases-loaded walks by Al Hrabosky to Bob Randall and John Castino.

May 21   The Twins score three runs in the ninth inning to defeat the Rangers 7–6 in Arlington. The runs were driven in on singles by Willie Norwood and John Castino and a double from Hosken Powell.

May 23   Al Oliver hits three homers for the Rangers during a 7–2 win over the Twins in Arlington.

May 31   The Twins rout the Athletics 13–2 at Metropolitan Stadium.

June 5   In the first round of the amateur draft, the Twins select outfielder Kevin Brandt from Nekoosa High School in Nekoosa, Wisconsin.

Brandt was one of the worst first-round selections in Twins history. He failed to make it past the Class A level. Fortunately, the club made one of its best selections ever in the first round of the secondary phase of previously drafted players by choosing third baseman Gary Gaetti from Northwest Missouri State University. Other future major leaguers drafted and signed by the Twins in 1979 were Randy Bush (second round), Tim Laudner (third round), Mike Kinnunen (tenth round) and Ed Holly (ninth round of the January draft).

June 14   Butch Wynegar has a hand in all four runs of a 4–2 win over the Yankees at Metropolitan Stadium. In the fourth inning, Wynegar hit a three-run double, then scored on a double by Dave Edwards.

Edwards had older twin brothers who both reached the majors. Twins Marshall and Mike were 18 months older than Dave. Mike played for the Pirates in 1977 and the Athletics from 1978 through 1980. Dave was the next to play in the big leagues as a member of the Twins from 1978 through 1980 and the Padres in 1981 and 1982. Marshall played for the Brewers from 1981 through 1983. Mike was primarily a second baseman while Dave and Marshall were outfielders.

June 26   After falling behind 6–0 in the fourth inning, the Twins rally to defeat the Brewers 8–7 at Metropolitan Stadium. The Twins took a 7–6 lead in the eighth but allowed Milwaukee to tie the contest in the top of the ninth. Jose Morales drove in the winning run with a two-out single in the bottom of the ninth.

June 27	After falling behind 9–0 in the fifth inning, the Twins score eight unanswered runs but lose 9–8 to the Brewers at Metropolitan Stadium.
June 30	The Twins score in seven consecutive innings from the second through the eighth and crush the White Sox 16–4 at Metropolitan Stadium.
July 3	The Twins go from one extreme to another with a 12–2 win and a 10–2 loss during a double-header against the Mariners at Metropolitan Stadium. In the opener, Ken Landreaux hit two doubles during a six-run rally in the seventh inning.
July 15	Dave Edwards hits a grand slam off Jim Clancy in the third inning of a 9–4 triumph over the Blue Jays in Toronto.
July 20	After falling behind 5–0, the Twins score four runs in the fourth inning and nine runs in the fifth and defeat the Tigers 14–6 at Metropolitan Stadium. During the nine-run rally, nine consecutive batters reached base on back-to-back home runs by Ken Landreaux and Glenn Adams, five singles, a walk and a fielder's choice.
July 22	The Twins score eight runs in the seventh inning and crush the Blue Jays 13–1 at Metropolitan Stadium. The rally started with six consecutive hits. Roy Smalley's double was followed by five straight singles from Ken Landreaux, Mike Cubbage, Glenn Adams, Butch Wynegar and Hosken Powell.
July 23	The Twins edge the Blue Jays 7–6 at Metropolitan Stadium. With one out in the ninth and the score 6–6, Bombo Rivera's triple off Mark Lemongello was followed by two intentional walks and a wild pitch.
August 12	Jerry Koosman pitches a ten-hit shutout to beat the Athletics 1–0 at Metropolitan Stadium. The lone run scored in the seventh inning when Danny Goodwin doubled home Mike Cubbage.
August 20	Ken Landreaux drives in six runs with a home run, triple and a double to lead the Twins to a 10–5 win over the Red Sox at Metropolitan Stadium.
August 29	Eddie Murray hits three home runs for the Orioles during a 7–4 win over the Twins in the second game of a double-header at Metropolitan Stadium. Baltimore also won the opener 4–0.
	The Twins and Orioles played each other in eight consecutive games with double-headers in Minnesota on August 27 and 29, and single contests in Baltimore on August 30 and 31 and September 1 and 2.
September 4	Jerry Koosman pitches a two-hitter to defeat the Royals 5–1 at Metropolitan Stadium. The only Kansas City hits were a home run by John Wathan in the sixth inning and a single by Willie Wilson with two out in the ninth.
September 9	The Twins field a starting line-up in which the oldest player is only 26 before losing 6–5 to the Rangers at Metropolitan Stadium. The starters were catcher Butch Wynegar (23), first baseman Ron Jackson (26), second baseman Rob Wilfong (26),

third baseman John Castino (24), shortstop Roy Smalley (26), left fielder Rick Sofield (22), center fielder Ken Landreaux (24), right fielder Hosken Powell (24), designated hitter Danny Goodwin (26) and pitcher Paul Hartzell (25).

September 13   Ken Landreaux leads off the 12th inning with a home run and the Twins add two insurance runs to defeat the Rangers 7–4 in Arlington.

September 16   The Twins score all six of their runs in a 6–2 win over the Rangers in Arlington in the second inning.

September 17   The Twins revive pennant hopes with a 10–3 win over the White Sox in Chicago.

With 12 games left on the schedule, the Twins had a 78–72 record and were in third place, three games behind the first-place Angels. The Royals were second, two games behind. The Twins lost eight of the last 12 games, however.

September 18   The Twins suffer a crushing 1–0 loss to the White Sox in ten innings at Comiskey Park. Dave Goltz pitched a complete game, allowing three straight singles in the tenth to take the loss. Ken Kravec pitched a three-hit shutout for Chicago.

September 21   The Twins score three runs in the ninth inning to top the Brewers 3–2 in Milwaukee. A walk to Roy Smalley was followed by back-to-back homers from Ken Landreaux and Butch Wynegar.

September 30   On the final day of the season, Jerry Koosman earns his 20th victory with a 5–0 win over the Brewers at Metropolitan Stadium. It was the only time all year that Milwaukee was held scoreless. The Brewers were last held without a run on August 10, 1978, a span of 213 games, which is the second-longest streak in major league history. The record for most games without being shut out is 308 games by the Yankees from 1931 through 1933. The Twins scored all five of their runs in the fifth inning.

October 23   Yankee manager Billy Martin fights a marshmallow salesman at a hotel in suburban Bloomington.

Martin was in the area following a four-day hunting trip in South Dakota with his close friend Howard Wong, a Minneapolis restaurateur. The two made a stop at L'Hotel de France in Bloomington late in the evening on October 23, and were engaged in a conversation with Joseph Cooper, a 52-year-old marshmallow salesman from Lincolnshire, Illinois. An altercation developed, and the salesman required 15 stitches to close his lip. Publicly, Martin denied hitting Cooper and claimed he had fallen. Both Yankee owner George Steinbrenner and Commissioner Bowie Kuhn launched investigations. Martin was then fired on October 28. Two days afterward, Cooper stated that Martin had become belligerent and sucker-punched him after a discussion about baseball. Cooper said he remained silent for a week because he didn't want Martin to lose his job but "couldn't stand the lies that went around." A few weeks later, Martin became manager of the Oakland Athletics.

November 14   Ten days after 66 Americans are taken hostage by followers of the Ayatollah Khomeni in Iran, the Dodgers sign Dave Goltz as a free agent.

In five seasons from 1975 through 1979, Goltz averaged 253 innings per season and won 77 games for some mediocre Twins teams. At the end of the 1979 season, he was 30-years-old and was the most highly sought free agent on the market. The Dodgers would regret signing him, however. After leaving the Twins, Goltz lasted only four more years in the majors and had a record of 17–32.

DECEMBER 3   The Twins draft Doug Corbett from the Reds organization.

Corbett was 27-years-old and had no major league experience when picked up by the Twins in the Rule 5 draft. He was brilliant as a rookie in 1980 with an 8–6 record and 23 saves with a 1.98 ERA in 73 games and 136$^1/_3$ innings. Corbett led the AL in games pitched with 54 of the 110 played by the Twins in the strike-shortened season of 1981, and compiled an earned run average of 2.57 in 87$^1/_3$ innings. He proved to be one of many Twins relievers burned out by a heavy workload. Like Bill Campbell, Tom Johnson and Mike Marshall before him, Corbett lost his effectiveness after a year or two of abuse. He was traded to the Angels for Tom Brunansky in 1982.

DECEMBER 20   Construction begins on the Hubert H. Humphrey Metrodome in downtown Minneapolis.

Baseball's first domed stadium was the Astrodome, which was the home of the Houston Astros from 1965 through 1999. Throughout the decade following the opening of the Astrodome, several ideas were floated concerning the construction of a domed facility in either Minneapolis, St. Paul or the surrounding suburbs. City officials in Minneapolis began aggressively pushing for a domed stadium in 1972, but public and political opposition prevented it from becoming a reality. Many Bloomington politicians and business leaders also desired to keep the Twins and Vikings in their community with their own proposals for a stadium. Meanwhile the leases on Metropolitan Stadium for both the Twins and Vikings expired in 1975. Each club signed one-year extensions while stating their displeasure with the Met and making threats about moving out of Minnesota should a new stadium fail to become a reality. Finally in 1977, the Minnesota state legislature voted to fund the project and appointed a seven-person commission to select a site for the new stadium. Eight locations were considered. There were two in Minneapolis, and one each in Bloomington, St. Paul, Brooklyn Center, Coon Rapids, and Eagan, along with a "Midway" site between Minneapolis and St. Paul. After six were eliminated from consideration, the choice came down to a 20-acre site in Industry Square in the eastern portion of downtown Minneapolis, and in Bloomington. The vote was 4–3 in favor of Minneapolis. The site was bounded by Chicago Avenue, South 4th Street, 11th Avenue South and South 6th Street. The commission wanted an "austere but a quality and aesthetically pleasing structure." The design team included Skidmore, Owings and Merrill, and Minneapolis-based Setter, Leach & Lindstrom, Inc. The facility opened as the Hubert Humphrey Metrodome in 1982. Humphrey served as mayor of Minneapolis (1945–49), a US Senator from Minnesota (1949–64), Vice-President of the United States (1964–69), and as a US Senator once more (1971 until his death in 1978).

1980s

THE STATE OF THE TWINS

The Twins floundered through the first seven years of the decade while fielding some of the youngest (and lowest-paid) rosters in the American League. Through 1986, the only non-losing season was in 1984, when the club was 81–81 and finished three games out of first in a weak field in the AL West. In 1987, the Twins won the division by three games, then stunned the heavily favored Tigers in the ALCS to win their first American League pennant since 1965. In the World Series, the Twins won all four games against the Cardinals at the Metrodome for the franchise's first world championship since 1924 when it was located in Washington. Overall, the Twins were 733–833 during the 1980s, a winning percentage of .468 which ranked 11th among 14 AL teams. AL pennant winners were the Royals (1980 and 1985), Yankees (1981), Brewers (1982), Orioles (1983), Tigers (1984), Red Sox (1986), Twins (1987) and Athletics (1988 and 1989). AL West winners were the Royals (1980, 1984 and 1985), Athletics (1981, 1988 and 1989), White Sox (1983), Twins (1987), Angels (1982 and 1986).

THE BEST TEAM

The 1987 Twins won the first world championship since the move to Minnesota after posting a regular season record of 85–77 while being outscored 806–786. The 1988 team posted the best regular season record with a mark of 91–71 but finished 13 games behind the Athletics in the AL West.

THE WORST TEAM

The 1982 Twins were 60–102, the most losses since the move to Minnesota and the most for the franchise since the 1949 Senators were 50–104.

THE BEST MOMENT

Willie McGee of the Cardinals grounded a Jeff Reardon pitch to third baseman Gary Gaetti for the final out of the seventh game of the World Series on October 25, 1987, at the Metrodome. The Twins won the game 4–2 and sealed the world championship.

THE WORST MOMENT

The low point of the decade was June 12, 1981, when the players went on strike with the Twins holding a miserable record of 17–39.

THE ALL-DECADE TEAM • YEARS W/TWINS

Player	Years
Tim Laudner, c	1981–89
Kent Hrbek, 1b	1981–94
John Castino, 2b	1979–84
Gary Gaetti, 3b	1981–90
Greg Gagne, ss	1983–92
Dan Gladden, lf	1987–91
Kirby Puckett, cf	1984–95
Tom Brunansky, rf	1982–88
Randy Bush, dh	1981–92
Frank Viola, p	1982–89
Bert Blyleven, p	1970–76; 1985–88
Jerry Koosman, p	1979–81
Mark Smithson, p	1984–87

Castino was primarily a third baseman but is listed here at second, where he played in 232 games. Blyleven was also on the 1970s All-Decade Team. Puckett is in the Hall of Fame. With the exception of Castino and Koosman, all of the players listed above played on the 1987 world championship team. The position players during the 1980s tended to remain in Minnesota for many years. Puckett, Hrbek, Gaetti, Bush, Gagne and Brunansky each played in over 900 games for the club. Since the move to Minnesota in 1961, only 16 players have reached that figure through the end of the 2009 season. With the exception of Viola, however, the pitching staffs had a large degree of turnover each season throughout the 1980s. Left fielder Gary Ward (1979–83) was another Twin who played a significant role during the decade.

THE DECADE LEADERS

Batting Avg:	Kirby Puckett	.323
On-Base Pct:	Kent Hrbek	.368
Slugging Pct:	Kent Hrbek	.496
Home Runs:	Kent Hrbek	201
RBIs:	Kent Hrbek	724
Runs:	Kent Hrbek	624
Stolen Bases:	Kirby Puckett	84
Wins:	Frank Viola	112
Strikeouts:	Frank Viola	1,287
ERA:	Frank Viola	3.86
Saves:	Jeff Reardon	104

THE HOME FIELD

After spending their first 21 seasons at Metropolitan Stadium, the Twins moved into the Metrodome in 1982 (see April 2, 1982). During their first season at the new downtown Minneapolis facility, the Twins drew only 921,186 fans as the club lost 102 games. It marked the sixth time in a span of nine years in which the Twins finished last in the AL in attendance. The Twins drew a franchise-record 3,030,872 in 1988 in the euphoria following the world championship season of 1987, but attendance was back under two million by 1990. The 1988 figure was a dramatic increase from the first four years of the decade, when the club attracted a combined 3,018,421 from 1980 through 1983. The Twins finished in the top half of the AL in attendance every year from 1961 through 1971, but have done so only three times since, finishing sixth in 1987, first in 1988 and fifth in 1992.

THE GAME YOU WISHED YOU HAD SEEN

Baseball doesn't get better than the home team winning the seventh game of a World Series. It happened at the Metrodome on October 25, 1987, when the Twins defeated the Cardinals 4–2.

THE WAY THE GAME WAS PLAYED

The 1980s had a little something for everybody. Trends that surfaced in the 1970s continued, with teams still emphasizing speed. In 1987, offense spiked in a year that combined the speed of the dead ball era with the power of the 1950s. AL teams averaged 124 stolen bases and 188 home runs.

THE MANAGEMENT

The Griffith family was a part of the franchise from 1912 until 1984. Clark Griffith was named manager of the Washington Senators in 1912 and by 1919 was owner, a position he held until his death in 1955. Clark's nephew and adopted son Calvin Griffith inherited the team and moved it to Minnesota in October 1960. Griffith sold the Twins to Carl Pohlad in 1984. Griffith always served as his own general manager, and the key front office positions were held by members of his family. The nepotism ended soon after Pohlad bought the club. Andy MacPhail served as general manager from 1985 through 1994. Field managers in the 1980s were Gene Mauch (1980), Johnny Goryl (1980–81), Billy Gardner (1981–85), Ray Miller (1985–86) and Tom Kelly (1986–2001).

THE BEST PLAYER MOVE

The best player move was the drafting of Kirby Puckett in 1982.

THE WORST PLAYER MOVE

The worst trade sent Tom Brunansky to the Cardinals for Tom Herr in April 1988.

1980

Season in a Sentence
The Twins win 12 games in a row in September and October after Johnny Goryl succeeds Gene Mauch as manager, but it's not enough to salvage a losing season.

Finish • Won • Lost • Pct • GB
Third   77   84   .478   19.5

Managers
Gene Mauch (54–71) and Johnny Goryl (23–13)

Stats   Twins • AL • Rank
Stat	Twins	AL	Rank
Batting Avg:	.265	.269	9
On-Base Pct:	.319	.331	11
Slugging Pct:	.381	.399	10
Home Runs:	99		12
Stolen Bases:	62		14
ERA:	3.93	4.03	7
Errors:	148		10
Runs Scored:	670		11
Runs Allowed:	724		7

Starting Line-up
Butch Wynegar, c
Ron Jackson, 1b
Rob Wilfong, 2b
John Castino, 3b
Roy Smalley, ss
Rick Sofield, lf-cf
Ken Landreaux, cf-lf
Hosken Powell, rf
Jose Morales, dh
Pete Mackanin, 2b
Mike Cubbage, 1b
Glenn Adams, dh

Pitchers
Jerry Koosman, sp
Geoff Zahn, sp
Darrell Jackson, sp
Roger Erickson, sp
Pete Redfern, sp-rp
Fernando Arroyo, sp-rp
Doug Corbett, rp
John Verhoeven, sp

Attendance
769,206 (14th in AL)

Club Leaders
Batting Avg:	John Castino	.302
On-Base Pct:	Roy Smalley	.359
Slugging Pct:	John Castino	.430
Home Runs:	John Castino	13
RBI:	John Castino	64
Runs:	John Castino	67
Stolen Bases:	Hosken Powell	14
Wins:	Jerry Koosman	16
Strikeouts:	Jerry Koosman	149
ERA:	Roger Erickson	3.25
Saves:	Doug Corbett	23

JANUARY 2 — Just 13 days after the start of construction on the Metrodome, bulldozers meet a 250,000-pound granite rock, believed to have been there about 11,000 years.

> *The rock resisted all attempts to dislodge it, move it, crush it or blast it. Meanwhile, the obstacle gained considerable media attention and public sentiment developed to save it. At the same time, First Bank Minneapolis was opening a branch in the western suburb of Plymouth. Bank officials decided to transport it to the new branch and dub it "Plymouth Rock." Nearly two months later, the rock was loaded onto two side-by-side flatbed trailers, a railroad car, and again onto flatbed trailers for the 15-mile trip to Plymouth.*

JANUARY 29 — Glenn Borgmann signs a contract as a free agent with the White Sox.

APRIL 10 — Seven weeks after the miracle win by the US hockey team at the Olympics in Lake Placid, New York, the Twins open the season with a 12-inning, 9–7 decision over the Athletics in Oakland. The Twins took a 5–0 lead until the A's scored seven runs in the seventh inning off Jerry Koosman and Mike Marshall. With two out in the top of the ninth, the Twins trailing 7–5, and runners on second and third, Willie Norwood hit a two-run single to tie the score. In the 12th, Roy Smalley and Rick Sofield both hit home runs. Making his major league debut, Doug Corbett pitched five innings of shutout relief and struck out six batters. The game was also Billy Martin's debut as manager of the A's. Martin was a native of nearby Berkeley and his 76-year-old mother threw out the ceremonial first pitch.

APRIL 14 Trailing 3–0, the Twins score a run in the eighth inning and four in the ninth to defeat the Angels 5–3 in Anaheim. In the ninth, Roy Smalley hit a three-run homer with two out to put Minnesota into the lead.

The Twins opened the season with a 12-game road trip to Oakland, Anaheim and Seattle and posted a record of 5–7.

Though he never quite fulfilled the promise he showed as a twenty-year-old rookie phenom, Butch Wynegar gave the Twins steady and heady play behind the plate for nearly seven years, winning fans with his take-charge, competitive attitude.

APRIL 16 The Angels foil the strategy of Gene Mauch to win 2–1 in ten innings in Anaheim. With a 1–0 lead and the bases full of Angels with one out in the ninth, Mauch deployed a five-man infield and a two-man outfield with Don Baylor batting. Baylor hit a sacrifice fly to tie the score, and Bobby Grich hit another sacrifice fly in the tenth for the California victory.

APRIL 22 In the home opener, the Twins beat the Angels 8–1 before 36,268 at Metropolitan Stadium. Roy Smalley, Hosken Powell and Ron Jackson each homered.

Because of the success of the San Diego Chicken during the 1970s, many big league clubs tried out similar mascots to entertain the fans. Some were unsuccessful, including the Twins incarnation, which was called Twinkie the Loon. According to Bruce Nash and Alan Zullo in their book The Baseball Hall of Shame 3, *"local entertainer Al Johnson dressed in a costume that made him look like a ne'er-do-well brother-in-law of Big Bird." After two seasons, Twinkie the Loon was benched. Johnson eventually moved to Los Angeles and found work in comedy clubs performing a juggling routine and as an actor.*

1980s

APRIL 23 — The Twins collect only one hit during a crushing 17–0 loss to the Angels at Metropolitan Stadium. Bruce Kison carried a no-hitter into the ninth inning before Ken Landreaux doubled with one out.

APRIL 27 — The Twins score ten runs in the first inning and outlast the Athletics 20–11 at Metropolitan Stadium. There were 42 hits during the contest, with the A's collecting 22 of them. The 20 Minnesota hits were garnered by 12 players. Twelve players also scored a run, and eleven players drove in at least one. The 20 hits consisted of 17 singles, two doubles and a triple. The ten runs in the first came on only five hits. Oakland pitchers walked five and hit a batter and another Twin reached on an error. Starting pitcher Geoff Zahn had an 18–4 lead after four innings, but couldn't earn a victory. He was relieved with two out in the fifth after allowing a total of eight runs and 14 hits.

> *The April 27 victory concluded a three-game series against the Athletics in which Oakland manager Billy Martin had to dodge marshmallows thrown by fans. During the April 25 contest, Martin had to be restrained from going into the stands after one of the fans. The marshmallow throwing was in response to Martin's fight with a marshmallow salesman in Bloomington six months earlier (see October 23, 1979).*

MAY 10 — The Twins need 11 innings to beat the Yankees 1–0 in New York. Darrell Jackson was the starter and allowed five hits in ten innings. Oddly, Bob Watson collected four of New York's five hits. Ken Landreaux drove in the lone run with a single. Doug Corbett earned the save by retiring all three batters to face him in the bottom of the 11th.

MAY 17 — Jose Morales grounds into double plays in three consecutive plate appearances during a 14–11 loss to the Brewers at Metropolitan Stadium.

MAY 31 — Two weeks after Mt. St. Helens erupts in Washington State, the 31-game hitting streak of Ken Landreaux comes to an end during an 11–1 loss to the Orioles in Baltimore.

> *The 31-game streak is a Minnesota club record. The longest in franchise history is 33 games by Heinie Manush with the Senators in 1933. Landreaux's streak lasted from April 23 through May 29. He batted .392 with 49 hits in 135 at-bats.*

JUNE 3 — In the first round of the amateur draft, the Twins select catcher Jeff Reed from Joliet High School in Joliet, Illinois.

> *Reed made his major league debut in 1984, and played the first three seasons of a 17-year career in a Minnesota uniform. He played for six big league clubs, mainly as a back-up catcher. Other future major leaguers drafted and signed by the Twins in 1980 were Tim Teufel (second round), Jim Weaver (also in the second round), Scotti Madison (third round), Rod Booker (fourth round), Andre David (eighth round), Jim Eisenreich (16th round) and Rich Yett (25th round).*

JUNE 6 — Geoff Zahn pitches a one-hitter to defeat the Blue Jays 5–0 at Metropolitan Stadium. Zahn had a no-hitter in progress until John Mayberry singled with two out in the seventh inning.

On the same day, the Twins released Mike Marshall. Marshall filed a grievance, claiming he was released because of his activities with the player's union. The Twins countered that Marshall was let go for performance-based reasons. He had a 6.12 ERA in 32 1/3 innings, although he had allowed just one earned run in his previous 11 innings on the mound. Marshall won the grievance, and the Twins had to pay for the remainder of his contract, which ran though the end of the 1981 season.

JUNE 15   Jorge Orta of the Indians collects six hits in six at-bats off three Twins pitchers to lead his club to a 14–5 win in Cleveland.

JUNE 19   Jose Morales hits a grand slam off Dan Schatzeder in the third inning of a 5–1 win over the Tigers at Metropolitan Stadium.

JUNE 23   Jerry Koosman ties a club record by striking out 15 batters during a 4–1 win over the Royals at Metropolitan Stadium.

JUNE 30   John Castino collects four hits, including a home run, and drives in five runs during a 12–3 clubbing of the Royals in Kansas City.

JULY 3   Ken Landreaux ties an American League record with three triples during a 10–3 victory over the Rangers at Metropolitan Stadium. He tripled in the third inning off Steve Comer, the sixth against John Henry Johnson and in the eighth facing Jim Kern.

Landreaux is the only player in Twins history with a three-triple game.

JULY 10   Jose Morales drives in six runs with a pair of three-run homers to lead the Twins to a 12–4 triumph over the Mariners in Seattle. The Twins collected 20 hits during the contest.

JULY 18   The Twins lose 1–0 to the Red Sox in Boston on a walk-off homer by Dave Stapleton off Roger Erickson.

JULY 30   Jerry Koosman pitches all ten innings of a 2–1 win over the Yankees at Metropolitan Stadium and allows only three hits. John Castino drove in the winning run with a double.

AUGUST 7   Doug Corbett pitches 6 2/3 innings of shutout relief, but the Twins lose 4–2 to the Angels in 15 innings at Anaheim. The game ended on a two-run homer by Rod Carew off Albert Williams.

AUGUST 12   Glenn Adams hits a walk-off homer in the ninth inning to beat the Athletics 3–2 at Metropolitan Stadium.

AUGUST 24   Gene Mauch resigns as manager and is replaced by 46-year-old Johnny Goryl.

Mauch was optimistic about his club's chances in 1980 after an 82–80 record the previous season with one of the youngest rosters in the American League. The club was 10–10 in April, but collapsed with an 8–19 May. A nine-game losing streak in August convinced Mauch to resign even though he had a contract that ran through the end of the 1981 season. The Twins were 54–71 when Goryl took over. Goryl spent six years in the majors as a utility infielder and played for the Twins from 1962 through 1964. He spent several years as a manager in Minnesota's minor league system before serving as Mauch's third base coach for two years. The Twins were 23–13 under Goryl over the remainder of the 1980 season. He was hired on an interim basis but was given the job permanently after the strong finish. Goryl was fired early in the 1981 campaign, however, with an 11–25 record. Mauch went on to manage the Angels in 1981 and 1982 and again from 1985 through 1987. The 1987 season was his 26th as a major league manager. No one managed longer in the majors without taking a team to the World Series. Mauch came excruciating close three times. His 1964 Phillies blew a 6½-game lead in the last two weeks of the season. The Angels had a two-games-to-none lead over the Brewers in the best-of-five American League Championship Series, then lost three in a row. Mauch's 1986 Angels led the Red Sox three games to one in the best-of-seven ALCS and held a three-run lead in the ninth inning of game five, but wound up losing the series.

August 28 — The Twins beat the Blue Jays 7–5 in 15 innings in Toronto. Dave Edwards drove home the go-ahead run with a single.

September 9 — The Twins collect 22 hits on 19 singles and three doubles and routed the Brewers 15–2 at Metropolitan Stadium. The Twins scored six runs in the fourth inning and six more in the sixth.

September 18 — Gary Ward hits for the cycle, but the Twins lose 9–8 to the Brewers in the first game of a double-header at County Stadium. Ward doubled in the first inning, singled in the third and homered in the fifth off Mike Caldwell, then hit a triple off Reggie Cleveland in the seventh. The Twins fell behind 7–1 in the second inning and rallied to take an 8–7 advantage, only to lose when Milwaukee scored twice in the ninth on a two-out, walk-off homer by Gorman Thomas off Doug Corbett. The Brewers also won the second tilt 5–0.

The cycle came in Ward's 14th big league game and sixth start, and fourth game of 1980. He played his first ten contests in the majors in 1979 and spent most of 1980 in the minors before earning a September call-up. Ward was a starting outfielder for the Twins from 1981 through 1983. His son Daryle made his big league debut with the Astros in 1998 and spent more than a decade in the majors.

September 22 — Jerry Koosman (eight innings) and Doug Corbett (one inning) combine to beat the Rangers 1–0 at Metropolitan Stadium. Roy Smalley drove in the lone run with a single in the first inning.

October 3 — The Twins extend their winning streak to 12 games with a 5–3 decision over the Royals in Kansas City.

October 4 — The 12-game winning streak comes to a stunning conclusion as the Royals crush the Twins 17–1 in Kansas City.

The 12-game winning streak was the fourth longest in franchise history and the second longest since the move to Minnesota. The 1912 Senators won 17 in a row.

The 1991 Twins put together a 15-game streak on the way to winning the World Series. In 1933, the Senators won 13 in a row.

DECEMBER 2   A month after Ronald Reagan defeats Jimmy Carter in the presidential election, the Angels sign Geoff Zahn as a free agent.

Zahn spent four seasons in the Angels starting rotation and had an 18–8 record in 1982.

1981

Season in a Sentence

The Twins change managers in May, a strike wipes out the middle third of the season, the club finishes last in the majors in attendance, and closes Metropolitan Stadium.

Finish • Won • Lost • Pct • GB

*   41   68   .376   *

* Because of the player's strike, the season was split into two halves. During the first half, the Twins finished in seventh place with a 17–39 record, 18 games behind. During the second half, the Twins finished in fourth place with a 24–29 record, six games behind.

Managers

Johnny Goryl (11–25) and Billy Gardner (30–43)

Stats

Stats	Twins	AL	Rank
Batting Avg:	.240	.256	13
On-Base Pct:	.293	.321	13
Slugging Pct:	.338	.373	13
Home Runs:	47		13
Stolen Bases:	34		13
ERA:	3.98	3.66	13
Errors:	96		12
Runs Scored:	378		13
Runs Allowed:	486		13

Starting Line-up

Sal Butera, c
Danny Goodwin, 1b
Rob Wilfong, 2b
John Castino, 3b
Roy Smalley, ss
Gary Ward, lf
Mickey Hatcher, cf
Dave Engle, rf
Glenn Adams, dh
Hosken Powell, rf
Pete Mackanin, 2b-ss
Ron Jackson, 1b
Butch Wynegar, c

Pitchers

Pete Redfern, sp
Albert Williams, sp
Fernando Arroyo, sp
Jerry Koosman, sp-rp
Roger Erickson, sp
Brad Havens, sp
Doug Corbett, rp
Jack O'Connor, rp
Don Cooper, rp

Attendance

469,090 (14th in AL)

Club Leaders

Batting Avg:	John Castino	.268
On-Base Pct:	Gary Ward	.325
Slugging Pct:	John Castino	.396
Home Runs:	Roy Smalley	7
RBI:	Mickey Hatcher	37
Runs:	Gary Ward	42
Stolen Bases:	Hosken Powell	7
Wins:	Pete Redfern	9
Strikeouts:	Pete Redfern	77
ERA:	Fernando Arroyo	3.93
Saves:	Doug Corbett	17

MARCH 30   On the day that President Ronald Reagan is shot and seriously wounded by John Hinckley in Washington, the Twins trade Ken Landreaux to the Dodgers for Mickey Hatcher, Kelly Snider and Matt Reeves.

Hatcher was known more for his ability to keep a team loose as a clubhouse comic than his play on the field during his six seasons with the Twins. He batted a respectable .284 in 672 games as an outfielder in Minnesota, but a lack of power kept him from becoming a fixture in the starting line-up.

APRIL 9 The Twins open the season with a 5–1 loss to the Athletics before 42,658 at Metropolitan Stadium. Jerry Koosman was the starting and losing pitcher. The Twins began the year by losing all four games of the Series against the A's.

The Opening Day crowd represented nearly ten per cent of the Twins attendance total in 1981. The club drew only 469,090 fans in 59 home dates in the strike-shortened 1981 season. The Twins finished last in the majors in attendance for the second year in a row and were last in the American League for the fifth time in eight seasons beginning in 1974. After the season opener, the largest crowd at the Met all season was 18,702 for a double-header against the Angels on April 26.

APRIL 18 Roy Smalley hits a grand slam off Bill Travers in the third inning of a 6–4 victory over the Angels in Anaheim.

APRIL 29 The Twins beat the rain to salvage a 7–7 tie against the Mariners at Metropolitan Stadium. The Twins trailed 7–4 heading into the bottom of the eighth. With one out and rain falling heavily, Danny Goodwin doubled in two runs and scored on a drive by Dave Engle, who was out on the play at the plate trying to complete an inside-the-park homer. The umpires ordered the field to be covered and an hour later the game was called.

The tie game was the only one involving the Twins between 1974 and 1999. Under today's rules, the contest would have been suspended and completed at a later date.

MAY 12 After the Red Sox score a run in the top of the tenth inning, Mickey Hatcher and Roy Smalley hit back-to-back homers with two out in the bottom half for a 4–3 win at Metropolitan Stadium.

MAY 22 With the Twins holding a record of 11–25, Johnny Goryl is fired as manager and replaced by 53-year-old Billy Gardner.

Goryl led the Twins to a 23–13 record over the last 36 games of 1980 and succeeding Gene Mauch but couldn't survive the wretched start to the 1981 season. Gardner played in 1,034 games for five franchises as an infielder from 1954 through 1963. He was part of the transition from Washington to Minnesota, playing for the Senators in 1960 and the Twins in 1961. He managed in the minors for 12 years. He was a coach for the Twins when appointed as a manager in the majors for the first time. He remained on the job until June 1985, a period in which the Twins were undergoing a youth movement. Gardner's best record in Minnesota was 81–81 in 1984. Goryl never managed another big league club. He became a coach with the Indians in 1982 and has served the organization in a variety of roles for more than a quarter of a century.

May 23	The Twins play 15 innings, only to lose 1–0 to the Royals in Kansas City. Roger Erickson (9 1/3 innings), Doug Corbett (2 2/3 innings) and Dan Cooper (2 2/3 innings) did the pitching for the Twins. Willie Wilson drove in the winning run with a two-out single. Paul Splittorf (11 innings) and Renie Martin (four innings) combined on the Kansas City shutout.
June 8	The Twins edge the Brewers 1–0 at Metropolitan Stadium. Ron Jackson drove in the lone run with a seventh-inning single. Ron Erickson (7 2/3 innings) and Doug Corbett (1 2/3 innings) combined on the shutout.
	On the same day, the Twins selected third baseman Mike Sodders from Arizona State University in the first round of the amateur draft. Sodders never reached the major leagues, but the Twins more than made up for the mistake by choosing Frank Viola in round two. Other future major leaguers drafted and signed by the Twins in 1981 were Curt Wardle (third round), Dave Meier (fifth round) and Steve Lombardozzi (ninth round).
June 11	In the last game before the player's strike, the Twins lose 7–2 to the Tigers at Metropolitan Stadium. The loss dropped the Twins record to 17–39.
June 12	Major league baseball players begin a strike that lasts 50 days and wipes out nearly two months of the 1981 season. The strike reduced the Twins record to 110 games (including one tie).
July 31	Two days after Prince Charles marries Lady Diana Spencer, the players and owners hammer out an agreement to end the strike.
August 6	The owners vote to split the 1981 pennant race with the winners of the two halves of the season to compete in an extra round of playoffs for the division title.
August 10	In the first game following the strike, the Twins defeat the Athletics 6–2 before 15,414 on a Monday night at Metropolitan Stadium. The Twins scored all six of their runs in the fifth inning. The crowd was the eighth largest of the season at the Met in 1981, and nearly double the season average of 7,951 per game.
August 14	Jeff Burroughs hits three homers for the Mariners during a 13–3 win over the Twins in the second game of a double-header at Metropolitan Stadium. The Twins won the opener 6–1.
August 23	The Twins trade Ron Jackson to the Tigers for Tim Corcoran.
August 24	Playing in his first major league game, Kent Hrbek leads off the 12th inning with a home run to beat the Yankees 3–2 in New York. The blow was struck off George Frazier in Hrbek's fifth at-bat.
	Hrbek played his entire 14-year major league career with the Twins and became one of the most popular players in club history. An intense competitor, he was an integral part of the 1987 and 1991 world championship teams. Hrbek attended Kennedy High School in Bloomington and was drafted by the Twins in the 17th round in 1978. When he made his big league debut, Hrbek was 21 and hadn't

played a game professionally above Class A. Despite his inexperience, He became the Twins starting first baseman in 1982 and made the All-Star team. It proved to be the only All-Star appearance of his career, but he had several seasons worthy of the honor, including 1984 when he was runner-up in the MVP voting. Nagging injuries shortened his career, and he retired following the 1994 season. The Twins later retired his number 14. On the club's all-time lists, Hrbek ranks third in games (17,747), fifth in at-bats (6,192), second in home runs (293), second in RBIs (1,086), second in walks (838), third in doubles (312), fourth in runs (903), fourth in hits (1,749) and fourth in slugging percentage (.481).

AUGUST 27   The Twins score four runs on only one hit in the ninth inning to stun the Tigers 4–3 at Metropolitan Stadium. Three walks and an error produced the first run and a ground out brought home a runner from third to make the score 3–2. With two out, Pete Mackanin delivered a two-run, walk-off single for the victory. Mackanin entered the game as a pinch-hitter for Kent Hrbek in the third inning after Hrbek left the contest with an injury.

AUGUST 28   In the third at-bat of his first major league game, Tim Laudner hits a home run to help the Twins to a 6–0 win over the Tigers at Metropolitan Stadium. It was struck in the seventh inning off Dave Rozema.

AUGUST 29   In the second at-bat of his second major league game, Tim Laudner hits a home run to help the Twins to a 7–1 victory over the Tigers at Metropolitan Stadium. It was struck in the third inning off Dan Schatzeder.

At Class AA Orlando, Laudner won the Southern League MVP Award. He batted .284 with 42 homers in 130 games. After five big league plate appearances, Laudner had two homers and two singles for a batting average of .800. He didn't hit another home run until June 22, 1982, however. Laudner had 102 at-bats between his second and third homers. He played his entire nine-year career with the Twins and clubbed 77 home runs in 2,038 at-bats.

AUGUST 30   The Twins trade Jerry Koosman to the White Sox for Ivan Mesa, Randy Johnson and Ronnie Perry.

Koosman won 36 games for the Twins in 1979 and 1980, but slumped to 3–9 in 1981 before the trade to Chicago. He pitched three more seasons as a starter with earned run averages around the league average for the White Sox and Phillies. The Twins received next to nothing in exchange for Koosman. The Randy Johnson acquired in the trade was not the famous pitcher, but a designated hitter who played only 101 games in the majors.

SEPTEMBER 7   Sal Butera ties a major league record for catchers with three assists in an inning during a 4–0 win over the Blue Jays at Metropolitan Stadium. It happened in the third. The first and third outs were recorded when Butera allowed a third strike to elude him, and he threw out the runner at first base. The second out occurred when he threw out Jesse Barfield trying to steal second base.

SEPTEMBER 8   A walk-off double by Rob Wilfong in the ninth inning downs the Blue Jays 1–0 at Metropolitan Stadium. Brad Havens pitched the shutout.

SEPTEMBER 13 — Trailing 6–2, the Twins score a run in the eighth inning and four in the ninth to defeat the White Sox 7–6 at Metropolitan Stadium. Gary Ward tripled in the first run of the ninth and scored on a single with two out to narrow the gap to 6–5. With two out and runners on first and second, Hosken Powell drew a walk to load the bases and Kent Hrbek drove in two with a double for the improbable victory.

After compiling a 17–39 record during the first half of the season, the Twins were in contention for a postseason berth with 15 games remaining in the second half. On September 18, the club was 19–19 and in second place, 3½ games behind the first-place Royals. The Twins lost ten of the final 15 games.

SEPTEMBER 20 — In his first major league plate appearance, Gary Gaetti hits a home run off Charlie Hough in the second inning of a 4–3 loss to the Rangers in Arlington. Gaetti was the third Twin in less than a month to homer in his first game, following Kent Hrbek (August 24) and Tim Laudner (August 28).

Gaetti was the Twins starting third baseman until 1990. His best years were from 1986 through 1988, when he hit 93 homers and drove in 297 runs. Gaetti slumped badly over the next two seasons, however, and many blamed a conversion to Christianity for the downslide as he seemed to lack the aggressiveness he displayed earlier. At the end of the 1990 season, Gaetti opted to sign with the Angels as a free agent. From 1991 through the end of his career in 2000, he played for five different clubs. During his 20 seasons in the majors, Gaetti struck 360 home runs. Through the 2009 season, he ranks sixth in Twins history in home runs (201) and fifth in RBIs (758).

SEPTEMBER 30 — The Twins play their last game at Metropolitan Stadium and lose 5–2 to the Royals before 15,900. Roy Smalley recorded the last out by popping up a Larry Gura pitch to shortstop U. L. Washington. After the game ended, Bill Schnobrick won home plate in a fan drawing.

OCTOBER 2 — The roof at the Metrodome is inflated.

OCTOBER 4 — In the last game of the season, the Twins lead 12–5 before allowing four runs in the eighth inning and four more in the ninth to lose 13–12 to the White Sox in Chicago.

NOVEMBER 19 — A heavy wet snow of ten inches causes the roof at the Metrodome to partially deflate. A rip in the roof was created when a bolt snapped and a sharp piece of steel tore through the fabric. The rip was repaired, and the roof was re-inflated four days later.

DECEMBER 20 — The Vikings play at Metropolitan Stadium for the last time and lose 10–6 to the Kansas City Chiefs.

For three years, Metropolitan Stadium sat unused and was heavily damaged by vandalism. Demolition began on January 28, 1985, and took four months. For years, the site sat vacant, although the nearby Met Center continued as an entertainment and sports venue, chiefly as the home of the Minnesota North Stars of the National Hockey League. The Mall of America, which opened in 1992, now stands on the former site of Metropolitan Stadium.

1982

Season in a Sentence
The Twins open the Metrodome, field the youngest team in the majors, lose a club-record 102 games, and finish last in the AL in attendance for the sixth time in nine years.

Finish • Won • Lost • Pct • GB
Seventh   60   102   .370   33.0

Manager
Billy Gardner

Stats   Twins • AL • Rank
Stat	Twins	AL	Rank
Batting Avg:	.257	.264	10
On-Base Pct:	.316	.328	10
Slugging Pct:	.396	.402	9
Home Runs:	148		7
Stolen Bases:	38		14
ERA:	4.77		14
Errors:	108		2 (tie)
Runs Scored:	657		11
Runs Allowed:	819		13

Starting Line-up
Tim Laudner, c
Kent Hrbek, 1b
John Castino, 2b
Gary Gaetti, 3b
Ron Washington, ss-2b
Gary Ward, lf
Bobby Mitchell, cf
Tom Brunansky, rf
Randy Johnson, dh
Lenny Faedo, ss
Mickey Hatcher, lf-rf-dh

Pitchers
Bobby Castillo, sp
Brad Havens, sp
Albert Williams, sp
Jack O'Connor, sp
Frank Viola, sp
Ron Davis, rp
Terry Felton, sp
Pete Redfern, rp-sp

Attendance
921,186 (14th in AL)

Club Leaders
Batting Avg:	Kent Hrbek	.301
On-Base Pct:	Tom Brunansky	.377
Slugging Pct:	Gary Ward	.519
Home Runs:	Gary Ward	28
RBI:	Kent Hrbek	92
Runs:	Gary Ward	85
Stolen Bases:	Gary Ward	13
Wins:	Bobby Castillo	13
Strikeouts:	Brad Havens	129
ERA:	Bobby Castillo	3.66
Saves:	Ron Davis	22

JANUARY 12   In the first round of the winter amateur draft, the Twins select outfielder Kirby Puckett from Triton Junior College in Illinois. After two full seasons and part of a third in the minors, Puckett made his debut with the Twins on May 8, 1984.

APRIL 3   The Twins play at the Metrodome for the first time and beat the Phillies 5–0 in an exhibition game. Kent Hrbek hit two home runs. The two clubs met again the following day, and the Twins lost 11–8.

APRIL 6   The Twins play their first regular season game at the Metrodome and lose 11–7 to the Mariners before 52,279. The first batter was Julio Cruz, who was struck out by Pete Redfern. Jim Eisenreich, in his major league debut, was the first Minnesota hitter and grounded out to shortstop facing Floyd Bannister. With two out in the first, Dave Engle homered to give the Twins a 1–0 lead. Gary Gaetti later hit two home runs, and Jim Maier and Al Cowens homered for Seattle. Gaetti also tripled and singled and drove in four runs.

The stadium is officially known as the Hubert H. Humphrey Metrodome. Among those in the Opening Night crowd was Muriel Humphrey Brown, the widow of Hubert Humphrey, who died in 1978. Pearl Bailey sang the

National Anthem. There were a few glitches, as overflowing toilets flooded corridors. Outside of the dome, it was a frigid 28 degrees.

APRIL 7   The Twins win their first game at the Metrodome in their second try with a 7–5 decision over the Mariners before 5,213. Randy Johnson collected two doubles and a single in his debut with the Twins.

The crowd at the second game was more typical of those at the Metrodome in 1982. Despite the attraction of a new ballpark, the Twins drew 921,186 and were the only big league club with an attendance figure under one million. It was the third year in a row in which Minnesota was last in the majors in attendance and the sixth time in nine seasons from 1974 through 1982 in which the franchise finished last in the AL in the category. A terrible start (16–54), the lowest average salary ($90,000) and the highest average ticket prices in baseball ($7.50) contributed to the problem in attracting fans.

APRIL 10   The Twins trade Roy Smalley to the Yankees for Ron Davis, Greg Gagne and Paul Boris.

Injuries had reduced Smalley's range at shortstop. He would return to play for the Twins from 1985 through 1987 primarily as a designated hitter. Gagne was the club's starting shortstop from 1985 through 1992. Davis was an inconsistent closer for the Twins from 1982 until 1985.

APRIL 19   The Twins score five runs in the ninth inning on six hits and beat the Athletics 5–2 in Oakland. Entering the ninth, Rick Langford had retired 24 of the 25 batters to face him, and 18 in a row, allowing only a double to Butch Wynegar leading off the third. In the ninth, Langford loaded the bases on two singles and a walk, but still had a 2–0 lead with two out when Kent Hrbek hit a three-run double. The Twins later added two insurance runs.

The Twins ended April with a 9–13 record. They followed with a horrendous May in which the club was 3–26. Things didn't get much better in early June. The Twins lost 41 of 48 games from May 1 through June 22 to fall to 16–54. It looked for a while like the Twins might threaten the 1962 New York Mets record of 120 losses in a season, but they managed a 44–48 record after June 22. Part of the problem was an extreme youth movement. The Twins fielded the youngest roster in club history in 1982. There were several games in September in which the Twins had nine rookies in the starting line-up. Among the youngsters playing as regulars were Tom Brunansky (age 21), Kent Hrbek (22), Brad Havens (22), Frank Viola (22), Lenny Faedo (22), Gary Gaetti (23), Randy Johnson (23), Jack O'Connor (24), Tim Laudner (24) and Terry Felton (24).

MAY 4   Twins rookie outfielder Jim Eisenreich is forced to remove himself from a 5–3 loss to the Red Sox when he is taunted mercilessly by bleacher fans in Boston and his violent twitching becomes uncontrollable.

A native of St. Cloud, Minnesota, Eisenreich was hitting .310 in 24 games after making the jump from Class A to the majors in one year. He was hospitalized on May 9 and later diagnosed with Tourette's Syndrome. He shook, twitched and gave off other signs of discomfort during games and had been mocked and teased since childhood. Doctors had declared him hyperactive before the correct diagnosis was found. Tourette's Syndrome is a genetic disorder that often causes rapid physical and verbal actions. Eisenreich made several attempts at a comeback with the Twins before retiring in 1984. With the help of medication, he returned to the majors in 1987 and played 12 more seasons in the big leagues with the Royals (1987–92), Phillies (1993–96), Marlins (1997–98) and Dodgers (1998). He played in the 1993 World Series with Philadelphia and won legions of fans for overcoming adversity.

May 10 — Gary Ward hits a grand slam off Mike Torrez in the fourth inning of a 9–5 loss to the Red Sox at the Metrodome. It was the first grand slam at the ballpark.

May 12 — The Twins send Doug Corbett and Rob Wilfong to the Angels for Tom Brunansky, Mike Walters and $400,000. On the same day, the Twins dealt Butch Wynegar and Roger Erickson to the Yankees for Pete Filson, Larry Milbourne, John Pacella and cash.

The Twins pulled off a positive deal with the Angels, as Corbett struggled for most of his five seasons in a California uniform and Wilfong was an infield reserve. Brunansky hit at least 20 homers for the Twins for six consecutive seasons from 1982 thorough 1987 with highs of 32 in both 1984 and 1987. The transaction with the Yankees helped neither team. Wynegar looked like the next Johnny Bench when he made the All-Star team as a 20-year-old rookie in 1976 but was never an All-Star again, though he remained a serviceable catcher during the team's stretch of mediocre-to-poor seasons. Erickson had excelled as a rookie with a 14–13 record in 1978 but was 21–40 over the rest of his career. None of the trio acquired from New York helped the Twins extract themselves from the basement in the AL West.

May 14 — The Twins lose a fight-filled game won by the Tigers 4–2 in 11 innings in Detroit. Five were ejected. The first fight occurred in the fourth when Chet Lemon charged Twins pitcher Pete Redfern after being hit with a pitch. It started a benches-clearing brawl that lasted five minutes. Lemon was ejected. In the 11th, Minnesota reliever Ron Davis brushed back Enos Cabell. The dugouts cleared again, and after the dust settled, Davis, Cabell, Richie Hebner of the Tigers and Jesus Vega of the Twins were ejected. Detroit pitcher Dave Rozema suffered a knee injury during the brawl that ended his season. Moments after play resumed, Kirk Gibson hit a two-run, walk-off homer off Terry Felton. Kent Hrbek went hitless in five at-bats, ending his hitting streak at 23 games.

May 29 — The Twins pull off a triple play that begins with a strikeout in the second inning of a 6–4 loss at the Metrodome. With New York runners Graig Nettles on first base and Bobby Murcer on second, Roy Smalley struck out on a 3–2 pitch. Murcer attempted to steal third, but the throw by Minnesota catcher Sal Butera beat him to the bag. Murcer attempted to retreat to second, only to find Nettles there. Third baseman Gary Gaetti tagged Murcer, and then threw to first baseman Kent Hrbek, who tagged out Nettles trying to make it back to first.

June 2 — The Twins extend their losing streak to 14 games by dropping a 4–2 decision to the Indians in Cleveland.

JUNE 4   The Twins break their 14-game losing streak by defeating the Orioles 6–0 at the Metrodome. Brad Havens (5 2/3 innings) and Terry Felton (3 1/3 innings) combined on the shutout.

The save was a rare moment of glory in Felton's career. Entering the 1982 season, he had pitched in seven big leagues games over three seasons and was 0–3 with an 8.57 ERA in 21 innings. During the 1982 season he was 0–13 to set records for the most losses without a victory in a season and the most consecutive defeats at the start of a career. Russ Miller of the 1928 Phillies and Steve Gerkin of the 1945 Philadelphia Athletics were both 0–12. The previous record for most losses at the start of a career was 13 by Guy Morton with the 1914 Indians. Morton recovered, however, and finished his career with 98 wins and 86 losses. Felton had no such luck. He didn't pitch in the majors after 1982 and finished his career with an 0–16 record and an earned run average of 5.53. Felton was 0–7 in ten starts and 0–9 in 45 relief appearances. At least he avoided the record for most consecutive losses. That's held by Anthony Young, who lost 27 in a row with the Mets in 1992 and 1993.

JUNE 7   Ron Washington, Tom Brunansky and Kent Hrbek hit consecutive homers in the eighth, but the Twins lose 5–4 to the Royals in ten innings at the Metrodome.

On the same day, the Twins selected Bryan Oelkers from Wichita State University in the amateur draft. He pitched only ten games for the club in 1983 and was 0–5 with an 8.65 ERA in 34 1/3 innings. Oelkers's only distinction is that he was the first player born in Spain to play the majors. Other future big leaguers drafted by the Twins in June 1982 and later signed were Allan Anderson (second round), Mark Davidson (11th round), Frank Eufemia (18th round) and Marty Pevey (19th round).

JUNE 18   With the Rangers leading 3–2 over the Twins at the Metrodome, two out, and no one on base in the 10th, Texas manager Don Zimmer orders an intentional walk to Kent Hrbek, placing the potential tying run on base. Jesus Vega followed Hrbek to the plate and grounded out to end the game.

At the time, Hrbek was hitting .336 with 15 homers in 55 games. He finished his rookie season with a .301 average and 23 home runs in 140 contests.

JUNE 23   Trailing 3–0, the Twins explode for six runs in the ninth inning to beat the White Sox 6–3 in Chicago. Jesus Vega drove in the first run with a single and Gary Gaetti tied the score with a two-run single. Tim Laudner snapped the deadlock by clubbing a three-run homer.

JULY 4   Gary Gaetti's walk-off homer in the ninth inning beats the Blue Jays 4–3 at the Metrodome.

JULY 15   The Tigers score 11 runs in the first inning off Jack O'Connor and John Pacella and squash the Twins 18–2 at the Metrodome.

JULY 19   Tom Brunansky hits an inside-the-park grand slam off Jerry Augustine in the third inning of a 6–4 triumph over the Brewers at the Metrodome. Center fielder Gorman Thomas just missed a diving catch of Brunansky's drive, and the ball rolled all the way to the wall.

1980s

The inside-the-park grand slam is the only one in Twins history.

July 20 — A fight mars a 5–3 win over the Brewers at the Metrodome. In the fifth inning, Kent Hrbek barreled into Brewers second baseman Jim Gantner on a play at second. A bench-clearing ten-minute scuffle ensued in the sixth after Robin Yount ran into Twins shortstop Lenny Faedo trying to break up a double play. Hrbek and Milwaukee's Bob McClure were ejected for throwing punches.

July 26 — Gary Gaetti hits a grand slam off Floyd Bannister in the first inning of a 10–4 win over the Mariners in Seattle.

August 2 — Trailing 6–0, the Twins score three runs in the seventh inning, three in the eight and three in the ninth to down the Angels 9–7 in Anaheim. The score was 7–6 in favor of California with one out in the ninth when Ron Washington put Minnesota ahead with a two-run single.

August 3 — Brad Havens gives up three home runs to Doug DeCinces but is the winning pitcher in a 5–4 decision over the Angels in Anaheim.

August 18 — The Twins pull out a thrilling 6–5 decision over the Orioles in ten innings at the Metrodome. With two out in the ninth, Dave Engle hit a two-run double to tie the score 4–4. After Baltimore plated a run in the top of the tenth, the Twins rallied for two tallies in their half for the victory. Kent Hrbek doubled in the first run and crossed the plate on a two-out single from Mickey Hatcher.

August 21 — The Vikings play their first exhibition game at the Metrodome and beat the Seattle Seahawks 7–3.

August 28 — The Twins rout the Indians 10–0 at the Metrodome. Jack O'Connor pitched the shutout.

September 10 — In Arlington, the Twins score all five of their runs in a 5–0 win over the Rangers in the seventh inning.

September 11 — The University of Minnesota football team plays their first game at the Metrodome and defeats Ohio University 57–3.

The Golden Gophers had played on campus at Memorial Stadium since 1924. By the 1970s, the stadium was in need of $10 million in repairs, and rather than upgrade it, the regents decided to move into the Metrodome. The Golden Gophers began playing at TCF Bank Stadium in 2009.

September 12 — The Vikings play their first regular season game at the Metrodome, and defeat the Tampa Bay Buccaneers 17–10.

September 13 — Tom Brunansky hits a two-run homer in the fourth inning to account for both runs of a 2–0 win over the Rangers at the Metrodome. Albert Williams (7 1/3 innings) and Ron Davis (1 2/3 innings) combined on the shutout.

Williams, who pitched for the Twins from 1980 through 1984, had an unusual path to the majors. A native of Nicaragua, he spent 16 months in 1977 and 1978 with guerrilla forces engaged in jungle fighting against the forces of Anastacio Somoza.

SEPTEMBER 19   Gary Gaetti hits a grand slam off Mike Armstrong in the fifth inning of a 9–4 win over the Royals at the Metrodome.

SEPTEMBER 28   Randy Bush's single leading off the ninth is the only Twins hit off Jim Clancy in a 3–0 loss to the Blue Jays in the first game of a double-header at Exhibition Stadium. Clancy had a perfect game in progress after retiring the first 24 batters to face him when Bush stepped to the plate. Toronto also won the second tilt 4–3 in ten innings.

SEPTEMBER 30   The Twins record their 100th loss of the season by dropping a 4–3 decision to the Blue Jays in Toronto.

OCTOBER 2   The Twins and the University of Minnesota football team play at the Metrodome on the same day. In the afternoon, the Twins lost 5–3 to the White Sox before only 3,888. In the evening, Minnesota lost 42–24 to Illinois.

DECEMBER 30   A crane clearing snow from the exterior of the Metrodome rips a hole in the roof, causing it to collapse.

The Metrodome

The Hubert H. Humphrey Metrodome opened in April 1982 to replace Metropolitan Stadium, which had served the Twins and Vikings since 1961. The stadium was part of a trend that began in the 1960s as cities built multi-purpose stadiums, mostly in downtown areas. In 1980 and 1981, 18 of the 26 Major League Baseball teams shared a stadium with a National Football League or Canadian Football League team. (The only three out of the 30 MLB clubs who shared a stadium with an NFL or CFL in 2010 were the Athletics, Blue Jays and Marlins.)

The Metrodome was only the third domed stadium in baseball following the Houston Astrodome that opened in 1965, and the Kingdome in Seattle (1977). Olympic Stadium, which opened in Montreal in 1977, was intended to be a retractable domed stadium, but by 1982 the roof wasn't yet fully operational. The Metrodome roof is an air-supported fiberglass fabric held in place by steel cables. The air pressure is generated by 20 90-horsepower fans. The roof was dark enough to permit outfielders to track a fly ball but translucent enough so that a passing cloud could be traced on the field. The exterior roof is coated with Teflon, giving the building a white glow. The original playing dimensions in the 54,711-seat Metrodome were 343 feet to left field, 408 feet to center and 327 to right. The dome, as its peak, is 186 feet above the Astroturf field.

The Metrodome cost roughly $68 million to build and came in $2 million under budget. Many believed the two million should have been spent on some architectural embellishments to the largely utilitarian structure. One stadium official said that all the facility was designed to do was "get fans in, let 'em see a game, and let 'em go home." Unimpressed writers have nicknamed it The Humpty-Dump, Homerdome, Thunderdome, Sweat Box, and Metrodish.

Although artificial and sterile, the Metrodome was filled with quirky nuances for baseball. The roof was low enough that fly balls could strike it. Dave Kingman and Craig Koskie both hit towering flies into the roof that disappeared into drainage holes and never came down. The grayish-white inner roof made it difficult to track balls hit into the air, particularly for first-time visitors. Glare from the lights compounded the difficulty. The height of the outfield fences varied. The park's signature feature was a seven-foot-high padded wall topped by a 16-foot piece of stretched canvas dubbed "The Hefty Bag." Balls hitting the hard padding shot back toward the infield, but balls hitting the Bag dropped straight to the ground. The bag covered some 7,600 retractable seats used for football.

For many years, the seven-foot padded left field wall was topped by a six-foot section of Plexiglas. The seven-foot center field fence was made from a thin piece of canvas that gave on impact. Another oddity was an irregular curve behind home plate that forced balls to bounce off the backstop toward first base.

During the early years of operation, the field was covered with a SuperTurf, which caused balls to bounce much higher than on other artificial surfaces. High pop ups that fell to the turf could bounce as much as 40 feet into the air, turning singles into extra-base hits. It wasn't uncommon for middle infielders to track down balls that rolled to the wall after they bounded over the heads of outfielders. Both baseball and football players complained that the surface was too hard. It was upgraded to Astroturf in 1987 and FieldTurf in 2004.

The air pressure that supported the roof affected fans entering the exiting the stadium as well. When entering through the revolving doors a quick rush of air made it feel like you were walking against the wind. When leaving the air rush practically vaulted you through the doors and onto the stadium plaza.

Then there was the noise level that reverberated through the stadium when full. The screams of fans waving homer-hankies in the 1987 World Series were measured at 118 decibels, about the same as a jet airplane on take-off. Counting the postseason, the Twins were 62–25 at home and 31–56 on the road that year.

The versatile Metrodome is the only building to host baseball's All-Star Game (1985), a World Series (1987 and 1991), a Super Bowl (1992) and a Final Four (1992) and 2001). But the multi-functions had a price as it failed to serve any one sport very well. Beginning in the 1990s, the multi-purpose stadiums were being phased out across North America and were replaced by separate facilities for baseball and football. The Twins, Vikings and the University of Minnesota each wanted stadiums of their own. The University of Minnesota was the first to leave as TCF Bank Stadium opened on campus in the fall of 2009.

By 2009, the Twins were playing in their 28th season at the Metrodome, but it was the seventh-oldest ballpark in the majors behind Fenway Park in Boston (1912), Wrigley Field in Chicago (1914), Dodger Stadium in Los Angeles (1962), Angel Stadium in Anaheim (1966), McAfee Coliseum in Oakland (1968) and Kauffman Stadium in Kansas City (1973). A little more than a decade after it opened, the Metrodome became an anachronism and was made obsolete by the building of all-grass, baseball-only parks with luxury suites and nostalgic, "retro" features, beginning with Camden Yards in Baltimore in 1992. In 2010, the Twins began playing at Target Field. The Vikings lease at the Metrodome expires in 2011 and their situation has yet to be fully resolved as this book went to press.

1983

Season in a Sentence
With nowhere to go but up, the Twins win 70 games, ten more than the previous season.

Finish • Won • Lost • Pct • GB
Fifth (tie)   70   92   .432   29.0

Manager
Billy Gardner

Stats   Twins • AL • Rank
Stat	Twins	AL	Rank
Batting Avg:	.261	.266	11
On-Base Pct:	.319	.328	12
Slugging Pct:	.401	.401	8
Home Runs:	141		8
Stolen Bases:	44		12
ERA:	4.66		14
Errors:	121		5 (tie)
Runs Scored:	789		9
Runs Allowed:	822		14

Starting Line-up
Dave Engle, c
Kent Hrbek, 1b
John Castino, 2b
Gary Gaetti, 3b
Ron Washington, ss
Gary Ward, lf
Darrell Brown, cf
Tom Brunansky, rf
Randy Bush, dh
Mickey Hatcher, rf-dh

Pitchers
Ken Schrom, sp
Albert Williams, sp
Frank Viola, sp
Bobby Castillo, sp
Brad Havens, sp
Ron Davis, rp
Rick Lysander, rp
Pete Filson, rp-sp
Jack O'Connor, rp
Len Whitehouse, rp

Attendance
858,939 (12th in AL)

Club Leaders
Batting Avg:	Kent Hrbek	.297
On-Base Pct:	Kent Hrbek	.366
Slugging Pct:	Kent Hrbek	.489
Home Runs:	Tom Brunansky	28
RBI:	Gary Ward	88
Runs:	John Castino	83
Stolen Bases:	Ron Washington	10
Wins:	Ken Schrom	15
Strikeouts:	Frank Viola	127
ERA:	Ken Schrom	3.71
Saves:	Ron Davis	30

APRIL 5   The Twins open the season with an 11–3 loss to the Tigers before 30,961 at the Metrodome. Starting pitcher Brad Havens allowed eight runs in 1 1/3 innings.

Counted on to be the number one starter in 1983, Havens was 5–8 with a horrendous 8.18 ERA in 80 1/3 innings.

APRIL 14   The Twins-Angels game at the Metrodome is postponed. The Angels couldn't reach Minneapolis because the airport was closed due to a snowstorm. Later in the evening, a chuck of ice ripped a hole in the roof of the Metrodome, causing it to deflate.

The Twins began their foray into pay television in 1983 by broadcasting some games over Spectrum TV.

APRIL 20   The Twins clobber the Mariners 11–2 at the Metrodome. Mickey Hatcher led off the first inning with a double and injured his leg. Hatcher was replaced by Darrell Brown, who drove in three runs in his debut with the Twins.

APRIL 30   The Twins score four runs in the ninth inning to defeat the Brewers 9–7 at the Metrodome. John Castino drove in the first run with a double and later scored on a sacrifice fly by Kent Hrbek. With two out, Tom Brunansky ended the game with a two-run homer.

1980s

MAY 16 Trailing 7–0, the Twins hit four homers in the ninth inning but wind up losing 7–6 at the Metrodome. Dave Engle led off with a pinch-hit homer and Bobby Mitchell followed with another home run. With two out, Gary Gaetti clubbed a two-run homer to make the score 7–4. Tom Brunansky walked, and Mickey Hatcher, pinch-hitting for Randy Bush, smacked the fourth Minnesota homer of the inning to pull the Twins with in a run. Lenny Faedo singled to keep the rally alive, but Engle struck out to end the game.

> *Engle started his career in the minors as a third baseman in 1978, and became an outfielder by the time he made his major league debut in 1981. During the 1983–84 off-season, Engle went to the Florida Instructional League for a conversion to catcher. He became the Twins starting catcher in 1984, and hit .305 with eight homers in 120 games.*

MAY 18 The Twins collect 20 hits and wallop the Athletics 16–5 at the Metrodome.

MAY 22 Ron Washington leads off the 13th inning with a home run to defeat the Red Sox 4–3 in Boston.

MAY 23 The Twins hit five home runs during a 12–4 triumph over the Orioles in Baltimore. Tom Brunansky hit two homers and drove in five runs. Gary Ward also struck for two home runs in addition to a double and a single. Dave Engle accounted for the fifth Minnesota homer.

JUNE 6 With the first overall pick in the amateur draft, the Twins select pitcher Tim Belcher from Mount Vernon Nazarene University.

> *The Twins failed to sign Belcher. He went back into the draft, was selected by the Yankees in 1984, and went on to play 14 seasons in the majors from 1987 through 2000. He compiled a record of 146–140. The Twins also failed to sign second rounder choice Bill Swift, who was 94–78 during a 12-year career. In the first round of the secondary phase, the Twins drafted outfielder Oddibe McDowell. The tight-fisted Minnesota front office of Calvin Griffith couldn't come to terms with him either. McDowell played seven seasons in the majors. None of the players drafted and signed by the Twins in 1983 played a single game in the big leagues. The trend continued in the January 1984 draft when the Twins selected Mark Grace but failed to sign him to a contract. Grace won the 1988 Rookie of the Year Award with the Cubs and remained in the majors until 2003.*

JULY 3 Ron Washington's walk-off single in the ninth inning downs the White Sox 4–3 at the Metrodome.

JULY 25 The Twins hit five home runs during a 17–3 rout of the Brewers at the Metrodome. Tom Brunansky led the way with two homers. Gary Ward, Kent Hrbek and Ron Washington also connected.

JULY 27 Gary Gaetti hits a home run, a triple and a double during a 13–9 loss to the Brewers at the Metrodome.

AUGUST 1 Rick Lysander allows 11 hits, walks three, and throws four wild pitches but manages a shutout to defeat the Angels 7–0 in the second game of a double-header at the Metrodome. California left 11 men on base. The Twins lost the opener 12–6.

> *The game was the 46th of Lysander's career, but his first starting assignment. It was the first of only five starts in 137 games in the majors. He made three more starts in 1983 and another one in 1985, and failed to last longer than 4 1/3 innings in any of them. In his four starts after the shutout, he combined to allow 17 earned runs in 12 1/3 innings, an ERA of 12.41, and lost all four of them. His final career record was 9–17.*

AUGUST 8   During a 4–2 win over the Angels in Anaheim, the Twins pull off a triple play and hit two homers in a span of three pitches. In the bottom of the fourth inning with Angels runners on first and second, Ron Jackson lined a Ken Schrom pitch into a triple play, which went from third baseman Gary Gaetti to second baseman John Castino to first baseman Kent Hrbek. On the first two pitches in the top of the fifth, Gaetti and Tom Brunansky homered off Tommy John.

> *Schrom was a pleasant surprise in 1983. Entering the season, he was 28 years old and had a 5.44 ERA in 46 1/3 major league innings. For the Twins in 1983, Schrom had a 15–8 record and an earned run average of 3.71 in 196 1/3 innings. His success didn't last long, unfortunately, as he was 14–23 in 1984 and 1985 before being traded to the Indians.*

AUGUST 17   A seven-run eruption in the second inning is enough to defeat the Mariners 7–4 in Seattle.

SEPTEMBER 1   Tom Brunansky drives in six runs during an 11–0 drubbing of the Red Sox in the first game of a double-header against the Red Sox at Fenway Park. Brunansky hit a two-run homer off Dennis Eckersley in the first inning and a grand slam against Luis Aponte in the seventh. Boston won the second contests 9–3.

SEPTEMBER 2   Frank Viola gives up a home run in the ninth inning to Ken Singleton to lose 1–0 to the Orioles at the Metrodome.

SEPTEMBER 9   Kent Hrbek hits a walk-off homer in the tenth inning to defeat the Royals 7–6 at the Metrodome.

> *Hrbek hit .297 with 41 doubles and 16 homers in 1983.*

SEPTEMBER 14   A walk-off single by Tim Teufel in the ninth inning beats the White Sox 1–0 at the Metrodome. Albert Williams (8 1/3 innings) and Ron Davis (two-thirds of an inning) combined on the shutout.

SEPTEMBER 16   Playing in only his tenth big league game, Tim Teufel stars in an 11–4 victory over the Blue Jays at the Metrodome. In five plate appearances, Teufel homered leading off the first inning, singled in the second, tripled in the fourth, singled again in the sixth, and clubbed his second home run in the eighth. He tied a club record by scoring five runs. The homers were the first two of Teufel's career. The triple was also his first.

Teufel collected 22 hits in his first 50 major league at-bats for an average of .440. He was the Twins starting second baseman in 1984 and 1985 before being dealt to the Mets.

SEPTEMBER 17   In a bad day at the Metrodome, the Twins drop a 13–3 decision to the Blue Jays in the afternoon, and the University of Minnesota is trounced 84–13 by Nebraska in the evening.

The Twins game began at 11:00 a.m. to allow sufficient time for the conversion to football. The Twins played many games that started on a Saturday morning during the next two decades on days in which a college football game was held at the Metrodome in the evening.

OCTOBER 29   Pete Redfern, who pitched for the Twins from 1976 through 1982, is paralyzed in a diving accident at Balboa Island off the Southern California coast. Redfern dove off of a wall not realizing the water was less than two feet deep.

DECEMBER 7   The Twins trade Gary Ward and Sam Sorce to the Rangers for Mike Smithson and John Butcher.

Ward produced two solid seasons in 1982 and '83, but the Twins desperately needed pitching and decided to sacrifice the budding star. At six-foot-eight, Smithson was the tallest player in the majors during the mid-1980s, and he proved a good addition to the team, winning 15 games for the Twins in both 1984 and 1985. Butcher gave the Twins a competent starting pitcher for two years, winning 13 in 1984 with a 3.44 ERA.

1984

Season in a Sentence

Calvin Griffith sells the club, the Twins hold a 5½ game lead on August 22, and draw over 1.5 million for the first time before finishing at .500, just three games out of first.

Finish • Won • Lost • Pct • GB

Second (tie) 81 81 .500 3.0

Manager

Billy Gardner

Stats   Twins • AL • Rank

Batting Avg:	.265	.264	6
On-Base Pct:	.318	.326	9
Slugging Pct:	.385	.398	9
Home Runs:	114		13
Stolen Bases:	39		13
ERA:	3.85	3.99	4
Errors:	120		1
Runs Scored:	673		11
Runs Allowed:	675		3

Starting Line-up

Dave Engle, c
Kent Hrbek, 1b
Tim Teufel, 2b
Gary Gaetti, 3b
Houston Jiminez, ss
Mickey Hatcher, lf
Kirby Puckett, cf
Tom Brunansky, rf
Randy Bush, dh
Tim Laudner, c
Darrell Brown, cf-lf

Pitchers

Frank Viola, sp
Mike Smithson, sp
John Butcher, sp
Ken Schrom, sp
Ed Hodge, sp-rp
Ron Davis, rp
Pete Filson, rp

Attendance

1,598,692 (tenth in AL)

Club Leaders

Batting Avg:	Kent Hrbek	.311
On-Base Pct:	Kent Hrbek	.383
Slugging Pct:	Kent Hrbek	.522
Home Runs:	Tom Brunansky	32
RBI:	Kent Hrbek	107
Runs:	Kent Hrbek	80
Stolen Bases:	Kirby Puckett	14
Wins:	Frank Viola	18
Strikeouts:	Frank Viola	149
ERA:	Frank Viola	3.21
Saves:	Ron Davis	29

JANUARY 10   Harmon Killebrew is elected to the Hall of Fame.

APRIL 3   The Twins lose 8–1 to the Tigers before an Opening Night crowd of 34,381 at the Metrodome. Albert Williams was the starting and losing pitcher.

> *Harmon Killebrew and Ted Robinson began announcing Twins games on television in 1984. Killebrew remained with the club until 1988 and Robinson until 1989. Robinson later announced events at the Winter Olympics for CBS in 1998 and on NBC in 2002 and 2006, and the Summer Olympics in 2008. He has also anchored NBC's Wimbledon coverage for many years.*

APRIL 7   The Twins rout the Orioles 13–4 at the Metrodome. The Twins had 16 hits in the contests, with eight different players collecting exactly two of them.

APRIL 14   Ron Washington hits a walk-off homer in the tenth inning to defeat the Mariners 4–3 at the Metrodome.

APRIL 16 — The Twins erupt for eight runs in the sixth inning and beat the Angels 9–2 at the Metrodome. Kent Hrbek started the rally with a single and drove in the last four runs of the rally with a grand slam off John Curtis.

MAY 1 — The Twins score seven runs in the third inning to take a 7–3 lead but wind up losing 11–8 to the Mariners in Seattle. There were eight hits during the seven-run rally, each of them singles.

MAY 4 — Dave Kingman of the Athletics disproves the adage that "what goes up must come down" in the fourth inning of a 3–1 Twins victory at the Metrodome. Kingman's high fly ball disappeared into one of the drainage holes in the Metrodome roof. He was awarded a ground rule double. Kingman later homered in the ninth for the only Oakland run.

MAY 7 — The Twins score five runs in the ninth inning to cap an 11–1 win over the Angels in Anaheim.

MAY 8 — In his major league debut, Kirby Puckett collects four hits in five at-bats during a 5–0 victory over the Angels in Anaheim. Batting leadoff and playing centerfield, Puckett grounded out in his first plate appearances before picking up four straight singles.

> *Standing five-foot-eight and weighing at 210 pounds, Puckett didn't look like a prototypical athlete, but his size didn't prevent him from becoming one of the best and most popular players in Twins history. Jovial and always smiling, he was involved in numerous charities and became an icon in Minnesota. When he made his major league debut, Puckett was 23 and had played only 21 games professionally above Class A. As a rookie, he batted .296 in 128 games but hit no homers and drew only 16 walks. Puckett was never particularly patient at the plate, but he developed a power stroke and clubbed 31 homers in 1986, the first of six seasons in which he would hit 20 or more. He collected over 200 hits four times and topped the circuit in the category four times. In 12 big league seasons, Puckett batted .300 or better nine times with a high of .356 in 1988 and a batting title in 1989. He made ten straight All-Star Game appearances from 1986 through 1995 but the run ended in the spring of 1996 when he was diagnosed with glaucoma. The ailment ended his career. He was elected to the Hall of Fame on the first ballot in 2001. On the all-time Twins lists, Puckett ranks second in games (1,783), first in at-bats (7,244), first in runs (1,071), first in hits (2,304), first in doubles (414), second in triples (57), second in batting average (.318), third in RBIs (1,085), fourth in stolen bases (134) and fifth in home runs (207).*

MAY 15 — A boneheaded play by catcher Dave Engle costs the Twins a victory against the Blue Jays at the Metrodome. The Twins led 1–0 in the top of the ninth with Toronto runners on second and first. Rick Leach hit a grounder that appeared to be an inning-ending double play, but Kent Hrbek dropped the throw at first base. Mitch Webster, who was the base runner at second, steamed home and Hrbek fired the ball toward the plate. Engle wasn't there, however. He was headed to the mound to congratulate pitcher Ron Davis on what Engle assumed was a victory. The gaffe allowed Webster to score the tying run. The Blue Jays scored four runs in the top of the tenth and won the contest 5–2.

Perhaps the most popular Twins player of the 1980s, first baseman Kent Hrbek, who grew up in Minneapolis, produced an outstanding season in 1984, when he finished runner-up for the MVP award.

MAY 16   The Twins lose 8–7 to the Blue Jays in a game in which the official attendance at the Metrodome was 51,863. There were only 6,346 actually in the stands, however.

When the Metrodome opened in 1982, Calvin Griffith signed a 30-year lease but it contained an escape clause that allowed him to break the agreement if the Twins failed to average 1.4 million in attendance over the first three seasons. Griffith threatened to move the Twins out of Minnesota after the club drew under a million in both 1982 and 1983. The "crowd" of 51,863 was part of a ticket-buying campaign to keep the Twins in state. When the year ended, the Twins had an attendance figure of 1,598,692, which was then a club record but still ranked only 18th among 26 teams in the majors in 1985.

MAY 19   Frank Viola pitches a three-hit shutout to defeat the Red Sox 7–0 at the Metrodome.

Viola came into the season with a career record of 11–25 and an ERA of 5.38. He came into his own in 1984 with an 18–12 mark and an earned run average of 3.21 in 257$^2/_3$ innings. It was the first of five consecutive excellent seasons for Viola, who was 93–46 for the Twins from 1984 through 1988 with a peak of

1980s

24–7 in his Cy Young season of 1988. The highlight of his years in Minnesota was a victory over the Cardinals in game seven of the 1987 World Series. A native of New York, Viola was traded to the Mets after an 8–12 start in 1989. On the all-time Twins lists, Viola ranks fourth in wins (112), third in losses (93), third in games started (259), fourth in innings (1,772 2/3), fourth in walks (521), and third in strikeouts (1,214).

JUNE 4 — In the first round of the amateur draft, the Twins select shortstop Jay Bell from Gonzalez Tate High School in Pensacola, Florida.

Bell became one of the most successful first round draft picks ever chosen by the Twins. Unfortunately, the success came after the club traded him (see August 1, 1985). The only other future major leaguer drafted and signed by the Twins in 1984 was Gene Larkin in round number 20.

JUNE 8 — Four batters into the game against the White Sox in Chicago, Frank Viola gives up four runs after a triple, two walks and a grand slam to Greg Luzinski. The Twins lost 6–1.

JUNE 9 — Greg Luzinski hits a grand slam off Twins pitching for the second game in a row with a seventh-inning blast off Mike Walters. The White Sox won 8–4 at Comiskey Park.

JUNE 10 — The Twins score seven runs in the fourth inning and defeat the White Sox 12–5 in Chicago. Mickey Hatcher led off the rally with a double and later added a two-run single.

JUNE 22 — In a home plate ceremony prior to an 8–6 loss to the White Sox at the Metrodome, Calvin Griffith signs the contract that turns the club over to new owner Carl Pohlad.

The Griffith family had been involved in the franchise since 1912 when Clark Griffith, the uncle and adopted father of Calvin Griffith, became manager of the Washington Senators. Clark was named president of the Senators in 1919. Upon Clark's death in 1955, Calvin ascended to the presidency and moved the franchise to Minnesota in 1960. The sale to Pohlad ended threats that the Twin Cities might lose the team. A Minneapolis banker, Pohlad was 68 and was rated by Fortune *magazine as one of the 100 wealthiest individuals in the United States. Newspaper accounts pegged his net worth at $500 million. The empire of banks and corporations he ran did $3 billion a year in business. Pohlad began negotiating to buy the Twins early in the year, but the sale was delayed after minority partner Gabe Murphy sold his 42 percent interest to a group from Tampa for $11.5 million. Griffith and his sister, Thelma Haynes, sold their 52 percent to Pohlad for $32 million. Three weeks later, Pohlad bought the shares from the Tampa group for $12.5 million. Calvin and five other family members received five-year contracts with the club. Calvin was named chairman of the board. Pohlad remained as owner of the Twins until his death on January 5, 2009, at the age of 93. The franchise won two world championships during his reign in 1987 and 1991, but the stewardship wasn't without controversy. In spite of Pohlad's enormous wealth, the Twins payroll usually ranked among the lowest in baseball. In 2001, he offered to sell the club back to Major League Baseball for $150 million, which would have effectively eliminated the Twins* because Commissioner Bug Selig advocated reducing the number of team in the majors from 30 to 28.

JUNE 24 — Shutout through eight innings, the Twins erupt for three runs in the ninth inning to defeat the White Sox 3–2 at the Metrodome. With one out and runners on first and second, Tim Teufel thrilled the crowd with a walk-off, three-run, inside-the-park homer. Teufel's "drive" landed 150 feet from the plate and bounced off the spongy turf over the head of right fielder Harold Baines and rolled to the wall.

JUNE 29 — In his first major league plate appearance, right fielder Andre David hits a home run sparking a 5–3 win over the Tigers in Detroit. The homer was struck in the second inning off Jack Morris. The Tigers won game two 7–5.

The home run proved to be the only one of David's career. He had only 53 big league at-bats and batted .245.

JULY 6 — The Twins score seven runs in the fourth inning and beat the Yankees 9–4 at the Metrodome. Kent Hrbek capped the rally with a three-run homer.

Hrbek was the runner-up to Tigers reliever Willie Hernandez in the MVP balloting in 1984. Kent hit .311 with 27 homers and 107 RBIs.

JULY 23 — The Twins clobber the Athletics 14–4 at the Metrodome.

JULY 28 — Randy Bush hits a grand slam off Jim Slaton in the fifth inning of a 6–1 victory over the Angels at the Metrodome.

Randy Bush spent his entire 12-year career with the Twins from 1982 through 1993 and played in 1,219 games. He was seldom an everyday player, however. Bush's career high in plate appearances was 466 in 1988, 36 plate appearances shy of qualifying for the batting title.

AUGUST 5 — The Twins regain a hold on first place with a 4–2 triumph over the Angels in Anaheim.

With the exception of two days (August 2 and August 4), the Twins held sole possession of first place from July 28 through September 4 and were tied for first from September 5 through September 8. Improved pitching was the key to the Twins vaulting into pennant contention. The club ERA of 4.66 in 1983 ranked 14th in the AL. In 1984, the team earned run average of 3.85 was fourth in the American League.

AUGUST 10 — The Twins collect 21 hits and outslug the Mariners 13–7 in Seattle.

AUGUST 19 — The Twins trade Jay Pettibone to the Cardinals for Chris Speier.

Speier was in the 14th season of a 19-year career in which he played in 2,260 games when acquired by the Twins. He was expected to take over as starting shortstop, a position held by Houston Jiminez, who batted .195 in 384 at-bats for the Twins in 1983 and 1984. Speier came to the Twins with a bruised heel, however, and the club tried to void the deal but Commissioner Bowie Kuhn turned down the request. Speier lasted only 12 games in Minnesota before exiting as a free agent.

AUGUST 22   The Twins take a 5½-game lead in the AL West with a 5–2 and 4–3 sweep of the Brewers in a double-header in Milwaukee.

The pair of victories gave the Twins a record of 67–58. The club was 14–23 the rest of the way, however, to wind up in a tie for second place three games behind the Royals.

SEPTEMBER 8   For the first time, both the Twins and the University of Minnesota football are winners at the Metrodome on the same day. In a contest that began at 11:00 a.m., the Twins downed the Rangers 5–4. In the evening, the Golden Gophers defeated Rice 31–24.

SEPTEMBER 15   Mike Smithson pitches the Twins to a 1–0 win over the Rangers in Arlington. Pat Putnam drove in the lone run with a single in the third inning.

The win allowed the Twins to remain in a first place tie with the Royals. Both clubs had records of 75–72. The Angels were in third one-half game back at 74–72. Although in first in the Western Division, the Twins and Royals were tied for the sixth- best record in the AL.

SEPTEMBER 17   Harold Baines hits three homers for the White Sox during a 7–3 win over the Twins at the Metrodome. The loss dropped the Twins out of first place.

SEPTEMBER 20   The Twins edge the White Sox 5–4 in 13 innings at the Metrodome. The winning run scored when Tom Brunansky walked and advanced on a sacrifice bunt, a passed ball and a wild pitch.

SEPTEMBER 23   The Twins move back into a tie for first place with the Royals by defeating the Indians 3–1 at the Metrodome.

SEPTEMBER 24   The Twins score seven runs in the sixth inning and defeat the White Sox 8–4 in Chicago.

Despite the victory, the Twins dropped out of first place because the Royals swept the Angels in a double-header in Anaheim. The pair of defeats all but eliminated the Angels from the pennant race. The Twins were 81–75 after the September 24 win, but lost the six remaining games on the schedule.

SEPTEMBER 27   Needing a win to stay one game behind the Royals in the pennant race, the Twins lead the Indians 3–0 in Cleveland but allow three runs in the eighth inning and one in the ninth to lose 4–3. The winning run scored off Ron Davis on a walk-off homer by Jamie Quirk, who entered the game in the top of the ninth as a substitute catcher.

Quirk played 18 seasons in the majors with eight clubs from 1975 through 1992. He was acquired by the Indians from the White Sox three days earlier. The game-winning homer came in his only plate appearance in a Cleveland uniform. He was released by the Indians on October 15.

SEPTEMBER 28   The Twins blow a 10–0 lead and suffer a shocking 11–10 loss to the Indians at Municipal Stadium. The loss put Minnesota three games behind the Royals with two games to play, thereby allowing Kansas City to clinch the AL West. The Twins took the ten-run advantage with a run in the first inning, six in the second and three in the third. The Indians came back with two runs in the third, seven in the sixth, one in the eighth and one in the ninth. Frank Viola gave up eight of the 11 Cleveland runs. Ron Davis surrendered the tallies in the eighth and ninth.

> *During the years that Calvin Griffith ran the Twins, the club had no general manager. Griffith headed the operation and made all of the trades. That changed during the 1984–85 off-season after Carl Pohlad bought the club and 31-year-old Andy MacPhail was hired. MacPhail's official title was vice-president, player personnel. He was a third-generation baseball executive. Andy's grandfather was Larry MacPhail, who was the general manager of the Reds (1934–36) and Dodgers (1938–42) and co-owner of the Yankees (1945–47). Andy's father, Lee, was general manager of the Yankees (1966–73) and president of the American League (1973–84). Andy headed the Twins front office until 1994 and put together two world championship clubs.*

DECEMBER 3   A month after Minnesota's Walter Mondale loses the presidential election to Ronald Reagan, the Twins draft Mark Salas from the Cardinals organization.

> *Salas looked like a steal when he won the Twins starting catcher job as a rookie in 1985 and hit .300 in 120 games. His average tailed off to .233 in 1986, however, and he was traded to the Blue Jays in 1987.*

1985

Season in a Sentence
The Twins expect to contend with a roster of rising young players, but a ten-game losing streak in May and June leads to the firing of Billy Gardner and a losing season.

Finish • Won • Lost • Pct • GB
Fourth (tie)   77   85   .475   14.0

Managers
Billy Gardner (27–35) and Ray Miller (50–50)

Stats

Stats	Twins	AL	Rank
Batting Avg:	.264	.261	5
On-Base Pct:	.326	.327	7
Slugging Pct:	.407	.406	7
Home Runs:	141		11
Stolen Bases:	68		13
ERA:	4.48	4.14	11
Errors:	120		3
Runs Scored:	705		11
Runs Allowed:	710		10

Starting Line-up
Mark Salas, c
Kent Hrbek, 1b
Tim Teufel, 2b
Gary Gaetti, 3b
Greg Gagne, ss
Mickey Hatcher, lf
Kirby Puckett, cf
Tom Brunansky, rf
Roy Smalley, dh-ss
Randy Bush, lf-dh

Pitchers
Frank Viola, sp
Mike Smithson, sp
John Butcher, sp
Ken Schrom, sp
Bert Blyleven, sp
Ron Davis, rp
Pete Filson, rp

Attendance
1,651,814 (ninth in AL)

Club Leaders
Batting Avg:	Kirby Puckett	.288
On-Base Pct:	Kent Hrbek	.351
Slugging Pct:	Tom Brunansky	.448
Home Runs:	Tom Brunansky	27
RBI:	Kent Hrbek	93
Runs:	Kirby Puckett	80
Stolen Bases:	Kirby Puckett	21
Wins:	Frank Viola	18
Strikeouts:	Frank Viola	135
ERA:	Frank Viola	4.09
Saves:	Ron Davis	25

JANUARY 28   Demolition begins on Metropolitan Stadium. In 1992, the Mall of America opened on the site.

FEBRUARY 11   The Dodgers sign Bobby Castillo as a free agent.

FEBRUARY 19   The Twins trade Randy Johnson and Ron Scheer to the White Sox for Roy Smalley.

The Twins made an excellent trade, as neither Johnson (the designated hitter not the pitcher) nor Scheer played in a big league game after leaving the Minnesota organization. Smalley, who previously played for the Twins from 1976 through 1982, served the club as a designated hitter and back-up shortstop for three seasons and played on the 1987 world champions.

APRIL 8   The Cubs sign Chris Speier as a free agent.

APRIL 9   The Twins open the season with a 6–2 win over the Angels in Anaheim. Tom Brunansky broke a 1–1 tie with a three-run homer in the eighth. Mickey Hatcher also homered and Kirby Puckett collected three hits. Frank Viola (7 2/3 innings) and Ron Davis (1 1/3 innings) did the pitching.

APRIL 13   With two out in the ninth inning and a 7–4 lead, Ron Davis walks Ivan Calderon to load the bases, then gives up a walk-off grand slam to Phil Bradley to lose 8–7 to the Mariners in Seattle.

APRIL 15   In the home opener, the Twins lose 5–0 to the Angels before 51,190 at the Metrodome. Former Twin Geoff Zahn pitched the shutout.

APRIL 21   Kirby Puckett accounts for both runs of a 2–0 victory over the Athletics in Oakland with a two-run single in the fifth inning. John Butcher pitched the shutout.

APRIL 24   The Twins rout the Mariners 10–0 at the Metrodome. Mike Smithson pitched the shutout.

APRIL 25   A walk-off single by Kirby Puckett in the ninth inning beats the Athletics 5–4 at the Metrodome.

APRIL 26   A walk-off homer by Tom Brunansky in the ninth inning defeats the Athletics 8–7 at the Metrodome. In was the second game in a row in which the Twins won in their last at-bat.

APRIL 27   Mickey Hatcher collects five hits, including a double, in five at-bats to lead the Twins to an 8–6 triumph over the Athletics at the Metrodome.

APRIL 28   Mickey Hatcher collects four hits, including two doubles, in five at-bats during a 10–1 thrashing of the Athletics at the Metrodome. The hits came in Hatcher's first four plate appearances to give him nine consecutive hits combined with his five-for-five performance the previous day. The nine-hit streak consisted of six singles and three doubles. The nine hits in a row tied a club record set by Tony Oliva in 1967. Todd Walker also had nine hits in succession in 1998.

APRIL 30   The Twins erupt for ten runs in the fourth inning and beat the Tigers 11–2 in Detroit. The ten runs scored on two homers (by Kent Hrbek and Tim Teufel), two doubles, five singles and two walks. Gary Gaetti drove in four of the runs on a single and a bases-loaded double. Tom Brunansky also singled and doubled. It was Minnesota's ninth win in a row.

MAY 1   The Twins extend their winning streak to ten games by beating the Tigers 7–3 in Detroit.

> *The Twins were an extremely streaky team early in 1985. The club won their first two games and then dropped nine in a row to fall to 2–9 before compiling a ten-game winning streak to raise their record to 12–9. The club was 21–16 on May 20, but 19 losses in 24 games from May 21 through June 25, which included another nine-game losing streak, wrecked the season.*

MAY 8   Gary Gaetti hits a grand slam off Joe Cowley in the first inning to spark an 8–6 victory over the Yankees at the Metrodome.

1980s

May 12 — Randy Bush hits a grand slam off Ken Dixon in the first inning to ignite a 7–3 triumph over the Orioles in Baltimore.

May 13 — The Twins blow an 8–0 lead and lose 9–8 to the Yankees in New York. Minnesota scored two runs in the first inning and six in the second for the eight-run advantage. The Yanks countered with a run in the fourth inning, five in the sixth and three in the ninth for the win. The Twins still held an 8–6 lead with two out in the ninth and a runner on first base. But Ron Davis walked Ken Griffey, Sr. and surrendered a three-run, walk-off homer to Don Mattingly for the shocking loss.

May 17 — Just four days after the disaster at Yankee Stadium, the Twins trail 6–0 before scoring a run in the eighth inning, five in the ninth and one in the 11th to stun the Blue Jays 7–6 at the Metrodome in one of the greatest come-from-behind wins in team history. Randy Bush led off the ninth with a triple and Roy Smalley followed with a homer, but the Twins were still behind 6–3. Two walks and a double from Mark Salas brought home another run. Kirby Puckett tied the score with a two-run single to tie the score 6–6 and there were still no outs. The Twins loaded the bases with one out on a single and an intentional walk but were unable to score again. Minnesota emerged victorious in the 11th, however, on Mickey Hatcher's lead-off double and Tom Brunansky's walk-off single.

June 3 — In the first round of the amateur draft, the Twins select pitcher Jeff Burngarner from Hanford High School in West Richland, Washington.

Burngarner never reached the majors. The only future big leaguers drafted and signed by the Twins in 1985 were Paul Abbott (third round) and Lenny Webster (20th round).

June 21 — In Ray Miller's debut as manager, the Twins score three runs in the ninth inning to defeat the Rangers 3–2 at the Metrodome. Mark Salas drove in the tying and winning runs with a two-out, two-run, walk-off single.

Earlier in the day, the Twins fired Billy Gardner as manager and replaced him with Miller, who was 40-years-old. Gardner became manager of the Twins in May 1981. After a 60–102 season in 1982, the club was 81–81 in 1984 and ended the year just three games out of first. Gardner seemed to have the young club headed in the right direction, but a 27–35 start to the 1985 campaign sealed his fate. Miller never played in the majors. He had been a pitching coach with the Orioles since 1978 when hired by the Twins as manager. Miller's only previous experience as a manager was in the winter leagues in Puerto Rico. After winning 16 of his first 22 games at the helm of the Twins, Miller guided the team to a 50–50 record over the remainder of 1985, but he was fired in September 1986 when the Twins were 59–80. Gardner later managed the Royals in 1987.

June 26 — Ken Schrom pitches a one-hitter to defeat the Royals 2–1 at the Metrodome. The only Kansas City hit was a single by Willie Wilson in the third inning. The Royals scored a run in the first without a hit, and the Twins still trailed 1–0 heading into the bottom of the ninth. With the bases loaded and one out, Roy Smalley delivered a two-run single for the victory.

June 29 — Dave Engle hits a home run off Britt Burns in the fourth inning to account for the lone run of a 1–0 win over the White Sox in Chicago. Mike Smithson (8 1/3 innings) and Frank Eufemia (two-thirds of an inning) combined on the shutout.

July 10 — Tom Brunansky hits a two-run homer in the ninth inning to defeat the Orioles 2–1 in Baltimore.

July 16 — The National League defeats the American 6–1 in the All-Star Game at the Metrodome before a crowd of 54,960. It was the second time that the Twins hosted the Midsummer Classic. The first one was at Metropolitan Stadium in 1965. The AL took a 1–0 lead in the first inning, but couldn't dent the plate again. Jack Morris of the Tigers and LaMarr Hoyt of the Padres were the starting pitchers.

> *Future Hall of Famers on the rosters of the two clubs were Wade Boggs, George Brett, Gary Carter, Goose Gossage, Tony Gwynn, Rickey Henderson, Paul Molitor, Eddie Murray, Jim Rice, Cal Ripken, Nolan Ryan, Ryne Sandberg, Ozzie Smith and Dave Winfield. Other outstanding players included Bert Blyleven, Steve Garvey, Don Mattingly, Dave Parker, Tim Raines, Pete Rose, Alan Trammell, Fernando Valenzuela and Lou Whitaker. Opposing managers Sparky Anderson and Dick Williams are also in the Hall of Fame.*

July 18 — A grand slam by Kent Hrbek off Brian Fisher in the seventh inning breaks a 4–4 tie and leads to an 8–4 victory over the Yankees at the Metrodome.

July 22 — Kent Hrbek hits a grand slam off Storm Davis in the second inning of a 5–2 victory over the Orioles at the Metrodome. It was Hrbek's second grand slam in a span of five days.

July 27 — The Twins score seven runs in the sixth inning and defeat the Tigers 11–4 at the Metrodome. The seven runs scored on only three hits, one of them a two-run homer by Roy Smalley. The Twins were aided by four walks and a wild pitch. Kent Hrbek started and finished the inning with outs.

August 1 — The Twins trade Jay Bell, Curt Wardle, Jim Weaver and Rich Yett to the Indians for Bert Blyleven.

> *Blyleven had previously starred for the Twins from 1970, when he was a 19-year-old rookie, until 1976. He was traded to the Rangers in June 1976 in the midst of a salary dispute with Calvin Griffith. By 1985, Griffith was no longer running the club, and swapping four players for a proven starting pitcher was a positive sign for Twins fans that things would be different under Carl Pohlad. In the short term, the Twins came out ahead on the deal, as Blyleven was 8–5 over the remainder of 1985, 17–14 in 1986 and 15–12 in 1987. It's doubtful the Twins would have raised the world championship banner in 1987 without Blyleven. In the long run, however, the team lost an excellent player. Bell had yet to play in a major league game when traded by the Twins, and wouldn't appear in one for over a year (see September 29, 1986). He struggled for several years before finding himself in 1990 as the starting shortstop for the Pirates and developing into one of the best middle infielders in baseball. Bell was a starter as late as 2001. His best season was in 1999 when he hit 38 homers and drove in 112 runs as a second baseman for the Diamondbacks.*

AUGUST 4	With a third-inning single off Frank Viola in Anaheim, Rod Carew collects the 3,000th hit of his career. Carew picked up 2,085 of the hits as a member of the Twins. The Angels won the game 6–5.
AUGUST 6	The Twins game against the Athletics in Oakland is postponed by a strike called by the players. The August 7 contest between the two clubs was also called off. The strike ended on August 8, and the two games were later made-up with double-headers.
AUGUST 12	The Twins sign Steve Howe as a free agent following his release by the Dodgers.

Howe was released by the Dodgers on July 3 after failing to overcome an addiction to cocaine. He was suspended for the entire 1984 season by Commissioner Bowie Kuhn to "protect the image of baseball." He was 2–3 with a 6.16 ERA and no saves in 13 relief appearances for the Twins. After admitting he had suffered a relapse of cocaine use during a series in Cleveland, the club released him on September 17 following a three-day disappearance for three days. After returning, Howe claimed he had to visit his grandfather in Michigan. The official Twins explanation for Howe's release was a "temporary recurrence" of his cocaine problem. Howe later pitched for the Rangers (1987) and Yankees (1991–96), but was never able to completely shed his drug addiction. He died in 2006 in an accident when his truck rolled over on a California highway.

AUGUST 15	The Twins score a run in the second inning, eight in the fourth and five in the fifth to take a 14–0 lead, and defeat the Mariners 14–5 at the Metrodome. Kent Hrbek hit his third grand slam of the season with a blast off Bob Long in the fifth.
AUGUST 17	Kent Hrbek hits a two-run homer in the fifth inning to account for all of the runs in a 2–0 victory over the Mariners at the Metrodome. Bert Blyleven pitched the shutout.
AUGUST 19	Roy Smalley's homer off Danny Darwin in the fifth inning is the only Twins hit in a 4–1 loss to the Brewers in Milwaukee.
AUGUST 24	Mike Smithson pitches the Twins to a 1–0 victory over the Red Sox in Boston.
AUGUST 31	Down 5–4 with two out in the ninth, the Twins rally to score twice and beat the Red Sox 6–5 at the Metrodome. Ron Washington drove in the winning run with a single.
SEPTEMBER 16	The Twins score two runs in the ninth inning and one in the 11th to defeat the Rangers 7–6 at the Metrodome. Kirby Puckett drove in the two tallies in the ninth with a one-out single. Gary Gaetti ended the contest with a walk-off homer.

1986

Season in a Sentence
Tom Kelly succeeds Ray Miller as manager during a dreary year in which the Twins post the highest ERA in the majors and lose 91 games.

Finish • Won • Lost • Pct • GB
Sixth 71 91 .438 21.0

Managers
Ray Miller (59–80) and Tom Kelly (12–11)

Stats

Stats	Twins	AL	Rank
Batting Avg:	.261	.262	7
On-Base Pct:	.325	.330	10
Slugging Pct:	.428	.408	3
Home Runs:	196		2
Stolen Bases:	81		12
ERA:	4.77	4.18	14
Errors:	118		5
Runs Scored:	741		8
Runs Allowed:	839		13

Starting Line-up
Mark Salas, c
Kent Hrbek, 1b
Steve Lombardozzi, 2b
Gary Gaetti, 3b
Greg Gagne, ss
Randy Bush, lf
Kirby Puckett, cf
Tom Brunansky, rf
Roy Smalley, dh
Mickey Hatcher, lf-dh
Tim Laudner, c

Pitchers
Bert Blyleven, sp
Frank Viola, sp
Mike Smithson, sp
Neal Heaton, sp
Mark Portugal, sp-rp
Keith Atherton, rp
Allan Anderson, rp-sp

Attendance
1,255,453 (13th in AL)

Club Leaders
Batting Avg: Kirby Puckett .328
On-Base Pct: Kirby Puckett .366
Slugging Pct: Kirby Puckett .537
Home Runs: Gary Gaetti 34
RBI: Gary Gaetti 108
Runs: Kirby Puckett 119
Stolen Bases: Kirby Puckett 20
Wins: Bert Blyleven 17
Strikeouts: Bert Blyleven 215
ERA: Bert Blyleven 4.01
Saves: Keith Atherton 10

JANUARY 16 — The Twins trade Tim Teufel and Pat Crosby to the Mets for Billy Beane, Joe Klink and Bill Latham. On the same day, Dave Engle was dealt to the Tigers for Chris Pittaro and Alejandro Sanchez. Teufel probably was the biggest name in the deals, and he gave the Mets adequate production. None of the other players involved contributed significantly to any of the teams.

APRIL 8 — The Twins open the season with a 3–2 win over the Athletics in Oakland. Frank Viola pitched the first seven innings for the victory. In the bottom of the ninth Roy Smith loaded the bases with one out and was relieved by Ron Davis, who ended the game by inducing Dusty Baker to hit into a double play.

> *Davis was the Twins closer from 1982 through 1985 and was expected to fill that role again in 1986. He saved only one more game after Opening Day, however, and was traded to the Cubs in August with an awful 9.08 ERA in 38⅔ innings.*

APRIL 11 — In the home opener, the Twins beat the Mariners 5–1 before 42,871 at the Metrodome. Tom Brunansky and Gary Gaetti hit home runs.

1980s

APRIL 16   Gary Gaetti hits a two-run, walk-off homer in the tenth inning to defeat the Athletics 7–5 at the Metrodome.

Gaetii batted .287 with 34 homers and 108 RBIs in 1986.

APRIL 26   The Twins lead 6–1 at the end of the eighth, but the Angels score six times in the ninth off Frank Viola and Ron Davis to win 7–6 at the Metrodome.

The six-run rally in the ninth wasn't the most bizarre event of the night. The game was halted for nine minutes in the eighth inning when strong winds tore a hole in the inner roof of the Metrodome. As the lights and speakers, suspended from the roof, sagged toward the playing field, players and fans scurried for safety. When all 20 blower fans used to inflate the inner roof were turned on, the roof rose to its accustomed height about 175 feet above the field and play resumed.

APRIL 29   Left fielder Billy Beane collects five hits, including a home run, in five at-bats during a 14–11 loss to the Yankees in New York. The home run was his first as a major leaguer.

The outburst came in Beane's 17th major league game, and fourth with the Twins. It was also only his fourth start in the majors and second with Minnesota. Entering the contest, he had three hits in 21 big league at-bats and was hitless in three at-bats in a Twins uniform. Beane closed his playing career in 1989 with a .219 average and three home runs in 148 games. He became the general manager of the Athletics in 1998 and won accolades for being able to put a winning team on the field with one of the lowest payrolls in baseball. He was the subject of Michael Lewis's best-selling 2003 book Moneyball. *Beane is an advocate of working the count and drawing walks, although it's a skill he failed to develop as a player. In 315 big league plate appearances, Beane drew only 11 base on balls and struck out 80 times.*

MAY 2   Leading off the first inning, Kirby Puckett hits a Jack Morris pitch for a home run to spark a 10–1 victory over the Tigers in Detroit.

MAY 3   For the second night in a row, Kirby Puckett hits the first pitch of the game for a home run. This time, it was off Walt Terrell, although the Twins lost 7–4 to the Tigers in Detroit.

Puckett failed to homer in 557 at-bats in the majors as a rookie in 1984, then hit only four in 691 at-bats in 1985. In 1986, he clobbered 11 home runs in the first 24 games of the season and finished the year with 31 homers, 96 RBIs, 119 runs scored, 223 hits, 37 doubles, and a .328 batting average. By the end of the season, Puckett was dropped into the third spot in the batting order, a position he held for most of the remainder of his career. He hit lead-off in 128 games as a rookie in 1984, 160 in 1985 and 128 more in 1986. From 1987 through the end of his career in 1995, Puckett started a game batting first only once. Over that period, he hit second six times, third in 1,261 games, and clean-up on 66 occasions.

MAY 10   The Twins score five runs in the first inning and rout the Tigers 12–2 at the Metrodome.

MAY 12 — Trailing 9–2 to the Yankees at the Metrodome, the Twins score six runs in the ninth inning but the rally falls short and results in a 9–8 defeat.

MAY 19 — Leading 7–6 with two out and no one on base against the Red Sox in Boston, Ron Davis allows five batters in a row to reach base and lose 8–7. Davis loaded the bases on a walk, a double and an intentional walk, then walked Jim Rice to force in the tying run and hit Mark Sullivan with a pitch to lose the game.

MAY 20 — The first six Red Sox batters reach base against Frank Viola in a 17–7 loss at Fenway Park. Combined with the debacle of the previous night, 11 straight Boston batters reached base on four doubles, two singles, four walks and a hit batsman.

MAY 30 — Switch-hitting Roy Smalley homers from both sides of the plate during a 13–5 win over the Red Sox at the Metrodome. Smalley homered off right-hander Rob Woodward in the third inning and lefty Joe Sambito in the seventh.

JUNE 2 — In the first round of the amateur draft, the Twins select catcher Derek Parks from Montclair High School in Upland, California.

> *Parks lasted only 45 games in the majors from 1992 through 1994, and hit .200 with one home run. Future major leaguers drafted and signed by the Twins in 1986 were Jeff Bonkey (second round), Mike Dyer (fourth round), Bryan Hickerson (seventh round), Jeff Reboulet (tenth round) and Scott Leius (13th round).*

JUNE 4 — The Twins hit five home runs during a 10–4 win over the Blue Jays in Toronto. Tom Brunansky and Roy Smalley each homered twice and Jeff Reed once. It was Reed's first major league home run.

> *The Twins hit 107 homers in the first 67 games of the 1986 season and finished the year with 196.*

JUNE 7 — Kent Hrbek collects five hits, including a home run and a double, in five at-bats during a 4–1 win over the Royals at the Metrodome.

> *Hrbek garnered 14 hits in 19 at-bats over a five-game span from June 6 through June 20.*

JUNE 10 — The Twins collect 20 hits but lose 14–10 to the Rangers at the Metrodome.

JUNE 11 — Allan Anderson allows two runs in ten innings in his major league debut, but the Twins lose 6–2 in 16 innings to the Rangers at the Metrodome.

JUNE 18 — The Twins score four runs in the ninth inning and one in the tenth to defeat the White Sox 10–9 at the Metrodome. The improbable ninth-inning rally began with a single by Steve Lombardozzi and a homer from Kent Hrbek. Tom Brunansky and Randy Bush also singled and advanced to second and third when the next two batters were retired. With the Twins down to their last out, Mickey Hatcher tied the score with a two-run single. In the tenth, Lombardozzi drove in the winning run with a walk-off triple.

June 20	The Twins use five homers to slip past the Blue Jays 9–8 at the Metrodome. The Minnesota home runs were all struck in the fifth and sixth innings by Kent Hrbek, Tom Brunansky, Ron Washington, Randy Bush and Tim Laudner. Bush's homer came as a pinch-hitter for Washington in the sixth.

On the same day, the Twins traded John Butcher to the Indians for Neal Heaton.

June 23	Randy Bush hits his second consecutive homer in a pinch-hit role, but the Twins lose 11–2 to the White Sox in Chicago.
July 5	Gary Gaetti hits a grand slam off Mike Flanagan in the first inning of a 7–6 win over the Orioles at the Metrodome.
July 18	Kirby Puckett and Gary Gaetti start the top of the first inning with back-to-back homers to spark a 7–3 win over the Orioles in Baltimore.

During the 1986 season, when the wife of sportscaster Bob Costas was pregnant with the couple's first child, Costas jokingly told Puckett if he was hitting .350 when the child was born he would name the baby Kirby. Puckett was batting .350 at the time of the birth, and Costas' son was named Keith Michael Kirby Costas.

July 21	The Twins edge the Tigers 1–0 in Detroit. Kent Hrbek drove in the lone run with a single in the sixth inning. Frank Viola (7 2/3 innings) and Keith Atherton (1 1/3 innings) combined on the shutout.
July 25	Gary Gaetti hits two homers and drives in five runs during a 9–5 triumph over the Yankees in New York.
July 28	The Twins take a thrilling 6–5 decision from the Mariners in ten innings at the Metrodome. Trailing 4–0, the Twins score four times in the eighth, three of them on a home run by Kirby Puckett. After Seattle scored in the top of the ninth, the Twins countered with a tally in their half on a two-out single from Kent Hrbek. Puckett drove in the winning run with a single in the tenth.

Puckett collected 13 hits in 18 at-bats over a four-game span from July 28 through August 1. The 13 hits included two homers, two triples and two doubles.

August 1	The Twins defeat the Athletics 10–1 on an eventful night at the Metrodome as Kirby Puckett hits for the cycle and Bert Blyleven fans 15, one of them his 3,000th career strikeout. Against Curt Young, Puckett tripled in the first inning, flied out to center field in the third, and doubled in the fifth. Facing Darrel Akerfelds, Kirby hit a single in the sixth and completed the cycle with a home run in the eighth. The 15 strikeouts by Blyleven tied a club record that stood until Johan Santana fanned 17 in a game in 2007. Blyleven came into the game with 2,992 strikeouts. His 3,000th victim was Mike Davis in the fourth inning. Blyleven also allowed only two hits in the contest, a single by Bruce Bochte in the fifth inning and a homer from Alfredo Griffin in the eighth.

Blyleven was 17–14 with a 4.01 ERA in 271 2/3 innings in 1986.

AUGUST 2   Mike Smithson pitches a two-hitter to defeat the Athletics 8–0 at the Metrodome. Smithson had a no-hitter in progress until Dwayne Murphy singled with one out in the seventh. The second Oakland hit was a single by Donnie Hill in the eighth. Smithson walked seven.

AUGUST 12   Kent Hrbek ties a major league record for first baseman by starting three double plays during a 12-inning, 5–4 loss to the Angels in Anaheim. Hrbek was also on the end of two other double plays.

AUGUST 13   The Twins trade Ron Davis and Dewayne Coleman to the Cubs for George Frazier, Ray Fontenot and Julius McDougal.

AUGUST 14   The Twins score seven runs in the fourth inning and demolish the Mariners 14–1 in Seattle. Billy Beane hit a single and a double during the rally.

AUGUST 15   Alvin Davis of the Mariners hits a walk-off homer off Keith Atherton with one out in the ninth inning to beat the Twins 1–0 in Seattle.

AUGUST 24   A pitcher makes the last out of ten-inning, 7–5 loss to the Blue Jays at the Metrodome. As the Twins rallied to tie the score 4–4 with a run in the ninth, manager Ray Miller used Mickey Hatcher as a pinch-hitter for Alvaro Espinosa, pinch-hit Tim Laudner for Greg Gagne, and pinch-ran Billy Beane for Jeff Reed. Because of earlier substitutions, Miller had only eight non-pitchers left to play. As a result, he had to move designated hitter Roy Smalley to shortstop, which meant that the Twins lost the use of the DH for the remainder of the game. Gary Gaetti also switched from third base to second. It was the first of only two times in his major league career in which Gaetti played second. The other one was with the Cardinals 12 years later in 1998. Toronto scored three runs in the top of the tenth off Keith Atherton and Ray Fontenot. With a run in, a runner on first, and two out in the bottom of the tenth, Fontenot was forced to bat, and struck out. He was the only Twins pitcher to bat in a regular season game between 1975 and 1989.

SEPTEMBER 1   Gary Gaetti hits two homers and drives in five runs during a 9–8 win over the Brewers at the Metrodome.

SEPTEMBER 12   The Twins fire Ray Miller as manager and replace him with 36-year-old Tom Kelly.

The Twins had a record of 59–80 at the time of the change. Kelly got the job after Jim Frey was offered the position as Twins manager, but declined the offer. Frey led the Cubs to a division title in 1984 before being fired in May 1986. Kelly's big league playing career lasted only 49 games, in which he hit just .181 for the Twins as a first-baseman-outfielder in 1975. As a minor league manager in the Twins system, he was named the Manager of the Year in the California League in both 1979 and 1980 and in the Southern League in 1981. Kelly became the club's third base coach in 1983. In his first full year as manager of the Twins, Kelly won the World Series, and followed with another world championship in 1991. He lasted as the Twins skipper until 2001 when he resigned citing burnout with a record of 1,140–1,244. Although only six of the 15 clubs he managed had winning records, and he endured a stretch of eight consecutive losing campaigns beginning in 1993, Kelly remained one of the most respected

1980s

managers in the game. After leaving the Twins, Miller was the Pirates pitching coach from 1987 through 1996 and managed the Orioles in 1997 and 1998.

SEPTEMBER 13   Bert Blyleven gives up five home runs in 5$\frac{1}{3}$ innings during a 14–1 loss to the Rangers at the Metrodome. Texas batters hit a total of seven homers during the contest, including two each by Darrell Porter and Ruben Sierra. Pete O'Brien, Pete Incaviglia and Steve Buechele also homered.

SEPTEMBER 21   Mark Portugal strikes out 13 batters in eight innings but winds up losing 2–1 to the Rangers in Arlington.

SEPTEMBER 23   Gary Gaetti drives in six runs with two homers and a single during a 9–2 triumph over the Royals at the Metrodome.

SEPTEMBER 24   Bert Blyleven strikes out 14 batters without issuing a walk, but winds up losing 2–1 to the Royals at the Metrodome.

SEPTEMBER 29   On the first pitch of his first major league at-bat, Indians shortstop Jay Bell homers off Bert Blyleven during the third inning of a 6–5 Twins victory at the Metrodome.

The home run by Bell was the 47th allowed by Blyleven in 1986, which broke the major league record of 46 set by Robin Roberts with the Phillies in 1956. Oddly, Bell was traded by the Twins to the Indians to acquire Blyleven (see August 1, 1985). Blyleven finished the season by surrendering 50 home runs, which is still the record.

SEPTEMBER 30   After the Indians score in the top of the tenth inning, the Twins rally with two in their half to win 10–9 at the Metrodome. Tom Brunansky drove in both tenth-inning runs with a one-out double. It was the 20th Minnesota hit of the game.

OCTOBER 3   Steve Lombardozzi hits a grand slam off Rich Dotson in the fourth inning of a 9–2 win over the White Sox at the Metrodome.

OCTOBER 4   Greg Gagne hits two inside-the-park homers and a triple during a 7–3 triumph over the White Sox at the Metrodome. Both inside-the-park homers were struck in consecutive plate appearances off Floyd Bannister in the second and fourth innings. Gagne tripled in the sixth facing Gene Nelson.

Only four major leaguers since 1940 have collected two inside-the-park homers in a single game. The others are Hank Thompson of the New York Giants in 1950, Dick Allen of the White Sox in 1972, and Ken Caminiti of the Padres in 1995.

OCTOBER 5   In the last game of the season, Frank Viola pitches a two-hitter to defeat the White Sox 3–0 at the Metrodome. The only Chicago hits were singles by John Cangelosi in the fourth inning and Ozzie Guillen in the eighth.

1987

Season in a Sentence
The Twins are outscored during the regular season, but win the division title, then stun the Tigers and Cardinals in the postseason to win the first world championship since the move to Minnesota and the first for the franchise since 1924.

Finish • Won • Lost • Pct • GB
First   85   77   .525 +2.0

AL Championship Series
The Twins defeated the Detroit Tigers four games to one.

World Series
The Twins defeated the St. Louis Cardinals four games to three.

Manager
Tom Kelly

Stats

Stats	Twins	AL	Rank
Batting Avg:	.261	.265	10
On-Base Pct:	.328	.333	9
Slugging Pct:	.430	.425	3
Home Runs:	196		5
Stolen Bases:	113		10
ERA:	4.63	4.46	10
Errors:	98		1
Runs Scored:	786		8
Runs Allowed:	886		9

Starting Line-up
Tim Laudner, c
Kent Hrbek, 1b
Steve Lombardozzi, 2b
Gary Gaetti, 3b
Greg Gagne, ss
Dan Gladden, lf
Kirby Puckett, cf
Tom Brunansky, rf
Roy Smalley, ss
Randy Bush, rf
Al Newman, ss-2b
Gene Larkin, dh-1b

Pitchers
Frank Viola, sp
Bert Blyleven, sp
Les Straker, sp
Mike Smithson, sp
Joe Niekro, sp
Jeff Reardon, rp
Juan Berenguer, rp
George Frazier, rp
Keith Atherton, rp

Attendance
2,081,976 (sixth in AL)

Club Leaders
Batting Avg:	Kirby Puckett	.332
On-Base Pct:	Kent Hrbek	.389
Slugging Pct:	Kent Hrbek	.545
Home Runs:	Kent Hrbek	34
RBI:	Gary Gaetti	109
Runs:	Kirby Puckett	96
Stolen Bases:	Dan Gladden	25
Wins:	Frank Viola	17
Strikeouts:	Frank Viola	197
ERA:	Frank Viola	2.97
Saves:	Jeff Reardon	31

JANUARY 9   The Twins sign Juan Berenguer, most recently with the Giants, as a free agent.

Berenguer gave the Twins four effective seasons as a reliever. He posted a won-lost record of 33–13 with the club.

FEBRUARY 3   The Twins trade Neal Heaton, Jeff Reed, Yorkis Perez and Al Cardwood to the Expos for Jeff Reardon and Tom Nieto.

Reardon was the Twins closer for three seasons and saved 104 games.

FEBRUARY 20 The Twins trade Mike Shade to the Expos for Al Newman.

Newman spent five seasons with the Twins as a light-hitting middle infielder and appeared in both the 1987 and 1991 World Series. He batted .231 with the club

1980s

and failed to hit a home run in 1,647 at-bats. During his eight-year major league career, Newman hit one homer in 2,107 at-bats and went 1,871 consecutive at-bats without a home run from 1976 through the end of his career in 1992.

FEBRUARY 22   Kirby Puckett is nearly arrested by a police officer during spring batting practice in Orlando. Puckett sent several shots over the left field wall into the parking lot of neighboring Orlando Stadium. The lot was full of cars and trucks from the crowd attending a tractor pull. Puckett's drive shattered the window of one vehicle and dented several others. Sergeant Robert Newsome climbed over the outfield wall and threatened Puckett with arrest if the batting practice didn't cease. Kirby continued hitting balls in a covered cage in the bullpen.

Closer Jeff Reardon celebrates the Twins victory in Game Seven of the 1987 World Series over the St. Louis Cardinals. Reardon appeared in four games in the Series, giving up no runs, walking no batters while striking out three.

MARCH 31   The Twins trade Bryan Hickerson, Jose Dominquez, and Ray Velasquez to the Giants for Dan Gladden and David Blakely.

Gladden was the Twins starting left fielder for five seasons from 1987 through 1991. He played in two World Series and won the hearts of Minnesota fans with his all-out hustle.

APRIL 7   Kent Hrbek hits a walk-off single in the tenth inning to defeat the Athletics 5–4 in the season opener before 43,548 at the Metrodome. It was his third RBI of the game. Earlier, he drove in runs with groundouts in the third and eighth innings, the second of which tied the score 4–4. Kirby Puckett homered and doubled. Bert Blyleven was the starting pitcher and went eight innings. George Frazier hurled two scoreless innings to earn the victory.

The Twins won their first four games in 1987.

APRIL 9 — The Twins score three runs in the ninth inning to down the Athletics 5–4 at the Metrodome. With one out, Gary Gaetti doubled and Tom Brunansky singled to score the first run. After a double by Roy Smalley and an intentional walk to Mark Salas, Dan Gladden hit a two-run single to seal the victory.

The springy turf that caused baseballs to bounce like tennis balls since the Metrodome opened in 1982 was replaced by Astroturf in 1987.

APRIL 20 — The Twins score six runs in the first inning and rout the Mariners 13–5 at the Metrodome.

The Twins sported new uniforms in 1987 to replace those introduced in 1972 (see April 25, 1972) as button-down fronts, belts and pinstripes returned. On the home uniforms, "Twins" was written across the front in unique and modern graphics. On the road, Minnesota appeared in more traditional block lettering. The pinstripes were also on the road grays. Instead of an interlocking "T" and "C" on the caps, there was an "M" representing Minnesota. The "T-C" monogram was moved to the shirtsleeves. The uniform design has changed little since 1987, though the team now switches between a variation of the old "T-C" hat and the "M" hat.

MAY 3 — After falling behind 3–0, the Twins use four solo homers to defeat the Yankees 4–3 at the Metrodome. The homers were by Gary Gaetti in the fourth inning, Dan Gladden in the fifth, Tom Brunansky in the sixth and Kirby Puckett in the eighth.

Puckett batted .332 with 207 hits and 28 homers in 1987.

MAY 5 — After being held without a hit through eight innings by Orioles pitcher Eric Bell, the Twins score four runs on five hits in the ninth but lose 5–4 at the Metrodome.

John Gordon joined Herb Carneal in the Twins radio booth in 1987. He was still with the club in 2009. Gordon is known for his intense style of play calling and his home run call "Touch 'em all," followed by the name of the player who hit the homer.

MAY 8 — Jeff Reardon gives up six runs in the ninth inning to lose 11–7 to the Yankees in New York. Rickey Henderson hit a two-run homer to tie the score. After loading the bases with two out, Reardon gave up a walk-off grand slam to Mike Pagliarulo.

MAY 15 — Kirby Puckett hits a two-run walk-off homer in the ninth inning to defeat the Red Sox 3–1 at the Metrodome.

MAY 17 — The Twins power past the Red Sox 10–8 in ten innings at the Metrodome. Boston scored seven runs in the eighth inning to take an 8–6 lead. Gary Gaetti led off the ninth with a home run, and with one out, Tom Brunansky tied the contest with another home run. Kent Hrbek walloped a two-run walk-off homer in the tenth for the win.

Hrbek batted .285 with 34 homers in 1987.

MAY 20 Tom Brunansky hits a grand slam off Tom Candiotti in the sixth inning of an 8–2 win over the Indians in Cleveland.

MAY 21 Cory Snyder hits three homers for the Indians during a 6–3 win over the Twins in Cleveland.

MAY 28 The Twins score six runs in the first inning and five in the third to take an 11–0 lead and clobber the Brewers 13–1 at the Metrodome.

MAY 29 After entering the game in the seventh inning as a substitute catcher for Tim Laudner, Mark Salas hits two homers and drives in five runs in two plate appearances, but the Twins lose 15–7 to the Tigers in Detroit.

MAY 31 The Twins sweep the Tigers 9–5 and 11–3 during a double-header in Detroit. There were 20 Minnesota hits in the second game.

JUNE 3 With the third overall pick in the amateur draft, the Twins select pitcher Willie Banks from St. Anthony's High School in Jersey City, New Jersey.

Banks made his major league debut in 1991 and was 16–17 with a 4.61 ERA in three seasons with the Twins. He pitched for six clubs from 1994 through 2002 and had a record of 17–22. Other future major leaguers drafted and signed by the Twins in 1987 were Terry Jorgensen (second round), Larry Casian (fifth round), Mark Guthrie (seventh round), Shawn Gilbert (12th round) and Chip Hale (17th round). The club also selected Bret Boone in the 28th round but failed to sign him.

JUNE 6 The Twins outlast the Rangers 3–2 in 13 innings at the Metrodome. Mark Salas led off the ninth inning with a pinch-hit homer to tie the score 2–2. Steve Lombardozzi drove in the game-winner with a single in the 13th. Frank Viola (nine), George Frazier (five), Jeff Reardon (two) and Keith Atherton (one) combined to strikeout 17 batters. The game would prove to be Salas's last with the Twins. He was traded the following day.

JUNE 7 The Twins trade Mark Salas to the Yankees for Joe Niekro.

Niekro was 42 years old and in his 21st big league season when acquired by the Twins. He is remembered by Minnesota fans more for carrying a nail file to the mound (see August 3, 1987) than for his pitching (a 5–10 record and a 6.67 ERA).

JUNE 14 Tim Laudner hits a grand slam off Jose DeLeon in the second inning of a 6–3 triumph over the White Sox in Chicago.

JUNE 17 A bench-clearing brawl mars an 8–5 loss to the Brewers in Milwaukee. In the sixth inning, Mark Clear hit Steve Lombardozzi with a pitch. Lombardozzi attempted to rush toward Clear but was restrained by umpire Ken Kaiser. Lombardozzi went to first base, and then bowled over second baseman Jim Gantner trying to break up a double play. Gantner leaped on Lombardozzi, causing both benches to empty. Gantner, Twins coach Tony Oliva and Minnesota catcher Sal Butera were all ejected as a result of the fracas.

June 19   Tim Laudner hits a walk-off homer in the ninth inning to defeat the White Sox 7–6 at the Metrodome.

June 24   The Twins outslug the Indians 14–8 at the Metrodome.

The Twins had a 42–29 record and a 4½-game lead in the AL West on June 25. The club was 43–48 over the remainder of the regular season but managed to hang onto first place.

July 6   The Twins collect only three hits off Ron Guidry but two are homers and result in a 2–0 win over the Yankees in New York. Tom Brunansky homered in the first inning and Kent Hrbek in the seventh. The only other Minnesota hit was a single by Brunansky with two out in the ninth. Frank Viola pitched the shutout.

Viola was 17–10 with a 2.90 ERA in 1987. Viola and Bert Blyleven were a combined 32–22 with a 3.64 ERA. The rest of the starters were 23–32 with an earned run average of 5.37.

July 7   After taking a 7–0 lead, the Twins allow seven runs in the seventh inning and five in the eighth to lose 12–7 to the Yankees in New York.

July 8   The Twins lose 13–4 to the Yankees in New York. In eight consecutive turns at bat over two games, the Yanks scored 25 runs off Minnesota pitching.

July 11   Solo homers by Randy Bush in the fourth inning and Gary Gaetti in the sixth are enough to beat the Orioles 2–1 in Baltimore.

July 19   The Twins retire Rod Carew's number 29 in ceremonies prior to a 7–6 win over the Blue Jays at the Metrodome. No one had worn number 29 since Carew was traded to the Angels in February 1979.

July 25   The Twins score seven runs in the sixth inning and beat the Blue Jays 13–9 in Toronto. Gene Larkin started the rally with a home run and singled in the seventh run.

July 26   Bert Blyleven strikes out 12 batters, but the Twins lose 4–2 to the Blue Jays in Toronto.

July 27   The Twins erupt for four runs in the ninth inning to defeat the Mariners 4–3 in Seattle. After a single and a walk, Steve Lombardozzi hit a three-run homer to tie the score. Two batters later, Gary Gaetti also homered.

Gaetti hit .257 with 31 homers and 109 RBIs in 1987.

July 31   The Twins trade Jeff Perry to the Indians for Steve Carlton.

Carlton had a 328–228 career record when acquired by the Twins, but he was 42 and was bouncing from team to team. From June 21, 1986, through August 4, 1987, Carlton pitched for the Phillies, Giants, White Sox, Indians and Twins. His last 13 appearances in the majors were with the Twins in 1987 and 1988, and he posted a 1–6 record and a horrendous 8.54 ERA in 52⅔ innings.

AUGUST 3 — Joe Niekro is ejected in the fourth inning of an 11–3 win over the Angels in Anaheim for carrying an emery board in his pocket. Tim Tschida, the home plate umpire, ordered Niekro to turn over his glove and empty his pockets after a pitch to Brian Downing. When Niekro turned his back pockets inside out, a five-inch emery board flew out and Tschida ejected the pitcher.

Niekro claimed he used the emery board to file his nails for his trademark knuckler and not on baseballs, but AL president Bobby Brown didn't believe him. Niekro was suspended for ten days on August 8.

AUGUST 8 — Kirby Puckett collects a homer, two doubles and a single and scores four runs during a 9–2 victory over the Athletics at the Metrodome.

AUGUST 15 — At the Metrodome, the Twins score eight runs in the first inning and three in the second on the way to sinking the Mariners 14–4.

On the same day, suspended pitcher Joe Niekro (see August 3, 1987) appeared on Late Night With David Letterman. *He came onto the stage carrying a power sander and a carpenter's apron.*

AUGUST 17 — The Twins take a five-game lead with a 4–2 win over the Mariners at the Metrodome. The lead vanished, however, with a stretch of nine losses in ten games.

AUGUST 28 — The Twins drop into second place behind the Athletics with a 1–0 loss to the Brewers in Milwaukee.

AUGUST 29 — Kirby Puckett collects four hits, two of them homers, in five at-bats to lead the Twins to a 12–3 victory over the Brewers in Milwaukee.

AUGUST 30 — Kirby Puckett collects six hits, on two homers, two doubles and two singles, in six at-bats to lead the Twins to a 10–6 triumph over the Brewers in Milwaukee. It was the second consecutive game in which Puckett homered twice. He also scored four runs and drove in four. Facing Juan Nieves, Puckett singled in the first inning, homered in the third and singled in the fifth. Kirby added a pair of doubles against Chuck Crim in the sixth and eighth. He capped the great afternoon with a home run off Dan Plesac in the ninth. If the six hits weren't enough, he also robbed Robin Yount of a potential grand slam by leaping above the fence for a catch in the sixth inning. The win put the Twins into first place. The club wouldn't relinquish the spot for the remainder of the season.

The ten hits on August 29 and 30 tied a modern (since 1900) major league record for most hits in consecutive nine-inning games. The only other individual to accomplish the feat is Rennie Stennett with the Pirates in 1975. In addition, Puckett is the only player in Twins history to garner six hits in a game. He did it again in 1991. The only other players in franchise history with six hits in a game are George Myatt and Stan Spence with the Senators, both in 1944. Over a four-game span from August 29 through September 2, Puckett had 13 hits in 17 consecutive at-bats.

SEPTEMBER 1   The Twins trade Enrique Rios to the Red Sox for Don Baylor.

Baylor was acquired to provide some veteran leadership and to play as a designated hitter in the drive for the pennant. He played in only 27 games as a Twin, seven of them in the postseason. Baylor is the only player to play in three consecutive Fall Classics with three different teams. The other two were the Red Sox in 1986 and the Athletics in 1988.

SEPTEMBER 3   The Twins score a run in the ninth inning and another in the tenth to beat the Red Sox 2–1 at the Metrodome. Kirby Puckett provided the first Minnesota run of the game with a homer in the ninth. The winning run scored on a bases-loaded walk by Wes Gardner to Al Newman.

SEPTEMBER 4   The Twins win 2–1 in extra innings for the second game in a row, this time in 12 innings against the Brewers at the Metrodome. Billy Beane drove in the winning run with a single. He was recalled from Class AAA Portland only three days earlier.

SEPTEMBER 5   The Twins win 2–1 with a run in their last at-bat for the third night in a row as Tom Brunansky leads off the ninth with a home run for a win against the Brewers at the Metrodome.

SEPTEMBER 9   The Twins collect only two hits, but both are homers that result in a 2–1 win over the White Sox at the Metrodome. Kirby Puckett homered off Dave LaPoint in the fourth inning. Tim Laudner led off the ninth with a walk-off home run against Jim Winn for the victory.

SEPTEMBER 11   After falling behind 7–1 in the fourth inning, the Twins rally to beat the Indians 13–10 in 11 innings in Cleveland. The Twins still trailed 10–7 heading into the ninth. Tom Brunansky drove in the first run of the ninth, and after a walk to Gene Larkin, Tim Laudner delivered a two-run single. In the 11th, Dan Gladden hit a two-out, three-run homer.

SEPTEMBER 13   The Twins score four runs in the tenth inning to down the Indians 7–3 in Cleveland. It was the Twins sixth win in their last at-bat in a span of ten games beginning on September 3.

The Twins started a six-game winning streak on September 18 that stretched the team's lead in the AL West from 3½ games to six and virtually wrapped up a division title.

SEPTEMBER 28   The Twins clinch the AL West title by beating the Rangers 5–3 in Arlington. In the second inning, left fielder Dan Gladden threw out runners on consecutive plays trying to stretch singles into doubles. Steve Lombardozzi tied the score with a three-run homer in the fourth inning and then broke the deadlock with a run-scoring single in the eighth. He ended the game by starting a double play.

1980s

The Twins met the Detroit Tigers in the American League Championship Series. Managed by Sparky Anderson, the Tigers were 98–64 in 1987. Detroit overcame a 3½-game deficit in the last week of the season and won the division title with a 1–0 win over the Blue Jays on the last day of the regular season. The Tigers were heavy favorites to quickly dispatch the Twins, who were 85–77 and had a 19–23 record since August 17. Minnesota had the fifth best record in the AL and was outscored by the opposition 806–786. The Twins also hadn't played in the postseason since 1970. In addition, Anderson was in his 18th season as a big league manager and had led three clubs to world championships in Cincinnati in 1975 and 1976 and Detroit in 1984. Kelly was in his first full season at the helm of the Twins. Despite the fact that the Tigers had the best record in the majors in 1987, the Twins had home field advantage in the ALCS. At the time, home field advantage was in the hands of the AL West winner in odd-numbered years and the AL East in even-numbered seasons. The Home Field edge was significant, because the Twins were 56–25 at home that season, and only 29–52 on the road. Since July 12, the Twins road record was 9–26.

October 7 — The Twins open the ALCS by beating the Tigers 8–5 before 53,269 at the Metrodome. Doyle Alexander, who had a 9–0 record for the Tigers after being acquired by the Braves on August 12, gave up six runs in 7⅓ innings. Gary Gaetti, playing in his first postseason game, gave the Twins a 1–0 advantage in the second inning with a homer and a 2–1 advantage with another home run in the fifth. The Twins fell behind 5–4, however, before scoring four times in the eighth. Kirby Puckett drove in the tying run with a double. After the bases were loaded with two walks, Don Baylor delivered a pinch-hit single.

Tom Brunansky was the star of the series with seven hits, including four doubles and two homers, in 17 at-bats. He also drove in nine runs.

October 8 — The Twins beat the Tigers 6–3 in game two before 55,245 at the Metrodome. After Detroit scored twice in the top of the second for a 2–0 lead, the Twins responded with three in their half and never gave up the advantage. Jack Morris was the losing pitcher. A native of St. Paul, Morris entered the game with a career record of 11–0 in Minnesota.

The series was carried on national television over NBC. The announcers were Bob Costas and Tony Kubek.

October 10 — The Tigers win game three 7–6 at Tiger Stadium in Detroit. The Tigers took a 5–0 lead in the third, but the Twins fought back with two runs in the fourth, sixth and seventh innings for a 6–5 lead. Greg Gagne and Tom Brunansky each homered during the comeback. The six runs came off Walt Terrell, who entered the game with a 32–7 career record at Tiger Stadium. Detroit won the game in the eighth on a two-run homer by Pat Sheridan off Jeff Reardon.

October 11 — The Twins move within one victory of the World Series by beating the Tigers 5–3 in Detroit. Trailing 1–0, the Twins took the lead on solo homers by Kirby Puckett in the third inning and Greg Gagne in the fourth.

October 12 — The Twins clinch their first American League championship since 1965 with a 9–5 triumph over the Tigers in Detroit. The Twins took a 4–0 lead with four runs in the second. Tom Brunansky led the offense with a homer, a double and a single and three RBIs. Dan Gladden contributed two doubles and a single and scored three runs.

The Twins played the St. Louis Cardinals in the World Series. Managed by Whitey Herzog, the Cards were 95–67 during the regular season and beat the Giants in seven games in the NLCS. St. Louis also won the NL pennant in 1982 and 1985. In 1982, the club beat the Brewers in seven games in the World Series, and in 1985 lost in seven games to the Royals.

OCTOBER 17   The Twins score seven runs in the fourth inning and demolish the Cardinals 10–1 before a raucous crowd of 55,171 at the Metrodome. The Twins were held hitless by Joe Magrane over the first three innings. Dan Gladden capped the seven-run rally with a grand slam off Bob Forsch. Steve Lombardozzi belted a two-run homer in the fifth and Gladden added his fifth RBI of the evening with a double in the seventh. Frank Viola pitched eight innings for the win. The game was also the first in World Series history to be played indoors.

Viola was supposed to be the best man at his brother's wedding that evening but had to back out when the Twins reached the World Series. ABC showed clips of the wedding throughout the game. The announcers on television were Al Michaels, Tim McCarver and Jim Palmer.

OCTOBER 18   The Twins score six runs in the fourth inning and beat the Cardinals 8–4 before a game two crowd of 55,257 at the Metrodome. Gary Gaetti started the scoring with a home run in the second. During the six-run rally, Randy Bush contributed a two-run double and Tim Laudner added a two-run single.

Both starting pitchers were born in Europe. Bert Blyleven hailed from the Netherlands, and Danny Cox was born in Northhampton, England.

OCTOBER 20   The Cardinals erase a 1–0 Twins lead with three runs in the seventh and win game three 3–1 in St. Louis. Les Straker started for the Twins and pitched six shutout innings. Reliever Juan Berenguer surrendered the three seventh-inning runs.

OCTOBER 21   The Cardinals even the series by beating the Twins 7–2 in St. Louis. The Cards broke a 1–1 tie by scoring six runs in the fourth inning. The highlight was a three-run homer by Tom Lawless off Frank Viola. During the regular season, Lawless batted .080 in 25 at-bats and failed to drive in a run. The homer was his first in the majors since 1984. Greg Gagne walloped a home run in the losing cause.

Kent Hrbek, Frank Viola, Gary Gaetti, Tom Brunansky, Tim Laudner, Sal Butera and Roy Smalley each played on the 1982 club that lost 102 games and on the 1987 world champions.

OCTOBER 22   The Cardinals take a three-games-to-two lead in the World Series by beating the Twins 4–2 in St. Louis. The Cards broke a scoreless tie with three runs in the sixth.

OCTOBER 24   The Twins force a seventh game by beating the Cardinals 11–5 before 55,293 at the Metrodome. The Twins trailed 5–2 before scoring four runs in the fifth inning and four in the sixth. The fifth-inning rally began with a single by Kirby Puckett, who scored on Gary Gaetti's double. Don Baylor followed with a home run to tie the score 5–5. Tim Laudner's single broke the deadlock. In the sixth, Kent Hrbek hit a grand slam off Ken Dayley. Puckett collected four hits in four at-bats, stole a base, and scored four runs.

The game started at 3:00 Minnesota time and 4:00 Eastern Standard Time. It is the last time that a World Series game started in the afternoon in the East.

OCTOBER 25   The Twins claim the world championship by beating the Cardinals 4–2 in game seven before 55,376 at the Metrodome. The club was 6–0 at home in the 1987 postseason. St. Louis took a 2–0 lead in the second off Frank Viola, who was making his third start of the series. Steve Lombardozzi drove in a run with a single in the second and Kirby Puckett delivered an RBI-double in the fifth to tie the score 2–2. An infield single by Greg Gagne with the bases loaded in the sixth gave Minnesota a 3–2 lead. An insurance run was added in the eighth. Jeff Reardon relieved Viola in the ninth and retired all three batters he faced. The last out was recorded when Willie McGee bounced out to Gary Gaetti.

The title was the first by a pro sports team in Minnesota since the Minneapolis Lakers won the NBA title in 1954. It was the first time the Senators/Twins franchise won a World Series since 1924. That was the only world championship won by the Senators in 60 seasons in Washington.

OCTOBER 29   The Twins are honored by President Ronald Reagan at the White House.

1988

Season in a Sentence

The defending world champions lead the AL in attendance by drawing over three million and win six more games than in 1987 but finish 13 games behind the Athletics.

Finish • Won • Lost • Pct • GB

Second 91 71 .562 13.0

Manager

Tom Kelly

Stats

Stats	Twins	AL	Rank
Batting Avg:	.274	.259	2
On-Base Pct:	.348	.324	2
Slugging Pct:	.421	.391	1
Home Runs:	151		3
Stolen Bases:	107		6
ERA:	3.93	3.97	6
Errors:	84		1
Runs Scored:	759		5
Runs Allowed:	672		5

Starting Line-up

Tim Laudner, c
Kent Hrbek, 1b
Tom Herr, 2b
Gary Gaetti, 3b
Greg Gagne, ss
Dan Gladden, lf
Kirby Puckett, cf
Randy Bush, rf
Gene Larkin, dh-1b
Steve Lombardozzi, 2b
Al Newman, 3b
John Moses, lf-rf

Pitchers

Frank Viola, sp
Allan Anderson, sp
Bert Blyleven, sp
Charlie Lea, sp
Freddie Toliver, sp
Les Straker, sp
Jeff Reardon, rp
Juan Berenguer, rp
Keith Atherton, sp

Attendance

3,030,672 (first in AL)

Club Leaders

Batting Avg:	Kirby Puckett	.356
On-Base Pct:	Kent Hrbek	.387
Slugging Pct:	Gary Gaetti	.551
Home Runs:	Gary Gaetti	28
RBI:	Kirby Puckett	121
Runs:	Kirby Puckett	109
Stolen Bases:	Dan Gladden	28
Wins:	Frank Viola	24
Strikeouts:	Frank Viola	193
ERA:	Allen Anderson	2.45
Saves:	Jeff Reardon	42

JANUARY 4   The Twins sign Brian Harper, most recently with the Athletics, as a free agent.

The move didn't make any headlines in the Twin Cities newspapers, but it proved to be one of the best transactions in club history. Entering the 1988 season, Harper was 28 and had a .233 batting average, and a .258 on-base percentage, with 11 home runs in 421 at-bats over eight seasons as an outfielder with five clubs. The Twins converted Harper into a catcher. After backing up Tim Laudner in 1988, he was the starter at the position from 1989 through 1993. In six seasons with the Twins, Harper batted .306 with 48 home runs in 730 games.

APRIL 5   The Twins open the season with an 8–0 loss to the Yankees in New York. Frank Viola was the Minnesota starter and allowed six runs in five innings. Rick Rhoden pitched a three-hit shutout.

The game was a rare bad outing that year for Viola, who put together one of the best seasons by a pitcher in Twins history. He was 24–7 with a 2.64 ERA and 193 strikeouts in 255 1/3 innings. He also won 19 straight regular season decisions at the Metrodome from May 27, 1987, through July 22, 1988. Counting the 1987 postseason, Viola won 21 in a row in Minneapolis.

1980s

April 6   Dan Gladden collects four hits, including two doubles, in five at-bats during a 5–3 loss to the Yankees in New York.

> *Jim Kaat rejoined the Twins as a television announcer in 1988. He remained with the club until 1993.*

April 8   The Twins win the home opener 6–3 over the Blue Jays before 53,067 at the Metrodome. Dan Gladden hit two homers, a double and a single and stole a base. It was his second straight game with four hits. Gary Gaetti also homered.

> *The Twins set a club attendance record in 1987 by drawing 2,081,976. Buoyed by a huge advance sale in the wake of the World Series victory, the Twins shattered that mark by attracting 3,030,672 in 1988. That figure is still the franchise standard by a wide margin heading into the 2010 season. The second largest season attendance is 2,482,428 in 1992. The Twins were also the first American League club to draw at least three million fans in a season. The only previous major league clubs to attract over three million in a season were the Los Angeles Dodgers (1978, 1980 and 1982 through 1986) and the New York Mets (1987).*

April 22   The Indians hit two grand slams and beat the Twins 11–6 at the Metrodome. Cory Snyder hit a slam off Bert Blyleven in the first inning, and Joe Carter duplicated the feat in the eighth against Keith Atherton. Blyleven also tied an American League record by hitting four batters with pitches in just $4^{2}/_{3}$ innings.

> *On the same day, the Twins traded Tom Brunansky to the Cardinals for Tom Herr. Herr didn't want to come to Minnesota, and almost immediately mounted a campaign to be traded back to the National League. After a mediocre season with the Twins in 1988, that request was granted as Herr was shipped to the Phillies. Brunansky had five seasons ahead of him as a regular in the majors with the Cardinals and Red Sox.*

April 24   Tim Laudner drives in six runs during a 13–7 victory over the Indians at the Metrodome. Laudner hit three-run homers in consecutive at-bats in the third and fourth innings.

April 27   The Twins release Steve Carlton with an 0–1 record and a 16–76 ERA in $9^{2}/_{3}$ innings. The release ended Carlton's career. He was elected to the Hall of Fame on the first ballot in 1994.

April 28   The Twins defeat the Orioles 4–2 at the Metrodome. The defeat dropped Baltimore's record to 0–21, the worst start in major league history.

> *The Orioles ended the 21-game losing streak by defeating the White Sox 9–0 in Chicago the following day.*

May 15   The Twins use five homers to defeat the Tigers 10–2 in Detroit. Kent Hrbek led the way with two home runs. The others were struck by Tom Herr, Kirby Puckett and Randy Bush.

> *Hrbek hit .312 with 25 homers in 1988.*

MAY 17   With the Twins trailing 5–4 with two out in the ninth inning, Gene Larkin delivers a two-run single to defeat the Royals 6–5 at the Metrodome.

MAY 22   In the second game of a double-header against the Rangers in Arlington, Gary Gaetti breaks a scoreless tie with a grand slam off Mitch Williams. The Twins survived a two-run Texas rally in the bottom half to win 4–2. The Twins also won the opener 15–5. Gaetti hit two singles during a seven-run rally in the seventh inning.

Gaetti batted .301 with 28 homers in 1988.

MAY 29   The Twins extend their winning streak to eight games with a 6–3 decision over the Tigers at the Metrodome.

Pitching more than 200 innings for seven straight seasons, Frank Viola was the Twins workhorse and most successful starter in the 1980s. In 1988, his best year, he won twenty-four games and the Cy Young award.

1980s

May 31 — Dan Gladden contributes three doubles and a single to an 8–6 win over the Rangers at the Metrodome.

June 1 — In the first round of the amateur draft, the Twins select pitcher Johnny Ard from Manatee Community College in Florida.

> *Ard never played in a major league game. The Twins drafted and signed five future major leaguers in Alan Newman (second round), Steve Dunn (fourth round), Pat Mahomes (sixth round), Doug Simons (ninth round), and J. T. Bruett (11th round), but none of them made much of an impact.*

June 3 — Greg Gagne hits a grand slam off Dave Stewart in the second inning for a 4–0 lead, but the Twins wind up losing 8–5 to the Athletics at the Metrodome.

June 19 — Bert Blyleven earns his 250th career victory by defeating the Mariners 3–1 at the Metrodome.

June 24 — The Twins break a 5–5 tie with six runs in the ninth inning and beat the Athletics 11–5 in Oakland.

June 26 — The Twins sweep the Athletics 11–0 and 5–0 in a double-header in Oakland. Dan Gladden started the day by homering on the first pitch of the opener off Curt Young. Charlie Lea (six innings) and Juan Berenguer (three innings) combined on the shutout in the first game. Frank Viola (6 $1/3$ innings) and Keith Atherton (2 $2/3$ innings) hurled game two.

> *Lea was born in Orleans, France.*

June 27 — Dan Gladden pitches the eighth inning of a 16–7 loss to the Angels in Anaheim. Gladden retired all three batters he faced on nine pitches.

> *On the same day, the Twins signed Dan Schatzeder, most recently with the Indians, as a free agent.*

June 29 — Brian Harper hits his first major league home run since August 26, 1984, during a 2–1 loss to the Angels in Anaheim.

July 4 — The Twins use three solo homers to defeat the Brewers 3–1 in Milwaukee. Kent Hrbek homered in the sixth inning and both Hrbek and Brian Harper went deep in the ninth.

July 12 — At Riverfront Stadium in Cincinnati, Frank Viola starts the All-Star Game and retires all six batters he faces to help the American League to a 2–1 victory. Tom Kelly was the AL manager.

> *The Twins had a 9–16 record on May 4 and were ten games out of first place. By July 17, the club was 51–39 and had pulled within three games of the Athletics. From July 18 through the end of the year, Minnesota was 41–32 but couldn't keep pace with Oakland. The Twins finished the year with the second best record in the AL but were 13 games behind the A's.*

JULY 25	With the Twins trailing 4–3 and a runner on first base and two out in the ninth, Randy Bush draws a walk and Kirby Puckett hits a two-run, walk-off double to defeat the Blue Jays 5–4 at the Metrodome.
JULY 31	The Twins score nine runs in the sixth inning to take a 12–0 lead and rout the Indians 12–4 in Cleveland. During the nine-run rally, Gene Larkin doubled and singled, Gary Gaetti singled twice, and Kent Hrbek drew two walks.
AUGUST 8	Dan Gladden starts a triple play during a 7–2 win over the Indians at the Metrodome. With Ron Washington on second base and Willie Upshaw on first, Joe Carter hit a lone drive to left. Running full speed, Gladden made the catch, caromed off the wall, and fired a strike to Steve Lombardozzi. The base runners were running on the play, and Lombardozzi stepped on second to retire Washington and threw to first baseman Kent Hrbek to force out Upshaw and complete the triple play.
AUGUST 13	After falling behind 2–0 in the second inning, the Twins score 12 unanswered runs and demolish the Yankees 12–2 at the Metrodome.
AUGUST 21	The Twins score six runs in the first inning and clobber the Rangers 12–2 at the Metrodome. The Twins scored the even dozen runs on only eight hits.
AUGUST 23	Kent Hrbek hits a two-run, walk-off homer in the tenth inning to down the Tigers 7–5 at the Metrodome. It was Hrbek's second home run of the game.
AUGUST 31	Frank Viola earns his 20th victory of the season with a 10–1 decision over the Rangers in Arlington.
SEPTEMBER 9	Freddie Toliver allows only one hit in eight innings of a 1–0 win over the White Sox in Chicago. The only hit off Toliver was a single by Steve Lyons leading off the seventh. Jeff Reardon pitched the ninth. Dan Gladden drove in the lone run with a single in the third inning. *Reardon finished the season with 42 saves and a 2.47 ERA in 63 games and 73 innings.*
SEPTEMBER 15	Jim Dwyer hits a pinch-hit grand slam off Donn Pall in the sixth inning of a 10–3 win over the White Sox at the Metrodome. *Kirby Puckett set a Twins record by driving in runs in 11 consecutive games from September 15 through September 25. He finished the year with a .356 batting average, 24 homers, 121 RBIs, 109 runs scored and league-leading figures in total bases (358) and hits (234).*
SEPTEMBER 28	Bert Blyleven ties a major league record by hitting three batters with pitches in the second inning of a 5–2 loss to the Athletics in Oakland. He started the inning by hitting Don Baylor and Ron Hassey with back-to-back pitches. Three batters later, Blyleven plunked Tony Phillips.
OCTOBER 2	On the last day of the season, the Twins create controversy by holding Allen Anderson out of a scheduled start to give him the AL earned run average title. Heading into the day, Anderson had an ERA of 2.446, while Milwaukee's Teddy

Higuera stood at 2.454. Higuera pitched the day before, and allowed three runs in 6²/₃ innings that increased his ERA four points from 2.41. Roy Smith pitched in place of Anderson, and the Twins won 3–2 over the Angels at the Metrodome.

Anderson was 24 years old in 1988 and had a 16–9 record. He began the year at Class AAA Portland and was recalled on April 25. He was 17–10 in 1989 and appeared to be in line for a long and productive career but was 7–18 in 1990 and 5–11 in 1991 before his days in the big leagues ended prematurely.

OCTOBER 24   The Twins trade Tom Herr, Tom Nieto and Eric Bullock to the Phillies for Shane Rawley.

NOVEMBER 3   Five days before George Bush defeats Michael Dukasis in the presidential election, the Twins trade Bert Blyleven and Kevin Trudeau to the Angels for Paul Sorrento, Mike Cook and Rob Wassenaar.

Blyleven was 10–17 with a 5.43 ERA for the Twins in 1988. He rebounded in 1989 by going 17–5 with an earned run average of 2.72 for California. He won 16 games from 1990 through 1992 before his career ended. Of the three players acquired in the deal, only Sorrento made an impact in the majors, and that was after the Twins traded him in 1992.

DECEMBER 4   The Twins trade Mark Portugal to the Astros for Todd McClure.

Portugal was 11–19 with a 5.13 ERA in four seasons with the Twins. He lasted in the majors until 1999, peaking with an 18–4 mark for Houston in 1993.

1989

Season in a Sentence
Suffering from year-long pitching problems, the Twins take an unexpected step backward, and post a losing record.

Finish • Won • Lost • Pct • GB
Fifth   80   82   .494   19.0

Manager
Tom Kelly

Stats   Twins • AL • Rank
Batting Avg: .276   .261   2
On-Base Pct: .334   .326   2
Slugging Pct: .402   .384   2
Home Runs: 117   10
Stolen Bases: 111   7
ERA: 4.28   3.88   12
Errors: 107   3
Runs Scored: 740   2
Runs Allowed: 738   11

Starting Line-up
Brian Harper, c
Kent Hrbek, 1b
Al Newman, 2b-3b
Gary Gaetti, 3b
Greg Gagne, ss
Dan Gladden, lf
Kirby Puckett, cf
Randy Bush, rf
Gene Larkin, dh-1b-rf
Wally Backman, 2b
Jim Dwyer, dh
Tim Laudner, c
John Moses, rf-lf
Carmen Castillo, rf

Pitchers
Allen Anderson, sp
Roy Smith, sp
Frank Viola, sp
Shane Rawley, sp
Jeff Reardon, rp
Juan Berenguer, rp
Gary Wayne, rp

Attendance
2,227,438 (seventh in AL)

Club Leaders
Batting Avg: Kirby Puckett   .339
On-Base Pct: Kirby Puckett   .379
Slugging Pct: Kirby Puckett   .465
Home Runs: Kent Hrbek   25
RBI: Kirby Puckett   85
Runs: Kirby Puckett   75
Stolen Bases: Al Newman   25
Wins: Allen Anderson 17
Strikeouts: Frank Viola   138
ERA: Frank Viola   3.79
Saves: Jeff Reardon   31

January 30   The Astros sign former Twin Dan Schatzeder as a free agent.

March 21   The Twins trade Steve Lombardozzi to the Astros for Ramon Cedeno and Gordon Farmer.

April 4   The Twins open the season with a 4–2 loss to the Yankees before 52,394 at the Metrodome. Frank Viola was the starting and losing pitcher.

> *In the midst of an acrimonious salary dispute with Twins management following a 24–7 season in 1988, Viola was booed by Twins fans when introduced before the game.*

April 5   The Twins score eight runs in the fifth inning and wipe out the Yankees 12–2 at the Metrodome. Greg Gagne contributed to the eight-run inning with a single and a double and Brian Harper capped the rally with a three-run homer.

April 11   The Twins score eight runs in the eighth inning and rout the Tigers 14–0 in Detroit. Batting for Kent Hrbek, Carmen Castillo hit a grand slam off Willie Hernandez. It was Castillo's first homer as a member of the Twins.

1980s

April 16 — Gary Gaetti drives in six runs, all off Tommy John, during a 9–4 win over the Yankees in New York. Gaetti homered twice and singled.

May 1 — Twins reliever Mike Cook walks seven in only 1 2/3 innings during a 13–6 loss to the Red Sox at the Metrodome. Starter Allan Anderson fared little better, allowing seven runs in one-third of an inning.

May 7 — The Twins lose a double-header to the Indians in Cleveland by scores of 5–4 and 12–1. To save wear and tear on a taxed pitching staff, Dan Gladden pitched the eighth inning of the second game and allowed a run. It was Gladden's second career pitching appearance (see June 27, 1988).

May 13 — Kirby Puckett ties a major league record with four doubles during a 10–8 win over the Blue Jays at the Metrodome. Puckett doubled off Dave Stieb in the first and fifth innings and against Tom Henke in the sixth and eighth.

Puckett is the only player in the history of the franchise, including the 60 years it was located in Washington, to pick up four doubles in a game.

May 14 — Kirby Puckett hits two more doubles during a 13–1 triumph over the Blue Jays at the Metrodome. The six doubles in consecutive games tied another major league record.

In an unusual scheduling move, the Twins opened the season with 34 consecutive games against teams from the AL East. The club didn't play a division opponent until May 15.

May 17 — The Twins score two runs in the ninth inning and one in the tenth to down the Royals 4–3 at the Metrodome. In the ninth, Kirby Puckett singled and Gary Gaetti walloped a two-run homer with one out. In the tenth, Puckett drove in the winning run with another single.

Puckett led the AL in batting average (.339) and hits (215) in 1989 (see October 1, 1989). He also contributed 45 doubles and nine home runs.

May 20 — Randy Bush drives in eight runs during a 19–3 thrashing of the Rangers in Arlington. Most of the Twins scoring was done late in the game with two runs in the sixth inning, two in the seventh, seven in the eighth and four in the ninth. There were 20 Minnesota hits in all. Bush's eight runs batted in tied a franchise record, including the Washington years. He singled in a run in the first inning, hit a sacrifice fly in the seventh, and followed with three-run homers in both the eighth and ninth.

May 23 — Shane Rawley (eight innings) and Juan Berenguer (two-thirds of an inning) combine on a two-hitter, but the Twins lose 2–1 to the Blue Jays in Toronto. The Blue Jays scored in the ninth on a three-base error by right fielder John Moses and a sacrifice fly. It was also the last time that the Twins played at Exhibition Stadium.

May 28 — The Rangers score six runs in the ninth after two are out off Steve Shields, Jeff Reardon and Lee Tunnell to stun the Twins 8–6 at the Metrodome. The three relievers combined to allow six straight hits (four singles and two doubles) after the second out was recorded.

May 30	The Twins score all seven of their runs in the second inning of a 7–1 victory over the Royals in Kansas City.
May 31	Dan Gladden hits a grand slam off Tom Gordon in the sixth inning of a 7–1 win over the Royals in Kansas City. Two pitches after Gladden's slam, the game was called by rain. All three games of the series in Kansas City were settled by 7–1 score. The Royals won 7–1 on May 29 and the Twins on May 30.
June 5	In the first round of the amateur draft, the Twins select shortstop Chuck Knoblauch from Texas A&M University.

> *The Twins moved the fiery Knoblauch to second base at the Class AA level in 1990, and in 1991, he won the Rookie of the Year Award with the world champions. Despite being only five-foot-nine, he starred at second base for the Twins for seven seasons before being traded to the Yankees. Knoblauch's on-base percentage of .391 as a Twin is the third highest in club history. Knoblauch set a single-season franchise record in 1996 by scoring 140 runs. The 1991 draft was arguably the most productive in club history. Other future major leaguers drafted and signed by the Twins were Denny Neagle (second round), Scott Erickson (fourth round), Marty Cordova (tenth round), Dan Masteller (11th round), Mike Trombley (14th round), George Tsamis (15th round) and Denny Hocking (52nd round).*

June 10	With the Twins trailing 8–7 and two out in the eighth inning, Jim Dwyer hits a grand slam off Bobby Thigpen to defeat the White Sox 11–8 at the Metrodome. Dwyer entered the game in the seventh as a pinch-hitter for Brian Harper and remained in the line-up as a designated hitter.
June 13	The Twins score a run in the ninth inning and one in the 11th to defeat the Mariners 4–3 at the Metrodome. The 11th inning rally was accomplished despite the fact the pitcher Allan Anderson was used as a pinch-hitter. During the ninth inning, Tom Kelly inserted John Moses into the game as a pinch-hitter for Tim Laudner. Brian Harper was the only other catcher on the roster and was already in the contest as a designated hitter. After Harper was moved behind the plate, the Twins lost the use of the DH for the rest of the game. The Twins also had no remaining position players on the bench. With runners on second and third and no one out in the 11th, Anderson pinch-hit for fellow pitcher Gary Wayne. Anderson struck out in what would prove to be his only career plate appearance. Fortunately, Al Newman saved the day with a walk-off single to give Wayne his first career victory.

> *Harper hit .325 with eight homers in 385 at-bats in 1989. He drew only 13 walks, but struck out just 16 times.*

June 18	After the Brewers score three runs in the top of the ninth to tie the score 6–6, Gary Gaetti delivers a two-run, walk-off homer in the bottom half for an 8–6 win at the Metrodome.
June 22	After falling behind 8–3, the Twins score four runs in the seventh inning and two in the ninth to defeat the Indians 9–8 in Cleveland. Tim Laudner tied the game 8–8 with a double and John Moses drove in the game winner with a sacrifice fly.
June 23	Gary Gaetti hits two homers and drives in five runs during a 10–0 win over the Red Sox in Boston.

June 26	Kirby Puckett hits a walk-off homer in the tenth inning to defeat the Athletics 4–3 at the Metrodome.
June 27	The Twins score eight runs in the sixth inning and defeat the Athletics 11–5 at the Metrodome. The Twins collected only four hits during the eight-run rally. Kent Hrbek drew two of the five walks issued by Oakland pitchers in the inning.
July 18	Gene Larkin collects five singles in five at-bats during a 5–4 win over the Indians at the Metrodome. Larkin also scored the winning run on a sacrifice fly by Jim Dwyer in the ninth inning. Joe Carter hit two homers for Cleveland.
July 19	Joe Carter hits three homers off Twins pitching during a 10–1 Indians victory in Cleveland. The five homers by Carter in consecutive games tied a major league record.
June 24	John Moses pinch-hits in the sixth inning and then plays as a right fielder, center fielder and pitcher during an 11–2 loss to the Red Sox in the second game of a double-header in Boston. Moses pitched a scoreless eighth. He faced four batters, walking one. The Twins also lost the opener 6–2.
July 30	The Twins bookend five runs in both the first and ninth innings and beat the Tigers 14–3 in Detroit.
July 31	The Twins trade Frank Viola to the Mets for Rick Aguilera, Kevin Tapani, David West, Tim Drummond and Jack Savage. The deal was finalized about a minute before the midnight trading deadline.
	After a 24–7 season in 1988, Viola was 8–12 in 1989 at the time of the trade. Twins fans were outraged by the deal, especially after Viola, a native of New York, was 20–12 for the Mets in 1990. But in the long run it was a positive transaction, and it's doubtful the 1991 world championship could have been accomplished without it. All five players acquired in exchange for Viola were pitchers. Aguilera became the closer and played in the All-Star Game in a Twins uniform in 1991, 1992 and 1993. At the end of the 2009 season, he ranks second in Twins history in games pitched (490) and first in saves (254). Tapani was a 16-game winner for Minnesota in 1991 and 1992.
August 26	The Twins edge the Mariners 1–0 at the Metrodome. David West (7 2/3 innings) and Jeff Reardon (1 1/3 innings) combined on the shutout. Kirby Puckett drove in the lone run with a single in the third inning.
August 27	The Twins score seven runs in the fifth inning and defeat the Mariners 8–5 at the Metrodome. John Moses doubled and singled during the rally.
August 28	The Twins trade Jim Dwyer to the Expos for Alonzo Powell.
September 1	The Twins play at SkyDome in Toronto for the first time and lose 7–3 to the Blue Jays.
September 5	Gene Larkin collects a homer, two doubles and a single during a 9–4 win over the Blue Jays in Toronto.
September 12	Kent Hrbek hits a grand slam off Duane Ward in the seventh inning of an 8–2 victory over the Blue Jays at the Metrodome.

SEPTEMBER 27 — Facing Shawn Hillegas, Dan Gladden hits the first pitch of the game for a home run sparking a 6–1 win over the White Sox in Chicago.

SEPTEMBER 29 — The Twins collect 24 hits and beat the Mariners 10–7 in 11 innings in Seattle. The even two-dozen hits consisted of a club-record 20 singles, plus a double, a triple and two homers. Dan Gladden had five singles and a sacrifice fly in six plate appearances. Minnesota won despite committing six errors, four of them from Al Newman at two different positions. Newman made errors as a third baseman in the second, third and fourth innings and as a second baseman in the ninth.

Gladden collected eight consecutive hits (six singles, a double and a homer) over three games on September 27, 29 and 30.

OCTOBER 1 — On the last day of the season, Kirby Puckett wins the batting title during a 3–1 loss to the Mariners in Seattle. Heading into the day, Puckett was hitting .3381 while Carney Lansford of the Athletics had an average of .3376. Against the Royals in Kansas City, Lansford was hitless in three at-bats, while Puckett went two-for-five at the Kingdome. Puckett won the batting title over Lansford .339 to .336.

NOVEMBER 8 — Three weeks after an earthquake interrupts the World Series between the Giants and Athletics, the Timberwolves play their first regular season home game and lose 96–87 to the Bulls before 35,427 at the Metrodome. Michael Jordan scored 45 points.

The Metrodome served as the home of the Timberwolves for one season. The club drew 1,027,572 in 41 home games to lead the NBA in attendance. The Metrodome is one of the two venues to serve as the home of a Major League team, an NFL team and another from the NBA. The other is the Kingdome in Seattle from 1978 through 1985.

NOVEMBER 22 — Kirby Puckett signs a three-year contract worth $9 million making him the first player in baseball history to earn at least $3 million in a season. The total deal of $9 million was also a record. Puckett's distinction as the highest paid player in baseball history lasted only six days. On November 28, Rickey Henderson inked a four-year, $12 million deal with the Athletics. On December 1, Mark Langston signed with the Angels for five years and $16 million. In the end, Puckett's $9 million deal was a Twins record for only two weeks. On December 6, the club retained Kent Hrbek for five years and $14 million.

DECEMBER 4 — The Twins select Shane Mack from the Padres in the Rule 5 draft.

Mack proved to be a steal. He played five seasons with the Twins, and hit .309 with 67 home runs. Among Twins with at least 2,000 plate appearances with the club, Mack's batting average ranks fourth behind Rod Carew, Kirby Puckett and Joe Mauer.

DECEMBER 6 — The Red Sox sign Jeff Reardon as a free agent.

Reardon had two seasons ahead of him as an effective closer for the Red Sox before heading into a decline. When he retired in 1994, he had 367 career saves.

THE STATE OF THE TWINS

After finishing last in the Western Division with the tenth-best record in the AL in 1990, the Twins won more games than any other team in the league in 1991 and won the World Series against the Braves. A 90–72 mark in 1992 was followed by eight straight losing seasons. Overall, the Twins were 718–833 during the 1990s, a winning percentage of .463 which was 12th among the 13 teams that were a part of the American League during the entire decade. The Twins beat out only the Tigers. AL champions during the 1990s were the Athletics (1990), Twins (1991), Blue Jays (1992 and 1993), Indians (1995 and 1997) and Yankees (1996, 1998 and 1999). There was no champion in 1994 because of the players' strike. AL West champs during the years that Minnesota was part of the division were the Athletics (1990 and 1992), Twins (1991) and White Sox (1993). The Indians won the AL Central every year from 1995 through 1999.

THE BEST TEAM

The Best Team was the 1991 world champions, which was 95–67 during the regular season and beat the Blue Jays and Braves in the postseason.

THE WORST TEAM

The 1995 team was 56–88 in the strike-shortened season to post a winning percentage of .389, the worst of any Twins team since 1982. The 1999 club lost the most games with a mark of 63–97.

THE BEST MOMENT

Gene Larkin's walk-off single in the tenth inning beat the Braves 1–0 in game seven of the 1991 World Series.

THE WORST MOMENT

Kirby Puckett was forced to retire in 1996 because of an eye ailment.

THE ALL-DECADE TEAM • YEARS W/TWINS

Brian Harper, c	1988–93
Kent Hrbek, 1b	1981–94
Chuck Knoblauch, 2b	1991–97
Scott Leius, 3b	1990–95
Pat Meares, ss	1993–98
Shane Mack, lf	1990–94
Kirby Puckett, cf	1984–95
Matt Lawton, rf	1995–2001
Paul Molitor, dh	1996–98
Kevin Tapani, p	1989–95
Brad Radke, p	1995–2006
Scott Erickson, p	1990–95
Rick Aguilera, p	1989–99

Hrbek was on the 1980s All-Decade Team. Molitor is in the Hall of Fame. Other prominent Twins players during the decade included left fielder Marty Cordova (1995–99) and pitcher Mike Trombley (1992–99, 2002). The club fielded strong outfields throughout the decade, but third base was a constant problem.

THE DECADE LEADERS

Batting Avg:	Shane Mack	.309
On-Base Pct:	Chuck Knoblauch	.391
Slugging Pct:	Shane Mack	.479
Home Runs:	Kent Hrbek	92
RBIs:	Kirby Puckett	579
Runs:	Chuck Knoblauch	713
Stolen Bases:	Chuck Knoblauch	276
Wins:	Kevin Tapani	73
Strikeouts:	Kevin Tapani	703
ERA:	Rick Aguilera	3.54
Saves:	Rick Aguilera	254

THE HOME FIELD

The Metrodome was in its ninth season in 1990. There were no major changes made to the facility during the decade. The Metrodome hosted the World Series in October 1991, the Super Bowl in January 1992 and the Final Four in April 1992.

THE GAME YOU WISHED YOU HAD SEEN

How does it get better than a spine-tingling game seven of the World Series. On October 27, 1991, the Twins beat the Braves 1–0 in ten innings at the Metrodome.

THE WAY THE GAME WAS PLAYED

Baseball experienced one of its pivotal transitions during the 1990s, as offensive numbers soared to new heights. Fueled by expansion to 30 teams, newer ballparks with fences closer to home plate, and the use by some players of performance-enhancing substances, the average number of home runs in the AL increased from 123 per team in 1989 to 188 per team in 1999, with a peak of 196 in 1996. The average number of runs per game increased from 8.6 in 1989 to 10.4 in 1999 with a high of 10.6 in 1996. The trend of the 1970s and 1980s toward artificial turf ended as every new ballpark that opened or was on the drawing board had a grass field. The "retro" look, beginning with Camden Yards in 1992, was the wave of the future as most of the new facilities tried to emulate the older classic venues like Fenway Park. Four new teams were added in Miami, Denver, St. Petersburg and Phoenix. Beginning in 1994, there were three divisions in each league, adding a new tier of playoffs. Interleague play started in 1997.

THE MANAGEMENT

Carl Pohlad owned the Twins from 1984 until his death in 2009. The general managers were Andy MacPhail (1984–94) and Terry Ryan (1994–2007). The field manager was Tom Kelly (1986–2001).

THE BEST PLAYER MOVE

The best player move sent a minor leaguer to the Marlins in December 1999 for Johan Santana and $500,000.

THE WORST PLAYER MOVE

The worst move occurred in March 1992 when the Twins traded Denny Neagle and Midre Cummings to the Pirates for John Smiley.

1990

Season in a Sentence
The Twins are 21–7 in May, 7–21 in June, outscore only two teams in the AL and finish in last place.

Finish • Won • Lost • Pct • GB
Sixth   74   88   .457   29.0

Manager
Tom Kelly

Stats   Twins • AL • Rank
Batting Avg: .265   .259   4
On-Base Pct: .324   .327   11
Slugging Pct: .385   .388   8
Home Runs: 100   13
Stolen Bases: 96   10
ERA: 4.12   3.91   11
Errors: 101   4
Runs Scored: 666   12
Runs Allowed: 729   10

Starting Line-up
Brian Harper, c
Kent Hrbek, 1b
Al Newman, 2b
Gary Gaetti, 3b
Greg Gagne, ss
Dan Gladden, lf
Kirby Puckett, cf
Shane Mack, rf-cf
Gene Larkin, dh-rf-1b
Fred Manrique, 2b

Pitchers
Kevin Tapani, sp
Allen Anderson, sp
Roy Smith, sp
David West, sp
Mark Guthrie, sp
Scott Erickson, sp
Rick Aguilera, rp
Juan Berenguer, rp
Tim Drummond, rp
Terry Leach, rp

Attendance
1,751,584 (11th in AL)

Club Leaders
Batting Avg: Kirby Puckett   .298
On-Base Pct: Kent Hrbek   .377
Slugging Pct: Kent Hrbek   .474
Home Runs: Kent Hrbek   22
RBIs: Kirby Puckett   80
Runs: Kirby Puckett   82
Stolen Bases: Dan Gladden   25
Wins: Kevin Tapani   12
Strikeouts: Kevin Tapani   101
               Mark Guthrie   101
ERA: Allen Anderson 4.53
Saves: Rick Aguilera   32

JANUARY 31   Wally Backman signs with the Pirates as a free agent.

FEBRUARY 15 The owners lock the players out of spring training because of a lack of progress in negotiations for a new basic agreement.

FEBRUARY 28 The Twins sign John Candelaria, most recently with the Expos, as a free agent.

MARCH 18   The labor dispute between the players and owners is resolved.

Spring training camps opened on March 20. The season, scheduled to start on April 2, was delayed a week, with missed games made up on open dates, with double-headers, and by extending the end of the campaign by three days.

APRIL 9   The Twins open the season with an 8–3 loss to the Athletics in Oakland. Allan Anderson was the starting and losing pitcher. Greg Gagne homered and Kirby Puckett collected three hits in the losing cause.

APRIL 10   Dan Gladden homers on the first pitch of the game from Bob Welch, but the Twins lose 5–3 to the Athletics in Oakland.

April 11	Kent Hrbek hits a three-run homer with one out in the first inning to account for all of the runs in a 3–0 win over the Athletics in Oakland. Kevin Tapani (six innings), Gary Wayne (one-third of an inning), Terry Leach (1 2/3 innings) and Rick Aguilera (one inning) combined on the shutout.
	Hrbek hit .287 with 22 homers in 1990.
April 20	In the home opener, the Twins score nine runs in the fifth inning and wallop the Angels 13–1 before 37,975 at the Metrodome. Gene Larkin singled twice during the rally and Kirby Puckett walked and homered.
April 24	The Twins erupt for seven runs in the sixth inning and rout the Tigers 16–4 at the Metrodome. Gene Larkin contributed a double and a single to the rally.
May 2	Gary Gaetti drives in six runs to lead the Twins to an 8–2 triumph over the Tigers in Detroit. Gaetti struck three-run homers off Jack Morris in the fourth and sixth innings.
May 3	Gary Gaetti hits a two-run homer in the tenth inning to down the Tigers 3–1 in Detroit.
May 5	Brian Harper breaks a 5–5 tie in the eighth inning with a grand slam off Dan Plesac to lift the Twins to a 9–5 victory over the Brewers in Milwaukee. The homer by Harper came on the second pitch following a 25-minute rain delay.
May 8	After the Indians score five runs in the first inning off David West, the Twins counter with a run in the second, another in the third, three in the fourth and one in the seventh to win 6–5 at the Metrodome. After the opening inning, West, Juan Berenguer (3 2/3 innings) and Rick Aguilera (one inning) combined to allow only one hit.
May 14	Kirby Puckett collects five hits, including two doubles, during a 6–2 win over the Athletics at the Metrodome.
May 16	In New York, Yankee pitcher Andy Hawkins retires all 13 Twins batters he faces, but they don't count in the official statistics because the game ends with one out in the top of the fifth because of rain (see July 6, 1990).
May 19	John Moses plays right field, center field and pitches during a 13–1 loss to the Red Sox in Boston. Moses pitched the eighth inning and allowed a run and two hits.
May 25	The Twins collect 19 hits and clobber the Red Sox 16–0 at the Metrodome. Roy Smith pitched the shutout. Boston outfielder Danny Heep pitched the eighth inning and allowed a run.
	The Twins started the season 7–12, but were 29–20 by June 2. A streak of 15 losses in 17 games beginning on June 3 dispelled any notions that the club would reach the postseason.

JUNE 4	With the 12th overall pick in the first round of the amateur draft, the Twins select pitcher Todd Ritchie from Duncanville High School in Duncanville, Texas.
	Ritchie played for the Twins in 1997 and 1998 at the start of an eight-year career. Overall, he was 43–54 with a 4.71 ERA. Other future major leaguers drafted and signed by the Twins in 1991 were Midre Cummings (also in the first round), Jayhawk Owens (second round), Rich Becker (third round), Brent Brede (fifth round), Pat Meares (12th round), Damian Miller (20th round), Eddie Guardado (20th round) and Brian Raabe (21st round). The club also signed Cory Lidle as an amateur free agent in August.
JUNE 5	Kirby Puckett collects five hits, including a double, in five at-bats during a 12–5 victory over the Blue Jays in Toronto.
JULY 1	The Twins play a regularly scheduled night game at home on a Sunday night, and win 4–3 over the Orioles. The game was televised nationally on ESPN.
JULY 6	The Twins score two runs in the 12th inning to defeat the Yankees 2–0 in New York. Gene Larkin and Brian Harper drove in the two tallies with singles off Andy Hawkins, who pitched 11 shutout innings before allowing the pair of 12th-inning runs. Allen Anderson (nine innings), Juan Berenguer (two innings) and Rick Aguilera (one inning) combined on the Minnesota shutout.
	In his previous start on July 1, Hawkins pitched a no-hitter against the White Sox at Comiskey Park but lost 4–0. The four Chicago runs scored in the eighth inning on three errors and two walks. In his first start after the 12-inning loss to the Twins, Hawkins was the losing pitcher in an 8–0 decision to the White Sox in New York in which Meildo Perez pitched a rain-shortened, six-inning no-hitter.
JULY 15	Kirby Puckett plays only six innings, but hits two homers and drives in five runs during a 10–3 win over the Orioles in Baltimore.
JULY 16	The Twins score two runs in the ninth inning to defeat the Red Sox 3–2 in Boston. Brian Harper drove in the tying run and scored on Paul Sorrento's triple. Sorrento was out trying to stretch the drive into an inside-the-park homer.
JULY 17	The Twins become the only major league team to turn two triple plays in one game but wind up losing 1–0 to the Red Sox at Fenway Park.
	The July 17 contest is the only one in major league history in which two triple plays have been recorded. They are also the only triple plays turned by the Twins between 1988 and 2006. Both triple plays were started by third baseman Gary Gaetti, who fielded a bases-loaded smash by Tom Brunansky in the fourth inning and Jody Reed's sharp grounder in the eighth with runners on first and second. On both plays, Gaetti stepped on third and threw to Al Newman on second, who relayed to Kent Hrbek at first. The Boston base runners retired were Reed and Carlos Quintana in the fourth and Tim Naehring and Wade Boggs in the eighth. The pitchers in the game for the Twins when the triple plays were completed were Scott Erickson in the fourth and John Candelaria in the eighth.

July 18 — A day after turning two triple plays, the Twins record six double plays, including five in the first five innings, but lose again 6–4 to the Red Sox at Fenway Park. The Sox completed four double plays of their own. The two clubs set a major league mark for the most double plays in a contest with ten. The six double plays by the Twins is one short of a record by one team in a contest. First baseman Kent Hrbek participated in all six Minnesota twin killings, one of them of the 3–6–3 variety. Second baseman Fred Manrique and shortstop Al Newman were in five double plays each.

July 27 — The Twins trade John Candelaria to the Blue Jays for Nelson Liriano and Pedro Munoz.

July 31 — After starting the game on the bench, John Moses plays center field in the eighth inning and pitches in the ninth during a 13–2 loss to the Angels at the Metrodome. As a pitcher, Moses allowed two runs and three hits. It was his third major league pitching appearance.

August 3 — A three-run homer by Randy Bush caps a four-run 13th inning that beats the Mariners 6–2 in Seattle.

August 4 — Brian Harper extends his winning streak to 25 games during a 4–3 loss to the Mariners in Seattle.

Harper's streak started on July 6. He collected 38 hits in 99 at-bats over the 25 games, an average of .384.

August 5 — Three days after Iraq invades Kuwait, and two days before Operation Desert Storm troops leave for Saudi Arabia, a frightening incident occurs in the fourth inning of a 4–0 loss to the Mariners at the Kingdome. A line drive off the bat of Gary Gaetti struck Seattle pitcher Bill Swift squarely on the forehead and caromed into the third-base stands for a ground-rule double. Felled by the drive, Swift was sprawled for four minutes before walking off the field with assistance and was later found to have suffered only a concussion.

August 16 — Kirby Puckett plays right field, third base, shortstop and second base during a 7–5 loss to the Indians in Cleveland. Puckett played the three infield positions during the eighth inning after Tom Kelly ran out of substitutes. Kirby played on the left side of the diamond against left-handed batters and second base against right-handers, shifting with Nelson Liriano and Al Newman. It was the first time in his career that Puckett played in the infield. He later played three more games at second, three at third and two at short.

August 29 — Greg Gagne homers and steals three bases, including home plate, during a 6–1 victory over the White Sox at the Metrodome. Gagne stole home in the fourth inning on a double steal in which Dan Gladden swiped second.

August 30 — A fluke inside-the-park grand slam gives the White Sox a 4–3 win over the Twins at the Metrodome. With the bases loaded in the fourth inning, Ron Karkovice hit a drive over the glove of shortstop Greg Gagne and rolled to the fence, where left fielder Dan Gladden had trouble fielding the ball.

SEPTEMBER 3	The Twins score five runs in the ninth inning to defeat the Brewers 9–5 in the second game of a double-header in Milwaukee. Al Newman drove in the tying run with a single and Gary Gaetti put Minnesota ahead with an RBI double. Shane Mack provided the insurance runs with a three-run double. The Twins also won the opener 6–0.
SEPTEMBER 4	The Twins leave 17 runners on base but beat the Brewers 7–1 in Milwaukee. Twins batters collected 19 hits and drew six walks.
SEPTEMBER 13	Paul Sorrento hits a two-run homer in the tenth inning to defeat the Athletics 3–1 in Oakland. Scott Erickson (eight innings) and Juan Berenguer (two innings) combined on a three-hitter.
SEPTEMBER 19	The Twins outlast the Royals to win 1–0 in 11 innings at the Metrodome. Shane Mack drove in the winning run with a two-out single. Mark Guthrie (nine innings) and Gary Wayne (two innings) combined on the shutout.
SEPTEMBER 22	Kent Hrbek's season comes to a premature end when he sprains his ankle while engaging in horseplay with teammates in the clubhouse.
SEPTEMBER 23	Gary Gaetti hits a grand slam off Charlie Hough in the first inning to spark a 6–4 victory over the Rangers at the Metrodome.
SEPTEMBER 26	The Twins play at the original Comiskey Park in Chicago for the last time and lose 3–1 to the White Sox.
NOVEMBER 2	The Timberwolves play their first regular season game at the Target Center, and beat the Dallas Mavericks 98–85.
DECEMBER 5	The Twins trade Johnny Ard and Jimmy Williams to the Giants for Steve Bedrosian.
	Bedrosian won the NL Cy Young Award as a reliever with the Phillies in 1987, but he was a disappointment in his only season in Minnesota. He had a 4.42 ERA in 56 games and 77 1/3 innings.

1991

Season in a Sentence
The Twins go from last place in the AL West in 1990 to the best record in the AL in 1991, and then defeat the Blue Jays in the ALCS and the Braves in one of the most thrilling World Series in history.

Finish • Won • Lost • Pct • GB
First   95   67   .586   +8.0

AL Championship Series
The Twins beat the Toronto Blue Jays four games to one.

World Series
The Twins beat the Atlanta Braves four games to three.

Manager
Tom Kelly

Stats   Twins • AL • Rank
Batting Avg: .280   .260   1
On-Base Pct: .344   .329   1
Slugging Pct: .428   .395   2
Home Runs: 140   6
Stolen Bases: 107   7
ERA: 3.69   4.09   3
Errors: 95   2
Runs Scored: 776   4
Runs Allowed: 652   3

Starting Line-up
Brian Harper, c
Kent Hrbek, 1b
Chuck Knoblauch, 2b
Mike Pagliarulo, 3b
Greg Gagne, ss
Dan Gladden, lf
Kirby Puckett, cf
Shane Mack, rf-lf
Chili Davis, dh
Gene Larkin, rf-1b
Al Newman, ss-2b
Scott Leius, 3b

Pitchers
Jack Morris, sp
Scott Erickson, sp
Kevin Tapani, sp
Allan Anderson, sp
Rick Aguilera, rp
Mark Guthrie, rp
Carl Willis, rp
Steve Bedrosian, rp
Terry Leach, rp

Attendance
2,293,842 (eighth in AL)

Club Leaders
Batting Avg: Kirby Puckett   .319
On-Base Pct: Chili Davis   .385
Slugging Pct: Shane Mack   .529
Home Runs: Chili Davis   29
RBI: Chili Davis   93
Runs: Kirby Puckett   92
Stolen Bases: Chuck Knoblauch   25
Wins: Scott Erickson   20
Strikeouts: Jack Morris   163
ERA: Kevin Tapani   2.99
Saves: Rick Aguilera   42

JANUARY 23 — Six days after the United States and its allies launch an air attack against Iraq to start the Persian Gulf War, Gary Gaetti signs with the Angels as a free agent.

Gaetti had been the Twins starting third baseman since 1982, but was 32 at the start of the 1991 season and was coming off of the worst season of his career in which he batted .229 with 16 homers in 154 games. Gaetti continued to struggle with the Angels before being released outright in June 1993. He soon signed a deal with the Royals and found new life in Kansas City, collecting 35 homers in 137 games in 1995. Gaetti played in the postseason with the Cardinals in 1996 and the Cubs in 1998 before his career ended in 2000. Meanwhile, the Twins searched for a competent replacement at the hot corner, a search that would take

1990s

far longer than expected. No one with the club played at least 100 games at third in consecutive seasons during the 1990s.

JANUARY 25   The Twins sign Mike Pagliarulo, most recently with the Padres, as a free agent. He would replace Gary Gaetti at third base.

JANUARY 29   The Twins sign Chili Davis, most recently with the Angels, as a free agent. On the same day, Juan Berenguer signed with the Braves as a free agent.

Davis became the first Jamaican-born player to reach the majors, with the San Francisco Giants in 1981. He earned his unusual nickname as a result of a bad haircut as a youth that a friend said looked like the barber used a chili bowl to do the cutting. Davis gave the Twins one great season as a designated hitter with a .277 average and 29 homers. After slumping in 1992, he returned to the Angels.

FEBRUARY 5   The Twins sign Jack Morris, most recently with the Tigers, as a free agent.

A native of St. Paul, Morris had long desired to pitch for the Twins. At the time he was signed, Morris was 35 and had a career record of 198–150, but was 21–32 over the previous two seasons. He pitched only one season in Minnesota, but it was unforgettable. Morris was 18–12 with a 3.43 ERA in 246 2/3 innings during the regular season, and then beat the Braves with a ten-inning, 1–0 win in game seven of the World Series, one of the most memorable games in team history.

FEBRUARY 20   The Twins open training camp in Ft. Myers, Florida. The move ended a long association with Orlando, where the franchise trained as the Washington Senators from 1936 through 1942 and again from 1946 through 1960, and as the Twins from 1961 through 1990. In 1943, 1944 and 1945, the Senators trained in College Park, Maryland, because of World War II travel restrictions. The Red Sox joined the Twins in Ft. Myers in 1993.

APRIL 9   Six weeks after President George Bush orders a ceasefire to end the Persian Gulf War, the Twins open the season with a 7–2 loss to the Athletics in Oakland. In his Twins debut, starter Jack Morris gave up seven runs, three of them earned, in 4 2/3 innings. Greg Gagne and Chili Davis homered to account for the two Minnesota runs. It was also Davis's first game with the Twins.

Morris set a major league record by making 14 consecutive Opening Day starts with the Tigers (1980–90), Twins (1991) and Blue Jays (1992–93).

APRIL 12   In the home opener, Kevin Tapani pitches a complete-game shutout to defeat the Angels 6–0 before 45,866 at the Metrodome.

Tapani was 16–9 with a 2.99 ERA in 244 innings in 1991.

APRIL 13   St. Paul native Dave Winfield has one of the greatest games of his Hall of Fame career with three homers, a double and single to lead the Angels to a 15–9 win over the Twins at the Metrodome. He also drove in six runs and scored four.

After training in Florida, the Twins opened the season in Oakland, traveled to Minnesota for a three-game series against the Angels, and then went back to the West Coast to play the Mariners and Angels. The brutal schedule may have contributed to a slow start. Through their first 11 games, the Twins had a record of 2–9.

APRIL 25 After the Mariners score in the top of the tenth inning, the Twins rebound with two in their half to win 4–3 at the Metrodome. With one out and the bases loaded in the tenth, and the Twins still down a run, Seattle pitcher Mike Jackson threw a wild pitch that brought Kirby Puckett home from third. Al Newman tried to score from second on the play, and was safe on an error when Jackson, covering home, dropped the throw from catcher Dave Valle.

APRIL 28 Jack Morris earns his 200th career victory with an 8–2 decision over the Mariners at the Metrodome.

MAY 1 Scott Erickson pitches a two-hitter to defeat the Red Sox 1–0 at the Metrodome. The only Boston hits were a single by Jody Reed in the sixth inning and a double from Tom Brunansky in the seventh. The only run scored on a home run by Dan Gladden off Jeff Gray in the eighth.

MAY 14 Jack Morris pitches a two-hitter to beat the Brewers 5–1 at the Metrodome. Jim Gantner collected both Milwaukee hits with doubles in the fourth and seventh innings.

MAY 23 Kirby Puckett collects six hits in seven at-bats during an 11-inning, 10–6 loss to the Rangers at the Metrodome. Puckett started the evening with singles off Jose Guzman in the first and third before flying out in the fourth. Kirby's last four hits came off four different pitchers with a single off John Barfield in the sixth, a single against Goose Gossage in the seventh, a triple versus Mike Jeffcoat in the ninth and a triple facing Jim Poole in the 11th.

Puckett also had a six-hit game on August 30, 1987. He is one of only three players since 1900 with two career games of six hits or more. The others are Jim Bottomley with the Cardinals in 1924 and 1931, and Jimmie Foxx for the Philadelphia Athletics in 1930 and 1932.

MAY 28 Dan Gladden hits the first pitch of the game from Jose Guzman to spark a 3–0 win over the Rangers in Arlington. Scott Erickson (eight innings) and Rick Aguilera (one inning) combined on the shutout.

The Rangers came into the contest riding a 14-game winning streak, while the Twins were floundering with a 20–24 record. The 3–0 victory ignited a turnaround as Minnesota was 24–3 from May 28 through June 25 and 75–43 over the rest of the regular season. During the stretch of 24 wins in 27 games in May and June, the Twins went from fifth place, 7½ games behind, to first with a 4½-game advantage.

JUNE 3 With the third overall pick in the first round of the amateur draft, the Twins select first baseman David McCarty from Stanford University.

McCarty played for the Twins from 1993 through 1995 at the start of a major league career that lasted until 2005. He never came close to living up to his billing and spent most of his career bouncing between the minors and majors. McCarty never accumulated more than 300 plate appearances in a season after his rookie year. He finished his stay in the majors with a .242 batting average and 36 homers in 1,493 at-bats. Nonetheless, the Twins had a successful draft by mining some bargain picks in LaTroy Hawkins (seventh round), Brad Radke (eighth round) and Matt Lawton (13th round). Other future major leaguers drafted and signed by the Twins in 1991 were Steve Stahoviak (also in the first round) and Mike Durant (second round).

JUNE 7 — Allan Anderson (eight innings) and Rick Aguilera (one inning) combine on a two-hitter to defeat the Indians 2–0 at the Metrodome. The only Cleveland hits were a single by Mike Huff in the fourth inning and a double from Joel Skinner in the eighth.

JUNE 12 — Pedro Munoz hits a grand slam off Jeff Johnson in the first inning of a 6–3 win over the Yankees at the Metrodome. It was the Twins 11th win in a row.

JUNE 14 — Shane Mack hits a grand slam off Reid Nichols in the fifth inning of a 7–0 triumph over the Indians in Cleveland. It was the Twins 13th win in a row.

Mack batted .310 with 18 home runs in 1991.

JUNE 16 — The Twins extend their winning streak to 15 games with a ten-inning, 4–2 decision over the Indians in Cleveland.

JUNE 17 — The Orioles score three runs in the ninth inning to defeat the Twins 6–5 in Baltimore and end the 15-game winning streak. The game ended on a two-out, two-run double by Randy Milligan.

After the tough loss on June 17, the Twins won the next four games. Were it not for the ninth-inning meltdown by Aguilera, the Twins would have won 20 in a row. The only other clubs since 1900 with 20 or more wins in succession are the 1916 New York Giants (26), 1935 Chicago Cubs (21) and 2002 Oakland Athletics (20). Still, the 15-game winning streak is the longest in Twins history. It was also the longest streak in the majors between 1977 (16 in a row by the Royals) and 2001 (15 straight by the Mariners). In franchise history, it has been exceeded only by the 1912 Washington Senators, a team that captured 17 in a row.

JUNE 19 — The Twins score five runs in the ninth inning to defeat the Orioles 8–4 at Memorial Stadium. The rally was aided by three wild pitches from Baltimore reliever Greg Olson, two while Shane Mack was at the plate. On one, Olson retrieved the ball and threw wildly home for an error.

JUNE 21 — Dan Gladden hits the first pitch of the game from Scott Sanderson for a home run, and the Twins defeat the Yankees 5–4 in New York.

JUNE 24 — Scott Erickson pitches a two-hitter to earn his 12th win in a row with a 5–0 decision over the Yankees in New York. The only hits off Erickson were a single from Don Mattingly in the first inning and a double from Matt Nokes in the second. The Twins pitcher retired 24 of the last 25 batters to face him.

The 12-game winning streak gave Erickson a record of 12–2. The 12-game streak set a club record later tied by Brad Radke in 1997 and Johan Santana in 2004. The franchise mark is 16 by Walter Johnson with the Senators in 1912, which is also the American League record. Erickson finished the season at 20–8 with a 3.18 ERA in 204 innings. He was only 23 and in his second season in the majors. After a 13–12 season in 1992, however, Erickson slumped to 8–19 in 1993 before being traded to the Orioles in 1995.

July 4 — The Twins edge the Blue Jays 1–0 in Toronto. David West (seven innings), Steve Bedrosian (one inning) and Rick Aguilera (one inning) combined on the shutout.

July 5 — The Twins play for the first time at the new Comiskey Park (now U.S. Cellular Field) and lose 4–2 to the White Sox.

July 9 — Jack Morris is the AL starting pitcher in the All-Star Game at Toronto's SkyDome and gives up a run in two innings. The American League went on to win 4–2.

July 11 — After dropping into second place in the last game prior to the All-Star break, the Twins retake sole possession of the top spot in the AL West with a 7–3 win over the Red Sox at the Metrodome.

The Twins remained in first for the rest of the season. The club pulled away from the pack in August by extending their lead from 1½ games on the 15th to eight games on the 26th.

July 14 — Tony Oliva's number 6 is retired in ceremonies prior to a 5–3 loss to the Red Sox at the Metrodome.

July 19 — Randy Bush hits a home run in his second straight pinch-hit at-bat during a 3–2 win over the Red Sox in Boston. The first one was also struck against the Red Sox on July 14 (see August 19, 1991). The winning run scored in the 11th when Chuck Knoblauch scored from first on a two-out pop-up by Mike Pagliarulo that fell between left fielder Steve Lyons and third baseman Mike Brumley.

July 21 — The Twins wallop the Red Sox 14–1 in Boston.

July 26 — The Twins tie a major league record with three successful sacrifice bunts in the eighth inning of a 6–3 victory over the Brewers at the Metrodome. The sacrifices were made by Greg Gagne, Al Newman and Jarvis Brown.

July 27 — Dan Gladden hits a three-run walk-off homer in the ninth inning to defeat the Brewers 7–4 at the Metrodome.

July 31 — The Twins score eight runs in the second inning and crush the Yankees 12–3 in New York. Kent Hrbek climaxed the rally with a grand slam off Scott Sanderson. It was one of 20 Minnesota hits.

August 3 — Trailing 5–0, the Twins erupt for seven runs in the eighth inning and defeat the Athletics 8–6 in Oakland. After the Twins scored four runs on a double, three singles and a walk before Brian Harper smacked a three-run homer for the 7–5 lead.

Harper hit .311 with ten homers in 1991.

AUGUST 16 — The Twins score two runs in the ninth inning and one in the 12th to down the Athletics 5–4 at the Metrodome. The two ninth-inning tallies scored off Dennis Eckersley. Mike Pagliarulo drove in the tying run with a single. Kent Hrbek's walk-off single was the game-winner.

AUGUST 19 — Randy Bush ties an American League record with his seventh consecutive pinch-hit at-bat during an 8–7 loss to the Athletics at the Metrodome. The record-tying hit was a double. The first six hits in the streak came on July 5 (single), July 14 (home run), July 19 (home run), July 27 (single), July 31 (single) and August 16 (double).

AUGUST 22 — The Twins pull a victory out of the fire with three runs in the ninth inning and one in the tenth to defeat the Mariners 5–4 at the Metrodome. Randy Bush deadlocked the contest with a three-run homer off Mickey Schooler with one out in the ninth. Schooler was still on the mound when Scott Leius hit a walk-off homer in the tenth. Leius entered the game in the top of the tenth as a defensive replacement in the top of the tenth.

AUGUST 24 — The Twins score four times in the ninth inning to defeat the Orioles 5–2 in Baltimore. Dan Gladden broke the 2–2 tie with a three-run triple.

AUGUST 25 — The Twins play at Memorial Stadium in Baltimore for the last time and lose 7–3 to the Orioles.

SEPTEMBER 1 — The Twins demolish the Orioles 14–3 at the Metrodome.

SEPTEMBER 2 — Shane Mack hits a grand slam off Steve Olin in the eighth inning of a 9–3 victory over the Indians at the Metrodome.

SEPTEMBER 13 — Kent Hrbek hits a three-run homer that caps a four-run rally in the tenth inning to defeat the Rangers 7–3 in Arlington.

SEPTEMBER 24 — Scott Erickson (seven innings) and Mark Guthrie (two innings) combine on a one-hitter to defeat the White Sox 9–2 at the Metrodome. The only Chicago hit was a two-run homer by Dan Pasqua with one out in the seventh inning.

Erickson, Jack Morris and Kevin Tapani combined for a 54–29 record and a 3.20 earned run average in 101 starts in 1991. The rest of the starters were 17–22 with an ERA of 5.15.

SEPTEMBER 25 — Chuck Knoblauch runs his hitting streak to 20 games during a 6–1 loss to the White Sox at the Metrodome.

SEPTEMBER 29 — The Twins lose 2–1 to the Blue Jays in Toronto, but they clinch the Western Division pennant because the second-place White Sox also lose 2–1 to the Mariners in Chicago.

OCTOBER 5 — Scott Erickson notches his 20th win of the season with a 3–1 decision over the Blue Jays at the Metrodome.

Kirby Puckett rounds the bases after hitting a game-winning home run in the 11th inning of Game Six of the World Series. Puckett had earlier tripled in a run and made a tremendous catch in centerfield. His home run—and emotional circling of the bases—is one of the most celebrated moments in team history.

The Twins played the Blue Jays in the final three regular season games, and six of the last ten, and then met them again in the American League Championship Series. Managed by Cito Gaston, the Blue Jays were 91–71 during the regular season.

OCTOBER 8   The Twins open the American League Championship Series with a 5–4 win over the Blue Jays before 54,766 at the Metrodome. The Twins scored two runs in the first inning, two more in the second, and another in the third for a 5–0 lead. Toronto countered with a run in the fourth and three in the sixth off Jack Morris, but relievers Carl Willis and Rick Aguilera shut out the opposition the rest of the way.

1990s

The Twins bullpen allowed no runs and only seven hits in 18 1/3 innings during the five games against the Blue Jays.

OCTOBER 9   The Blue Jays even the series by beating the Twins 5–2 before 54,816 at the Metrodome. Kevin Tapani was the starting and losing pitcher. Heading into the contest, the Twins had a 7–0 postseason record at the Metrodome.

OCTOBER 11   The Twins take a two-games-to-one lead in the ALCS with a 3–2 victory in ten innings over the Blue Jays in Toronto. The Blue Jays scored twice in the first inning but were shut out the rest of the way by Scott Erickson, David West, Carl Willis, Mark Guthrie and Rick Aguilera. Pinch-hitting for Scott Leius, Mike Pagliarulo homered off Mike Timlin in the tenth to provide the winning run.

The series was telecast nationally over CBS with Dick Stockton and Jim Kaat serving as announcers.

OCTOBER 12   The Twins move within one win of the American League pennant with a 9–3 trouncing of the Blue Jays in Toronto. The Twins erased a 1–0 deficit with four runs in the fourth inning. Kirby Puckett homered and singled twice, and Dan Gladden collected three singles.

OCTOBER 13   The Twins reach the World Series by coming from behind to beat the Blue Jays 8–5 in Toronto. Trailing 5–2, the Twins scored three runs in the sixth inning and three more in the eighth. Minnesota had runners on first and third with one out in the sixth when Dan Gladden hit a ground ball to third baseman Kelly Gruber, who threw home to stop Shane Mack from scoring but catcher Pat Borders missed the tag on Mack. Chuck Knoblauch then doubled home two runs to tie the score 5–5. Kirby Puckett broke the deadlock with a two-out single in the eighth.

The Twins met the Atlanta Braves in the World Series. Like the Twins, the Braves went from last place to first in one season. In 1990, Atlanta was 65–97. Managed by Bobby Cox, the club went 94–68 in 1991 and then beat the Pirates in seven games in the NLCS. It was the first time the Braves had been in the World Series since the move to Atlanta in 1966. The last time the franchise won a National League pennant was 1958, when it was located in Milwaukee.

OCTOBER 19   The Twins open the World Series with a 5–2 win over the Braves before 55,108 at the Metrodome. Greg Gagne extended the Minnesota lead from 1–0 to 4–0 with a three-run homer in the fifth inning. Jack Morris went seven innings for the win.

The 1991 World Series was telecast nationally by CBS. The announcers were Jack Buck and Tim McCarver.

OCTOBER 20   The Twins edge the Braves 3–2 in game two before a crowd of 55,145 at the Metrodome. Chili Davis rifled a homer with two out in the first inning for a 2–0 lead. After Atlanta responded with runs in the second and fifth to tie the score 2–2, Scott Leius homered off Tom Glavine in the eighth for the win. Leius came into the game with six career regular-season homers in 224 at-bats.

The game included a controversial call by first base umpire Drew Coble. In the third inning, Atlanta's Ron Gant tried to retreat to first base after hitting a single. Kent Hrbek, who weighed 250 pounds, took a throw from pitcher Kevin Tapani. The 172-pound Gant stepped on the bag before Hrbek applied the tag, but the Twins first baseman appeared to lean into Gant lifting the runner off the base. Coble ruled that Gant's momentum carried him off the bag, and not Hrbek's tag and called Gant out.

OCTOBER 22   The Braves claim their first victory of the series by defeating the Twins 5–4 in 12 innings at Atlanta-Fulton County Stadium. The Braves led 4–1 after six innings before the Twins tied the contest. Kirby Puckett hit a solo home run in the seventh and Chili Davis added a two-run, pinch-homer in the eighth. Davis started the game on the bench because the designated hitter rule isn't used in National League parks. Unaccustomed to managing without the DH, Tom Kelly ran out of position players in the 11th. In the top of the 12th, the Twins loaded the bases with two out. Rick Aguilera pinch-hit for Mark Guthrie and struck out. It was Aguilera's first plate appearance since 1989. He took the mound in the bottom of the inning and gave up the winning run. Mark Lemke ended the 12-inning struggle with a single. Before Aguilera gave up the run, Twins relievers had combined for 27 consecutive scoreless innings in the 1991 postseason.

OCTOBER 23   The Braves even the series by beating the Twins 3–2 in Atlanta. Mark Pagliarulo homered in the seventh inning to give the Twins a 2–1 lead, but the Braves rallied with runs in the seventh and ninth. The winning run scored on a triple by Mark Lemke and a sacrifice fly from Jerry Willard. Lemke scored on a close play following a throw home from right fielder Shane Mack. The Twins argued vociferously that Lemke was out on a tag by Brian Harper, but replays appeared to confirm the call by home plate umpire Terry Tata. Willard had only three hits during the 1991 regular season.

Harper made two key defensive plays in the fifth inning. Lonnie Smith tried to score from second on a double from Terry Pendleton and bowled over Harper on a play at the plate, but the Twins catcher held onto the ball. Later, Pendleton tried to score from third on a wild pitch and was tagged out by Harper, who retrieved the ball and made a successful lunge at the Braves base runner.

OCTOBER 24   The Braves take a three-games-to-two lead by walloping the Twins 14–5 in Atlanta.

David West faced six batters in the third and fifth games and allowed all six to reach base on four walks, a single and a home run. West pitched in the World Series again for the Phillies against the Blue Jays in 1993 and allowed the first four batters to reach base on three doubles and a single, running the streak to ten before he finally retired a hitter. Overall, West pitched one official inning in World Series play and surrendered seven hits, five walks, and seven runs for an ERA of 63.00.

OCTOBER 26   The Twins force a seventh game with a walk-off homer by Kirby Puckett off Charlie Leibrandt in the 11th inning that beat the Braves 4–3 before 55,155. The Twins scored twice in the first. Kirby Puckett drove in the first run with a triple and scored on Shane Mack's single. In the third, Puckett leaped high above the wall to rob Ron Gant of an extra bases. After Atlanta tied the contest 2–2 in the top of the fifth, Puckett broke the deadlock in the bottom half with a sacrifice fly. The Braves tied the game again in the seventh, setting the stage for more Puckett heroics.

1990s

The Twins are 11–1 in the postseason and 8–0 in the World Series at the Metrodome. Since the move to Minnesota, the club is 11–1 at home and 0–9 on the road in the World Series. Including the 1924, 1925 and 1933 World Series when the franchise was located the Washington, the Senators/Twins are 17–5 at home and 2–17 on the road.

OCTOBER 27   The Twins win the world championship with a ten-inning, 1–0 nail-biter over the Braves in game seven before 55,118. Jack Morris pitched the complete game shutout, allowing seven hits and two walks. The Braves blew an opportunity to win in the eighth inning. Lonnie Smith led off with a single and Terry Pendleton followed with a double. Smith lost sight of the ball, however, and hesitated rounding second base. He only reached third. Still, Atlanta had runners on second and third with none out. Morris bore down and induced Ron Gant to ground out to first baseman Kent Hrbek with the runners holding. After David Justice was intentionally walked to load the bases, Sid Bream hit into a double play, Hrbek to catcher Brian Harper and back to Hrbek. Dan Gladden started the tenth with a double off Alejandro Pena and was sacrificed to third by Chuck Knoblauch. After intentional walks to Kirby Puckett and Hrbek, Gene Larkin pinch-hit for Jarvis Brown and delivered a championship-winning single.

The 1991 World Series was one of the most exciting ever played. Five games were decided by one run, the winning run scored in the last half of the last inning of four contests, and a record three games went into extra innings, including the last two.

OCTOBER 31   The Twins are honored by President George Bush in a Rose Garden ceremony at the White House.

On the same day, Halloween festivities were canceled in the Twin Cities because of a blizzard that dumped 28.5 inches on Metro area before it ended on November 2.

DECEMBER 17   Steve Bedrosian signs with the Braves as a free agent.

DECEMBER 18   Jack Morris signs with the Blue Jays as a free agent.

Morris was 21–6 for the Blue Jays in 1992 and played for a world champion for the second year in a row. Like he had with the Tigers in 1984 and the Twins in 1991, Morris started game one of the 1992 Fall Classic. He went into a sharp decline after 1992, however, and was out of baseball after compiling a 17–18 record and a 5.91 ERA for the Blue Jays and Indians in 1993 and 1994.

DECEMBER 20   Dan Gladden signs a contract as a free agent with the Tigers.

1992

Season in a Sentence

The Twins hold a three-game lead in the AL West in late July with the best record in the majors, but an August and September collapse results in a second-place finish.

Finish • Won • Lost • Pct • GB

Second   90   72   .556   6.0

Manager

Tom Kelly

Stats

Stats	Twins	AL	Rank
Batting Avg:	.277	.259	1
On-Base Pct:	.341	.328	2
Slugging Pct:	.391	.385	7
Home Runs:	104		10
Stolen Bases:	123		8
ERA:	3.70	3.94	3
Errors:	95		4
Runs Scored:	747		3
Runs Allowed:	653		2

Starting Line-up

Brian Harper, c
Kent Hrbek, 1b
Chuck Knoblauch, 2b
Scott Leius, 3b
Greg Gagne, ss
Shane Mack, lf
Kirby Puckett, cf
Pedro Munoz, rf
Chili Davis, dh
Gene Larkin, 1b-rf

Pitchers

John Smiley, sp
Kevin Tapani, sp
Scott Erickson, sp
Bill Krueger, sp
Rick Aguilera, rp
Carl Willis, rp
Tom Edens, rp
Mark Guthrie, rp
Gary Wayne, rp

Attendance

2,482,428 (fifth in AL)

Club Leaders

Batting Avg:	Kirby Puckett	.329
On-Base Pct:	Shane Mack	.394
Slugging Pct:	Shane Mack	.490
Home Runs:	Kirby Puckett	19
RBI:	Kirby Puckett	110
Runs:	Chuck Knoblauch	104
	Kirby Puckett	104
Stolen Bases:	Chuck Knoblauch	34
Wins:	John Smiley	16
	Kevin Tapani	16
Strikeouts:	John Smiley	163
ERA:	John Smiley	3.21
Saves:	Rick Aguilera	41

JANUARY 26   The Super Bowl is played at the Metrodome with the Washington Redskins defeating the Buffalo Bills 37–24.

MARCH 6   Mike Pagliarulo suffers a perforated eardrum when hit in the head by a pitch from David West during an intrasquad game. Pagliarulo was limited to just 42 games in 1992 because of that injury and another in April when he broke a bone in the palm of his hand while swinging a bat during batting practice.

MARCH 17   The Twins trade Denny Neagle and Midre Cummings to the Pirates for John Smiley.

The deal was a good one for a year but was one they would regret in the long term. Smiley gave the Twins a fine season with a 16–9 record and a 3.21 ERA in 1992. At the end of the year, he opted for free agency, however, and signed with the Reds. Only 23 at the time of the trade, Neagle struggled with the Pirates in 1992 but developed into an excellent starting pitcher. From 1995 through 2000 with the Pirates, Braves and Reds, Neagle had a record of 89–47.

1990s

MARCH 28   The Twins trade Paul Sorrento to the Indians for Curt Leskanic and Oscar Munoz.

Sorrento was 26 at the time of the trade, had shown little indication that he would develop into a starting first baseman, and his path to the position was blocked by Kent Hrbek. Sorrento moved on to give the Indians and Mariners a half-dozen seasons of above-average offensive production. Leskanic never played a game for the Twins, while Munoz appeared in only ten ineffective contests with the club as a pitcher in 1995.

APRIL 6   In the opening game of the season, the Twins score two runs in the ninth inning to defeat the Brewers 4–2 in Milwaukee. Chuck Knoblauch broke the deadlock with a single, moved to third on Kirby Puckett's double and then crossed the plate on a pinch-hit sacrifice fly by Luis Quinones. It was Knoblauch's fourth hit of the game. The RBI by Quinones would prove to be the only one he collected in a Twins uniform and the last of his big league career. Kirby Puckett homered in the third. Scott Erickson was the starting pitcher and went six innings. Carl Willis notched the win and Rick Aguilera recorded the save. Vice-President Dan Quayle threw out the ceremonial first pitch.

On the same day, the NCAA championship basketball game was played at the Metrodome, with Duke defeating Michigan 71–51. Two days earlier in the semifinals, Duke defeated Indiana and Michigan downed Cincinnati. In a span of a little over six months, the Metrodome hosted the World Series, the Super Bowl and the Final Four.

APRIL 8   The Brewers score five runs in the ninth inning to defeat the Twins 9–5 at County Stadium. With two out in the ninth, Rick Aguilera had a 5–4 lead with Milwaukee runners on first and second when he surrendered a run-scoring single, a walk, and a grand slam to B. J. Surhoff.

APRIL 10   In the home opener, the Twins defeat the Rangers 7–1 before 53,031 at the Metrodome. Shane Mack homered leading off the first inning, and later added three singles and a stolen base. It was Mack's first plate appearance since being removed from a game two days earlier after he was hit in the head with a pitch.

Mack hit .315 with 16 homers in 1992.

MAY 2   Three days after riots begin in the South Central section of Los Angeles, resulting in the deaths of 52 people, the Twins hit four homers in the fourth inning of a 7–6 win over the Yankees in New York. All four were struck off Scott Sanderson in a span of six batters and 18 pitches. Shane Mack led off the inning with a homer that snapped a 2–2 tie. After Chuck Knoblauch flied out, Kirby Puckett and Kent Hrbek clouted back-to-back home runs. Following a ground out by Brian Harper, Randy Bush added the fourth Minnesota homer of the inning. The Yanks came back, however, to tie the score 6–6 with four tallies in the sixth. The game-winner was a home run by Chili Davis in the eighth.

Puckett batted .329 and added 19 homers, 110 RBIs and 104 runs scored in 1992.

MAY 6	The Twins play at Camden Yards in Baltimore for the first time, and lose 6–2 to the Orioles.
MAY 24	The Twins demolish the Tigers 15–0 in Detroit. Shane Mack hit a grand slam off Frank Tanana in the fourth inning. Bill Krueger (seven innings), Carl Willis (one inning) and Bob Kipper (one inning) combined on the shutout.
MAY 29	The Twins continue to strafe Tigers pitching with a 17–5 rout at the Metrodome. The Twins scored eight runs in the fourth inning, highlighted by a grand slam from Kirby Puckett off Les Lancaster and a double and a homer from Chili Davis. It was the first grand slam of Puckett's career, which began in 1984. He hit another one five days later.
MAY 30	Rob Deer of the Tigers has an unusual day during a 7–5 Twins victory at the Metrodome. After homering in the second inning, Deer hit drives off the roof for outs in consecutive plate appearances in the sixth and the eighth. Both balls deflected to shortstop Greg Gagne, who caught them on the fly.
JUNE 1	In the first round of the amateur draft, the Twins select pitcher Dan Serafini from Serra High School in San Mateo, California. *Serafini attended the same high school as Barry Bonds but had a far less successful career. Serafini pitched for six teams from 1996 through 2007 with a 15–16 record and a 6.04 ERA. The only other future major leaguers chosen by the Twins in a weak draft were Gus Ganderillas (third round), Dan Naulty (14th round) and Scott Watkins (23rd round).*
JUNE 3	Kirby Puckett hits a grand slam off Juan Guzman in the third inning of an 11–3 triumph over the Blue Jays at the Metrodome.
JUNE 4	The Twins break a 12–12 tie with three runs in the ninth inning and defeat the Rangers 15–12 in Arlington. Chuck Knoblauch broke the tie with an RBI single and scored on a home run by Kirby Puckett. The Twins had leads of 5–0 in the second inning, 6–5 in the third and 12–10 in the fifth, but Texas came back to tie the score on each occasion.
JUNE 7	Juan Gonzalez hits three homers for the Rangers during a 5–4 win over the Twins in Arlington.
JUNE 18	The Twins utilize three solo homers to defeat the Royals 3–1 at the Metrodome. The homers were by Shane Mack in the third inning, Kent Hrbek in the fourth and Pedro Munoz in the eighth.
JUNE 19	Greg Briley's homer leading off the first inning holds up for a 1–0 Mariners victory over the Twins at the Metrodome.
JUNE 24	Kevin Tapani pitches a two-hitter to defeat the Angels 11–0 at the Metrodome. The only California hits were a single by Rene Gonzales in the first inning and a double from Junior Felix in the seventh. Tapani also fanned ten without issuing a walk.

JUNE 26	An unusual play highlights a 4–3 win over the Athletics in Oakland. In the sixth inning, Mike Bordick of the A's hit a shot off the foot of Twins pitcher Willie Banks that caromed into foul territory. Hustling catcher Brian Harper dove for the ball and threw out Bordick at first base.
JUNE 27	The Twins trounce the Athletics 12–2 in Oakland.
JUNE 28	The Twins bunch all ten of their runs in the fourth inning of a 10–2 victory over the Athletics in Oakland. The ten runs were accomplished with nine hits (two homers, two doubles and five singles), two walks and a stolen base. Kirby Puckett contributed a home run and a single and Chuck Knoblauch and Chili Davis both doubled and singled. Greg Gagne walloped a three-run homer. The victory put the Twins into a tie for first place.
JUNE 30	Bill Krueger pitches a two-hitter to defeat the Angels 2–0 in Anaheim. The only California hits were singles by Luis Sojo in the fifth inning and Gary DiSarcina in the sixth.
JULY 4	The Twins take a thrilling 15-inning 3–2 decision from the Orioles at the Metrodome. Baltimore scored in the top of the 15th and the first two Minnesota batters in the bottom half struck out against Greg Olson. But the Twins quickly loaded the bases on singles by Chuck Knoblauch and Kirby Puckett and a walk to Kent Hrbek. Chili Davis followed with a two-run single to win the game.
JULY 5	The Twins come from behind in their last at-bat for the second day in a row with two runs in the ninth inning to defeat the Orioles 2–1 at the Metrodome. The tying run scored on a bases-loaded ground out by Chuck Knoblauch with one out. After a walk, Kent Hrbek delivered the game-winner with a single. An unusual incident occurred in the sixth inning when a drive by Chili Davis seemed headed for a home run but struck a speaker and deflected to second baseman Mark McLemore for an out.
JULY 14	Tom Kelly manages the American League to a 13–6 win in the All-Star Game at Jack Murphy Stadium in San Diego.
JULY 17	Kirby Puckett plays musical positions during a ten-inning, 3–2 win over the Red Sox at the Metrodome. After spending the first eight innings in his customary spot in center field, Puckett played second base, shortstop and third base in the ninth and tenth after Tom Kelly ran out of infielders. Puckett played at second against right-handed batters and short and third against lefties, alternating with Chuck Knoblauch and Jeff Reboulet. It was the second time that Puckett played three infield positions in a game (see August 16, 1990). It would happen again three years later (see September 10, 1995). Knoblauch drove in the winning run with a single.
JULY 19	After falling behind 5–0, the Twins score two runs in the fifth inning, one in the sixth, three in the seventh and one in the eighth to defeat the Red Sox 7–5 at the Metrodome. In the seventh, Chili Davis tied the score with a two-out, two-run single, and Brian Harper drove home the go-ahead tally with another single.

Harper hit .307 with nine homers in 1992.

July 24	Scott Erickson pitches a one-hitter to defeat the Red Sox 5–0 in the first game of a double-header at Fenway Park. The only Boston hit was a single by Tom Brunansky leading off the second inning. The Red Sox won the second game 5–4.
July 25	The Twins score all three of their runs along with their only three hits in the seventh inning of a 3–1 win over the Red Sox at Fenway Park. After Boston hurler Danny Darwin retired the first 18 batters to face him, the Twins loaded the bases on two walks around a single by Kent Hrbek. Chili Davis drove in two with a single and Brian Harper followed with another run-scoring single.
July 29	With one out in the ninth inning and leading 4–2, Rick Aguilera gives up a three-run homer to Eric Fox, which results in a 5–4 loss to the Athletics at the Metrodome. The loss capped a three-game series sweep by the A's.

The Twins overcame a 9–13 start to the 1992 season to win 51 of their next 76 games. Heading into the three-game series against Oakland that started on July 27, the Twins held a three-game lead in the AL West and had a 60–38 record, the best in the majors. But the sweep by the Athletics set the stage for a slide that saw the Twins go 30–34 over the rest of the season and finish six games out of first as the A's won their fourth AL West crown in a span of five years. The Twins wouldn't post another winning season until 2001.

August 1	Brian Harper hits a grand slam off Doug Henry in the eighth inning of a 9–6 win over the Brewers at the Metrodome.
August 4	The Twins lose a 19–11 slugfest to the White Sox in Chicago. Both teams had 19 hits. Willie Banks allowed ten runs, all earned, in 1 2/3 innings.
August 5	The Twins drop out of first place with a 9–5 loss to the White Sox in Chicago. The Twins never regained the top spot in the AL West over the rest of the season.
August 14	Kirby Puckett drives in six runs during a 9–6 victory over the Mariners in Seattle. Puckett started the day with a two-run homer off Brian Fisher in the first inning, and then added a grand slam off Fisher in the third. It was Puckett's third slam of the season.
August 26	Brian Harper hits a walk-off homer off John Kiely with one out in the ninth inning to beat the Tigers 1–0 at the Metrodome. John Smiley pitched the shutout.
August 28	The Twins outlast the Yankees 4–3 in 14 innings at the Metrodome. The winning run scored on doubles by Shane Mack and Lenny Webster.
August 29	A 6–3 loss to the Yankees at the Metrodome is delayed for 23 minutes by a power failure.
September 4	The Blue Jays tie a major league record with ten consecutive hits in the second inning of a 16–5 win over the Twins in Toronto. Kevin Tapani gave up three singles, a double, another single and a triple before being relieved. Tom Edens followed by surrendering two singles, a triple and a double.

SEPTEMBER 20	The Twins score three runs in the ninth inning to defeat the Angels 7–5 in Anaheim. Kirby Puckett drove in the tying run with a double and scored the go-ahead tally on another double from Brian Harper.
SEPTEMBER 22	The Twins edge the Rangers 1–0 in 13 innings in Arlington. Pedro Munoz drove in the winning run on a two-out single off Kenny Rogers. John Smiley (nine innings), Gary Wayne ($1^1/_3$ innings), Tom Edens (one-third of an inning), Larry Casian ($1^1/_3$ innings) and Rick Aguilera (one inning) combined on the shutout.
SEPTEMBER 29	The Twins score four runs in the ninth inning to stun the White Sox 5–4 at the Metrodome. The first three runs were driven in by three different players on a double by Randy Bush, a sacrifice fly from Chili Davis, and a double by Bernardo Brito. The winning tally came on a two-out error by Chicago shortstop Esteban Beltre. Brito was playing in his sixth big league game and the double was his first extra-base hit.
OCTOBER 2	Chili Davis homers from both sides of the plate during a 5–1 win over the Royals in Kansas City. Davis homered in the first inning batting left-handed against Craig Shifflett and in the sixth hitting right-handed against Chris Haney.
NOVEMBER 17	Two weeks after Bill Clinton defeats George Bush in the presidential election, the Twins lose Jayhawk Owens and Curt Leskanic to the Rockies and Tom Edens to the Marlins in the expansion draft.
DECEMBER 1	John Smiley signs as a free agent with the Reds.
DECEMBER 8	Greg Gagne signs as a free agent with the Royals.
DECEMBER 9	The Twins sign Jim Deshaies, most recently with the Padres, as a free agent.
DECEMBER 11	Chili Davis signs with the Angels as a free agent.
	Davis proved to be a loss, as he had five productive years ahead of him. He hit at least 20 homers every year from 1993 through 1997.
DECEMBER 17	The Twins sign Dave Winfield, most recently with the Blue Jays, as a free agent.
	Winfield grew up in St. Paul and starred at the University of Minnesota in both basketball and baseball. During his college years he had a 13–1 record as a pitcher in addition to his slugging prowess as an outfielder. Because of his athletic ability, Winfield was drafted by the Padres as the fourth overall pick in the 1973 amateur draft as well as being picked by the Atlanta Hawks (fifth round of the NBA draft), Utah Stars (sixth round of the ABA draft) and Vikings (15th round of the NFL draft). He chose baseball as a career path and went straight from the campus to the major leagues. When he signed with the Twins, Winfield was 41 and was coming off a season in which he helped the Blue Jays win a world championship with a .290 batting average, 26 homers and 108 RBIs. In two seasons with the Twins, he batted .264 and had 31 home runs and 119 RBIs in 922 at-bats. He achieved a milestone with his 3,000th career hit on September 26, 1993.

1993

Season in a Sentence
After a world championship in 1991 and 90 wins in 1992, the Twins begin a stretch of eight straight losing seasons in 1993.

Finish • Won • Lost • Pct • GB
Fifth (tie)   71   91   .438   23.0

Manager
Tom Kelly

Stats   Twins • AL • Rank
Batting Avg: .264   .267   8
On-Base Pct: .327   .337   13
Slugging Pct: .385   .408   12
Home Runs: 121   12
Stolen Bases: 83   11
ERA: 4.71   4.32   13
Errors: 100   3 (tie)
Runs Scored: 693   11
Runs Allowed: 830   12

Starting Line-up
Brian Harper, c
Kent Hrbek, 1b
Chuck Knoblauch, 2b
Mike Pagliarulo, 3b
Pat Meares, ss
Shane Mack, lf-cf
Kirby Puckett, cf-rf
Dave McCarty, rf-1b-lf
Dave Winfield, dh
Pedro Munoz, rf
Jeff Reboulet, ss-3b

Pitchers
Kevin Tapani, sp
Willie Banks, sp
Jim Deshaies, sp
Scott Erickson, sp
Eddie Guardado, sp
Rick Aguilera, rp
Mike Trombley, rp
Mike Hartley, rp
Carl Willis, rp
Larry Casian, rp
George Tsamis, rp

Attendance
2,048,673 (tenth in AL)

Club Leaders
Batting Avg: Brian Harper   .304
On-Base Pct: Chuck Knoblauch   .354
Slugging Pct: Kirby Puckett   .474
Home Runs: Kent Hrbek   25
RBI: Kirby Puckett   89
Runs: Kirby Puckett   89
Stolen Bases: Chuck Knoblauch   29
Wins: Kevin Tapani   12
Strikeouts: Kevin Tapani   150
ERA: Willie Banks   4.04
Saves: Rick Aguilera   34

JANUARY 8   The Twins sign Bert Blyleven, most recently with the Angels, as a free agent.

Blyleven previously pitched for the Twins from 1970 through 1976 and again from 1985 through 1988. He was invited to training camp on a minor league contract at the age of 41 after posting an 8–12 record and a 4.74 record for the Angels in 1992. The Twins released Blyleven on March 31, ending his career with a record of 287–250.

APRIL 6   Six weeks after a terrorist bomb explodes in the parking garage of the World Trade Center, killing six people, the Twins open the season with a 10–5 loss to the White Sox before 51,617 at the Metrodome. Kevin Tapani started for the Twins, and allowed nine runs, eight of them earned, in 3 1/3 innings. Kirby Puckett and Dave Winfield homered in the losing cause. It was Winfield's debut in a Minnesota uniform.

APRIL 20   On the day after the raid on the Branch Davidian compound in Waco, Texas, the Twins bombard the Brewers 10–0 at the Metrodome. Willie Banks (6 1/3 innings), Pat Mahomes (1 2/3 innings) and Brett Merriman (one inning) combined on the shutout.

APRIL 21　　Kent Hrbek breaks a 3–3 tie with a grand slam off Graeme Lloyd in the fifth inning, but the Twins wind up losing 10–8 in ten innings to the Brewers at the Metrodome. Pedro Munoz contributed a triple, two doubles and a single in four at-bats.

APRIL 23　　Dave Winfield ties the score 4–4 with a grand slam off Mike Moore in the third inning, but the Twins wind up losing 12–4 to the Tigers at the Metrodome.

APRIL 24　　The Tigers trample the Twins 17–1 at the Metrodome. Starter Pat Mahomes surrendered ten runs in $2^{2}/_{3}$ innings.

APRIL 25　　Ahead 5–1 at the end of the sixth inning, the Twins give up eight runs in the seventh inning and seven in the eighth to lose 16–5 to the Tigers at the Metrodome. Reliever Brett Merriman gave up nine runs in two-thirds of an inning. The debacle completed a three-game series against the Tigers in which the Twins were outscored 45–10.

APRIL 26　　The Twins pitching staff gives up double digits in runs for the fourth game in a row, and the fifth time in the last six outings, with a 10–3 loss to the Brewers in Milwaukee.

The Twins gave up 99 runs in ten games from April 21 through April 30.

MAY 10　　The Twins collect 22 hits and wallop the Angels 13–3 in Anaheim.

Although St. Paul native Dave Winfield's Hall of Fame career was nearly over by the time he joined the Twins, he was a popular player and still feared by opposing pitchers.

MAY 17 — Dave Winfield collects his 500th career double during an 11–5 loss to the Yankees at the Metrodome. It was struck off Jimmy Key in the fourth inning.

MAY 26 — The Twins break an eight-game losing streak by defeating the Athletics 12–11 in Oakland. Trailing 8–5, the Twins scored four runs in the eighth inning to take a 9–8 lead, the last two on a double by Gene Larkin off Dennis Eckersley, but fell behind again in the bottom half when the A's scored on two bases-loaded walks by Rick Aguilera. Three tallies in the top of the ninth when the game. Pat Meares tied it 10–10 with an RBI triple, and Kirby Puckett broke the deadlock with a two-run single.

JUNE 3 — With two picks in the first round of the amateur draft, the Twins select outfielder Torii Hunter from Pine Bluff High School in Pine Bluff, Arkansas, and catcher Jason Varitek from Georgia Tech University.

> *The Twins picked 20th and 21st in the draft in 1993 and chose two longtime major leaguers. The extra selection came as a result of losing John Smiley as a free agent to the Reds. Hunter made the major leagues in 1997 and played 11 seasons for the Twins. The club failed to sign Varitek, however, and he spent another season playing collegiate baseball. He was drafted and signed by the Mariners in 1994, and following a trade, made his big league bow with the Red Sox in 1997. Other future major leaguers drafted and signed by the Twins in 1993 were Dan Perkins (second round), Javier Valentin (third round), Benj Sampson (sixth round), Kevin Ohme (ninth round), Bryan Radmanovich (14th round), Shane Bowers (21st round) and Bob Radiosky (23rd round).*

JUNE 8 — Pedro Munoz homers in the tenth inning to defeat the Rangers 3–2 in Arlington.

JUNE 12 — Kirby Puckett hits a grand slam off Bobby Witt in the third inning of a 7–2 win over the Athletics at the Metrodome. Puckett also robbed Terry Steinbach of a home run by leaping above the center field fence. The two Oakland runs scored on back-to-back homers by Rickey Henderson and Craig Paquette off Jim Deshaies to lead off the first inning.

> *The St. Paul Saints, an independent team in the Northern League, began play in 1993 at Midway Stadium. The principal owner was Mike Veeck, son of the legendary Bill Veeck, who owned the Cleveland Indians (1946–49), St. Louis Browns (1951–53) and Chicago White Sox (1959–61 and 1975–79). The Saints moved from the Northern League to the American Association in 2006. Veeck is no longer the principal owner but has a stake in the club. Actor Bill Murray is also a part owner.*

JULY 2 — After falling behind 10–5, the Twins score two runs in the sixth inning, three in the seventh, and one in the ninth to down the Brewers 11–10 at the Metrodome. Brian Harper ended the game with a walk-off single.

JULY 5 — The Twins score seven runs in the third inning and defeat the Tigers 13–3 at the Metrodome. The highlight of the rally was a rare three-run single by Chuck Knoblauch with two out. Dave McCarty raced home from first base on the play. Kirby Puckett singled and doubled during the big inning, and Dave Winfield contributed a home run and a single.

July 13	Kirby Puckett is the MVP in the All-Star Game, a 9–3 AL win at Camden Yards in Baltimore. Puckett homered off Terry Mulholland in the second inning and doubled in a run in the fifth.
	There have been only four All-Star Game home runs by Twins batters. The other three were by Harmon Killebrew in 1961, 1965 and 1971.
July 28	Ken Griffey, Jr. ties a major league record by homering in his eighth consecutive game during a 5–1 Twins victory over the Mariners in Seattle.
	The only other players with homers in eight straight games are Dale Long of the Pirates in 1956 and Don Mattingly with the Yankees in 1987.
July 29	The Twins prevent Ken Griffey, Jr. from breaking the record for homering in consecutive games but lose 4–3 to the Mariners in Seattle. Griffey singled and doubled in four at-bats against Scott Erickson and Larry Casian.
August 6	Gene Larkin hits a walk-off single in the ninth inning to defeat the Yankees 4–3 at the Metrodome.
August 7	The Twins win with a walk-off single in the ninth inning for the second game in a row when Kirby Puckett delivers with two out to down the Yankees 7–6 at the Metrodome.
August 13	Kent Hrbek hits two homers, both off Ron Darling, in his first two plate appearances to account for all of the Twins runs in a 5–2 win over the Athletics in Oakland. Hrbek hit a three-run homer in the first inning and a two-run shot in the third.
August 14	Willie Banks strikes out 13 batters in eight innings and the Twins defeat the Athletics 5–1 in 12 innings in the first game of a double-header in Oakland. Jeff Reboulet capped the four-run rally in the 12th with a three-run double. The Twins completed the sweep with a 6–2 victory in the second tilt.
August 15	The Twins use six homers to power past the Athletics 12–5 in Oakland. Kirby Puckett had a five-hit game with two homers and three singles in five at-bats. Left fielder Bernardo Brito also homered twice. The other Minnesota homers were by Jeff Reboulet and Brian Harper. On the same day, the Twins traded Mike Pagliarulo to the Orioles for Erik Schullstrom.
	Brito, who was a 29-year-old rookie in 1993, came into the contest with one career homer. He hit only five home runs in 48 games in 76 at-bats in three seasons in the majors.
August 27	The Twins score five runs in the tenth inning to defeat the White Sox 7–2 in Chicago. Bernardo Brito capped the rally with a three-run homer in his first start since homering twice in a game on August 17. The Twins actually scored four runs during Brito's at-bat. He stepped to the plate with the bases loaded. Kent Hrbek scored from third on a wild pitch before the home run.
August 28	The Twins trade Jim Deshaies to the Giants for Andres Duncan, Greg Brumlett and Aaron Fultz.

August 31	The Twins outlast the Indians 5–4 in a 22-inning marathon at the Metrodome. The game consumed six hours and 17 minutes and ended at 1:22 a.m. The Twins trailed 4–1 before scoring two runs in the eighth inning and one in the ninth. After the first two batters in the ninth were retired, Dave McCarty and Terry Jorgensen hit back-to-back doubles. Minnesota relievers Larry Casian (two-thirds of an inning), Carl Willis (2²/₃ innings), Rick Aguilera (2²/₃ innings), Mike Hartley (four innings), George Tsamis (two innings) and Brett Merriman (three innings) combined for 15 innings of scoreless pitching while allowing six hits. Pedro Munoz ended the long night with a walk-off homer off Jason Grimsley.

The homer by Munoz is tied for the second latest in major league history. Harold Baines of the White Sox ended the longest game in AL history with a 25th-inning homer to beat the Brewers 7–6 in Chicago on May 9, 1984. Jack Reed of the Yankees in 1962 and Rick Dempsey of the Dodgers in 1989 also homered in the 22nd inning of a game, but unlike the one by Munoz, neither was a walk-off shot. The 22-inning affair on August 31, 1993, is also the longest in the history of the Senators/Twins franchise to be completed in one day. The Brewers beat the Twins 4–3 in 22 innings at Metropolitan Stadium in a contest started on May 12, 1972, and completed a day later.

September 9	The Twins play at Municipal Stadium in Cleveland for the last time, and defeat the Indians 5–3 in ten innings.

On the same day, Major League Baseball announced a three-division alignment and an extra round of playoffs, to be put into effect for the 1994 season. The Twins were placed in the Central Division with the White Sox, Indians, Royals and Brewers. In 1998, the Brewers were transferred to the National League and the Tigers moved from the AL East to the AL Central.

September 11	Kirby Puckett hits a grand slam off Roger Pavlik of the Rangers in the fifth inning in Arlington for a 4–3 lead but the Twins lose 7–4.
September 12	The Twins play at Arlington Stadium for the last time and defeat the Rangers 4–2.
September 16	Dave Winfield collects his 3,000th career hit with a single off Dennis Eckersley in the ninth inning of a thrilling 13-inning 5–4 win over the Athletics at the Metrodome. Winfield came into the contest with 2,998 career hits. Number 2,999 was a single in the seventh. The Twins trailed 2–0 heading into the ninth. Winfield's single drove in the first run. The game was delayed for several minutes while fans cheered and threw debris onto the field. Scott Stahoviak drove in the tying tally with a two-out single, also against Eckersley. It was Stahoviak's first major league RBI. The A's scored two runs in the top of the 13th, but Minnesota countered with three in the bottom half for the victory. Chuck Knoblauch drove in the first run with a double. Chip Hale drove in the game-winner with a single. Hale entered the contest as a pinch-hitter in the ninth and remained in the batting order as a first baseman.
September 21	Pedro Munoz drives in all five Twins runs with a pair of home runs during a 5–2 win over the Yankees in New York. Munoz smacked a three-run homer in the fourth inning and a two-run bomb in the sixth, both off Jim Abbott.

SEPTEMBER 28   The Twins score twice in the ninth for a 2–1 triumph over the Angels at the Metrodome. Kirby Puckett drove in the tying run with a double and crossed the plate on Brian Harper's single.

SEPTEMBER 29   The Twins win with a walk-off hit for the second game in a row when Pedro Munoz singles home Kirby Puckett in the tenth inning to defeat the Angels 3–2 at the Metrodome.

NOVEMBER 24   The Twins trade Willie Banks to the Cubs for Dave Stevens and Matt Walbeck.

1994

Season in a Sentence

The Twins are 36–27 and only a game out of first place in June but lose 33 of their next 50 and compile the highest ERA (5.68) in the majors before a player's strike ends the season on August 12.

Finish • Won • Lost • Pct • GB

Fourth   53   60   .469   14.0

Manager

Tom Kelly

Stats   Twins • AL • Rank

Batting Avg:	.276	.273	5
On-Base Pct:	.340	.345	7
Slugging Pct:	.427	.434	8
Home Runs:	103		12
Stolen Bases:	94		3
ERA:	5.68	4.60	14
Errors:	75		2
Runs Scored:	594		6
Runs Allowed:	688		13

Starting Line-up

Matt Walbeck, c
Kent Hrbek, 1b
Chuck Knoblauch, 2b
Scott Leius, 3b
Pat Meares, ss
Shane Mack, lf
Alex Cole, cf
Kirby Puckett, rf
Dave Winfield, dh
Pedro Munoz, lf
Jeff Reboulet, ss

Pitchers

Kevin Tapani, sp
Scott Erickson, sp
Pat Mahomes, sp
Jim Deshaies, sp
Carlos Pulido, sp
Rick Aguilera, rp
Carl Willis, rp
Mark Guthrie, rp
Larry Casian, rp

Attendance

1,398,565

Club Leaders

Batting Avg:	Shane Mack	.333
On-Base Pct:	Shane Mack	.402
Slugging Pct:	Shane Mack	.564
Home Runs:	Kirby Puckett	20
RBI:	Kirby Puckett	112
Runs:	Chuck Knoblauch	85
Stolen Bases:	Chuck Knoblauch	35
Wins:	Kevin Tapani	11
Strikeouts:	Scott Erickson	104
ERA:	Kevin Tapani	4.62
Saves:	Rick Aguilera	23

JANUARY 13   The Twins sign Jim Deshaies, most recently with the Giants, as a free agent.

The Twins traded Deshaies to the Giants the previous August and re-signed him as a free agent. The club should have passed. Deshaies was 6–12 with a 7.39 ERA in 130 1/3 innings in 1994.

FEBRUARY 13	The Brewers sign Brian Harper as a free agent.

Harper batted .306 in six seasons with the Twins, including .304 in 147 games in 1993, but went into a sudden decline after leaving Minnesota, appearing in only 66 more big league games before his career ended in 1995.

FEBRUARY 16	The Twins sign Alex Cole, most recently with the Rockies, as a free agent.
APRIL 5	The Twins open the season with an 8–2 loss to the Angels before 41,012 at the Metrodome. Starting pitcher Kevin Tapani allowed seven runs in 3½ innings. Dave Winfield and Pedro Munoz homered in the losing cause.

An additional 900 seats were added for Twins games in 1994 by moving both dugouts forward and adding three rows of seats. Section 113 in the right field corner was also added.

APRIL 8	Kirby Puckett collects five hits, including a double, in six at-bats, but the Twins lose 10–9 in ten innings to the Athletics at the Metrodome. The first of the five hits was the 2,000th of Puckett's career. It was a single off Bob Welch in the third inning. The Twins trailed 7–1 at the end of the sixth before battling back to force extra innings.

After eight games, the Twins were 1–7 and allowed 72 runs. Pitching was a problem all year. The club's 5.68 ERA was last in the major leagues. Despite the horrendous pitching, the Twins rebounded and were 36–27 and only a game out of first on June 15. The club was unable to sustain the momentum, however, and was 53–60 when the strike was called in August.

APRIL 14	The Twins erupt for four runs in the ninth inning off Dennis Eckersley after two are out to beat the Athletics 5–4 in Oakland. With two out and a runner on second, the four runs crossed the plate on a run-scoring single by Matt Walbeck, a pinch-single from Chip Hale, and RBI-single by Alex Cole, and Chuck Knoblauch's two-run double.

Knoblauch hit .312 with five homers and a league-leading 45 doubles in 1994.

APRIL 24	Alex Cole leads off the first inning with a home run to spark a 7–3 win over the Blue Jays in Toronto. It was the first home run of Cole's career and it came in his 1,317th at-bat. Cole made his major league debut in 1990 with the Indians and also played for the Pirates and Rockies before arriving in Minnesota.

Cole finished his career in 1996 with five homers, four of them as a Twin, in 2,016 at-bats.

APRIL 25	The Twins play at Jacobs Field (now known as Progressive Field) in Cleveland for the first time and defeat the Indians 9–7.
APRIL 27	Scott Erickson pitches a no-hitter to defeat the Brewers 6–0 before 17,988 at the Metrodome. It was the first no-hitter by a Twin pitcher since Dean Chance threw one on August 25, 1967, the first at the Metrodome, and the first in Minnesota since Jack Kralick's gem on August 26, 1962. Erickson threw 128 pitches, walked four, and struck out six. The ninth inning started with ground outs by Jody Reed from second

baseman Chuck Knoblauch to first baseman Kent Hrbek, and another by Alex Diaz to Hrbek unassisted. Just one out from the no-hitter, Erickson walked Bill Spiers and Turner Ward before inducing Greg Vaughn to fly out to left fielder Alex Cole.

> *Erickson entered the game with a 9–24 record in his last 40 starts over three seasons. The 1994 season was an otherwise disappointing one for Erickson, who was 8–11 with an ERA of 5.44. The no-hitter was his only shutout between August 23, 1992, and September 5, 1995.*

APRIL 30 — The Twins outslug the Blue Jays 11–9 at the Metrodome.

MAY 4 — Matt Walbeck hits a grand slam off Jesse Orosco in the sixth inning of an 8–7 win over the Brewers in Milwaukee.

MAY 6 — The Twins play at the Ballpark at Arlington for the first time and lose 7–0 to the Rangers.

MAY 14 — Dave Winfield hits two homers and drives in five runs during an 8–5 triumph over the Orioles at the Metrodome.

MAY 18 — The Twins trounce the Yankees 13–5 at the Metrodome.

MAY 20 — In the first game after scoring 13 runs, the Twins collect 22 hits and clobber the Red Sox 21–2 at the Metrodome. All 21 Minnesota runs crossed the plate in the first five innings with one in the first, five in the second, four in the third, and 11 in the fifth. The 11-run explosion consisted of ten hits (a home run, a double and eight singles), two walks, a hit batsmen and a wild pitch. The ten hits were achieved by ten different players as Tom Kelly used three pinch-hitters the second time through the line-up. Each of the pinch-hitters collected hits. There were eight consecutive hits from Dave McCarty (single), Matt Walbeck (single), Pat Meares (single), Jeff Reboulet (single), Scott Leius (single), Scott Dunn (double), Shane Mack (single) and Chip Hale (single). In four plate appearances, Puckett drove in seven runs on a sacrifice fly, two singles, and a home run.

MAY 21 — In the first game after winning 21–2, the Twins edge the Red Sox 1–0 at the Metrodome. Kevin Tapani (8 1/3 innings) and Rick Aguilera (two-thirds of an inning) combined on the shutout. Chuck Knoblauch drove in the lone run with a single in the fifth inning.

JUNE 2 — In the first round of the amateur draft, the Twins select second baseman Todd Walker from Louisiana State University.

> *Walker made his major league debut in 1996 and played five seasons for the Twins at the start of a career that lasted until 2007. He hit .289 with 107 home runs for seven clubs. Other future major leaguers chosen and signed by the Twins in a productive draft in 1994 were Travis Miller (supplemental first round pick), Cleatus Davidson (second round), A. J. Pierzynski (third round), David Dellucci (11th round), Corey Koskie (26th round) and Brandon Puffer (27th round).*

JUNE 4 — The Twins collect 24 hits and rout the Tigers 21–7 in Detroit. In the process, the Twins became the first team since the 1950 Red Sox to score at least 20 runs twice in a season (see May 20, 1994). The 21-run explosion occurred with a run in the first inning, six in the second, six more in the third, one in the fifth, another in the sixth, two in the seventh and three in the eighth. The 24 hits consisted of 17 singles, three doubles and four homers. Nine players (Chuck Knoblauch, Alex Cole, Shane Mack, Pedro Munoz, Scott Leius, Dave McCarty, Derek Parks, Pat Meares and Chip Hale) had at least two hits. Munoz led the way with seven runs batted in on two home runs, a single and a sacrifice fly. He also committed one of the five Minnesota errors during the game.

JUNE 5   Chuck Knoblauch and Tony Phillips both hit home runs leading off the first inning during a 5–3 loss to the Tigers in Detroit. Knoblauch homered off Mike Moore and then added another one against Moore in the eighth. Phillips also hit two home runs, both off Scott Erickson. Like Knoblauch, the second one occurred in the eighth inning. Phillips' second blast also led off the inning. The two would combine to hit lead-off homers again (see September 8, 1995).

JUNE 10   The Twins shock the White Sox with five runs in the ninth inning and two in the tenth to win 8–6 at the Metrodome. Chuck Knoblauch drove in the first ninth-inning run with a single and Kent Hrbek added a sacrifice fly, but the Twins still trailed 6–3 with two out and a runner on first. After Dave Winfield singled to keep the rally alive, Shane Mack clouted a three-run homer. Alex Cole won the game with a two-run, walk-off homer. It was only Cole's third career homer in 1,451 at-bats.

JUNE 19   Two days after 95 million Americans tune in to the eight-hour police chase of O. J. Simpson through the streets and highways of Greater Los Angeles, Pat Meares hits his first two career homers during a 10–4 win over the Orioles in Baltimore.

Meares entered the game without a home run in 498 career at-bats. He didn't hit another home run until May 6, 1995.

JUNE 29   The film *Little Big League* premieres.

The film's plot centers on a 12-year-old boy, played by Luke Edwards, who inherits the Minnesota Twins from his grandfather (Jason Robards) and decides to manage the team himself. In the end, the Twins lose the big game to the Mariners when Ken Griffey, Jr., playing himself, robs a Twins player of a home run. Other real life players and managers in the movie included Randy Johnson, Sandy Alomar, Jr., Tim Raines, Mickey Tettleton, Carlos Baerga, Paul O'Neill, Ivan Rodriguez, Rafael Palmeiro, Wally Joyner, Leon Durham, Kevin Elster and Lou Piniella. Twins broadcaster John Gordon played a fictitious announcer named Wally Holland. Chris Berman also made an appearance. The actors who played ballplayers underwent a training regimen led by Kirby Puckett and Kent Hrbek. Many scenes were shot at the Metrodome.

JUNE 30   Rick Aguilera strikes out four of the five batters to face him, including all three in the ninth inning, to close out a 6–4 win over the Rangers at the Metrodome. In the ninth, Aguilera fanned Jose Canseco, Will Clark and Juan Gonzalez.

JULY 7   The Twins tie a major league record for a nine-inning game with 19 putouts by the outfielders in a 4–3 loss to the Blue Jays at the Metrodome. The putouts were by right fielder Pedro Munoz (ten), center fielder Alex Cole (five) and left fielder Shane Mack (four).

July 8	Shane Mack hits a grand slam off Jason Grimsley in the first inning of an 8–6 win over the Indians at the Metrodome.
	Mack hit .333 with 15 homers in 1994. He declared himself a free agent after the season ended and played for the Yomiyuri Giants in Japan in 1995 and 1996. He closed out his major league career with the Red Sox, Athletics and Royals in 1997 and 1998.
July 12	At Three Rivers Stadium in Pittsburgh, Kirby Puckett is the starting right fielder in the All-Star Game and drives in a run in the sixth inning that ties the score 4–4, but the AL loses 8–7 in ten innings.
July 14	Two balls strike the roof during a 6–4 loss to the Brewers in the Metrodome. In the second inning, a fly ball by Pedro Munoz bounced from the roof to first baseman Kevin Seitzer, who caught it for an out. In the third, Kent Hrbek's drive off the roof fell for a double.
July 22	The Twins score two runs in the ninth inning and one in the 13th to defeat the Brewers 6–5 in Milwaukee. Chuck Knoblauch's single drove in the tying tally. Jeff Reboulet's double brought home the game-winner.
July 27	The Twins edge the Rangers 1–0 in Arlington. Pat Mahomes (6 2/3 innings), Mark Guthrie (one inning), Dale Stevens (one-third of an inning) and Rick Aguilera (one inning) combined on the shutout.
August 4	Kent Hrbek announces his retirement effective at the end of the season, citing nagging injury problems and a desire to spend more time with his wife and daughter. Hrbek was 34 years old and had been the Twins starting first baseman from the time he made his major league debut in August 1981.
August 10	With the strike deadline looming, the Twins score eight runs in the seventh inning and rout the Red Sox 17–7 at the Metrodome. Kirby Puckett drove in seven runs with a grand slam off Scott Bankhead in the second inning and a three-run blast against Tony Fossas in the seventh. Puckett also walked three times, twice intentionally.
	Puckett finished the year with a .317 average, 32 doubles, 20 homers and 112 RBIs in 108 games.
August 12	With about 70 percent of the season completed, the major league players go on strike.
	The strike, baseball's eighth interruption since 1972, had been anticipated all season. The owners wanted to put a lid on escalating payrolls by capping salaries and revising, if not eliminating, salary arbitration procedures. The players, who were obviously not interested in these reforms, had only one weapon once talks broke down: a strike.
August 15	Pat Mahomes is hospitalized following a car crash on a bridge in downtown Minneapolis. His Jeep crossed the center line, hit a guardrail, and turned over. Mahomes was knocked unconscious.

August 31	The Twins sell Dave Winfield to the Indians. When he played his last game for the Twins, three weeks earlier, Winfield was 42 years and ten months of age. He is the oldest non-pitcher to appear in a game in Twins history.
	The Indians purchased Winfield for the pennant race should the strike end. The remainder of the season was canceled two weeks later. Winfield hit only .191 in 46 games for Cleveland in 1995 and then retired. He was elected to the Hall of Fame on the first ballot in 2001.
September 9	Andy MacPhail resigns as general manager of the Twins to take a position as president and chief executive officer of the Cubs. MacPhail had been the Twins general manager since 1985.
September 13	The Twins hire 39-year-old Terry Ryan as general manager to replace Andy MacPhail.
	Drafted by the Twins out of high school in 1972, Ryan was a promising pitcher until injuries ended his playing career in 1976. He went to college and received a degree in physical education from the University of Wisconsin in 1979. He spent several years as a scout before joining the Twins as scouting director in 1986. He was promoted to vice-president and player personnel director in 1992. He ran the Twins front office until 2007. He didn't experience a winning season until 2001, but from that point forward became well-respected in baseball circles for putting together several teams that reached the postseason on a limited budget.
September 14	The owners of the 28 major league clubs vote 26–2 to cancel the remainder of the season, including the playoffs and the World Series.

1995

Season in a Sentence

The season is shortened by 18 games because of the players' strike, which started in August 1994, but the Twins find time to lose 88 games and compile an ERA of 5.76 just four years after winning the World Series.

Finish • Won • Lost • Pct • GB

Fifth   56   88   .389   44.0

In the wild card race, the Twins were tied for tenth (last), 23 games behind.

Manager

Tom Kelly

Stats	Twins	AL	Rank
Batting Avg:	.279	.270	4
On-Base Pct:	.346	.344	7
Slugging Pct:	.419	.427	9
Home Runs:	120		13
Stolen Bases:	105		8
ERA:	5.76		14
Errors:	100		7
Runs Scored:	703		10
Runs Allowed:	889		14

Starting Line-up

Matt Walbeck, c
Scott Stahoviak, 1b
Chuck Knoblauch, 2b
Scott Leius, 3b
Pat Meares, ss
Marty Cordova, lf
Rich Becker, cf
Kirby Puckett, rf
Pedro Munoz, dh
Jeff Reboulet, ss-3b
Dan Masteller, 1b
Matt Merullo, c

Pitchers

Brad Radke, sp
Kevin Tapani, sp
Mike Trombley, sp
Frank Rodriguez, sp
Scott Erickson, sp
Rick Aguilera, rp
Pat Mahomes, rp
Eddie Guardado, rp
Dale Stevens, rp

Attendance

1,057,667 (14th in AL)

Club Leaders

Batting Avg:	Chuck Knoblauch	.333
On-Base Pct:	Chuck Knoblauch	.424
Slugging Pct:	Kirby Puckett	.515
Home Runs:	Marty Cordova	24
RBI:	Kirby Puckett	99
Runs:	Chuck Knoblauch	107
Stolen Bases:	Chuck Knoblauch	46
Wins:	Brad Radke	11
Strikeouts:	Kevin Tapani	88
ERA:	Kevin Tapani	4.92
Saves:	Rick Aguilera	12

JANUARY 13   Major league owners vote to use replacement players during the 1995 season if the players' strike, begun on August 12, 1994, is not settled.

FEBRUARY 26   Jim Deshaies signs with the Phillies as a free agent.

APRIL 2   The 234-day strike of major league players comes to an end.

> *The opening of the season, originally scheduled to begin on April 3, was pushed back to April 26 with each team playing 144 games. The replacement players were either released or sent to the minors.*

APRIL 26   Seven days after a truck bomb explodes outside an Oklahoma City federal office building, killing 168 people, the Twins open the season with a 9–0 loss to the Red Sox at Fenway Park. Scott Erickson was the starter, and allowed two runs in $4^{2}/_{3}$ innings. Boston broke the game open with seven runs in the sixth off Carl Willis and Vince Horsman. Five pitchers combined on the shutout.

APRIL 27	In the home opener, the Twins defeat the Orioles 7–4 before 26,426 at the Metrodome. Rick Aguilera closed out the game by striking out all three batters he faced in the ninth.

The Twins drew 3,030,672 fans in 1988 to lead the AL in attendance. In 1995, the club attracted just 1,057,667, the lowest figure in the league.

APRIL 27	After falling behind 6–0 in the third inning, the Twins rally to beat the Orioles 12–9 at the Metrodome. Minnesota still trailed 9–6 before plating a run in the seventh and five in the eighth. Three consecutive RBI-singles by Kirby Puckett, Matt Merullo and Alex Cole put the Twins into the lead.

The Twins tried out several former players as broadcasters on television between 1994 and 1999, including Al Newman, Tommy John, Kent Hrbek, Bert Blyleven and Paul Molitor. Of those, only Blyleven, who started in 1995, lasted more than two years. He was in his 15th season in the booth in 2009.

MAY 3	After falling behind 7–1 in the third inning, the Twins rally to beat the Royals 10–9 at the Metrodome. Minnesota took a 9–7 lead with three runs in the third inning, two in the fifth and three in the sixth, but allowed Kansas City to tie the contest 9–9 in the seventh. Alex Cole drove in the winning run with a double in the eighth.
MAY 7	The Twins use nine pitchers in a 17-inning marathon in Cleveland, and lose 10–9. The nine pitchers, who combined to surrender 26 hits, were Kevin Tapani, Eddie Guardado, Kevin Campbell, Rich Robertson, Dale Stevens, Rick Aguilera, Mo Sanford, Vince Horsman and Mark Guthrie. The Twins used a total of 24 players during the contest. It took six hours and 36 minutes to complete.

The Twins had an ERA of 5.76 in 1995, the highest in a single season in the history of the franchise, including the years in Washington.

MAY 18	The Twins score seven runs in the sixth inning, but lose 15–9 to the Angels at the Metrodome. Pedro Munoz and Marty Cordova homered during the rally.

Cordova homered in five consecutive games from May 16 through May 20. The five homers came over 17 at-bats and drove in 12 runs. Cordova won the AL Rookie of the Year Award in 1995 by batting .277 with 24 homers. He had another good year in 1996 with a .309 average, 46 doubles, 16 home runs and 111 runs-batted-in. He became a fan favorite and looked like one of the cornerstones of the franchise, but his production dropped after 1996. He left Minnesota as a free agent after the 1999 season and was out of baseball by 2003.

MAY 25	Mark Guthrie strikes out 12 batters in six innings of relief, and the Twins defeat the Tigers 4–3 in Detroit. Guthrie pitched from the third inning though the eighth.
MAY 30	Center fielder Alex Cole suffers a broken right leg, a dislocated ankle, and torn ankle ligaments while attempting a diving catch during a 5–3 loss to the Brewers in Milwaukee. Cole was batting .360 at the time of the injury and didn't play again until September 23.
JUNE 1	In the first round of the amateur draft, the Twins select pitcher Mark Redman from the University of Oklahoma.

Redman didn't make his major league debut until 1999, pitched three seasons with the Twins, and spent a decade in the majors moving from team to team. Other future major leaguers drafted and signed by the Twins in 1995 were A. J. Hinch (third round), Doug Mientkiewicz (fifth round), Mike Moriarty (seventh round) and Jeff Harris (26th round).

JUNE 16   Kirby Puckett hits a grand slam off Randy Johnson in the sixth inning of a 10–1 triumph over the Mariners in Seattle.

JUNE 19   Chip Hale hits a three-run, pinch-hit double in the tenth inning to beat the Athletics 8–5 in Oakland.

JUNE 30   Playing for the Indians, Eddie Murray collects his 3,000th career hit with a single off Mike Trombley in the sixth inning of a 4–1 Cleveland win over the Twins at the Metrodome.

JULY 6   The Twins trade Rick Aguilera to the Red Sox for Frank Rodriguez and J. J. Johnson. Aguilera was summoned from the bullpen during a game against the Red Sox at the Metrodome to be informed of the trade. It came one day before he became a ten-year veteran with five years with one club, which would have given him the right to veto any trade.

By July, the Twins had no hope of posting a winning record and were last in the league in attendance, a combination that led to trades involving high-salaried players. After helping the Red Sox nail down the AL East title, Aguilera returned to the Twins as a free agent five months later (see December 11, 1995). Rodriguez was drafted by the Red Sox as a shortstop in 1990 and converted into a pitcher in 1992. He spent four undistinguished seasons with the Twins.

JULY 7   The Twins trade Scott Erickson to the Orioles for Scott Klingenbeck and Kimera Bartee.

After posting a 20–8 record for the Twins in 1991, Erickson was a combined 20–36 for the club from 1993 through 1995. He regained his form in Baltimore and won 69 and lost 48 from 1995 through 1999. Klingenbeck had an 8.30 ERA in 77 innings for the Twins over two seasons. Bartee never played a game in a Minnesota uniform.

JULY 13   Chuck Knoblauch hits the first pitch of the game from Jack McDowell for a home run, but the Twins lose 7–2 to the Yankees in New York.

Knoblauch hit .333 with 11 home runs and 107 runs scored in 1995.

JULY 28   Dan Masteller hits a two-run, walk-off homer off Jack McDowell in the ninth inning to defeat the Yankees 5–3 at the Metrodome.

The home run was the first of Masteller's big league career. He hit only three in 198 at-bats in the majors.

JULY 31   The Twins trade Kevin Tapani and Mark Guthrie to the Dodgers for Ron Coomer, Greg Hansell, Jose Parra and Chris Latham.

From 1995 through 1998 with the Dodgers, White Sox and Cubs, Tapani had a record of 45–24. After seven seasons with the Twins, Guthrie played for seven clubs through 2003 but was an effective reliever at nearly every stop. Among the four players acquired for the pair of pitchers, only Coomer spent a significant amount of time with the Twins. He was a starter at both third and first base from 1997 through 2000 and had several productive seasons.

Reliable Brad Radke pitched his entire twelve-year career, beginning in 1995, with the Twins. He won 148 games for the team, including twelve in twelve consecutive starts in 1997.

August 5 Matt Merullo hits a grand slam off Billy Brewer in the seventh inning of a 13–8 defeat of the Royals at the Metrodome.

The home run was the first for Merullo since October 6, 1991 when he played for the White Sox. It was also the only one he collected in 216 at-bats for the Twins and the last of seven he had as a major leaguer.

August 13 Kent Hrbek's number 14 is retired in ceremonies prior to a 2–1 loss to the Angels at the Metrodome.

August 15 The Twins score five runs after two are out in the ninth inning to stun the Mariners 7–6 at the Metrodome. With two out and runners on first and second, Chuck Knoblauch singled in a run to make the score 6–3. Rich Becker narrowed the gap to two runs with another single before Kirby Puckett clouted a three-run, walk-off homer.

Puckett batted .314 with 23 home runs in 1995 and made the All-Star team for the tenth consecutive season.

August 20 Chip Hale homers in the tenth inning to beat the Tigers 8–7 in Detroit.

August 21 The Rangers erupt for 11 runs in the first inning off Scott Klingenbeck and Oscar Munoz and beat the Twins 12–5 in Arlington.

AUGUST 29	Chuck Knoblauch homers, hits two doubles, and scores both runs in a 2–0 triumph over the Rangers at the Metrodome. Brad Radke pitched a three-hit shutout.

> *Radke was a 22-year-old rookie in 1995 and the shutout was the first of his career. He played his entire 12-year career with the club. Among Twins pitchers, Radke ranks third in wins (148), third in losses (139), second in games started (377), fourth in innings (2,461) and fourth in strikeouts (1,467).*

SEPTEMBER 2	Kirby Puckett hits a walk-off homer in the ninth inning to defeat the Brewers 6–5 at the Metrodome.
SEPTEMBER 8	Chuck Knoblauch and Tony Phillips each lead off the first inning with home runs during a 9–3 loss to the Angels in Anaheim. It was the second time that the pair accomplished the feat (see June 5, 1994). Knoblauch homered against Mike Langston and Phillips facing Jose Parra.
SEPTEMBER 10	After falling behind 7–1 in the fourth inning, the Twins rally to defeat the Angels 9–8 in ten innings in Anaheim. Dan Masteller homered leading off the ninth to tie the score 8–8. The winning run scored on a walk and a two-out error. Kirby Puckett began the game as a designated hitter, then played third base, shortstop and second base during the ninth and tenth innings when Tom Kelly ran out of infielders after pinch-hitting for Jeff Reboulet, Scott Leius and Pat Meares.
SEPTEMBER 11	The Twins outlast the Mariners 12–10 in Seattle. Rich Becker collected a triple, two doubles, and a single.
SEPTEMBER 23	Lance Johnson of the White Sox collects six hits, including three triples, in six at-bats to lead his club to a 14–4 victory over the Twins at the Metrodome.
SEPTEMBER 26	The Twins trounce the Indians 13–4 at the Metrodome.
SEPTEMBER 28	Kirby Puckett suffers a broken jaw when hit by a pitch from Dennis Martinez during a 12–4 loss to the Indians at the Metrodome. After he was struck with the pitch, Puckett bled profusely from the nose and mouth before being rushed to the hospital.

> *No one knew it at the time, but it would prove to be Puckett's last regular season game (see March 28, 1996).*

DECEMBER 5	The Twins sign Paul Molitor, most recently with the Blue Jays, as a free agent.

> *A native of St. Paul, Molitor played three seasons with the University of Minnesota before he was the third overall pick in the 1977 draft, selected by the Brewers. Molitor played for Milwaukee from 1978 through 1992 and in Toronto from 1993 through 1995. During that time, he led the AL in hits twice, runs three times, and doubles and triples once while collecting 2,789 hits. He also appeared in seven All-Star Games and two World Series. In the 1993 Fall Classic, Molitor was chosen the MVP after batting .500 with 12 hits and ten RBIs for the Blue Jays against the Phillies. Injuries early in his career as a second baseman and third baseman probably cost him 500 games, and he became primarily a designated hitter in 1991. He celebrated his first season in his hometown by leading the AL in hits again with 225, which included the 3,000th of his career. Molitor became the first 40-year-old to reach the 200-hit mark in a*

season. He also had 41 doubles and batted .341. After batting .305 in 1997 and .281 in 1998, he retired with 3,319 hits, the ninth highest in major league history at the time. In addition, Molitor had 605 doubles and 504 stolen bases. He was elected to the Hall of Fame on the first ballot in 2004.

DECEMBER 11   The Twins sign Rick Aguilera, most recently with the Red Sox, as a free agent.

First acquired by the club in a trade with the Mets on July 31, 1989, Aguilera was the Twins closer until dealt to Boston on July 6, 1995. After coming back to the Twins as a free agent, he remained in a Minnesota uniform until another trade with the Cubs on May 21, 1999. He had an unsuccessful conversion to a starting pitcher in 1996, in part because of a spring training injury in which he developed tendonitis in his right wrist after he picked up his wife's suitcase to load it onto a moving truck. Aguilera was the closer again from 1997 until the deal with the Cubs.

1996

Season in a Sentence

Kirby Puckett retires prematurely because of an eye ailment, but the Twins record a record of 78–84 which is a vast improvement over the previous season.

Finish • Won • Lost • Pct • GB

Fourth   78   84   .481   21.5

In the wild card race, the Twins finished in tied for sixth place, ten games behind.

Manager

Tom Kelly

Stats   Twins • AL • Rank

Batting Avg:	.288	.277	2
On-Base Pct:	.357	.350	7
Slugging Pct:	.425	.445	11
Home Runs:	118		14
Stolen Bases:	143		3
ERA:	5.28	4.99	12
Errors:	94		3
Runs Scored:	877		8
Runs Allowed:	900		9

Starting Line-up

Greg Myers, c
Scott Stahoviak, 1b
Chuck Knoblauch, 2b
Dave Hollins, 3b
Pat Meares, ss
Marty Cordova, lf
Rich Becker, cf
Matt Lawton, rf
Paul Molitor, dh
Roberto Kelly, rf-cf
Jeff Reboulet, 3b-ss-2b
Ron Coomer, 1b

Pitchers

Frank Rodriguez, sp
Brad Radke, sp
Rich Robertson, sp
Scott Aldred, sp
Rick Aguilera, sp
Dave Stevens, rp
Greg Hansell, rp
Eddie Guardado, rp
Mike Trombley, rp
Dan Naulty, rp

Attendance

1,437,352 (11th in AL)

Club Leaders

Batting Avg:	Chuck Knoblauch	.341
	Paul Molitor	.341
On-Base Pct:	Chuck Knoblauch	.448
Slugging Pct:	Chuck Knoblauch	.517
Home Runs:	Marty Cordova	16
RBIs:	Marty Cordova	111
Runs:	Chuck Knoblauch	140
Stolen Bases:	Chuck Knoblauch	45
Wins:	Frank Rodriguez	13
Strikeouts:	Brad Radke	148
ERA:	Brad Radke	4.46
Saves:	Dave Stevens	11

1990s

JANUARY 2   The Twins sign Dave Hollins, most recently with the Red Sox, as a free agent.

JANUARY 22   Alex Cole signs with the Red Sox as a free agent.

Cole played one season with the Red Sox, his last in the majors. In 2002, he pled guilty to a charge of conspiring to possess with the intent to distribute heroin and was sentenced to 18 months in federal prison.

JANUARY 29   The Twins sign Roberto Kelly, most recently with the Dodgers, as a free agent.

MARCH 28   Kirby Puckett wakes up with blurred vision in his right eye.

At the time, Puckett was tearing up the Grapefruit League with a .360 batting average. The blurred vision was later diagnosed as glaucoma. He had laser surgery on April 17 and took batting practice on May 28, but his vision problems persisted. Two more laser procedures in June showed irreversible damage to his retina and forced his retirement, which was formally announced on July 12. Puckett was only 35 and ended his 12-year career with a batting average of .318. He was elected to the Hall of Fame on the first ballot in 2001.

APRIL 1   The Twins open the season with an 8–6 win over the Tigers before 30,185 at the Metrodome. Brad Radke started and allowed only one run in six innings before three relievers combined to surrender five runs. Scott Stahoviak hit a home run.

A retractable curtain displaying the banners from the Twins championship years was hung in right-center prior to the 1996 season. A plaza was also added along Kirby Puckett Place on the west side of the Metrodome and served as a gathering spot for Twins fans prior to games. The area included tents for groups of 100 to 1,000 and featured a wide variety of food and beverage items. Twins management began campaigning for a baseball-only stadium in 1996, citing an inability to compete with large market clubs because of an unsatisfactory lease agreement and the poor sight lines for baseball at the Metrodome that they claimed held down attendance figures.

APRIL 2   Pat Meares falls just short of a cycle with a home run, triple and double, but the Twins lose 10–6 to the Tigers at the Metrodome.

APRIL 3   The Twins fall behind 6–2 in the third inning, but rally to rout the Tigers 16–7 at the Metrodome.

APRIL 8   The Twins-Red Sox game in Boston is postponed because of snow.

APRIL 12   The only two Twins hits off Mike Mussina are home runs in a 3–2 loss to the Orioles in Baltimore. Chuck Knoblauch homered in the fourth inning and Scott Stahoviak in the ninth. Mussina allowed only one other base runner, walking Knoblauch leading off the first inning.

APRIL 17   After falling behind 7–2, the Twins score three runs in the fifth inning and four in the sixth and defeat the Indians 9–8 at the Metrodome. A three-run homer by Pat Meares put the Twins into the lead.

April 20   Rick Aguilera makes his first start since 1989 and gives up four runs in three innings of a 7–6 loss to the Yankees at the Metrodome.

April 24   The Twins defeat the Tigers 24–11 at Tiger Stadium. The Twins scored in eight of the nine innings with three in the first, three in the second, one in the third, four in the fifth, three in the sixth, two in the seventh, five in the eighth and three in the ninth. After the Twins took a 7–2 advantage in the third, Detroit rallied to lead 10–7 before the Twins scored the four runs in the fifth. From the fifth through the ninth, the Twins scored 17 unanswered runs. Paul Molitor hit a home run and a triple, tied a team record with five runs scored, and drove in five. Chip Hale pinch-hit for Molitor in the ninth, and hit a three-run homer that gave Minnesota six runs and eight RBIs out of the number three spot in the batting order. Greg Myers also starred with five hits, including two doubles, with five RBIs in six at-bats. The Twins had 19 hits in all and drew 12 walks from seven Tiger pitchers. The 24 runs is a franchise record for a game, including the Washington years. The previous high was 21 by the Senators in 1929 and by the Twins twice in 1994. The 35 combined runs is one shy of the American League record and the most in a game involving the original Senators or the Twins. Tom Kelly was apologetic. "That wasn't very pretty, and all I can do is apologize to the fans in the stands who sat through the so-called exhibition of major league baseball," said the Twins manager. "The only thing good about the game is that we won."

Like Dave Winfield a few years earlier, Paul Molitor was a St. Paul native who returned to his hometown late in a Hall of Fame career. Also like Winfield, Molitor reached the 3,000-hit mark while with the Twins.

April 25   The Twins clobber the Tigers in Detroit for the second day in a row, winning 11–1.

April 30   Trailing 7–4, the Twins erupt for ten runs in the fifth inning and go on to defeat the Royals 16–7 at the Metrodome. The ten runs scored before an out was recorded as the first 11 batters reached base on a triple, a double, three singles, five walks and a fielder's choice. Marty Cordova started the rally with a single and hit a bases-loaded triple on the second time around the batting order.

MAY 1   Paul Molitor is hit by a pitch from Jeff Montgomery with the bases loaded in the tenth inning to lift the Twins to a 6–5 victory over the Royals at the Metrodome.

MAY 7   Sacrifice flies by Dennis Hocking in the fifth inning and Jeff Reboulet in the ninth account for the only runs of a 2–0 win over the Mariners in Seattle. Jose Parra (six innings), Pat Mahomes (one inning), Eddie Guardado (one inning) and Dave Stevens (one inning) combined on the shutout.

MAY 10   Ernie Young hits three homers for the Athletics during a 15–5 win over the Twins in Oakland. Young came into the game with three career homers in 164 at-bats.

MAY 26   The Twins break a 3–3 tie with six runs in the ninth inning and defeat the Blue Jays 9–3 in Toronto.

JUNE 1   Trailing 5–3, the Twins erupt for six runs in the ninth inning and defeat the Rangers 9–5 in Arlington. Rich Becker broke the 5–5 tie with a single, and Chuck Knoblauch followed with a three-run homer.

> *Knoblauch set a franchise record with 140 runs scored in 1996, breaking the mark of 128 set by Rod Carew in 1977. Knoblauch also hit .341 with 197 hits, 35 doubles, 14 triples, 13 home runs and 45 stolen bases.*

JUNE 2   The Twins rally in the ninth inning once again with three runs to defeat the Rangers 6–5 in Arlington. Dave Hollins tied the game with a two-out, two-run homer. The winning run was accomplished with three consecutive singles from Scott Stahoviak, Roberto Kelly and Pat Meares.

JUNE 4   With the second overall pick in the amateur draft, the Twins select first baseman Travis Lee from San Diego State University.

> *Major League Baseball made Lee a free agent on June 19 because the Twins did not offer him a proper contract within 15 days, a violation of the rules of the draft. Lee signed with the Diamondbacks and made his debut with the club in 1998. He played nine seasons in the majors and appeared in 1,099 games but never came close to fulfilling his promise. Other future major leaguers drafted and signed by the Twins in 1996 were Jacque Jones (second round), Chad Allen (fourth round), Michael Ryan (fifth round), Chad Loeller (seventh round) and Mike Lincoln (13th round).*

JUNE 5   The Twins score nine runs in the fourth inning and beat the Angels 14–3 at the Metrodome. Chuck Knoblauch capped the rally with a grand slam off Mark Eichhorn. Paul Molitor contributed a pair of singles.

JUNE 10   The Twins utilize five homers to pave the way for a 13–6 win over the Mariners at the Metrodome. Greg Myers hit two homers and Paul Molitor, Ron Coomer and Scott Stahoviak each added one. The Mariners hit four homers during the game.

June 11	In his first start since returning from the disabled list, Rick Aguilera gives up ten runs in three innings and the Twins lose 18–8 in Seattle.
June 15	With the score tied 4–4 in the seventh, Cecil Fielder hits a ball off the Metrodome roof that falls for a two-run double and a 6–4 defeat against the Tigers.
June 18	Brad Radke retires the first 20 batters to face him but winds up losing 2–0 to the Yankees in New York. Paul O'Neill broke up the perfect game bid with a double with two out in the seventh inning and Tino Martinez followed with a home run.
June 29	Marty Cordova runs his hitting streak to 23 games during a 12–7 victory over the Royals in Kansas City.
June 30	Matt Lawton hits a grand slam off Mark Gubicza in the third inning of a 5–2 triumph over the Royals in Kansas City.
July 5	The Twins score a run in the eighth inning and five in the ninth to shock the Royals 9–8 at the Metrodome. With one out in the ninth, doubles by Chuck Knoblauch, Paul Molitor and Scott Stahoviak and a single from Rick Becker produced three runs to make the score 8–7. After Dave Hollins struck out, however, the Twins were down to their last out. But Greg Myers walked and Chip Hale hit a two-run double for the improbable victory.

Knoblauch had ten multi-hit games in a row from June 29 through July 11. During that span he collected 22 hits in 42 at-bats. Among the 22 hits were six doubles, three triples and four home runs. He also scored 15 runs and drove in 13.

July 12	Kirby Puckett announces his retirement because of vision problems (see March 28, 1996).
July 13	Rich Becker has a career day during a 19–11 loss to the Indians at the Metrodome. Becker tied a franchise record for most extra base hits in a game with two homers, a triple and a double in six at-bats. The hits came in four consecutive plate appearances with the double in the first inning, the home runs in the third and fifth, and the triple in the sixth. He also drove in six runs. In addition, the Indians set an American League record by recording 12 doubles during the game. The Twins had six doubles of their own for a combined 18 by the two clubs. The 18 doubles broke an American League record that lasted until 2003 when the Yankees and Royals combined for 19.

Becker drove in 16 runs during a five-game span from July 11 through July 15.

July 14	Paul Molitor hits a walk-off homer in the ninth inning to defeat the Indians 5–4 at the Metrodome.
July 15	The Twins score six runs in the sixth inning to take a 16–1 lead and beat the White Sox 16–5 at the Metrodome.
July 25	The Twins score seven runs in the fourth inning and add six more in the fifth during a 16–6 thrashing of the Red Sox at the Metrodome. During the seven-run rally, Scott Stahoviak hit a home run and a single. The Twins also established a club record

with eight doubles. Paul Molitor and Marty Cordova each collected two with Rich Becker, Denny Hocking, Dave Hollins and Pat Meares adding the others.

AUGUST 8 — Two weeks after a bomb explodes in an Atlanta park filled with people attending the Olympics, the Twins trounce the Angels 13–5 in Anaheim.

AUGUST 14 — Chuck Knoblauch leads off the first inning with a home run on the first pitch from Dave Telgheder to spark a 13–7 victory over the Athletics in Oakland.

AUGUST 17 — The Twins clobber the Blue Jays 11–1 in Toronto.

AUGUST 20 — The Twins collect 20 hits and defeat the Brewers 12–7 at the Metrodome.

AUGUST 27 — Paul Molitor collects five hits in five at-bats during an 11-inning, 6–4 victory over the Blue Jays in Toronto.

AUGUST 29 — The Twins trade Dave Hollins to the Mariners for David Ortiz.

> *This trade would rank as one of the greatest in club history if the Twins had hung onto Ortiz (see December 16, 2002).*

SEPTEMBER 1 — Chuck Knoblauch leads off the first inning with a home run off Tim Van Egmond to ignite a 6–2 win over the Brewers in Milwaukee.

SEPTEMBER 2 — For the second game in a row, Chuck Knoblauch leads off the first time with a home run, this time off Ken Hill of the Rangers, to lead the Twins to a 6–4 victory in Arlington.

SEPTEMBER 7 — The Twins stage a tribute to Kirby Puckett prior to a 6–3 win over the Angels at the Metrodome. The event attracted a crowd of 51,011.

SEPTEMBER 15 — Entering the game with 2,998 hits, Paul Molitor misses a chance to record his 3,000th career hit in front of a hometown crowd when he goes hitless in a 7–0 loss to the Mariners at the Metrodome.

SEPTEMBER 16 — Paul Molitor collects his 3,000th career hits during a 6–5 loss to the Royals in Kansas City. He collected number 2,999 with a single off Jose Rosado in the first inning. Rosado was still on the mound in the fifth when Molitor tripled for his 3,000th hit. The game was delayed for several minutes as teammates mobbed Molitor.

> *Through the 2009 season, 27 players have 3,000 or more hits. Molitor is the only one to accomplish the feat in a season in which he collected 200 or more hits. He is also the only one to triple for his 3,000th hit. Molitor is also the second player to record his 3,000th hit as a member of the Twins. Dave Winfield was the first in 1993. Both Molitor and Winfield were born in St. Paul and both had their 3,000th hit on September 16.*

SEPTEMBER 29 — In the last game of the season, the Twins score two runs in the tenth inning to defeat the White Sox 5–4 at the Metrodome. Chuck Knoblauch drove in the tying run with a two-out triple, and scored on a walk-off single by Pat Meares.

DECEMBER 5   A month after Bill Clinton wins re-election to the presidency by defeating Bob Dole, the Twins sign Terry Steinbach, most recently with the Athletics, as a free agent.

> Steinbach was born in New Ulm, Minnesota, and attended the University of Minnesota. He was the Twins starting catcher for three years.

DECEMBER 12   The Twins sign Bob Tewksbury, most recently with the Padres, as a free agent.

DECEMBER 18   The Twins sign Greg Swindell, most recently with the Indians, as a free agent.

Native Born Sons

Jack Morris, Dave Winfield and Paul Molitor played the bulk of their careers outside of their home state of Minnesota, but each made an impact in Twins history during the 1990s. Morris pitched a ten-inning shutout in game seven of the 1991 World Series, while Winfield and Molitor each collected their 3,000th hit in a Twins uniform. On the other hand, Twin Cities natives Kent Hrbek and Joe Mauer became longtime stars with the club. The following is a list of players born in Minnesota who played for the Twins through the 2009 season.

Player	Years With Twins	Birthplace
Fred Bruckbauer	1961	New Ulm
Tom Burgmeier	1974–77	St. Paul
Jim Eisenreich	1982–84	St. Cloud
Bob Gebhard	1971–72	Lamberton
Paul Giel	1961	Winona
Dave Goltz	1972–79	Pelican Rapids
Kent Hrbek	1981–94	Minneapolis
Tom Johnson	1974–78	St. Paul
*Tom Kelly	1975	Graceville
Jerry Kindall	1964–65	St. Paul
Jerry Koosman	1979–81	Appleton
Mike Mason	1988	Faribault
Joe Mauer	2004–09	St. Paul
Paul Molitor	1996–98	St. Paul
Jack Morris	1991	St. Paul
Greg Olson	1989	Marshall
Glen Perkins	2006–09	St. Paul
Mike Poepping	1975	Little Falls
Brian Raabe	1995–96	New Ulm
Michael Restovich	2002–04	Rochester
Terry Steinbach	1997–99	New Ulm
Dick Stigman	1962–65	Nimrod
Jerry Terrell	1973–77	Waseca
George Thomas	1971	Minneapolis
Charlie Walters	1969	Minneapolis
Dave Winfield	1993–94	St. Paul

* Kelly also managed the Twins from 1986 through 2001. He is the only Minnesota native to manage the Twins.

1997

Season in a Sentence
Buoyed by the improvement shown in 1996, the Twins expect to post a winning record in 1997 but lose 94 games.

Finish • Won • Lost • Pct • GB
Fourth 68 94 .420 18.5

In the wild card race, the Twins finished in ninth place, 26 games behind.

Manager
Tom Kelly

Stats   Twins • AL • Rank
Batting Avg: .270   .271   8
On-Base Pct: .333   .340   11
Slugging Pct: .409   .428   11
Home Runs: 132   14
Stolen Bases: 151   2
ERA: 5.00   4.56   13
Errors: 101   5
Runs Scored: 772   10
Runs Allowed: 861   13

Starting Line-up
Terry Steinbach, c
Scott Stahoviak, 1b
Chuck Knoblauch, 2b
Ron Coomer, 3b
Pat Meares, ss
Marty Cordova, lf
Rich Becker, cf
Matt Lawton, rf-lf
Paul Molitor, dh
Dennis Hocking, ss
Roberto Kelly, rf

Pitchers
Brad Radke, sp
Bob Tewksbury, sp
Rich Robertson, sp
LaTroy Hawkins, sp
Rick Aguilera, rp
Frank Rodriguez, rp-sp
Greg Swindell, rp
Mike Trombley, rp
Eddie Guardado, rp
Todd Ritchie, rp

Attendance
1,411,064 (12th in AL)

Club Leaders
Batting Avg: Paul Molitor   .305
On-Base Pct: Chuck Knoblauch   .390
Slugging Pct: Ron Coomer   .438
Home Runs: Marty Cordova   15
RBI: Paul Molitor   89
Runs: Chuck Knoblauch   117
Stolen Bases: Chuck Knoblauch   62
Wins: Brad Radke   20
Strikeouts: Brad Radke   174
ERA: Brad Radke   3.87
Saves: Rick Aguilera   19

JANUARY 26 Carl Pohlad offers 49 percent of the Twins to the state in exchange for funding for a new stadium. Pohlad desired a retractable dome stadium as the new home of the ball club. The Twins ranked last in the major leagues in stadium revenue because of an unsatisfactory lease arranged at the Metrodome, which opened in 1982 and was owned by the state.

Stories about an impending move of the franchise from Minnesota dominated the sports pages all year. In June, the Twins received permission from Major League Baseball to talk to buyers who might want to relocate the club. On October 3, Pohlad signed a letter of intent with a group of North Carolina businessmen who planned to move the Twins to either the Piedmont Triad area of the state, which consisted of the cities of Greensboro, Winston-Salem and High Point, or to Charlotte. On November 18, baseball appointed a five-man committee to guide the Twins through the sport's relocation rules. This came two weeks after the Minnesota legislature defeated a proposal to finance a new stadium. "If there's no new ballpark, baseball will not survive in Minneapolis," said commissioner Bud Selig. The Twins offended many in Minnesota with their campaign for the stadium. The low point was a series of commercials produced by Pohlad's son Bill. In one, Marty Cordova visited a young cancer patient. The voice-over intoned: "If the Twins leave Minnesota, an eight-year-old from Wilmar will never get a visit from Marty Cordova." The boy wasn't even from Minnesota, and worst of all, he had died a few months before the spot aired (see May 5, 1998). In the end, the club alienated its dwindling fans base with its crude attempts to persuade the legislature into building a new ballpark. After the ballpark package was turned down, Carl Pohlad fielded a team with the lowest payroll in the American League in both 1999 and 2000.

APRIL 1   On Opening Day, the Twins overcome a five-run deficit to defeat the Tigers 7–5 before 43,216 at the Metrodome. After Detroit took a 5–0 lead off starter Brad Radke, the Twins scored three runs in the fifth inning and four in the eighth for the victory. Pat Meares broke the 5–5 tie with a two-run homer.

APRIL 3   The Twins score seven runs in the second inning and defeat the Tigers 10–6 at the Metrodome. Matt Lawton hit a three-run homer and Paul Molitor belted a grand slam, both off Willie Blair.

APRIL 24   The Twins lose a heart-rending 12–11 decision in 11 innings to the Athletics in Oakland. Minnesota was down 8–1 before scoring a run in the fifth inning, two in the sixth and seven in the eighth for a 11–8 lead. With two out in the eighth, Terry Steinbach hit a three-run homer to put the Twins into the lead 9–8, and a hit batsman and three singles produced two more runs. Steinbach, who played for the A's from 1986 through 1996, entered the game as a pinch-hitter in the seventh. But Oakland scored three in the ninth off Rick Aguilera. He was still on the mound in the 11th when his wild pitch scored the winning run from third base. The Twins collected 21 hits during the contest.

The loss was the second of an eight-game losing streak that sent the Twins record from 11–8 to 11–16. The club never got back over the .500 mark again.

MAY 5   Bob Tewksbury goes on the disabled list after breaking the pinky on his left hand in the bathroom door of the team bus. He was out of action for three months.

MAY 12   The Twins collect 20 hits and rout the Blue Jays 12–2 at the Metrodome. Greg Myers had four hits, two of them doubles, and scored four runs.

MAY 16   Batting twice with the bases loaded, center fielder Darrin Jackson drives in six runs with a two-run double in the third inning against Chris Hammond and a grand slam off Tom Borland in the fourth to lead the Twins to a 11–5 victory over the Red Sox at the Metrodome.

Incredibly, the game was Jackson's first with the Twins and his first in the majors since 1994. He played for four clubs from 1985 through 1994 and then spent two seasons in Japan. Jackson began the 1997 campaign with the Twins Triple A affiliate in Salt Lake City. He appeared in 49 games for the Twins and hit three homers with a .254 batting average before being dealt to the Brewers.

MAY 23   Paul Molitor collects five hits, including a double, but the Twins lose 8–4 to the Athletics at the Metrodome.

May 25	Kirby Puckett's number 34 is retired in ceremonies prior to a ten-inning, 7–6 triumph over the Athletics at the Metrodome.
	Puckett was the fifth Twins player to have his number retired following Harmon Killebrew (3), Rod Carew (29), Tony Oliva (6) and Kent Hrbek (14). In addition, number 42 was retired in 1997 throughout baseball in honor of Jackie Robinson. In 2009, two others numbers were in "limbo" and weren't issued to anyone on the Twins roster. Those are numbers 4 (Paul Molitor) and 10 (Tom Kelly).
May 27	The Twins stage an unbelievable rally by overcoming a 10–4 deficit with a run in the eighth inning and six in the ninth to defeat the Mariners 11–10 at the Metrodome. Playing in his first game in five weeks after recovering from a foot injury, Marty Cordova homered in the eighth. Rich Becker drove in the first run of the ninth with a double, moved to third on a wild pitch, and scored on a sacrifice fly by Paul Molitor to make the score 10–7. After a double by Terry Steinbach and a walk, Cordova belted his second consecutive homer to tie the score 10–10. The Twins loaded the bases with two walks and a single, before Chuck Knoblauch drew a walk from Norm Charlton to force home the winning run.
	Knoblauch hit .291 with nine homers and scored 117 runs batted in 1997.
June 3	In the first round of the amateur draft, the Twins select shortstop Michael Cuddyer from Great Bridge High School in Chesapeake, Virginia.
	Cuddyer made his major league debut in 2001 and was still with the Twins as the club's starting right fielder in 2009. Other future major leaguers drafted and signed by the Twins in 1997 were Matt LeCroy (supplemental first round), Michael Restovich (third round) and J. C. Romero (21st round).
June 13	The Twins play a National League team during the regular season for the first time and beat the Astros 8–1 at the Astrodome.
June 14	During a 6–1 victory over the Astros in Houston, Rich Robertson singles to become the first Twins pitcher to collect a hit since 1972.
June 16	The Twins play a National League opponent at the Metrodome for the first time during the regular season and lose 8–6 to the Pirates.
June 17	The Twins wallop the Pirates 13–1 at the Metrodome. All nine starters drove in at least one run.
June 28	The Twins score seven runs in the eighth inning and defeat the White Sox 11–5 at the Metrodome. The Twins collected eight singles during the rally, including two by Scott Stahoviak.
June 30	The Twins play the Cardinals for the first time during the regular season and lose 2–1 in St. Louis.
July 4	The Twins erupt for 23 hits and trounce the Brewers 13–1 in Milwaukee.

Tough little second baseman Chuck Knoblauch won many fans with his fierce determination as well as excellent fielding, hitting, and base-stealing skills. His insistence on being traded in 1997, however, turned fans against him, and he was always loudly booed when he returned to play for opposing teams.

JULY 13   To honor Jackie Robinson on the 50th anniversary of his first season in the major leagues, the Twins wear replica uniforms of the 1909 St. Paul Colored Gophers, a barnstorming team of African-Americans that existed from 1907 through 1910. The Twins lost 13–5 to the Brewers at the Metrodome.

JULY 17   The Twins break two extra-inning ties with home runs and beat the Mariners 9–7 in 12 innings at the Kingdome. Chuck Knoblauch homered in the tenth to give Minnesota a 7–6 advantage, but Seattle scored in the bottom half. Marty Cordova led off the 12th with a solo homer before the Twins added an insurance run.

JULY 20   Brad Radke fans ten without a walk in a complete game shutout which beats the Athletics 1–0 in Oakland.

JULY 29   Trailing 3–0, the Twins score eight runs in the third inning and outlast the Royals 11–8 in Kansas City.

JULY 30   The Twins explode for eight runs in the first inning and clobber the Royals 11–1 in Kansas City. It was the second day in a row in which the Twins produced an eight-run inning. After Chuck Knoblauch flied out, nine straight batters (Roberto Kelly, Paul Molitor, Terry Steinbach, Ron Coomer, Marty Cordova, Greg Colbrunn, Darrin Jackson, Dennis Hocking and Knoblauch) reached base on four singles, two doubles, a triple and two walks. Given an eight-run lead before throwing a pitch, Brad Radke coasted to his 11th consecutive victory.

Hocking played seven defensive positions and as a DH in 1997. The only positions he didn't play were pitcher and catcher.

AUGUST 4 — Brad Radke records his 12th consecutive victory with a 5–4 decision over the Blue Jays at the Metrodome. Greg Colbrunn hit a pinch-hit grand slam off Omar Daal in the fifth inning.

Radke put together his 12-game winning streak in 12 consecutive starts. It began on June 7 when he had a record of 4–5 with a 5.00 ERA and a career record of 26–35. During the 12 victories, Radke had a 1.87 earned run average in 91 1/3 innings. He finished the season 20–10 with a 3.87 ERA in 239 1/3 innings and a league-leading 35 starts. Radke won 20 on a team that was 68–94. No other Twins pitcher that season won more than eight games.

AUGUST 19 — The Twins extend their losing streak to ten games with an 8–2 defeat at the hands of the Tigers in Detroit.

The Twins were 2–17 from August 5 through August 25.

AUGUST 20 — The Twins break their ten-game losing streak with an 11–1 thrashing of the Tigers in Detroit.

On the same day, the Twins traded Roberto Kelly to the Mariners for Joe Mays and Jeremy Palki.

AUGUST 29 — The Twins play the Reds for the first time during the regular season and lose 5–3 at the Metrodome.

SEPTEMBER 1 — The day after Princess Diana dies following a car accident in Paris, the Twins play the Cubs for the first time during the regular season, and win 7–6 in Chicago.

SEPTEMBER 2 — During a 9–3 loss to the Cubs at Wrigley Field, Bob Tewksbury becomes the first Twins pitcher since 1972 to collect an RBI.

SEPTEMBER 11 — Ivan Rodriguez wallops three homers for the Rangers during a 7–0 win over the Twins in Arlington.

SEPTEMBER 14 — The Twins collect 21 hits and rout the Rangers 11–1 in Arlington.

SEPTEMBER 20 — LaTroy Hawkins (six innings), Mike Trombley (two innings) and Greg Swindell (one inning) combine on a two-hitter to defeat the Brewers 6–1 at the Metrodome. Hawkins had a no-hitter in progress until Jeff Cirillo doubled and Julio Franco singled in the sixth.

SEPTEMBER 21   Brad Radke pitches a ten-inning complete game to record his 20th victory of 1997 with a 2–1 decision over the Brewers at the Metrodome. Paul Molitor drove in the winning run with a walk-off triple.

SEPTEMBER 22   Damian Miller hits a grand slam off Jeff D'Amico in the second inning of a 5–2 win over the Brewers at the Metrodome.

SEPTEMBER 27   Matt Lawton leads off the tenth inning with a home run, and the Twins add an insurance run to defeat the Indians 6–4 in Cleveland.

NOVEMBER 18   In the expansion draft, the Twins lose Brent Brede and Damian Miller to the Diamondbacks.

DECEMBER 11   The Twins sign Otis Nixon, most recently with the Dodgers, as a free agent.

DECEMBER 12   The Twins trade Rich Becker to the Mets for Alex Ochoa.

DECEMBER 16   The Twins sign Mike Morgan, most recently with the Reds, as a free agent.

Morgan played for 12 clubs during a career that lasted from 1978 through 2002. He appeared in 18 contests for the Twins before going to the Cubs in an August 1998 trade.

1998

Season in a Sentence
The year begins with an offer on the table to sell the club to a group that would move it to North Carolina and ends with 92 losses and the lowest attendance figure in the AL.

Finish • Won • Lost • Pct • GB
Fourth   70   92   .432   19.0

In the wild card race, the Twins were in ninth place, 22 games behind.

Manager
Tom Kelly

Stats

Stats	Twins	AL	Rank
Batting Avg:	.266	.271	9
On-Base Pct:	.328	.340	11
Slugging Pct:	.389	.432	13
Home Runs:	115		13
Stolen Bases:	112		10
ERA:	4.75	4.65	8
Errors:	108		7
Runs Scored:	734		11
Runs Allowed:	818		8

Starting Line-up
Terry Steinbach, c
David Ortiz, 1b
Todd Walker, 2b
Ron Coomer, 3b-1b
Pat Meares, ss
Marty Cordova, lf
Otis Nixon, cf
Matt Lawton, rf
Paul Molitor, dh
Brent Gates, 3b
Alex Ochoa, rf
Dennis Hocking, ss-2b-lf

Pitchers
Brad Radke, sp
LaTroy Hawkins, sp
Eric Milton, sp
Bob Tewksbury, sp
Mike Morgan, sp
Rick Aguilera, rp
Mike Trombley, rp
Greg Swindell, rp
Eddie Guardado, rp
Hector Carrasco, rp

Attendance
1,165,976 (14th in AL)

Club Leaders
Batting Avg: Todd Walker .316
On-Base Pct: Matt Lawton .387
Slugging Pct: Matt Lawton .478
Home Runs: Matt Lawton 21
RBI: Matt Lawton 77
Runs: Matt Lawton 91
Stolen Bases: Otis Nixon 37
Wins: Brad Radke 12
Strikeouts: Brad Radke 146
ERA: Brad Radke 4.20
Saves: Rick Aguilera 38

JANUARY 14   The Twins sign Orlando Merced, most recently with the Blue Jays, as a free agent.

FEBRUARY 6   The Twins trade Chuck Knoblauch to the Yankees for Christian Guzman, Eric Milton, Brian Buchanan, Danny Mota and cash. Though fans were upset to watch another star leave the team, the deal actually turned out in Minnesota's favor.

> *Knoblauch was unhappy in Minnesota because the club seemed years away from contending and seemed poised to relocate to North Carolina. He had two decent offensive seasons with the Yankees, although nowhere near his peak years with the Twins, but he suffered a steep decline beginning in 2000 and was soon out of the majors. In his last year in 2002, he batted only .210 in 80 games with the Royals at the age of 34. A Gold Glover in 1997, Knoblauch also fell apart defensively and had difficulty making routine throws from second base. Because of his troubles, the Twins came out ahead in the trade. Guzman was the club's starting shortstop for six seasons beginning in 1999, and he led the AL in triples*

in 2000, 2001 and 2003. Milton spent five years in Minnesota's starting rotation, pitched a no-hitter in 1999, and was 41–26 from 2000 through 2002.

APRIL 1   The Twins open the season with a 3–2 loss to the Blue Jays in Toronto. Bob Tewksbury was the starting and losing pitcher. Brent Gates, in his first game with the Twins, hit a home run.

APRIL 3   The Twins blow a 4–0 lead and lose the home opener 9–5 against the Royals before 43,848 at the Metrodome. David Ortiz homered in the losing cause.

APRIL 4   On the final play of a ten-inning 3–2 loss to the Royals at the Metrodome, Otis Nixon is kicked in the face by Kansas City shortstop Felix Martinez while trying to break up a double play.

Martinez claimed the kick was accidental, but replays appeared to indicate that it was intentional. Nixon suffered a broken jaw on the play.

APRIL 5   The Twins score seven runs in the eighth inning to cap a 10–1 rout of the Royals at the Metrodome.

APRIL 7   The Twins clobber the Blue Jays 12–2 at the Metrodome. Roger Clemens started for Toronto, but left after seven pitches because of a groin strain. Bob Tewksbury retired the last 18 batters he faced in a seven-inning appearance.

APRIL 8   The Twins offense erupts again with a 13–2 trouncing of the Blue Jays at the Metrodome.

APRIL 13   The Twins play a regular season game in St. Petersburg for the first time, and collect 22 hits in a 14-inning, 13–12 loss to the Devil Rays. Minnesota led 7–1 before Tampa Bay scored five in the sixth. After the Twins scored three in the top of the seventh, the Devil Rays responded with their second straight five-run inning to take an 11–10 advantage. Matt Lawton hit a two-run single in the ninth to put the Twins back ahead 12–11, but the bullpen allowed a run in the bottom of the inning and another in the 14th resulting in the defeat. After Lawton's single, the Twins didn't put another runner on base.

APRIL 25   The Twins break a 2–2 tie with six runs in the ninth inning to defeat the Athletics 8–2 in Oakland. Ron Coomer capped the rally with a grand slam off Heathcliff Slocumb.

APRIL 26   Terry Steinbach has a hand in both runs of a 2–0 win over the Mariners in Seattle. In the seventh inning, Steinbach doubled home Ron Coomer and then scored on a single from Marty Cordova. Brad Radke ($6^{1}/_{3}$ innings), Mike Trombley ($1^{1}/_{3}$ innings), Greg Swindell (one-third of an inning) and Rick Aguilera (one inning) combined on the shutout.

APRIL 29   The Twins play the Devil Rays at the Metrodome for the first time and win 2–0. Bob Tewksbury (eight innings) and Rick Aguilera (one inning) combined on the shutout.

MAY 2   Ron Coomer homers in the 11th inning to down the Orioles 8–7 in Baltimore.

MAY 5	Voters in Forsyth and Guilford counties in North Carolina defeat a proposed referendum that would have raised taxes to fund construction of a ballpark in the Triad region (Greensboro, High Point and Winston-Salem). On October 3, 1997, Carl Pohlad signed a letter of intent to sell the club to a group of North Carolina businessmen, headed by Don Beaver. The passage of the referendum was necessary for the sale to be complete. Beaver also talked to Charlotte officials about moving the Twins there but found little interest in public funding of a stadium.
MAY 9	Matt Lawton hits a grand slam off Andy Pettitte in the sixth inning of an 8–1 triumph over the Yankees at the Metrodome.
MAY 17	David Wells of the Yankees pitches a perfect game to defeat the Twins 4–0 in New York. Wells fanned 11 and threw 123 pitches. It was the second perfect game hurled against the Twins in franchise history. The first was by Catfish Hunter of the A's on May 8, 1968. In the ninth inning, Wells retired Jon Shave on a fly ball to right fielder Paul O'Neill, struck out Javier Valentin, and set down Pat Meares on another fly ball to O'Neill.
MAY 19	In their first game since suffering a perfect game, the Twins score four runs in the first inning and defeat the Tigers 8–3 at the Metrodome.
MAY 20	The Twins score eight runs in the bottom of the first inning to take an 8–2 lead but wind up losing 12–11 to the Tigers at the Metrodome. Todd Walker started the rally with a single and drove in the final three runs of the inning with a home run.
	Walker hit .316 with 41 doubles and 12 home runs in 1998.
MAY 25	The Twins score eight runs in the third inning and defeat the Rangers 9–3 in Arlington. Third baseman Jon Shave started the rally with a single and drove in the final three runs with a homer.
	The home run by Shave was his only one in the majors and it was struck when he was 30 years old. He played 19 games with 43 at-bats as a member of the Twins and 79 contests and 178 at-bats as a big leaguer.

Rick Aquilera was the primary closer for the Twins throughout the 1990s. During those years he was considered one of the top closers in the game.

May 31	The Twins lose 6–5 to the Angels in a game at the Metrodome played with a temporary left-field foul pole. A white ten-foot pole was erected after a violent rainstorm the previous evening snapped the cable connecting the 45-foot pole normally in place to the roof, causing the pole to fall over.
June 2	In the first round of the amateur draft, the Twins select pitcher Ryan Mills from Arizona State University.

> *Mills never reached the majors, nor did any of the others chosen in the first eight rounds. Players drafted and signed by the Twins who played in the majors were Saul Rivera (ninth round), Mike Gosling (14th round), Kevin Thompson (18th round), Juan Padilla (24th round), Kevin Frederick (24th round) and Tommy Watkins (38th round). The draft consisted more of quantity than quality, as none of the six who reached the majors had much of an impact for the Twins.*

June 5	The Twins play a regular season game in Pittsburgh for the first time and lose 6–1 to the Pirates at Three Rivers Stadium. The lone Minnesota run was scored by Mike Morgan. He was the first Twins pitcher to score a run since 1972.
June 8	The Cubs play at the Metrodome for the first time and beat the Twins 8–1.
June 21	Brent Gates hits a grand slam off Jason Bere in the fourth inning of a 6–1 victory over the White Sox in Chicago.
June 26	The Twins play a regular season game against the Cardinals at the Metrodome for the first time and win 5–1.
June 28	Bob Tewksbury twice uses 44-mile-per-hour lob pitches to retire Mark McGwire with ground outs during a 3–2 win over the Cardinals at the Metrodome. Tewksbury also set down Ray Lankford with a lob to the plate.
June 30	The Twins play in Cincinnati for the first time and lose 6–3 to the Reds at Cinergy Field.
July 25	Trailing 5–0, the Twins score three runs in the fourth inning, two in the sixth and two in the eighth and beat the Rangers 7–6 at the Metrodome. David Ortiz broke a 5–5 tie in the eighth with a two-run double.
July 26	Todd Walker collects four hits, including a home run, in four at-bats during an 11–3 win over the Rangers at the Metrodome. The four-for-four game gave Walker eight consecutive hits over three games. He also had a streak of reaching base in ten straight plate appearances counting two walks, one of them intentional.
July 28	Todd Walker collects his ninth straight hit and reaches base in his 11th consecutive plate appearance with a single in the second inning of a 3–0 victory over the Royals in Kansas City.

> *Walker's nine hits were six singles, two doubles and a home run. The nine straight hits tied a franchise record set by Sam Rice with the Senators in 1925 and tied by Tony Oliva in 1967 and Mickey Hatcher in 1985. From July 21*

1990s

through July 28, Walker had 16 hits in 20 at-bats and reached base in 19 of 23 consecutive plate appearances.

JULY 31 — The Twins trade Greg Swindell and Orlando Merced to the Red Sox for Joe Thomas, Matt Barnes and Joe Kinney.

Merced was traded after he became a disruptive force in the clubhouse by complaining about his lack of playing time and by likening manager Tom Kelly to Fidel Castro.

AUGUST 8 — Paul Molitor collects five hits, including a double, in five at-bats, but the Twins lose 6–3 to the Orioles in Baltimore. Molitor also stole the 500th base of his career.

AUGUST 22 — With Dennis Eckersley pitching for the Red Sox, Paul Molitor bunts home Pat Meares from third base with two out in the ninth inning for a 4–3 victory at the Metrodome.

AUGUST 25 — The Twins trade Mike Morgan to the Cubs for Scott Downs.

SEPTEMBER 2 — Matt Lawton hits a two-run walk-off triple in the tenth inning to beat the Devil Rays 6–5 at the Metrodome.

SEPTEMBER 3 — The Twins win with an extra-inning walk-off hit for the second game in a row when Terry Steinbach singles in the 12th for a 5–4 decision over the Devil Rays at the Metrodome. The Twins tied the score 3–3 with a run in the ninth. After Tampa Bay plated a run in the top of the tenth, Matt Lawton homered in the bottom half.

SEPTEMBER 19 — The Twins extend their losing streak to ten games by dropping an 11-inning, 8–7 decision to the Tigers in Detroit.

SEPTEMBER 20 — In his first major league start, Benj Sampson pitches six shutout innings and is the winning pitcher in a 3–0 decision over the Tigers in Detroit.

Sampson began his big league career with $13 1/3$ consecutive scoreless innings over two starts and three relief appearances. In 1999, however, he had an 8.11 ERA in 71 innings and never pitched in the majors again.

SEPTEMBER 23 — Trailing 6–0, the Twins score two runs in the seventh inning, one in the eighth, three in the ninth, and one in the 12th to defeat the White Sox 7–6 at the Metrodome. The Twins still trailed 6–3 with two out in the ninth when Brent Gates hit a three-run homer. Chris Latham drove in the winning run with a single. Latham entered the game in the seventh inning as a defensive replacement in left field.

SEPTEMBER 24 — David Ortiz drives in both runs of a 2–0 win over the Indians at the Metrodome with a double in the sixth inning. Brad Radke ($7 1/3$ innings), Eddie Guardado (one-third of an inning), Mike Trombley (one-third of an inning) and Rick Aguilera (one inning) combined on the shutout.

SEPTEMBER 27 — On the last day of the season, Mike Trombley strikes out the first six batters he faces in a perfect $2 1/3$-inning relief appearance to close out a 6–2 win over the Indians at the Metrodome. Paul Molitor played in his last major league game and collected two singles in four at-bats.

Molitor was elected to the Hall of Fame on the first ballot in 2004. He is one of three players born in Minnesota to be enshrined in Cooperstown. The other two are Dave Winfield and Chief Bender.

NOVEMBER 3   Minnesota voters elect former wrestler Jesse Ventura as Governor.

The election would have an impact on the Twins, because for most of his four years in office, Ventura was an outspoken critic of using public funding for a new ballpark for the club.

DECEMBER 1   Otis Nixon signs with the Braves as a free agent.

1999

Season in a Sentence

With a full-fledged commitment to rebuilding with a youth movement, the Twins post the worst record in the American League.

Finish • Won • Lost • Pct • GB

Fifth   63   97   .394   33.0

In the wild card race, the Twins finished in 11th (last) place, 30 games behind.

Manager

Tom Kelly

Stats   Twins • AL • Rank

Stat	Twins	AL	Rank
Batting Avg:	.264	.275	11
On-Base Pct:	.328	.347	12
Slugging Pct:	.384	.439	14
Home Runs:	105		14
Stolen Bases:	118		5
ERA:	5.00	4.86	9
Errors:	92		2
Runs Scored:	686		14
Runs Allowed:	795		9

Starting Line-up

Terry Steinbach, c
Doug Mientiewicz, 1b
Todd Walker, 2b
Ron Coomer, 3b-1b
Christian Guzman, ss
Chad Allen, lf
Torii Hunter, cf
Matt Lawton, rf
Marty Cordova, dh
Corey Koskie, 3b
Dennis Hocking, ss-2b-lf
Jacque Jones, cf
Brent Gates, 3b-2b
Javier Valentin, c

Pitchers

Brad Radke, sp
Eric Milton, sp
LaTroy Hawkins, sp
Mike Trombley, rp
Bob Wells, rp
Travis Miller, rp
Eddie Guardado, rp
Joe Mays, rp-sp
Dan Perkins, rp-sp

Attendance

1,202,829 (14th in AL)

Club Leaders

Batting Avg:	Marty Cordova	.285
On-Base Pct:	Marty Cordova	.365
Slugging Pct:	Marty Cordova	.464
Home Runs:	Marty Cordova	14
RBI:	Marty Cordova	70
Runs:	Chad Allen	69
Stolen Bases:	Matt Lawton	26
Wins:	Brad Radke	12
Strikeouts:	Eric Milton	163
ERA:	Brad Radke	3.75
Saves:	Mike Trombley	24

1990s

February 20 — Eight days after President Bill Clinton is acquitted following his impeachment trial in the House of Representatives, Pat Meares signs a contract with the Pirates as a free agent.

April 6 — The Twins open the season with a 6–1 win over the Blue Jays before 45,601 at the Metrodome. Each fan in the crowd was guaranteed a free ticket to another game if the Twins had lost. Matt Lawton led the offense with three hits, including a double. Brad Radke was the starting pitcher, and went seven innings. There were four rookies in the starting line-up (center fielder Torii Hunter, left fielder Chad Allen, first baseman Doug Mientiewicz and shortstop Christian Guzman). There were ten rookies on the 25-man Opening Day roster.

April 8 — The Twins take a 7–1 lead after three innings and hold on to defeat the Blue Jays 11–9 at the Metrodome.

April 12 — Eric Milton (7 1/3 innings), Mike Trombley (three innings) and Rick Aguilera (1 2/3 innings) combine on a brilliant 12-inning, three-hit shutout to defeat the Tigers 1–0 at Tiger Stadium. Milton (19) and Trombley (three) combined to retire 22 batters in a row from the second through the ninth innings. The three Minnesota pitchers faced 40 batters, just four over the minimum. The Twins had only three hits off Detroit pitching over the first 11 innings before Todd Walker led off the 12th with a home run off Scott Runyan.

On the same day, assistant general manager Joe McIlvaine was arrested for nude sunbathing on Jensen Beach in Florida. McIlvaine's explanation was that he thought he was on a private beach.

April 17 — The Twins use two big innings to defeat the Indians 13–8 in 11 innings in the second game of a double-header at Jacobs Field. Trailing 7–1, the Twins erupted for seven runs in the eighth inning to take an 8–7 lead. Brent Gates doubled and singled during the rally and Matt Lawton walloped a grand slam off Joey Spradlin. Cleveland tied the score with a run in the ninth to send the contest into extra innings. In the 11th, the Twins scored five runs, two of them on a double by Lawton that gave him six runs batted in during the game. The Indians won the opener 5–1.

April 26 — Torii Hunter hits a grand slam off Tim Wakefield in the fourth inning of a 6–2 victory over the Red Sox at the Metrodome.

May 18 — Edgar Martinez of the Mariners hits three homers off Twins pitching to lead his club to a 10–1 win in Seattle.

May 19 — The Twins play at the Kingdome for the last time and lose 7–0 to the Mariners.

May 21 — The Twins slip past the Athletics 2–1 in a 15-inning marathon at the Metrodome. Todd Walker led off the 15th with a double and scored on a single by Doug Mientiewicz. The pitchers were LaTroy Hawkins (6 1/3 innings), Eddie Guardado (two-thirds of an inning), Bob Wells (two innings), Mike Trombley (five innings) and Travis Miller (one inning).

On the same day, the Twins traded Rick Aguilera and Scott Downs to the Cubs for Kyle Lohse and Jason Ryan. Aguilera left the club with club records in games pitched (494), relief appearances (464) and saves (254). He pitched for the Cubs through the end of the 2000 season before retiring. Lohse was a member of the Twins starting rotation from 2001 through 2006.

MAY 22 Todd Walker hits a walk-off homer just inside the left-field foul pole in the tenth inning to defeat the Athletics 2–1 in ten innings at the Metrodome. It was the Twins second straight 2–1, extra-inning victory.

The Twins fielded the youngest club in the American League in 1999. Regulars included Christian Guzman (age 21), Javier Valentin (23), Torii Hunter (23), Eric Milton (23), Joe Mays (23), Dan Perkins (24), Jacque Jones (24), Chad Allen (24), Doug Mientiewicz (25), Todd Walker (26), Corey Koskie (26), Brad Radke (26) and LaTroy Hawkins (26). David Ortiz (23) was expected to be the starting first baseman, but lost his job to Mientiewicz in spring training. Recalled in September, Ortiz was hitless in 20 at-bats with 12 strikeouts.

JUNE 2 In the first round of the amateur draft, the Twins select outfielder B. J. Garbe from Moses Lake High School in Moses Lake, Washington.

Garbe was the fifth overall pick in the draft but never advanced past the Class AA level. The Twins chose high school catchers in the second and third rounds in Bob Bowen and Justin Morneau. Both reached the majors in 2003 but had entirely different career paths. Bowen has been largely ineffective, while Morneau switched his position to first base and became a star. Other future big leaguers drafted and signed by the Twins in 1999 have been Brian Wolfe (sixth round), Travis Bowyer (20th round), Willie Eyre (23rd round) and Terry Tiffee (26th round).

JUNE 4 The Astros play at the Metrodome for the first time and beat the Twins 7–6. Dennis Hocking hit a grand slam off Mike Hampton in the second inning.

JUNE 6 The Twins collect 21 hits and beat the Astros 13–6 at the Metrodome. Every starter (Todd Walker, Dennis Hocking, Brent Gates, Marty Cordova, Matt Lawton, Corey Koskie, Ron Coomer, Javier Valentin and Cleatus Davidson) had at least two hits. Valentin had a homer, triple and a double.

The two hits by Davidson were the first two of his career. He didn't collect the third and final base hit of his career until September 10, when he finished his brief stay in the majors with a .154 average in 22 at-bats.

JUNE 7 Mike Trombley strikes out all three batters he faces in the ninth inning to close out an 8–6 triumph over the Reds at the Metrodome.

JUNE 8 Matt Lawton is hit in the face by a pitch from Dennys Reyes in the eighth inning of a 5–2 win over the Reds at the Metrodome. Lawton suffered two broken bones in his eye socket and missed six weeks.

JUNE 23 The Twins take a 12–3 lead in the sixth inning and hang on to defeat the White Sox 12–10 in Chicago.

June 26	The Twins edge the Tigers 1–0 in Detroit. Chad Allen drove in the lone run of the contest with a single in the sixth inning. Joe Mays (six innings), Bob Wells (1 2/3 innings) and Mike Trombley (1 1/3 innings) combined on the shutout. It was Mays' second career start.
June 27	The Twins play at Tiger Stadium for the last time and win 12–7. Dennis Hocking collected five hits, three of them doubles, in six at-bats.
July 3	Jacque Jones leads off the home half of the first inning with a homer on the first pitch from Nelson Cruz to spark a 7–2 win over the Tigers at the Metrodome. It was also Jones' first major league home run.
July 17	Dennis Hocking hits the first pitch of the game for a home run off Terry Mulholland to ignite an 8–0 victory over the Cubs in Chicago. The game started 20 minutes late because of rain.
July 18	For the second day in a row, Dennis Hocking hits the first pitch of the game for a home run. It came on a 3–1 pitch from Darren Oliver of the Cardinals in St. Louis. There was no more scoring until the ninth inning, when the Twins plated four runs and the Cards two for a 5–2 victory.
July 24	Corey Koskie hits a grand slam off Frank Rodriguez in the fifth inning of a 10–3 win over the Mariners at the Metrodome.
August 6	Trailing 7–1, the Twins score three runs in the sixth inning, two in the seventh, and three in the eighth to defeat the Royals 9–8 in Kansas City. Ron Coomer tied the score 8–8 with a two-run single in the eighth. Chad Allen drove in the winning run with another single. In the ninth, Mike Trombley walked three to load the bases and then fanned Carlos Beltran to end the game.
August 11	Eric Milton strikes out 12 batters in seven innings, but the Twins lose 6–3 to the Blue Jays at the Metrodome.
August 30	In only his second major league game, Jason Ryan pitches a two-hitter but winds up losing 2–1 to the Blue Jays at SkyDome. The only Toronto hits were an RBI-single by Tony Fernandez in the first inning and a homer from Tony Batista in the second. After Batista's home run, Ryan retired 19 batters in a row.

In his first start, six days earlier, Ryan repeatedly crossed up catcher Terry Steinbach. The club figured that Ryan couldn't read the catcher's signs and had him fitted for glasses. The vision correction worked in the August 30 start, but the improvement in his pitching acumen didn't stick. Ryan finished his brief two-year big league career with a record of 1–5 and an ERA of 5.94. |
| August 31 | The Twins score seven runs in the fourth inning to take a 12–0 lead and defeat the Blue Jays 14–3 in Toronto. Jacque Jones capped the fourth-inning rally with a three-run homer. Paul Spoljaric threw the first pitch following Jones' homer over the head of Christian Guzman. Guzman charged the mound and tackled Spoljaric, causing both benches to empty. Spoljaric left with a black eye and both he and Guzman were ejected. |

SEPTEMBER 6 — Trailing 7–6, the Twins score six runs in the sixth inning and defeat the Devil Rays 13–7 in St. Petersburg. The Twins scored 13 runs despite striking out 14 times.

SEPTEMBER 11 — Eric Milton pitches a no-hitter to defeat the Angels 7–0 at the Metrodome. He struck out 13, walked two, and threw 121 pitches. Milton fanned at least one batter in every inning. In the ninth, Milton retired Trent Durrington on a pop up to first baseman Doug Mientkiewicz, Andy Sheets on a grounder from second baseman Cleatus Davidson to Mientiewicz, and Jerry Davanon on a strikeout. Milton retired the last 18 batters to face him.

> *There were many unusual aspects to Milton's no-hitter. He came into the game with a career record of 14–25 and an ERA of 5.26. The game began at 11:00 a.m. because the University of Minnesota played a football game that night at the Metrodome against Louisiana-Monroe. The Twins allowed any wearing pajamas to be admitted for free. The official attendance was 11,222. Because of the early starting time, Anaheim manager Joe Maddon rested most of his regulars.*

SEPTEMBER 15 — The Twins lose 8–3 to the Rangers at the Metrodome to finish the season with an 0–12 record against the Texas club.

SEPTEMBER 17 — The Twins play at Safeco Field in Seattle for the first time, and lose 4–3 to the Mariners.

SEPTEMBER 24 — Joe Mays (eight innings) and Bob Wells (one inning) combine on a two-hitter to defeat the White Sox 6–2 at the Metrodome. The only Chicago hits were a single by Josh Paul and a double from Greg Norton, both in the sixth inning.

> *In October, Carl Pohlad came to an agreement to sell the Twins for $120 million to Glen Taylor, owner of the NBA's Minnesota Timberwolves, and Robert Naegele, Jr., managing partner of the NHL's Minnesota Wild. The deal was contingent on the approval of voters in St. Paul of a half-cent sales tax increase to finance one-third of the cost of a new stadium, with the other two-thirds coming from the Twins and the state. St. Paul voters rejected the referendum on November 2.*

OCTOBER 20 — Calvin Griffith, who owned the Washington Senators and Minnesota Twins from 1955 until 1984, dies at the age of 87. Griffith was buried in Washington, a city he rarely visited after he moved the franchise to Minnesota in October 1960.

NOVEMBER 18 — Mike Trombley signs with the Orioles as a free agent.

DECEMBER 13 — The Twins trade Jared Camp to the Marlins for Johan Santana. The deal was made moments after the Marlins selected Santana from the Astros organization in the Rule 5 draft. The Twins had the first pick in the draft that year and the Marlins second. The two clubs made a deal in which the Twins would draft Camp and the Marlins would choose Santana. The trade was then made, with the Twins receiving $500,000.

> *The trade generated little notice at the time it was announced, but it proved to be one of the best in Twins history. Santana was 20 years old at the time of*

the transaction and had yet to make an appearance above the Class A level. He struggled in his first two seasons in the majors with a 5.90 ERA in 129$^2/_3$ innings in 45 games, nine of them starts, over the 2000 and 2001 campaigns. He became a regular member of the starting rotation during the second half of the 2003 season and developed into one of the best pitchers in the majors. From 2003 through 2007, he posted a record of 82–35 for the Twins. While in Minnesota, Santana led the AL three times in strikeouts, twice in ERA, and once each in wins, innings and games started. He was also the Cy Young Award winner in 2004 and 2006. Camp didn't pitch a single game in the majors.

THE STATE OF THE TWINS

In the midst of a youth movement, the Twins were 69–93 in 2000, the club's eighth straight losing season. But from 2001 through 2009, the team experienced eight winning campaigns out of nine, reaching the post-season in 2002, 2003, 2004, 2006 and 2009, all with AL Central titles. In the process, the franchise became the model on how to win with a limited payroll. Overall, the Twins were 6–18 in the playoffs, however. During the decade, the team had a record of 863–758, a winning percentage of .532, which ranked fifth in the AL behind the Yankees, Red Sox, Angels and Athletics. AL Central champions outside of Minnesota during the decade were the White Sox (2000, 2005 and 2008) and Indians (2001 and 2007). AL champions were the Yankees (2000, 2001, 2003 and 2009), Angels (2002), Red Sox (2004 and 2007), White Sox (2005), Tigers (2006) and Rays (2008).

THE BEST TEAM

The 2006 Twins were 96–66 during the regular season, the most victories by any Minnesota team from 1970 to the present.

THE WORST TEAM

The Twins had a 69–93 record in 2000. It was the fourth consecutive season of 90 or more losses, the first time that had happened to the franchise since 1955 through 1959, when the club had five years in a row of 90 or more defeats as the Washington Senators.

THE BEST MOMENT

During the 2009 season, the Twins overcame impossible odds to beat out the Tigers for the AL Central title.

THE WORST MOMENT

Commissioner Bud Selig tried to contract the Twins out of existence from 2001 through 2003, and owner Carl Pohlad did nothing to stand in the way of the plan.

THE ALL-DECADE TEAM • YEARS W/TWINS

Joe Mauer, c	2004–09
Justin Morneau, 1b	2003–09
Luis Rivas, 2b	2000–05
Corey Koskie, 3b	1998–2004
Christian Guzman, ss	1999–2004
Jacque Jones, lf	1999–2005
Torii Hunter, cf	1997–2007
Michael Cuddyer, rf	2001–09
Jason Kubel, dh	2004, 2006–09
Johan Santana, p	2000–07
Brad Radke, p	1995–2006
Scott Baker, p	2005–09
Joe Nathan, p	2004–09

Brad Radke was also on the 1990s All-Decade Team. Joe Mauer is headed for an almost certain berth in the Hall of Fame. Second base, designated hitter and starting pitching depth were problems for the Twins throughout the decade.

THE DECADE LEADERS

Batting Avg:	Joe Mauer	.327
On-Base Pct:	Joe Mauer	.408
Slugging Pct:	Justin Morneau	.501
Home Runs:	Torii Hunter	183
RBIs:	Torii Hunter	674
Runs:	Torii Hunter	620
Stolen Bases:	Torii Hunter	116
Wins:	Johan Santana	93
Strikeouts:	Johan Santana	1,381
ERA:	Johan Santana	3.22
Saves:	Joe Nathan	246

THE HOME FIELD

The Twins closed out 28 seasons at the Metrodome following the 2009 season. Changes during the decade included the installation of Field Turf in 2004. The club finished fifth in attendance in the AL in 2009, the first time the club was in the top half of the AL in the category since 1992. The club moved into Target Field in 2010.

THE GAME YOU WISHED YOU HAD SEEN

The Twins won the Al Central on October 6, 2009, in a thrill-a-minute, 12-inning, 6–5 win over the Tigers in a one-game playoff.

THE WAY THE GAME WAS PLAYED

The offensive explosion of the 1990s continued into the 2000s, as did the trend toward baseball-only ballparks with grass fields. About mid-decade, allegations of the use of performance-enhancing drugs became a hot topic, and Major League Baseball instituted much harsher penalties for players caught using the substances. The disparity in payrolls and success on the field between the large and small-market clubs continued to increase.

THE MANAGEMENT

Part of the reason for the success of the Twins has been stability at the top of the organization. Carl Pohlad owned the club from 1984 until his death in January 2009. His son Jim took over the day-to-day operation of the franchise. General managers have been Terry Smith (1994–2007) and Bill Smith (2007–present). Field managers have been Tom Kelly (1986–2001) and Ron Gardenhire (2002–present).

THE BEST PLAYER MOVE

The best player move was the drafting of Joe Mauer with the first overall pick in the amateur draft in June 2001.

THE WORST PLAYER MOVE

The Twins released David Ortiz in December 2002. He was picked up by the Red Sox a month later and helped Boston win two world championships.

2000

Season in a Sentence

The Twins field the youngest team in the American League, have the lowest payroll in the majors, finish last in the AL in attendance for the third year in a row, and lose more games than any other club in the circuit.

Finish • Won • Lost • Pct • GB

Fifth   69   93   .426   26.0

In the wild card race, the Twins finished in 11th (last) place, 22 games behind.

Manager

Tom Kelly

Stats   Twins • AL • Rank

Batting Avg:	.270	.276	10
On-Base Pct:	.337	.349	13
Slugging Pct:	.407	.443	13
Home Runs:	116		14
Stolen Bases:	90		8
ERA:	5.14	4.91	11
Errors:	102		4
Runs Scored:	748		13
Runs Allowed:	880		10

Starting Line-up

Matt LeCroy, c
Ron Coomer, 1b
Dennis Hocking, 2b-of
Corey Koskie, 3b
Christian Guzman, ss
Jacque Jones, lf-cf
Torii Hunter, cf
Matt Lawton, rf-lf
David Ortiz, dh
Jay Canizaro, 2b
Butch Huskey, dh

Pitchers

Brad Radke, sp
Eric Milton, sp
Mark Redman, sp
Joe Mays, sp
LaTroy Hawkins, rp
Bob Wells, rp
Hector Carrasco, rp
Travis Miller, rp
Eddie Guardado, rp
Johan Santana, rp

Attendance

1,059,715 (14th in AL)

Club Leaders

Batting Avg:	Matt Lawton	.305
On-Base Pct:	Matt Lawton	.405
Slugging Pct:	Jacque Jones	.463
Home Runs:	Jacque Jones	19
RBI:	Matt Lawton	88
Runs:	Christian Guzman	89
Stolen Bases:	Christian Guzman	28
Wins:	Eric Milton	13
Strikeouts:	Eric Milton	160
ERA:	Brad Radke	4.45
Saves:	LaTroy Hawkins	14

JANUARY 19 — Eighteen days after the dawn of the new millennium and the end of worries about the Y2K problem, Marty Cordova signs a contract with the Red Sox as a free agent.

APRIL 3 — The Twins open the season with a 7–0 loss to the Devil Rays before 43,830 at the Metrodome. Brad Radke was the starting and losing pitcher.

The Twins opened the season with a payroll of $16.5 million. Dodgers pitcher Kevin Brown, at $15.7 million, earned nearly that much by himself.

APRIL 4 — The Twins score two runs in the ninth inning to defeat the Devil Rays 6–5 at the Metrodome. Christian Guzman doubled home the tying run and scored on a two-out walk-off single by David Ortiz.

The Twins changed the caps on the home team uniforms in 2000 switching from the letter "M" to an interlocking "T" and "C." The T and C combination was on the team's caps from 1961 through 1986. The "M" still remained on the hats when the club played on the road.

APRIL 5   Trailing 7–1, the Twins stage one of the greatest comebacks in club history with six runs in the eighth inning and three in the ninth to defeat the Devil Rays 10–7 at the Metrodome. The six-run rally in the eighth happened after the first two batters were retired. The next seven batters reached base on singles by Christian Guzman and Matt Lawton, a run-scoring double from Butch Huskey, Corey Koskie's RBI-single, a walk to Ron Coomer to load the bases, a single by Jacque Jones that plated the third run of the inning and kept the sacks filled, and a three-run double by Midre Cummings that tied the contest 7–7. In the ninth, three runs scored before an out was recorded on singles by Todd Walker and Guzman and Lawton's three-run, walk-off home run. It was the club's second walk-off win in a row.

Dan Gladden joined Herb Carneal and John Gordon in the Twins broadcast booth in 2000.

APRIL 9   The Twins bang six home runs to defeat the Royals 13–7 in Kansas City. Ron Coomer homered twice, with Matt Lawton, Butch Huskey, Jacque Jones and Matt LeCroy adding the remainder. In the sixth inning, Coomer, Jones and LeCroy hit three consecutive homers in a span of four pitches off Brad Rigby. It was LeCroy's first major league home run. Eric Milton retired the first 20 batters to face him before Carlos Beltran's two-out double in the seventh. The Twins built a 13–0 lead, but the Royals scored seven times in the eighth to make things interesting. During that rally, Beltran, Jermaine Dye and Mike Sweeney hit consecutive homers. It was the first game in major league history in which both teams hit three homers in a row.

The home run outburst was an unusual sight for Twins fans in 2000. The team hit 116 homers to rank last in the majors, well behind the Phillies, who clouted 144 to rank 29th among the 30 big league clubs.

APRIL 14   Down 9–4, the resilient Twins score six times in the eighth inning to defeat the Orioles 10–9 at the Metrodome. Matt LeCroy and Torii Hunter each hit two-run doubles to make the score 9–8. Christian Guzman drove in the tying tally with a single. Matt Lawton broke the deadlock with a sacrifice fly.

Despite the dramatic comebacks during the first two weeks of the season, the Twins had a 4–10 record after 14 games.

APRIL 15   Entering the game with 2,997 hits, Cal Ripken lines three consecutive singles to reach the 3,000-hit level during a 6–4 Orioles win at the Metrodome. Ripken's milestone came off Hector Carrasco.

Mike Trombley and Tom Kelly were both in uniform to witness the 3,000th career hits of Dave Winfield (1993), Eddie Murray (1995), Paul Molitor (1996) and Ripken. Trombley gave up Murray's 3,000th hit.

APRIL 21   Ron Coomer drives in seven runs during a 10–5 win over the Rangers in Arlington. He belted three-run homers in the fourth and ninth innings and drove in a run with a single in sixth. The win broke a 13-game losing streak against the Rangers dating to September 1998. The Twins were 0–12 against Texas in 1999.

May 7	Tom Kelly records his 1,000th win as manager of the Twins with a 4–0 decision over the Tigers at the Metrodome.
May 9	The Twins overcome a 5–0 deficit with six runs in the fifth inning and hang on to defeat the Indians 6–5 at the Metrodome. Jay Canizaro tied the score 5–5 with a two-run single and Matt Lawton drove in the winning run with a sacrifice fly.
May 10	The Twins put together another tremendous comeback to defeat the Indians 10–9 at the Metrodome after trailing by seven runs. Cleveland led 8–1 before the Twins scored sixth in the seventh to narrow the gap to one. The Indians scored in the top of the ninth to make the score 9–7, but the Twins rallied with three in their half for the victory. With one out in the ninth, Matt Lawton doubled and Ron Coomer singled for the first run. After Butch Huskey flied out, Midre Cummings hit a two-run walk-off homer for the victory. Cummings entered the game as a pinch-hitter in the six-run seventh and drove in a run with a single. It was the first time since the club moved to Minnesota that it overcame a seven-run deficit.
May 18	Dennis Hocking collects five hits in six at-bats during a 10–5 triumph over the Athletics in Oakland. He had a home run, two doubles, and two singles.

Hocking's wife gave birth to twins in 2000, making him the first player in Twins history to become the father of twins. The twins were fraternal daughters named Penelope and Iliana.

May 19	Jacque Jones hits the first pitch of the game from Gil Heredia for a home run to spark a 3–2 win over the Athletics in Oakland.
May 23	The Twins select Casey Blake off waivers from the Blue Jays.
June 3	Sean Bergman's double during a 9–3 loss to the Reds in Cincinnati is the first extra-base hit by a Twins pitcher since 1972.

Bergman was a disaster on the mound for the Twins in 2000. He had a horrendous ERA of 9.66 in 68 innings. Batters hit .374 with a slugging percentage of .630 against him.

June 5	The Twins play at Enron Field (now Minute Maid Park) in Houston for the first time and lose 8–2 to the Astros.

On the same day, the Twins selected pitcher Adam Johnson from California State University at Fullerton with the second pick in the amateur draft. Johnson proved to be a complete bust. He pitched only 26 1/3 innings in the majors over nine games, four of them starts, and had a dreadful ERA of 10.25. Other future major leaguers drafted and signed by the Twins in 2000 were J. D. Durbin (second round), Jason Miller (fourth round), Josh Rabe (11th round) and Jason Kubel (12th round).

June 7	Jay Canizaro hits a two-run homer in the seventh inning to account for the only runs of a 2–0 victory over the Astros in Houston. Joe Mays (six innings), Travis Miller (two-thirds of an inning), LaTroy Hawkins (two innings) and Eddie Guardado (one-third of an inning) combined on the shutout.

JUNE 12 — Eric Milton and Travis Miller combine for 16 strikeouts during a 7–2 victory over the Athletics at the Metrodome. Milton fanned 11 in seven innings and Miller struck out five in two innings.

JUNE 21 — Bob Wells faces only five batters but finds time to record four fielding chances, two of them errors, during a 7–5 loss to the Rangers in Arlington. Wells entered the contest in the sixth and fielded a ground ball from Gabe Kapler, only to throw wildly to first base and Kapler was safe. Kapler went to second on a sacrifice by Royce Clayton that Wells fielded and threw to first baseman Butch Huskey. The next batter was Luis Alicea, who bounced out, Wells to Huskey. Wells then tried to pick Kapler off second, but threw the ball into center field for the second error of the inning. Following a walk and a single, Wells was relieved.

JULY 1 — Three days after Elian Gonzalez is returned to Cuba following a bitter legal battle, the Twins rally to beat the Indians 4–3 in ten innings in Cleveland. Trailing 2–1 with two out in the ninth, Christian Guzman delivered a run-scoring triple to tie the score. Dennis Hocking drove in two with a single in the tenth and the Indians tallied in the bottom half before the Twins closed out the victory.

> *Guzman hit 20 triples in 2000 to tie a franchise record set by Hall of Famer Goose Goslin with the 1925 Washington Senators. Guzman broke the Minnesota record of Rod Carew, another member of the Hall of Fame. Carew had 16 triples in 1968. In addition, Guzman was the first major league shortstop with 20 or more triples in a season since Hall of Famer Honus Wagner collected 20 for the Pirates in 1912.*

JULY 3 — David Ortiz collects three RBIs without an official plate appearance during a 14–8 loss to the Red Sox at the Metrodome. Ortiz drew a bases-loaded walk and hit two sacrifice flies before being lifted for a pinch-hitter in the sixth inning.

JULY 11 — During a three-run rally in the ninth inning, Matt Lawton drives in a run and later scores to help the American League to a 6–3 victory in the All-Star Game at Turner Field in Atlanta.

JULY 15 — The Twins trade Todd Walker and Butch Huskey to the Rockies for Todd Sears and cash.

> *Walker talked his way out of Minnesota with his outspoken criticism of Tom Kelly and Twins management. After the trade, Walker was a starting second baseman in the majors until 2006, but he drifted from team to team, playing for the Rockies, Reds, Red Sox, Cubs and Padres.*

JULY 29 — Eric Milton (eight innings) and LaTroy Hawkins (one inning) combine on a two-hitter to defeat the Yankees 6–2 at the Metrodome. The only New York hits were back-to-back singles by Jose Vizcaino and Derek Jeter in the sixth inning that helped produce two runs. The Twins overcame the 2–0 deficit with six runs in the eighth. With the score tied 2–2 and two out, Chad Moeller hit a three-run, inside-the-park homer. He circled the bases after left fielder Ryan Thompson missed an attempt at a diving catch and the ball rolled to the wall. It was also Moeller's first major league home run and the only one he struck as a member of the Twins.

AUGUST 1	Mike Mussina of the Orioles pitches a one-hitter and strikes out 15 batters to defeat the Twins 10–0 in Baltimore. The only Minnesota hit was a single by Ron Coomer in the seventh inning.
AUGUST 4	The Twins play at Comerica Park in Detroit for the first time and lose 3–1 to the Tigers.
AUGUST 11	Matt Lawton drives in five runs with a homer and two doubles during a 9–4 victory over the Blue Jays at the Metrodome.
AUGUST 25	Jay Canizaro hits a grand slam off Willie Blair in the sixth inning of an 8–3 win over the Tigers at the Metrodome. The slam broke a 3–3 tie.

Matt Kinney, who made his major league debut with the Twins in 2000, grew up in Bangor, Maine, as a neighbor of famed author Stephen King and was a classmate and baseball teammate of King's son Owen. Kinney and Owen played on a Little League team coached by King that won the state championship in 1989. In the process, Kinney became the central figure in a King essay that appeared in the middle of a collection of King short stories.

SEPTEMBER 7	Six batters into the game, the Twins hold a 5–0 lead but wind up losing 11–6 to the Red Sox at Fenway Park. David Ortiz drove in the first four runs with a grand slam, and Corey Koskie followed with a solo shot, both off Ramon Martinez.

The Twins flew from Minneapolis to Boston for this one game to make up a postponement due to rain in July. After the contest, the club boarded a plane for Seattle for a series against the Mariners.

SEPTEMBER 17	Brad Radke pitches a complete game shutout to defeat the Angels 1–0 at the Metrodome. The lone run scored in the first inning on a lead-off single by Christian Guzman and a triple from Luis Rivas. The three-bagger came in Rivas's second major league game and accounted for his first extra base hit and RBI.
SEPTEMBER 19	The Twins pound out 20 hits and defeat the Rangers 15–7 at the Metrodome.

The Twins had hoped to play the three-game series against the Rangers from September 18 through September 20 at a makeshift 25,000-seat stadium at the Mall of America, which was built on the former site of Metropolitan Stadium, home to the Twins from 1961 through 1981. The move was designed to drum up support for an outdoor stadium for the club. The Metropolitan Sports Facilities Commission, which operated the Metrodome, refused to allow the Twins to break their lease and play the games at the outdoor facility.

SEPTEMBER 24	Trailing 5–0, the Twins score four runs in the seventh inning, one in the eighth and one in the tenth to defeat the White Sox 6–5 at the Metrodome. Matt Lawton ended the game with a home run.
SEPTEMBER 25	The Twins are involved in a three-team doubleheader at Jacobs Field. On the original schedule, the Indians were scheduled to play the Twins in a night game. However, the Indians were rained out against the White Sox in Cleveland on September 10, and because of the pennant implications of the teams involved, the American

League decreed that the contest be made up as part of a day game preceding the Twins-Indians nighttime affair on September 25. It was the first time that a club played two teams on one day since September 13, 1951, when the Cardinals squared off against the New York Giants and Boston Braves in St. Louis. It was also only the second three-team match-up in the majors since 1899, and the first in the AL. The historic twin bill caused a logistical nightmare with four team buses, two equipment trucks, three TV and radio crews, nearly 100 players, 80,000 fans, and eight umpires. The Indians defeated the White Sox 9–2 and then lost to the Twins 4–3.

SEPTEMBER 26   Doug Mientiewicz hits a ninth-inning homer to lift the U. S. to a 3–2 win over South Korea in the semi-final game of the Olympics in Sydney, Australia. Six days earlier, Mientiewicz hit a grand slam to defeat the South Koreans 4–0. The U.S. went on to defeat Cuba and won the gold medal.

> *Mientiewicz was the Twins starting first baseman as a rookie in 1999, but he spent nearly all of the 2000 campaign in the minors at the club's Triple A affiliate in Salt Lake City. The demotion made him eligible for the Olympics. The trip did not begin well. Shortly after arriving in Australia, Mientiewicz became involved in an altercation at a casino and was hit over the head by a purse wielded by a female patron. Three days after his dramatic homer in the Olympics, Mientiewicz played in the first of his three major league games during the 2000 season. He won back his job as the Twins starting first baseman in 2001.*

OCTOBER 1   On the last game of the season, the Twins and Tigers combine to use 15 pitchers in a contest won by Detroit 12–11 at Comerica Park. The Tigers used eight pitchers and the Twins seven. One of the Detroit hurlers was Shane Halter, who became the fourth player in major league history to play all nine positions in a game. Halter faced one batter in the eighth inning and issued a walk on five pitches to Matt LeCroy. The second of the four individuals to play all nine positions in a game was Cesar Tovar with the Twins on September 22, 1968.

2001

Season in a Sentence
The Twins stun the baseball world by holding first place into August and winning 85 games, the first season above .500 since 1992.

Finish • Won • Lost • Pct • GB
Second   85   77   .525   6.0

In the wild card race, the Twins were in second place, 17 games out of first.

Manager
Tom Kelly

Stats   Twins • AL • Rank
Batting Avg:	.272	.267	4
On-Base Pct:	.337	.334	5
Slugging Pct:	.433	.428	8
Home Runs:	164		9
Stolen Bases:	146		4
ERA:	4.51	4.47	7
Errors:	108		5
Runs Scored:	771		8
Runs Allowed:	776		7

Starting Line-up
A. J. Pierzynski, c
Doug Mientiewicz, 1b
Luis Rivas, 2b
Corey Koskie, 3b
Christian Guzman, ss
Jacque Jones, lf
Torii Hunter, cf
Matt Lawton, rf
David Ortiz, dh
Dennis Hocking, ss

Pitchers
Joe Mays, sp
Brad Radke, sp
Eric Milton, sp
Kyle Lohse, sp
LaTroy Hawkins, rp
Hector Carrasco, rp
Bob Wells, rp
Eddie Guardado, rp
Travis Miller, rp
Jack Cressend, rp

Attendance
1,782,929 (11th in AL)

Club Leaders
Batting Avg:	Doug Mientiewicz .306
On-Base Pct:	Doug Mientiewicz .387
Slugging Pct:	Corey Koskie .488
Home Runs:	Torii Hunter 27
RBI:	Corey Koskie 103
Runs:	Corey Koskie 100
Stolen Bases:	Christian Guzman 31
Wins:	Joe Mays 17
Strikeouts:	Eric Milton 157
ERA:	Joe Mays 3.16
Saves:	LaTroy Hawkins 28

JANUARY 10 Four weeks after the U. S. Supreme Curt declares George Bush the winner over Al Gore in the disputed 2000 Presidential election, Ron Coomer signs with the Cubs as a free agent.

JANUARY 16 Kirby Puckett and Dave Winfield are elected to the Hall of Fame on the first ballot.

MARCH 30 The semifinals of the Final Four of the NCAA basketball tournament are held at the Metrodome, with Duke defeating Maryland 95–84 and Arizona downing Michigan State 80–61. Two days later, Duke beat Arizona 81–72 in the championship game.

APRIL 3 The Twins open the season with a 3–2 win over the Tigers in Detroit. David Ortiz homered in the fourth to give Minnesota a 2–0 lead. Brad Radke allowed one run in eight innings.

APRIL 5 The Twins score five runs in the tenth inning and defeat the Tigers 9–5 in Detroit.

April 9 — In the home opener, the Twins beat the Tigers 11–5 before 46,101 at the Metrodome. Christian Guzman and Doug Mientiewicz homered.

After spending all but three games of the 2000 season in the minors (see September 26, 2000), Mientiewicz was off to a blazing start in 2001. His average was .403 in 42 games and 144 at-bats. He finished the year with a batting mark of .306.

April 11 — The Twins score seven runs in the eighth inning of a 12–1 walloping of the Tigers at the Metrodome.

April 15 — Eric Milton strikes out eight of the first ten batters he faces, and the Twins defeat the White Sox 4–3 at the Metrodome. Milton finished with ten strikeouts in seven innings.

April 17 — Corey Koskie hits a two-run, walk-off single in the ninth inning to defeat the Royals 6–5 at the Metrodome. It was his fourth hit of the game.

April 21 — The Twins run their record to 14–3 with a 4–2 victory over the White Sox in Chicago. The Twins led the AL Central by three games.

April 25 — Torii Hunter breaks a 3–3 tie with a three-run double in the tenth inning, and the Twins down the Red Sox 6–4 in Boston.

May 2 — A 4–2 win over the Yankees at the Metrodome is delayed several times when fans throw debris at Chuck Knoblauch.

Knoblauch had been a hero in Minnesota while playing for the Twins from 1991 through 1997 but forced the club to trade him before the start of the

For sixteen seasons, Tom Kelly managed the Twins, winning two pennants and two world championships. Sometimes saddled with less-than-stellar teams, Kelly found a way to get the most from his players.

1998 season (see February 6, 1998). He had always been booed heavily by the Metrodome crowds when the Yankees played there between 1998 and 2000, but a move from second base to left field in 2001 made him a tempting target and put him within range of the crowd. Fans threw coins, plastic bottles, a golf ball, a piece of metal, and a full cup of beer at him. The barrage continued even after repeated warnings by the public address announcer and manager Tom Kelly. In the sixth inning, the game was delayed six minutes when the Yankees left the field and nearly resulted in a forfeit. The contest was also delayed twice in the eighth and Knoblauch gestured angrily at the crowd of 36,825. More than 40 fans were ejected.

May 5   The Twins suffer a tough 12–10 loss to the Royals in 12 innings in Kansas City. The Royals scored twice in the ninth off LaTroy Hawkins, who ended his streak of converting 23 consecutive save opportunities dating back to 2000. One of the ninth-inning runs scored on an odd play when first baseman Doug Mientiewicz tumbled into the stands to catch a foul pop-up. According to the rules, when a fielder falls out of play, runners advance a base, which allowed Joe Randa to cross the plate from third base on a sacrifice fly.

May 8   Christian Guzman scores both runs of a 2–0 win over the Yankees in New York. Guzman broke the scoreless tie with a homer in the third inning. Eric Milton pitched a complete game shutout.

Guzman hit .302 with ten homers and a league-leading 14 triples in 2001.

May 10   The Twins defeat the Yankees 5–4 in ten innings in New York. The winning run scored when A. J. Pierzynski doubled, advanced to third on a single, and crossed the plate on a passed ball.

May 11   The Twins win in extra innings for the second day in a row with a 5–4 decision in 11 innings over the Royals at the Metrodome. After Kansas City scored in the top of the tenth, Matt Lawton tied the contest with a solo homer in the bottom half. Luis Rivas drove in the winning run with a single.

May 22   The Twins take an 8–0 lead with eight runs in the third inning, then hang on to defeat the Mariners 12–11 at the Metrodome. A. J. Pierzynski and Christian Guzman both hit a double and a single during the big third-inning rally.

May 26   The Twins score two runs in the ninth inning and one in the tenth to beat the Athletics 7–6 at the Metrodome. Torii Hunter led off the ninth with a home run. Doug Mientiewicz tied the score 6–6 with a two-out single. Hunter then drove in the winning run with a walk-off single.

After eight straight losing seasons from 1993 through 2000, and the worst record in the AL in both 1999 and 2000, the Twins were 34–16 on May 30 in 2001. During one stretch in April and May, the Twins won 12 games in a row.

June 4   The Twins outlast the Indians 11–10 at the Metrodome. Minnesota led 8–2 at the end of the second inning before allowing Cleveland to come back and deadlock the contests at 10–10. The winning run scored on a walk-off single by Christian Guzman in the ninth inning. Guzman was also involved in a strange play in the seventh. With a runner on third, he bunted and catcher Eddie Taubensee overthrew Jim Thome at first base. Guzman was able to round the bases on the play when Juan Gonzalez took a wrong angle in right field and allowed the ball to get past him.

JUNE 5   With the first overall pick in the first round of the amateur draft, the Twins select catcher Joe Mauer from Cretin-Derham Hall High School in St. Paul, Minnesota. (Paul Molitor attended the same high school.) Mauer turned down a football scholarship to play quarterback at Florida State University to sign with the Twins.

After choosing Mauer, the Twins took some heat for passing over players considered to be better prospects to take the local hero. Pitcher Mark Prior was thought to be the best player available and was picked by the Cubs as the second selection. But so far, Mauer has more than justified being the number one pick in the 2001 draft. After signing, he hit .400 in 110 at-bats for Elizabethtown in the Appalachian League and reached the majors in 2004. Others future major leaguers drafted and signed by the Twins in 2000 include Jose Morales (third round), Kevin Cameron (13th round) and Nick Blackburn (29th round).

JUNE 8   After falling behind 6–1, the Twins score two runs in the fourth inning and five in the fifth to defeat the Pirates 8–6 at the Metrodome. With the Twins still down 6–4 and two out in the fifth, Torii Hunter belted a grand slam off Omar Olivares. The slam came after Matt Lawton was intentionally walked to load the bases.

JUNE 19   The Twins survive three homers by Ellis Burks to win 10–9 in 12 innings over the Indians at Jacobs Field. The Twins led 6–0 in the fifth inning before Burks keyed a Cleveland comeback by hitting homers in the sixth and eighth inning. The contest went into extra innings with the score 8–8. A. J. Pierzynski hit a two-run double in the top of the 12th. Burks belted a solo shot in the bottom of the inning for his third homer.

JUNE 22   Matt Lawton leads off the top of the first inning with a homer on the first pitch from Dave Mlicki, but the Twins lose 5–4 to the Tigers in Detroit.

JUNE 24   The Twins break open a close game with seven runs in the seventh inning to thrash the Tigers 14–5 in Detroit. All seven runs scored after two were out. Christian Guzman capped the rally with a grand slam off Dave Borkowski to finish the game with six runs batted in. Guzman's slam was only the second hit of the seven-run seventh. The Twins were helped by four walks, a hit batsman and an error.

JUNE 26   The Twins score four runs in the ninth inning to stun the White Sox 7–6 at the Metrodome. Matt Lawton and Doug Mientiewicz drove in the first-inning runs with singles. With two out and the Twins still trailing 6–5, Dennis Hocking hit a two-run, pinch-hit triple for the victory.

JULY 5   Corey Koskie hits a home run, a triple and a double and drives in five runs during a 12–2 triumph over the White Sox at the Metrodome.

JULY 10   Joe Mays pitches a perfect fifth inning to help the American League to a 4–1 victory in the All-Star Game at Safeco Field in Seattle. Mays set down Larry Walker, Mike Piazza and Chipper Jones.

Mays was 17–13 with a 3.16 ERA in 233 2/3 innings in 2001. It proved to be the only good season of his eight-year career. Mays entered 2001 with a 13–26 career record and a 4.94 ERA. After 2001, he was 18–31 and had an earned run average of 6.15 with three clubs.

JULY 12   The Twins play at Miller Park in Milwaukee for the first time and wallop seven home runs and defeat the Brewers 13–5. Torii Hunter, Jacque Jones and Corey Koskie each homered twice with Doug Mientiewicz accounting for the other one. Koskie also doubled twice to tie a club record with four extra base hits. Jones hit a grand slam off Jimmy Haynes in the second inning. In the third, Mientiewicz, Koskie and Jones hit consecutive homers off Haynes during a sequence of six pitches.

The Twins took a five-game lead in the AL Central with the July 12 victory. The club had a 56–32 record on that date, but lost 29 of 38 between July 13 and August 21. The Twins dropped out of first place for good on August 12 during a four-game sweep at the hands of the lowly Devil Rays in St. Petersburg and were out of the pennant race by the beginning of September. A 5–14 record against the Indians contributed to the failure to win the pennant. The Twins finished six games behind Cleveland.

JULY 19   The Twins collect 20 hits and defeat the Athletics 12–10 at the Metrodome. The Twins trailed 4–0 in the fourth inning before coming back for the victory. The line-up was filled with reserves as Tom Kelly gave many of his regulars the day off. Bench players Brian Buchanan, Tom Prince and Casey Blake combined for nine hits.

JULY 28   The Twins trade Mark Redman to the Tigers for Todd Jones.

JULY 30   The Twins trade Matt Lawton to the Mets for Rick Reed.

Reed was acquired to bolster the starting rotation. The Twins had few options in 2001 beyond Joe Mays, Eric Milton and Brad Radke. Those three combined for 47–31 record and a 3.89 ERA, while the rest of the starters were 13–25 with a 5.58 earned run average. Reed was a disappointment during the 2001 pennant drive, posting a 4–6 record and a 5.19 ERA, but he was 15–7 for the Twins in 2002. The trade broke up the "Soul Patrol" outfield of Lawton, Jacque Jones and Torii Hunter. Lawton was a starter for the Mets, Indians and Pirates through 2005, posting batting numbers around the league average for outfielders.

AUGUST 3   After the Royals score a run in the top of the tenth, the Twins rally for two in their half to win 8–7 at the Metrodome. David Ortiz drove in the tying run with a double and Chad Allen came in as a pinch-runner for Ortiz. Jacque Jones beat out an infield single and Allen scored all the way from second on the play to score the winning run.

AUGUST 10   First baseman Doug Mientiewicz records an unusual unassisted double play at third base in the second inning of a 4–2 loss to the Devil Rays in St. Petersburg. Tampa Bay had Toby Hall on third base and Randy Winn on first with no outs. Aubrey Huff hit a weak grounder to Mientiewicz, who crossed the mound to chase Hall back to third. Hall made it back to third base safely, but during the play Winn also advanced to third and was tagged out. Hall thought that he was the one who was out, wandered off the bag and was also tagged by the Twins first baseman. The inning ended on a foul pop-up by Jared Sandberg to Mientiewicz.

Mientiewicz was a high school teammate of Alex Rodriguez.

AUGUST 23   During an adventurous ninth inning of a 6–2 loss to the Blue Jays at the Metrodome, Torii Hunter throws out two runners trying to stretch singles into doubles but then commits an error.

SEPTEMBER 2   Dennis Hocking hits a walk-off homer in the ninth inning to beat the Angels 5–4 at the Metrodome.

SEPTEMBER 5   The Twins pound out 20 hits and clobber the Rangers 12–2 in Arlington. Christian Guzman contributed a home run, a triple and two singles.

SEPTEMBER 8   Corey Koskie hits a grand slam off Pat Rapp in the fourth inning of a 6–4 victory over the Angels in Anaheim.

Koskie hit .276 with 26 homers and 103 RBIs in 2001.

SEPTEMBER 11   After the infamous terrorist attacks leave 3,000 people dead, baseball commissioner Bud Selig cancels the slate of games scheduled for that day, including the Twins-Tigers match in Detroit. With planes grounded, the Twins took a bus from Detroit to Minneapolis. The contests were made up by extending the regular season by a week. When play resumed, an air of heightened security and patriotism imbued every game. Fans endured close scrutiny by stadium personnel. "God Bless America" replaced "Take Me Out to the Ballgame" as the song of choice during the seventh-inning stretch.

SEPTEMBER 18   In the first game following the September 11 terrorist attacks, the Twins defeat the Tigers 8–3 at the Metrodome. Brad Radke took a no-hitter into the eighth inning before giving up home runs to Shane Halter and Chris Wakeland.

SEPTEMBER 28   Eric Milton (seven innings), Jack Cressend (two-thirds of an inning) and Eddie Guardado ($1\frac{1}{3}$ innings) combine on a shutout to defeat the Indians 1–0 in Cleveland.

OCTOBER 4   The Twins score two runs in the ninth inning to defeat the Tigers 5–4 in Detroit. A. J. Pierzynski drove in the tying run with a double and scored on a single from Dennis Hocking.

OCTOBER 12   Five days after the United States launches a sustained air attack in Afghanistan against al-Qaeda, Tom Kelly retires as manager of the Twins.

Kelly had been on the job since September 1986, at the time the longest tenure in North American pro sports. He cited burnout as the reason for his retiring at the age of 51. Kelly's Twins won the World Series in 1987 and 1991 before he endured eight consecutive losing seasons from 1992 through 2000. Overall, his record was 1,140–1,244. Because of contraction issues (see November 6, 2001), a successor to Kelly was not immediately announced.

NOVEMBER 6   Major League Baseball announces plans to pursue contraction from 30 teams to 28. Among the teams considered for contraction were the Twins, Montreal Expos,

Florida Marlins and Tampa Bay Devil Rays. The vote was 28–2. Baseball hadn't reduced teams since 1900 when the National League went from 12 franchises to eight. Owners hoped that contraction could take place before the 2002 spring training camps opened.

> *The action didn't come as a surprise because contraction had been discussed for months, but once the decision became official the negative reaction was swift and vociferous, particularly in Minnesota. Mike Hatch, the state's Attorney General, threatened to file a lawsuit against MLB in federal court. The Metropolitan Sports Facilities Commission, owner of the Metrodome, filed a lawsuit compelling the Twins to honor their lease and won a temporary restraining order in Hennepin County District Court to block any changes in the team's situation. Judge Harry Crump later granted a temporary injunction ordering the team to play its 2002 schedule in the Metrodome. MLB and the Twins appealed, asking the Minnesota Supreme Court to take the case. The Supreme Court refused. Senator Paul Wellstone of Minnesota and representative John Conyers of Michigan introduced bills to limit baseball's exemption from antitrust laws (see December 6, 2001). Owner Carl Pohlad raised no objection to contraction, reasoning he could make more money by selling his franchise to Major League Baseball and having it fold than by selling it to an outside buyer or by keeping it in operation.*

NOVEMBER 14   Former Players Association Director Marvin Miller accuses Commissioner Bud Selig of a conflict of interest in the contraction proposal because the elimination of the Twins would benefit the Milwaukee Brewers, a franchise in which Selig had an ownership stake. Selig put his controlling interest in the Brewers in a trust when he became commissioner, and his daughter was the club's CEO. Miller reasoned that the Brewers would be able to draw fans from Minnesota if the Twins no longer existed.

DECEMBER 6   Bud Selig testifies before the House Judiciary Committee. The commissioner said that baseball's financial system was badly flawed, which led to the decision to eliminate two teams. He claimed that baseball lost $519 million in 2001. He was challenged by several members of the committee, who criticized Selig's lack of detail. Minnesota Governor Jesse Ventura, on hand as a witness, stated, "I have a hard time believing it, Mr. Selig, that they're losing that kind of money and still paying the salaries they're paying." (See January 9, 2002.)

2002

Season in a Sentence
Under the threat of contraction, the Twins win 94 games and the AL Central under new manager Ron Gardenhire before losing the ALCS to the Angels.

Finish • Won • Lost • Pct • GB
First 94 67 .584 +13.5

AL Division Series
The Twins defeated the Oakland Athletics three games to two.

AL Championship Series
The Twins lost to the Anaheim Angels four games to one.

Manager
Ron Gardenhire

Stats	Twins	AL	Rank
Batting Avg:	.272	.264	5
On-Base Pct:	.332	.331	8
Slugging Pct:	.437	.424	5
Home Runs:	167		8
Stolen Bases:	79		8
ERA:	4.12	4.46	6
Errors:	74		1
Runs Scored:	768		9
Runs Allowed:	712		6

Starting Line-up
A. J. Pierzynski, c
Doug Mientkiewicz, 1b
Luis Rivas, 2b
Corey Koskie, 3b
Christian Guzman, ss
Jacque Jones, lf
Torii Hunter, cf
Dustan Mohr, rf
David Ortiz, dh
Bobby Kielty, rf-cf
Dennis Hocking, 2b-ss

Pitching
Rick Reed, sp
Kyle Lohse, sp
Eric Milton, sp
Brad Radke, sp
Johan Santana, sp-rp
Joe Mays, sp
Eddie Guardado, rp
Tony Fiore, rp
J. C. Romero, rp
LaTroy Hawkins, rp
Mike Jackson, rp
Bob Wells, rp

Attendance
1,924,473 (ninth in AL)

Club Leaders
Batting Avg:	Jacque Jones	.300
On-Base Pct:	Corey Koskie	.368
Slugging Pct:	Torii Hunter	.524
Home Runs:	Torii Hunter	29
RBI:	Torii Hunter	94
Runs:	Jacque Jones	96
Stolen Bases:	Torii Hunter	23
Wins:	Rick Reed	15
Strikeouts:	Johan Santana	137
Saves:	Eddie Guardado	45

JANUARY 4   The Twins appoint 44-year-old Ron Gardenhire as manager, replacing Tom Kelly, who retired on October 12, 2001. At the time of Gardenhire's hiring, it was uncertain whether or not the Twins would even field a team in 2002 because of contraction issues which were tied up in court.

> Born in West Germany and raised in Oklahoma, Gardenhire had a five-year career as a utility infielder with the Mets from 1981 through 1985. Prior to becoming manager of the Twins, he was the club's third base coach from 1991 through 2001. Gardenhire's aggressive style of managing was in direct contrast to the calm and stoic Tom Kelly, who was ejected only five times in 15 seasons as manager. During his first eight years as manager, Gardenhire averaged more than five ejections per season. A 2006 television commercial made light of Gardenhire's

frequent animated discussions with umpires by depicting him arguing with a Twin Cities office worker who wanted to go home rather than to a Twins game.

JANUARY 9 — Representative John Conyers of Michigan calls for Bud Selig to resign because of a conflict of interest. Conyers accused Selig of violating major league rules by obtaining a loan in 1995 from a bank controlled by Twins owner Carl Pohlad.

JANUARY 11 — Todd Jones signs a contract as a free agent with the Rockies.

JANUARY 22 — The three-judge Court of Appeals in Minnesota unanimously upholds the injunction requiring that the Twins play their entire schedule at the Metrodome in 2002 (see November 6, 2001). Major League Baseball appealed this ruling to the state's Supreme Court, but the court refused to take the case on February 5.

JANUARY 23 — The Twins sign Mike Jackson, most recently with the Astros, as a free agent.

MARCH 5 — Bud Selig announces that baseball has postponed plans for contraction of 30 teams to 28 until 2003 (see May 29, 2002).

APRIL 1 — Trailing 6–4, the Twins score four runs in the seventh inning and beat the Royals 8–6 in Kansas City in the season opener. Jacque Jones put Minnesota into the lead with a three-run homer. It was his second home run of the game. The first one led off the first inning on an 0–1 pitch from Jeff Suppan. David Ortiz, Torii Hunter and Brian Buchanan also homered to give the Twins five during the contest. After Brad Radke allowed six runs in $4^{2}/_{3}$ innings, four relievers (Jack Cressend, J. C. Romero, Mike Jackson and Eddie Guardado) shut out the Royals the rest of the way.

Torii Hunter provided Gold Glove defense in centerfield as well as a productive bat throughout much of the 2000s.

Guardado played for the Twins from 1993 through 2003 but was primarily a set-up reliever or left-handed specialist over his first nine seasons with the club. In 2002, he became the closer and recorded 45 saves. Among pitchers in Twins history, Guardado ranks first in games pitched (648) and third in saves (116).

APRIL 3 Eric Milton (seven innings), J. C. Romero (two-thirds of an inning), Bob Wells (one-third of an inning) and Eddie Guardado (one inning) combine to defeat the Royals 1–0 in Kansas City. Milton retired the last 19 batters to face him. David Ortiz drove in the lone run with a single in the third inning.

APRIL 12 In the home opener, the Twins defeat the Tigers 4–2 before 48,244 at the Metrodome.

APRIL 14 Trailing 7–5, the Twins erupt for eight runs in the eighth inning and defeat the Tigers 13–7 at the Metrodome. The loss dropped Detroit's record to 0–11 in 2002. Bobby Kielty tied the score with a two-run homer. David Ortiz broke the deadlock with a three-run triple. A. J. Pierzynski helped keep the rally alive with two singles. The triple by Ortiz was the only one he collected in 2002.

APRIL 18 Eddie Guardado strikes out all three batters he faces in the ninth inning to close out a 4–1 win over the Royals at the Metrodome.

The Twins featured a starting batting order in 2002 of players all under 30 years of age in A. J. Pierzynski (25), Doug Mientiewicz (25), Luis Rivas (22), Christian Guzman (24), Corey Koskie (29), Jacque Jones (27), Torii Hunter (26), Dustan Mohr (26) and David Ortiz (26).

APRIL 25 The Twins score five runs in the ninth inning to defeat the Indians 6–2 in Cleveland. A. J. Pierzynski drove in the tying run with a single and scored on a double from Doug Mientiewicz.

MAY 2 Trailing 6–0, the Twins score four runs in the seventh inning, two in the ninth and one in the tenth to win 7–6 over the Devil Rays at the Metrodome. With two out in the ninth and still trailing 6–4, Doug Mientiewicz hit a two-run single on an 0–2 pitch to tie the score. Corey Koskie ended the contest with a home run in the tenth. It was Koskie's second homer of the game.

MAY 15 Jacque Jones hits a home run leading off the first inning and adds another one in the sixth to lead the Twins to an 8–6 win over the Royals in Kansas City.

Jones hit a club record 11 home runs leading off the first inning in 2002.

MAY 16 The Twins clout five homers during a 14–5 thrashing of the Royals in Kansas City. Torii Hunter led the way with two home runs. Jacque Jones, Christian Guzman and Tom Prince added the others.

MAY 17 The Twins suffer through a tough 13–12 loss to the Yankees in 14 innings in New York. Minnesota took a 9–8 lead with six runs in the sixth inning, but New York tied the score 9–9 on a Bernie Williams home run with one out in the ninth. The Twins scored three times in the top of the 14th and seemed to have the game in hand, but in the bottom half, Mike Trombley loaded the bases before surrendering a walk-off grand slam to Jason Giambi.

MAY 22 The plan to save the Twins receives a boost when Governor Jesse Ventura approves a financing plan for a new stadium. Previously, Ventura had been an outspoken critic of public financing for new stadiums for either the Twins or Vikings. At the same time, Major League Baseball agreed to keep the Twins in Minnesota at least through the end of the 2003 season, forestalling a possible contraction once more.

> *The bill was the result of a seven-year effort by the Twins to secure help from the state to build a new stadium, but it received tepid support from the club because it was required to chip in $120 million toward the construction of the facility. The bill also obligated the Twins to a 30-year lease.*

MAY 24 Jacque Jones hits the first pitch of the first inning from Ramon Ortiz for a home run to spark a 5–1 win over the Angels in Anaheim.

MAY 27 The Twins take sole possession of first place with a 5–2 victory over the Rangers at the Metrodome.

> *The Twins remained in first place for the rest of the year and built an insurmountable lead. Minnesota led by 2½ games at the end of May, six at the end of June and 14 at the close of July. The peak was a 17-game advantage on August 24.*

MAY 28 Jacque Jones hits a grand slam off Chan Ho Park in the second inning of an 11–4 win over the Rangers at the Metrodome.

MAY 29 Bud Selig says that Major League Baseball has not backed off on plans to contract two teams before the start of the 2003 season, but that the Minnesota Twins will not be one of the two franchises eliminated. The Twins were not entirely safe, however. Selig left open the possibility that the club might be moved or abolished in 2004. That threat ended when a new collective bargaining agreement was signed by the players and owners on August 30, 2002, that stipulated that Major League Baseball must maintain at least 30 teams through 2006.

MAY 30 The Twins overcome a 5–0 deficit to defeat the Angels 7–6 in ten innings at the Metrodome. Christian Guzman drove in the winning run with a sacrifice fly.

JUNE 4 The Twins batter the Indians 23–2 at the Metrodome. The Twins scored one run in the first inning, two in the third, two in the fourth, four in the fifth, four in the sixth, and ten in the seventh. The club collected 25 hits to set a franchise record. The 25 hits were three homers, a triple, six doubles and 15 singles. Dustin Mohr, A. J. Pierzynski, Luis Rivas and Jacque Jones each had four hits. Batting ninth in the order, Rivas tied a franchise record by scoring five runs and also drove in five. It was his first game since going on the disabled list on April 4. Jones also drove in five runs. During the ten-run seventh, Bobby Kielty hit two doubles.

> *On the same day, the Twins selected outfielder Denard Span from Tampa Catholic High School in Tampa, Florida. Span reached the majors in 2008 and became the club's starting center fielder. Other future major leaguers drafted*

and signed by the Twins in 2002 include Jesse Crain (second round), Pat Neshek (sixth round) and Evan Meek (11th round).

June 7   The Twins play the Marlins for the first time during the regular season and win 12–7 at the Metrodome.

June 10   In a match-up of the 1991 World Series participants, the Twins play the Braves for the first time during the regular season and win 6–5 in 15 innings at the Metrodome. The Twins scored five runs in the first to take a 5–0 lead, then failed to score for 13 straight innings. Christian Guzman drove in Tom Prince with the winning run on a single with two out in the 15th. Prince, who was running with the pitch, scored all the way from first base. Mike Jackson, J. C. Romero, Eddie Guardado and Tom Fiore combined for eight innings of shutout relief.

Fiore had a 10–3 record and a 3.16 ERA in 48 games and 91 innings as a 30-year-old rookie in 2002. He pitched in only one more season, appearing in 21 games for the Twins in 2003.

June 18   The Twins play the Mets for the first time during the regular season and win 6–1 at Shea Stadium.

June 21   The Twins play the Phillies for the first time during the regular season and lose 3–0 at Veterans Stadium.

June 24   Security guard Gary Baggott is ejected during the eighth inning of a 5–4 win over the White Sox at the Metrodome. After Jacque Jones was called out at third base, the 63-year-old guard, who was stationed in the bullpen, bolted down the line and offered his glasses to umpire Joe West. The guard was ejected from the premises.

July 5   The Twins erase a 4–0 deficit with eight runs in the seventh inning and beat the Mariners 8–4 in Seattle. Torii Hunter broke the 4–4 tie with a grand slam off Jeff Nelson.

July 9   In the first inning of the All-Star Game at Miller Park in Milwaukee, Torii Hunter leaps above the center field fence to rob Barry Bonds of a home run. As Hunter trotted off the field, he was met by Bonds, who playfully lifted Hunter over his shoulder. In his next plate appearance in the third inning, Bonds hit a home run far out of the reach of any of the outfielders. Eddie Guardado came into the game with one out in the sixth and fanned Chipper Jones and Jose Hernandez. The game ended after 11 innings in a 7–7 tie when both squads ran out of pitchers.

July 15   After falling behind 7–1, the Twins score four runs in the fifth inning, two in the seventh and three in the eighth and defeat the Angels 10–8 at the Metrodome. Minnesota still trailed 8–7 with two out in the eighth inning when Christian Guzman delivered a three-run homer.

July 17   Torii Hunter fires a ball back at Indians pitcher Danys Baez during an 8–5 win in Cleveland. Hunter was angry at being hit in the left side in the fifth inning and retaliated by picking up the ball and firing it at Baez, who was about 40 feet away, hitting him in the upper leg. Hunter was ejected by the umpires. Hunter was later suspended for three games.

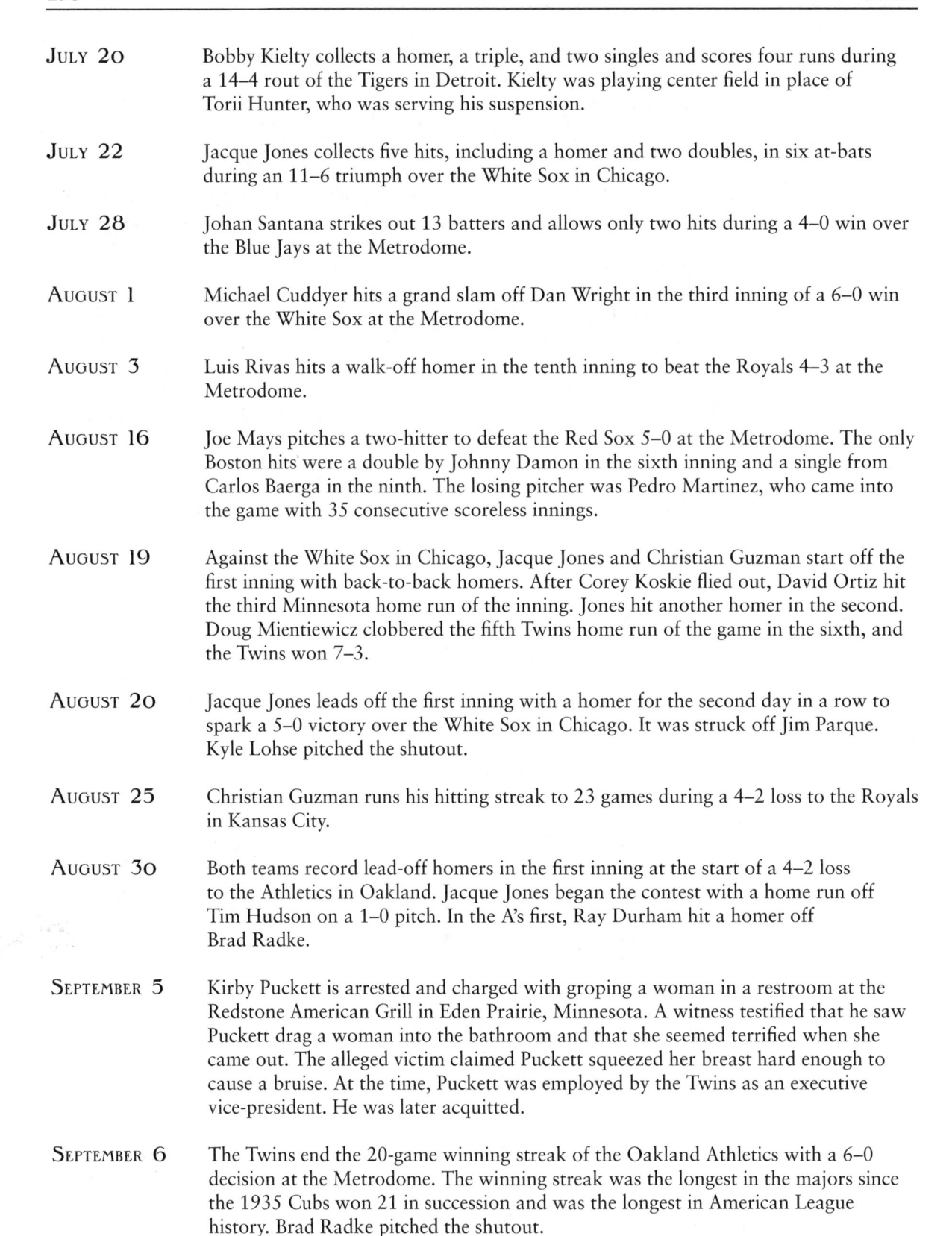

July 20	Bobby Kielty collects a homer, a triple, and two singles and scores four runs during a 14–4 rout of the Tigers in Detroit. Kielty was playing center field in place of Torii Hunter, who was serving his suspension.
July 22	Jacque Jones collects five hits, including a homer and two doubles, in six at-bats during an 11–6 triumph over the White Sox in Chicago.
July 28	Johan Santana strikes out 13 batters and allows only two hits during a 4–0 win over the Blue Jays at the Metrodome.
August 1	Michael Cuddyer hits a grand slam off Dan Wright in the third inning of a 6–0 win over the White Sox at the Metrodome.
August 3	Luis Rivas hits a walk-off homer in the tenth inning to beat the Royals 4–3 at the Metrodome.
August 16	Joe Mays pitches a two-hitter to defeat the Red Sox 5–0 at the Metrodome. The only Boston hits were a double by Johnny Damon in the sixth inning and a single from Carlos Baerga in the ninth. The losing pitcher was Pedro Martinez, who came into the game with 35 consecutive scoreless innings.
August 19	Against the White Sox in Chicago, Jacque Jones and Christian Guzman start off the first inning with back-to-back homers. After Corey Koskie flied out, David Ortiz hit the third Minnesota home run of the inning. Jones hit another homer in the second. Doug Mientiewicz clobbered the fifth Twins home run of the game in the sixth, and the Twins won 7–3.
August 20	Jacque Jones leads off the first inning with a homer for the second day in a row to spark a 5–0 victory over the White Sox in Chicago. It was struck off Jim Parque. Kyle Lohse pitched the shutout.
August 25	Christian Guzman runs his hitting streak to 23 games during a 4–2 loss to the Royals in Kansas City.
August 30	Both teams record lead-off homers in the first inning at the start of a 4–2 loss to the Athletics in Oakland. Jacque Jones began the contest with a home run off Tim Hudson on a 1–0 pitch. In the A's first, Ray Durham hit a homer off Brad Radke.
September 5	Kirby Puckett is arrested and charged with groping a woman in a restroom at the Redstone American Grill in Eden Prairie, Minnesota. A witness testified that he saw Puckett drag a woman into the bathroom and that she seemed terrified when she came out. The alleged victim claimed Puckett squeezed her breast hard enough to cause a bruise. At the time, Puckett was employed by the Twins as an executive vice-president. He was later acquitted.
September 6	The Twins end the 20-game winning streak of the Oakland Athletics with a 6–0 decision at the Metrodome. The winning streak was the longest in the majors since the 1935 Cubs won 21 in succession and was the longest in American League history. Brad Radke pitched the shutout.

SEPTEMBER 15   The Twins clinch the AL Central with a 5–0 win over the Indians in Cleveland. Kyle Lohse (six innings), Johan Santana (two innings) and Eddie Guardado (one inning) combined on a three-hitter.

SEPTEMBER 19   The Twins score nine runs in the first inning against the Tigers in Detroit, but it all goes for naught when the game is called by rain in the second. The postponement came after a wait of one hour and 25 minutes. Left fielder Mike Ryan, making his major league debut, hit two singles and scored twice in the big inning, but the statistics didn't count.

Ryan's first hit that counted came on September 27 in his 11th official big league at-bat. His second hit in the majors didn't happen until August 12, 2003. Ryan batted .393 with five home runs in 61 at-bats during a tight pennant race in 2003, but his big league career ended in 2005 with a .265 average in 127 games.

SEPTEMBER 25   David Ortiz hits a two-run, walk-off homer in the 12th inning to down the Indians 7–5 at the Metrodome.

The Twins met the Oakland Athletics in the American League Division Series. managed by Art Howe, the A's were 103–59 in 2002. From June 7 through the end of the regular season, Oakland had a record of 74–29 and were 35–8 after August 13.

OCTOBER 1   In the first game of the Division Series, the Twins overcome a four-run deficit to defeat the Athletics 7–5 in Oakland. The A's scored three runs in the first inning and two in the second off Brad Radke to take a 5–1 advantage. Radke settled down and pitched three innings of shutout ball before giving way to relievers Johan Santana, J. C. Romero and Eddie Guardado. Corey Koskie hit a two-run homer in the third to make the score 5–3. The Twins went ahead with three in the sixth. Doug Mientiewicz led off the inning with a home run. Two more runs crossed the plate on two singles, a double by Jacque Jones, a walk, and a run-scoring ground out from Koskie. A. J. Pierzynski collected four hits, including a triple, in four at-bats.

The series was carried on national television over the ABC Family network. The announcers were Jon Miller and Joe Morgan in games one, two and five, and Dave O'Brien, Rick Sutcliffe and Tony Gwynn in games three and four.

OCTOBER 2   The Athletics trounce the Twins 9–1 in Oakland. Starter Joe Mays gave up six runs in $3^{2}/_{3}$ innings.

OCTOBER 4   The Athletics take a two-games-to-one lead in the best-of-five series by beating the Twins 6–3 before 55,932 at the Metrodome. Rick Reed gave up four home runs. Ray Durham started the contest with an inside-the-park homer, and Scott Hatteberg followed Durham to the plate with another homer. The Twins battled back to tie 3–3, but Jermaine Dye broke the deadlock with a home run.

OCTOBER 5   The Twins stay alive in the Division Series by clobbering the Athletics 11–2 before 55,960 at the Metrodome. The Twins broke a 2–2 tie with seven runs in the fourth inning. Doug Mientiewicz hit two singles during the big rally and homered in the seventh.

OCTOBER 6   The Twins complete the upset of the Athletics in the Division Series with 5–4 victory in Oakland. The score was 2–1 after eight innings. In the ninth, A. J. Pierzynski hit a two-run homer for a 4–1 lead. Christian Guzman singled, stole second, and crossed the plate on a double from David Ortiz. The run proved to be necessary when Eddie Guardado gave up three runs in the bottom of the ninth. The game ended when Ray Durham fouled out to second baseman Dennis Hocking with a runner on first base.

After the game, Hocking broke his hand when someone stepped on it during the postgame celebration. In the Championship Series, the Twins met the Anaheim Angels. Managed by Mike Scioscia, the Angels were 99–63 during the regular season and won the wild card. In the Division Series, the Angels upset the Yankees in four games. The Yanks came into the 2002 postseason having won the four previous AL championships and were 103–58 during the regular season.

OCTOBER 8   The Twins open the Championship Series by beating the Angels 2–1 before 55,562 at the Metrodome. Joe Mays went eight innings and allowed one unearned run and four hits. Corey Koskie broke a 1–1 tie with an RBI-double in the fifth.

The Series was telecast nationally on the FOX network. The announcers were Thom Brennaman and Steve Lyons.

OCTOBER 9   The Angels even the series by defeating the Twins 6–3 before 55,990 at the Metrodome. In the second, Anaheim scored three times, one of them on a controversial play. Scott Spezio was caught in a rundown after trying to steal home. Spezio knocked the ball away from Twins catcher A. J. Pierzynski, but was not called out for interference. Doug Mientiewicz collected three hits in the losing cause.

OCTOBER 11   The Angels edge the Twins 2–1 in Anaheim to take a two-games-to-one lead in the Championship Series. Troy Glaus broke the 1–1 tie with a homer off J. C. Romero in the eighth inning.

OCTOBER 12   In game four, the Angels defeat the Twins 7–1 in Anaheim. The game was scoreless until the Angels scored two runs in the seventh. Five Twins relievers combined to allow five runs in the eighth.

OCTOBER 13   The Angels advance to the World Series by pounding the Twins 13–5 in Anaheim. With the help of two home runs from Adam Kennedy, the Angels led 3–2 after six innings. In the top of the seventh inning, the Twins scored three to move ahead 5–3. After loading the bases on a single by A. J. Pierzynski with one out, the Twins went ahead on a walk, a wild pitch and a sacrifice fly. But in the bottom half, the Twins fell under an avalanche of ten Anaheim runs. During the rally, Kennedy hit his third homer of the game. He hit only seven during the regular season.

OCTOBER 14   The Twins release Casey Blake.

The release of Blake has turned out to be one of the worst miscalculations in Twins history, although it wasn't the worst of the 2002–03 off-season (see December 16, 2002). When let go, Blake was 29-years-old and had played in only 49 big league games with three clubs, including 29 contests with the Twins. He signed with the Indians on December 18 and became a starter in Cleveland at third base in 2003, a position he held until a trade with the Dodgers in 2008. Blake was still a productive player in Los Angeles in 2009.

DECEMBER 16   In one of the worst transactions in club history, the Twins release David Ortiz.

Ortiz spent six seasons with the Twins and teased the club with his enormous potential, but it never developed to the satisfaction of club management. He was let go in part because he was eligible for arbitration, and the Twins didn't want to pay for what was expected to be a large boost in salary. At the time of his release, Ortiz was 27 years old. He had played in 479 big league games and had a batting average of .266 with a .461 slugging percentage and 58 home runs in 1,693 at-bats. Ortiz signed with the Red Sox on January 22, 2003, and immediately became a star and one of the most popular athletes in New England. He finished in the top five in the MVP voting five consecutive seasons from 2003 through 2007. During those five years, he batted .302, had a slugging percentage of .612, and average 42 homers and 128 RBIs per season. Ortiz led the AL twice in runs batted in and walks and once in on-base percentage and home runs (54 in 2006). He also had numerous clutch hits in the postseason, including the 2004 and 2007 World Series.

2003

Season in a Sentence
After falling four games below .500 at the All-Star break, the Twins rally to win their second straight AL Central title before falling to the Yankees in the playoffs.

Finish • Won • Lost • Pct • GB
First   90   72   .556   +4.0

AL Division Series
The Twins lost three games to one to the New York Yankees.

Manager
Ron Gardenhire

Stats   Twins • AL • Rank
	Twins	AL	Rank
Batting Avg:	.277	.267	3
On-Base Pct:	.341	.333	5
Slugging Pct:	.431	.428	6
Home Runs:	155		9
Stolen Bases:	94		7
ERA:	4.41	4.52	7
Errors:	87		2
Runs Scored:	801		6
Runs Allowed:	758		6

Starting Line-up
A. J. Pierzynski, c
Doug Mientiewicz, 1b
Luis Rivas, 2b
Corey Koskie, 3b
Christian Guzman, ss
Jacque Jones, lf
Torii Hunter, cf
Dustan Mohr, rf
Matt LeCroy, dh
Shannon Stewart, lf
Bobby Kielty, rf
Dennis Hocking, 2b-3b-ss

Pitchers
Brad Radke, sp
Kyle Lohse, sp
Kenny Rogers, sp
Rick Reed, sp
Joe Mays, sp
Eddie Guardado, rp
Juan Rincon, rp
LaTroy Hawkins, rp
J. C. Romero, rp
Johan Santana, rp-sp

Attendance
1,946,011 (eighth in AL)

Club Leaders
Batting Avg:	A. J. Pierzynski	.312
On-Base Pct:	Doug Mientiewicz	.393
	Corey Koskie	.393
Slugging Pct:	A. J. Pierzynski	.464
	Corey Koskie	.464
Home Runs:	Torii Hunter	26
RBI:	Torii Hunter	102
Runs:	Torii Hunter	83
Stolen Bases:	Christian Guzman	18
Wins:	Brad Radke	14
	Kyle Lohse	14
Strikeouts:	Johan Santana	169
ERA:	Brad Radke	4.49
Saves:	Eddie Guardado	41

JANUARY 9	The Twins sign Chris Gomez, most recently with the Devil Rays, as a free agent.
MARCH 17	The Twins sign Kenny Rogers, most recently with the Rangers, as a free agent.
	Rogers was 38 and had a career record of 145–106 when signed by the Twins. In his lone season in Minnesota, Rogers was 13–8 with a 4.57 ERA.
MARCH 31	The Twins open the season with a 3–1 victory over the Tigers in Detroit. It was the first time that the Twins played a regular season game in March. Dustan Mohr started the scoring with a two-run homer in the second inning. A. J. Pierzynski added a solo shot in the eighth. Brad Radke pitched 6⅔ innings and allowed a run and three hits.
	Pierzynski batted .312 with 11 homers in 2003.
APRIL 4	In the home opener, the Twins lose 7–2 to the Blue Jays before 48,617 at the Metrodome. Doug Mientiewicz homered in the losing cause.
	The first seven series involving the Twins, and nine of the first 11, resulted in sweeps. Minnesota opened with three straight wins against the Tigers in Detroit, then dropped three in a row at home to the Blue Jays. That was followed by a road trip in which the Twins lost all three against the Yankees in New York and won three in succession versus in Toronto. The homestand from April 15 through April 21 featured three wins against the Tigers and four losses to the Yankees. In a series in Kansas City, reduced to two games by a rainout, the Twins lost both. The ninth and eleventh series of 2003 were sweeps of the Devil Rays. The streaky Twins were involved in 20 two-game, three-game or four-game sweeps over the course of the season.
APRIL 7	The Twins-Yankees game in New York is postponed by snow.
APRIL 8	With the first-pitch temperature a frigid 35 degrees, the Twins lose 7–3 to the Yankees in New York.
APRIL 21	In a start against the Yankees at the Metrodome, Rick Reed allows 11 runs, ten of them earned, in 4⅓ innings and the Twins lose 15–1.
MAY 6	Jacque Jones collects five hits on two homers, a double and two singles in five at-bats to lead the Twins to a 7–3 triumph over the Devil Rays in St. Petersburg. Jones also stole a base.
MAY 7	Trailing 6–4, the Twins bust loose with seven runs in the fifth inning and defeat the Devil Rays 11–6 in St. Petersburg. A. J. Pierzynski hit a grand slam off Joe Kennedy.
MAY 9	Entering the contest with three career runs batted in, designated hitter Todd Sears drives in four during a 5–0 victory over the Red Sox at the Metrodome. Sears also hit his first career homer, a three-run shot off Pedro Martinez.
MAY 13	Todd Sears hits a two-run, walk-off homer in the tenth inning to beat the Royals 4–2 at the Metrodome. Sears entered the game as a pinch-hitter in the eighth and remained as a first baseman.

Sears never hit another major league homer. He finished his career with two home runs in 85 at-bats.

MAY 16 — The Twins collect 20 hits and wallop the White Sox 18–3 at the Metrodome. During a seven-run fourth inning, A. J. Pierzynski garnered a single and a double and Torii Hunter belted a three-run homer.

MAY 27 — The Twins are held to three hits but beat the Athletics 4–3 at the Metrodome. Oakland pitcher Barry Zito was working on a one-hitter in the eighth inning before giving up a double to Dustan Mohr, hitting A. J. Pierzynski with a pitch, and yielding a three-run, pinch-hit homer to Bobby Kielty.

JUNE 1 — Kenny Rogers allows hits to the first seven batters to face him in a 9–5 loss to the Mariners at the Metrodome. Rogers gave up five straight singles to Randy Winn, Carlos Guillen, Bret Boone, Edgar Martinez, and Mike Cameron, a triple to Greg Colbrunn, and another single to Jeff Cirillo. Rogers lasted 1 1/3 innings and gave up seven runs and ten hits while facing 13 hitters.

JUNE 3 — The Twins play the Giants for the first time during the regular season and lose 6–4 in San Francisco.

On the same day, the Twins selected third baseman Matthew Moses from Mills E. Godwin High School in Richmond, Virginia. In 2009, Moses was still in the Twins organization, struggling at the Class AA level. The club chose future big leaguers Scott Baker in the second round and Levale Speigner in the 14th.

JUNE 6 — The Twins play the Padres for the first time during the regular season and win 7–5 in 11 innings at Qualcomm Stadium in San Diego.

JUNE 7 — Jacque Jones homers on the first pitch of the first inning, then belts another homer on a 1–1 offering in the third, to lead the Twins to a 6–2 triumph over the Padres in San Diego. Both were struck off Carlton Loewer.

JUNE 10 — The Twins play the Rockies for the first time and lose 5–0 at the Metrodome. Batting clean-up as the designated hitter, Justin Morneau made his major league debut and collected two of the Twins three hits in four at-bats. Both were singles.

Morneau collected six hits in his first 11 at-bats but finished his rookie season with a .226 average and four homers in 40 games.

JUNE 12 — The Twins use a pair of seven-run innings to down the Rockies 15–3 at the Metrodome. The seven spots were put up in the first and seventh. A. J. Pierzynski drove in seven runs. He hit a grand slam in the first inning off Darren Oliver and a three-run shot against Javier Lopez in the seventh. Lew Ford hit a single and a double in the first, and Corey Koskie did likewise in the seventh.

Koskie hit .292 with 14 homers in 2003.

JUNE 13 — The Twins play the Diamondbacks for the first time, and win 3–1 at the Metrodome.

JUNE 16   Trailing 8–0 after six innings in Kansas City, the Twins rally to tie the score 8–8 with two runs in the seventh, three in the eighth and three in the ninth, only to lose 9–8 when the Royals score in the bottom of the ninth.

JUNE 17   Leading 3–1, the Twins allow 12 runs in the sixth inning and lose 14–7 to the Royals in Kansas City. The even dozen runs in the sixth were allowed by Kenny Rogers (six), J. C. Romero (three) and Mike Nakamura (three). Facing Albie Lopez in the eighth, Justin Morneau hit his first major league homer.

Nakamura was born in Japan and raised in Australia.

JUNE 19   The Twins erupt for 23 hits and trounce the Royals 16–2 in Kansas City. The Twins scored seven runs in the fifth. During the rally, Torii Hunter hit a single and a double. Corey Koskie finished the evening with six RBIs on two homers and two doubles. Christian Guzman collected four hits and scored four runs.

JUNE 25   Jacque Jones hits a walk-off homer in the 11th inning to defeat the White Sox 6–5 at the Metrodome.

JUNE 29   The Twins score two runs in the ninth inning and one in the tenth to defeat the Brewers 5–4 at the Metrodome. Doug Mientiewicz drove in the tying run in the ninth with a sacrifice fly to score Christian Guzman. The game ended an inning later on Guzman's walk-off single.

With the victory, the Twins were 43–37 and tied for first place. The club lost 12 of the next 13 contests, however, to fall to 44–49 on July 13 in third place 7½ games behind.

JULY 16   The Twins trade Bobby Kielty and Dan Gassmer to the Blue Jays for Shannon Stewart.

Stewart helped the Twins capture the AL Central title by hitting .322 in 65 games with the club and finished fourth in the MVP voting. He remained with Minnesota until 2006, but his batting numbers declined each season.

JULY 27   Former Metrodome superintendent Dick Ericson tells the *Minneapolis Star Tribune* that he tried to manipulate the outcome of Twins games by the use of electric fans in the late innings. Ericson retired in 1995. The power of the electric fans needed to be increased near the end of games to keep the roof inflated as doors were opened for the fans to leave. Ericson said he would increase the number of fans blowing from behind home plate between first and third base starting in the last of the eighth if the Twins were trailing, thus giving the home team the chance of two turns at bat under these conditions compared to one for the visitors. Ericson's admission was backed by another employee. Opposing managers, coaches and players had complained for two decades about the flow of the fans, which they claimed favored the Twins. Ericson said he acted on his own and not at the direction of the ball club or the Metropolitan Sports Facilities Commission, which operated the Metrodome. After Ericson's confession, a professor of fluid dynamics at the University of Minnesota conducted tests with some of his students and concluded that balls traveled 3½ feet farther with the fans turned on.

JULY 31   After falling behind 9–5, the Twins score two runs in the seventh inning, two in the ninth and one in the tenth to defeat the Orioles 10–9 in ten innings at the Metrodome. With two out in the ninth, the Twins still trailed 9–7 with runners on first and second. A. J. Pierzynski singled home Luis Rivas to cut the margin to one. Mike Restovich swung and missed at a Jorge Julio pitch for what should have ended the game, but the ball eluded Baltimore catcher Brook Fordyce. Restovich hesitated before running to first base, and Fordyce had time to throw him out, but the throw bounced in front of first baseman Jeff Conine and Restovich was safe. Doug Mientkiewicz scored from second on the play with the tying run. With the bases loaded in the tenth, Baltimore employed a five-man infield with Jacque Jones at-bat. Jones hit a high chopper through the infield that drove in the winning run with a single.

AUGUST 9   A two-run homer by Torii Hunter in the tenth inning caps a four-run rally that beats the Tigers 8–4 in Detroit.

AUGUST 13   The Indians break open a scoreless duel with five runs in the 14th inning to defeat the Twins 5–0 at the Metrodome. Through the first 13 innings, Johan Santana (eight innings), LaTroy Hawkins (two innings), Eddie Guardado (two innings) and Juan Rincon (one inning) combined to allow only six hits. But Rincon faltered in the 14th, giving up three runs before J. C. Romero surrendered two more.

Romero had a couple of odd injuries in 2003. In August he was whacked in the head with a foul ball off the bat of Ben Broussard of the Indians during batting practice. In September, Romero sat on a knife, requiring stitches in his rear end.

"Everyday" Eddie Guardado earned his nickname through numerous appearances out of the bullpen, both in middle relief and as a closer. He pitched for the Twins from 1993 to 2003 and then again in 2008.

AUGUST 16	The Twins score in seven of nine innings and rout the Royals 14–5 in Kansas City.
AUGUST 17	The Twins use three pitchers in a 5–4 loss to the Royals in Kansas City, and none of them strikes out or walks a batter. The trio consisted of Rick Reed (three innings), Joe Mays (four innings) and LaTroy Hawkins (one inning).
AUGUST 29	Carlos Pulido makes his first major league appearance in nine years during an 8–5 triumph over the Rangers in Arlington. Pulido pitched two shutout innings.

A native of Venezuela, Pulido made his major league debut with the Twins in 1994 and pitched 19 games for the club that season. During the nine-year interval between 1994 and 2003, he pitched in the minors for the Twins, Cubs, Expos and Mets organizations and played professionally in Mexico, Japan and Taiwan. He pitched in seven games for the Twins in 2003 and six more in 2004 and had a 6.00 ERA in 27 innings.

AUGUST 30	With a single in the sixth inning, Shannon Stewart drives in both runs of a 2–0 victory over the Rangers in Arlington. Johan Santana (six innings), Juan Rincon (1 2/3 innings), LaTroy Hawkins (one-third of an inning) and Eddie Guardado (one inning) combined on the shutout.

From the time he made his major league debut as a 21-year-old in 2000 through July 5, 2003, Johan Santana pitched in 102 big league games, 26 of them starts, and had a 15–10 record with an ERA of 4.20. His last 15 appearances in 2003 were all starts, and he was 8–2 in 92 1/3 innings and had an earned run average of 3.22. In addition, Santana went 20 consecutive starts without a defeat from July 29, 2003, through May 13, 2004. He had ten wins and ten no decisions during that stretch.

AUGUST 31	The Twins trade Juan Padilla to the Yankees for Jesse Orosco.

Orosco was 46 years old and in his 24th major league season. He became the oldest player in Twins history. The eight games he pitched for the club in 2003 were the last of his all-time record of 1,252. The Twins were Orosco's ninth club. He was ineffective in a Minnesota uniform, with a 6.23 ERA in 4 1/3 innings.

SEPTEMBER 3	The Twins score two runs to defeat the Angels 6–5 at the Metrodome. With the score 5–4, the first two batters in the ninth were retired, and the Angels were one strike from a win before Troy Percival walked Dustan Mohr on a 3–2 pitch. Shannon Stewart hit a drive down the left field line and Mohr raced home. Anaheim left fielder Garret Anderson threw to shortstop Wilson Delgado, who fired home in an attempt to nab Mohr. Mohr crashed into Anaheim catcher Bengie Molina, who suffered two broken bones above his left wrist on the play. As the ball rolled away from Molina, Stewart raced home with the winning run. To add insult to injury, Molina was charged with an error. Stewart was credited with a double and a two-base advance on Molina's error.

The win lifted the Twins into a first-place tie with the White Sox with a record of 73–66. The Royals were in third, one game back. The Twins posted an 18–3 record from September 2 through September 24.

SEPTEMBER 13   Solo homers by Christian Guzman in the sixth inning and Torii Hunter in the seventh, both off Jason Stanford, beat the Indians 2–0 in Cleveland. Kyle Lohse (7 1/3 innings), LaTroy Hawkins (two-thirds of an inning) and Eddie Guardado (one inning) combined on the shutout.

SEPTEMBER 15   The Twins take sole possession of first place with a 13–6 victory over the Indians in Cleveland. Minnesota scored eight runs in the sixth inning to take a 9–2 lead.

With the win, the Twins took a half-game lead over the White Sox. The next three games, on September 16, 17 and 18, were against the Sox in Chicago. The Twins took all three by scores 5–2, 4–2, and 5–3. The three victories gave the Twins a 3 1/2 game advantage in the AL Central.

SEPTEMBER 23   The Twins clinch the AL Central pennant with a 4–1 win over the Indians at the Metrodome.

SEPTEMBER 24   The Twins extend their winning streak to 11 games with a 3–2 decision over the Indians at the Metrodome.

SEPTEMBER 26   Michael Cuddyer homers in the 11th inning to beat the Tigers 5–4 in Detroit.

The loss was the 119th of the season for the Tigers, who were one defeat away from the modern record of 120 set by the New York Mets in 1962. The Tigers had two games remaining, both against the Twins in Detroit, and won both to finish the year with a 43–119 record.

SEPTEMBER 27   The Twins lead 8–0 in the fifth inning but wind up losing 9–8 to the Tigers in Detroit. With the score 8–8 in the ninth, Jesse Orosco walked Alex Sanchez, who proceeded to steal second and third with Warren Morris at-bat. On a 2–2 pitch, Morris swung and missed at a pitch for a strikeout, but the ball sailed past A. J. Pierzynski for a wild pitch and Sanchez scored. It was Orosco's last pitch in the majors. He ended his career with an all-time record of 1,252 games as a pitcher.

The Twins played the New York Yankees in the American League Division Series. Managed by Joe Torre the Yankees posted the best won-lost record in the AL in 2003 at 101–61. The 90 victories by the Twins were the fifth-best in the AL. The Twins were 0–7 against the Yankees during the 2003 regular season, and were 0–6 in 2002. Minnesota's last win against the Yanks was on May 10, 2001.

SEPTEMBER 30   The Twins break their 13-game losing streak to the Yankees with a 3–1 victory at Yankee Stadium in the first game of the Division Series. The Twins scored a run in the third inning and two more in the sixth. The lone New York run came in the ninth. Johan Santana was the starting pitcher and went four innings. LaTroy Hawkins was credited with the victory for pitching two shutout innings (the seventh and eighth) while fanning four.

The television announcers for the Series were Jon Miller and Joe Morgan (game one on ESPN), Joe Buck and Tim McCarver (game two on FOX), and Chris Berman, Jeff Brantley and David Justice (games three and four in ESPN).

OCTOBER 2 The Yankees even the Division Series by beating the Twins 4–1 in New York. The Yanks broke a 1–1 tie with three runs in the seventh off Brad Radke and LaTroy Hawkins.

OCTOBER 4 The Yankees take game three 3–1 before 55,915 at the Metrodome. The Yanks scored three runs before A. J. Pierzynski homered in the bottom of the third. There was no scoring over the last six innings.

OCTOBER 5 The Yankees move on to the Championship Series by downing the Twins 8–1 before 55,875 at the Metrodome. New York broke a scoreless tie with six runs in the fourth inning.

The Twins scored only six runs in the four games against the Yankees.

NOVEMBER 14 The Twins send A. J. Pierzynski and cash to the Giants for Joe Nathan, Boof Bonser and Francisco Liriano.

This trade has become one of the greatest in club history, although the final chapter is some years away because all four players were still active in professional baseball in 2009. Pierzynski has been a starting catcher with the Giants and White Sox since the trade, but the Twins had a far superior option in Joe Mauer, who made his major league debut in 2004. Nathan quickly established himself as the best closer ever to wear a Minnesota uniform. After a breakout year in 2006, Liriano has been beset by injuries and inconsistency.

DECEMBER 3 The Twins trade Eric Milton to the Phillies for Nick Punto, Carlos Silva and Bobby Korecky. On the same day, LaTroy Hawkins signed with the Cubs as a free agent.

Milton has struggled with several teams since leaving the Twins. Silva produced several good years for the team, and Punto has been a valuable role player.

Hawkins spent nine seasons with the Twins and tantalized the club with his potential, but in the end had a 44–57 record and a 5.05 earned run average while in Minnesota. He had a tremendous year in 2003, however, with a 9–3 record and 1.86 ERA in 74 games and 77$^{1}/_{3}$ innings. Since leaving Minnesota, Hawkins has had sporadic success with a half-dozen teams.

DECEMBER 8 Chris Gomez signs with the Orioles as a free agent.

DECEMBER 16 Eddie Guardado signs a contract as a free agent with the Mariners.

Guardado had two excellent seasons as Seattle's closer before injuries sent him into the decline phase of his career.

2004

Season in a Sentence
Backed by a pitching staff that leads the league in ERA, the Twins cruise to their third straight AL Central title and lose to the Yankees in the first round of the playoffs for the second year in a row.

Finish • Won • Lost • Pct • GB
First   92   70   .568   +9.0

AL Division Series
The Twins lost to the New York Yankees three games to one.

Manager
Ron Gardenhire

Stats

Stats	Twins	AL	Rank
Batting Avg:	.266	.270	10
On-Base Pct:	.332	.338	9
Slugging Pct:	.431	.433	9
Home Runs:	191		6
Stolen Bases:	116		3
ERA:	4.03	4.63	1
Errors:	101		6
Runs Scored:	780		7
Runs Allowed:	715		1

Starting Line-up
Henry Blanco, c
Doug Mientiewicz, 1b
Luis Rivas, 2b
Corey Koskie, 3b
Christian Guzman, ss
Lew Ford, lf-cf
Torii Hunter, cf
Jacque Jones, rf
Matt LeCroy, dh-c-1b
Shannon Stewart, lf
Michael Cuddyer, 3b-2b
Justin Morneau, 1b

Pitchers
Johan Santana, sp
Carlos Silva, sp
Brad Radke, sp
Kyle Lohse, sp
Joe Nathan, rp
Juan Rincon, rp
J. C. Romero, rp
Joe Roa, rp
Aaron Fultz, rp
Terry Mulholland, rp-sp

Attendance
1,911,490 (tenth in AL)

Club Leaders
Batting Avg:	Lew Ford	.299
On-Base Pct:	Lew Ford	.381
Slugging Pct:	Corey Koskie	.495
Home Runs:	Corey Koskie	25
RBI:	Torii Hunter	81
Runs:	Lew Ford	89
Stolen Bases:	Torii Hunter	21
Wins:	Johan Santana	20
Strikeouts:	Johan Santana	265
ERA:	Johan Santana	2.61
Saves:	Joe Nathan	44

JANUARY 10   Kenny Rogers signs with the Rangers as a free agent.

Rogers was 39 but still had some life left in his left arm. He was 18–9 for the Rangers in 2004 and 17–8 with the AL champion Tigers in 2006.

FEBRUARY 6   The Twins sign Jose Offerman as a free agent. After playing for four big league clubs from 1990 through 2002, Offerman spent the entire 2003 season with the Bridgeport Bluefish in the independent Atlantic League.

FEBRUARY 10   Dennis Hocking signs with the Rockies as a free agent.

APRIL 2   The Twins purchase Terry Mulholland from the Mariners.

APRIL 5 The Twins open the season with a thrilling 11-inning, 7–4 win over the Indians before 49,584 at the Metrodome. The Twins trailed 4–0 before tying the score with four runs in the eighth inning. With two out in the 11th, Shannon Stewart walloped a three-run walk-off homer for the victory. Six Minnesota pitchers, beginning with starter Brad Radke, allowed 17 hits but stranded 14 base runners. Joe Mauer made his major league debut, and collected two hits in three at-bats. He also walked twice.

Mauer was limited to 35 games because of a knee injury suffered in the second game of the season when he attempted to catch a foul ball behind the plate. He batted .308 with six home runs.

APRIL 6 The Twins score two runs in the ninth inning and one in the 15th to win 7–6 over the Indians at the Metrodome and start the season with back-to-back, extra-inning victories. In the ninth, Jacque Jones hit a two-out, two-run homer to tie the score 6–6. Jose Offerman, making his debut with the Twins, drove in the winning run with a single in the 15th. Offerman entered the game as a pinch-runner in the 12th and remained in the contest as the designated hitter.

The Twins used 15 designated hitters in 2004. Jose Offerman led the club in games played (38) and games started (33) at the position.

APRIL 10 The Twins hit six homers to defeat the Tigers 10–5 in Detroit. Henry Blanco hit his first two homers as a member of the Twins during the game. The other home runs were struck by Luis Rivas, Corey Koskie, Jose Offerman and Lew Ford.

The game was Ford's first since being called up from Triple A Rochester to replace the injured Torii Hunter. Ford became a regular outfielder, playing in 154 of the Twins last 158 games. He hit .299 with 15 home runs.

APRIL 27 The Twins score four runs in the ninth inning to defeat the Blue Jays 7–4 at the Metrodome. Singles by Shannon Stewart, Doug Mientiewicz and Torii Hunter produced one run and tied the score 4–4. Jacque Jones broke the deadlock with a three-run, walk-off homer.

Field Turf was installed at the Metrodome during the 2003–04 off-season. Compared to the previous artificial surfaces, Field Turf slowed down ground balls and turned the Metrodome into a ballpark that favored pitchers.

MAY 7 Christian Guzman collects five hits, including two doubles, in six at-bats, but the Twins lose 11–9 in 13 innings to the Athletics in Oakland.

MAY 13 The Twins edge the Mariners 1–0 at the Metrodome. Michael Cuddyer drove in the lone run of the game with a double in the second inning. Johan Santana (seven innings), Terry Mulholland (one-third of an inning), J. C. Romero (two-thirds of an inning) and Joe Nathan (one inning) combined on the shutout.

Nathan entered the season as a 29-year-old who had only one career save in four seasons in the majors. In 2004, his first season with the Twins, he recorded 44 saves and had a 1.62 ERA in 73 games and 72 1/3 innings. He pitched 29 consecutive scoreless innings over 28 games from June 9 through August 18.

At the end of the 2009 season, he had 246 saves as a Twin, eight shy of Rick Aguilera's team record.

MAY 15 — Torii Hunter collects two homers, a double and a single in four at-bats to lead the Twins to a 4–1 win over the White Sox in Chicago.

MAY 19 — With the Twins trailing 5–2 and one out in the ninth inning against the Blue Jays in Toronto, pinch-hitter Matt LeCroy hits a grand slam off Terry Adams for a 6–5 win.

The homer was the first of three consecutive pinch-hit at-bats in which LeCroy hit a home run, which tied a major league record. The other two were on June 1 and June 17.

One of baseball's elite pitchers throughout the 2000s, Johan Santana was the Twins ace, winning Cy Young awards in 2004 and 2006.

JUNE 1 — With Twins wallop five homers and trounce the Devil Rays 16–4 in St. Petersburg. Corey Koskie led the way with two home runs. The others were struck by Matt LeCroy, Torii Hunter and Jacque Jones.

JUNE 4 — Torii Hunter hits a walk-off homer in the ninth inning to defeat the Tigers 3–2 at the Metrodome.

JUNE 7 — With three picks in the first round of the amateur draft, the Twins select shortstop Trevor Plouffe from Crespi Camelite High School in Encino, California, pitcher Glen Perkins from the University of Minnesota, and pitcher Steven Waldrop from Farragut High School in Knoxville, Tennessee. The Twins had two extra picks as compensation for losing Eddie Guardado and LaTroy Hawkins in free agency. Perkins reached the majors in 2006 and became a regular in the Twins starting rotation in 2008. Plouffe and Waldrop were still in the minors in 2009. Matt Tolbert, who made his major league debut in 2008, was chosen in the 16th round.

JUNE 8 — The Twins play the Mets at the Metrodome for the first time, and win 2–1.

JUNE 10	The Twins outlast the Mets 3–2 in 15 innings at the Metrodome. Jose Offerman tied the score 2–2 with a pinch-hit double with two out in the ninth. Mike Ryan drove in the winning run in the 15th with a single. Ryan entered the game as a pinch-runner in the tenth and remained as the designated hitter. Kyle Lohse (seven innings), Aaron Fultz (one inning), Juan Rincon (two innings), Joe Nathan (one inning), Joe Roa (2$^{1}/_{3}$ innings) and Grant Balfour (1$^{2}/_{3}$ innings) combined on an eight-hitter. It was Balfour's first major league victory.
	Balfour was born in Sydney, Australia. Roa was 32 years old in 2004 and had been in professional baseball since 1989. The Twins were his seventh, and last, big league team. The 2004 season was the only one in which Roa spent the entire season in the majors.
JUNE 11	The Twins play the Phillies at the Metrodome for the first time and lose 11–6.
JUNE 15	The Twins play in Montreal for the first time and beat the Expos 8–2 at Olympic Stadium.
JUNE 16	The Twins score a run in the eighth inning, two in the ninth, and one in the 11th to defeat the Expos 5–4 in Montreal. A homer by Luis Rivas in the 11th broke the 4–4 tie, although replays indicated the drive was foul.
	At the end of the 2004 season, the Expos moved to Washington and were renamed the Nationals.
JUNE 20	Johan Santana and Joe Nathan combine for 15 strikeouts to defeat the Brewers 4–2 in Milwaukee. Santana fanned 12 in eight innings and Nathan three in the ninth to nail down the save.
	Santana had a 7–6 record on July 11 and went on to win 13 in a row. He finished the season with a 20–6 record, a 2.61 ERA, and a league-leading 265 strikeouts in 228 innings. The strikeouts broke the Twins single-season of 258 by Bert Blyleven in 1973. (Walter Johnson holds the franchise record with 313 for the Senators in 1910.) During the 13-game winning streak, accomplished over 15 starts, Santana had a dominating 1.21 earned run average in 104$^{1}/_{3}$ innings. He threw 33 consecutive scoreless innings over six starts from August 28 through September 24. Santana was the unanimous choice for the Cy Young Award.
JULY 1	Johan Santana strikes out 12 batters in eight innings, but the Twins lose 2–1 to the White Sox in Chicago.
JULY 2	The Twins play the Diamondbacks in Phoenix for the first time and win 6–5.
JULY 5	The Twins shut down the Royals 9–0 at the Metrodome. Brad Radke pitched a complete game.
	Before the game, the Twins gave away G. I. Joe action figures to the first 5,000 children attending as a gesture to honor local military personnel. In an effort to appease protesting groups who believed the promotion glorified war, the Twins asked Hasbro, the maker of the toy, to remove the customary gun from G. I. Joe's side, but the hand grenade remained visible.

July 6	Johan Santana strikes out 13 batters and pitches a three-hit complete game shutout to defeat the Royals 4–0 at the Metrodome.
July 7	The Twins shut out the Royals for the third game in a row with Kyle Lohse pitching the club a 12–0 triumph at the Metrodome. Each of the three shutouts were complete games. It was the first time since moving to Minnesota in 1961 that the Twins had three shutouts in a row.
July 11	Johan Santana (eight innings) and Joe Nathan (one inning) combine on a two-hitter, but the Twins lose 2–0 to the Tigers at the Metrodome. Both Detroit hits came in the second inning on a double by Marcus Thames and a homer from Eric Munson. Santana (18) and Joe Nathan (3) combined to retire the last 21 batters to face them. Santana also struck out 11.
July 13	Pitching in the seventh inning of the All-Star Game at Minute Maid Park in Houston, Joe Nathan retires all three batters to face him, two of them on strikeouts. The American League won 9–4.
July 16	Both lead-off batters start the first inning with home runs in a 12–3 loss to the Royals in Kansas City. Shannon Stewart started the Twins first with a homer off Darrell May. David DeJesus began the Royals first with a homer against Brad Radke.
July 17	One start after combining on a two-hitter, Johan Santana (eight innings) and Joe Nathan (one inning) join forces on a one-hitter to down the Royals 4–1 in Kansas City. The only hit off Santana was a double by Angel Berroa leading off the second inning.
July 21	The Twins score eight runs in the fourth inning and clobber the Devil Rays 12–2 at the Metrodome. Justin Morneau doubled and singled during the rally.
July 22	Nick Punto hits a grand slam off Jesse Colome in the seventh inning of a 7–5 victory over the Devil Rays at the Metrodome.
July 25	The Twins move into first place with an 8–4 win over the Orioles in Baltimore.
	The Twins remained in first for the rest of the year.
July 27	Corey Koskie is hit by pitches in three consecutive plate appearances during a 7–3 win over the White Sox in Chicago.
July 28	Justin Morneau has a strange day during a 10-inning, 5–4 win over the White Sox at U.S. Cellular Field by having two home runs reversed. In the second, Morneau hit a fly ball to left field that third base umpire Ed Montague ruled a home run. But after an argument by Chicago manager Ozzie Guillen and left fielder Carlos Lee, the arbiters huddled and ruled the play a double because it was determined that the ball hit the top of the wall and bounced back into the field of play. In the fifth, a drive by Morneau down the right field line was initially signaled a home run by first base umpire Matt Hollowell. It was changed to a foul ball after Guillen and right fielder Timo Perez objected and the umps conferred again. Replays were inconclusive. Morneau returned to the plate and flied out.

July 31 — As part of a four-team trade, the Twins send Doug Mientiewicz to the Red Sox and receive minor league pitcher Justin Jones from the Cubs. The Expos were also involved in the transaction, which also included Nomar Garciaparra (who went from the Red Sox to the Cubs) and Orlando Cabrera (Expos to Red Sox).

Mientiewicz would catch the last out of the 2004 World Series, which gave the Red Sox their first world championship since 1918. He played for six teams between 2004 and 2009. Mientiewicz was dealt to clear room in the starting line-up for Justin Morneau. Justin Jones has yet to reach the major leagues.

August 1 — Johan Santana (eight innings) and Joe Nathan (one inning) combine to allow only two hits in a 4–3 win over the Red Sox at the Metrodome. Santana struck out 11. He allowed home runs to Orlando Cabrera in the first inning and Manny Ramirez in the fourth. Boston scored a run without a hit in the seventh to take a 3–2 advantage. The Twins responded with two tallies in the eighth for the win.

August 2 — Carlos Silva allows 11 hits and walks two but beats the Angels 10–0 at the Metrodome.

August 8 — The Twins lose 6–5 in 18 innings to the Athletics at the Metrodome. The Twins tied the score 3–3 with a run in the eighth, and there was no more scoring until the 18th. J. C. Romero (two innings), Aaron Fultz (one inning), Jesse Crain (one inning), Joe Nathan (one inning) and Joe Roa (five innings) combined for ten innings of shutout ball while allowing only three hits from the seventh through the 17th. In the 18th, the A's scored three off Terry Mulholland. Justin Morneau hit a two-run homer in the bottom half with no one out, but the Twins couldn't dent the plate again.

Romero pitched 36 consecutive scoreless innings over 32 relief appearances from June 26 through September 11.

August 12 — Joe Nathan strikes out all three batters he faces in the ninth inning to close out a 6–3 win over the Mariners in Seattle.

Nathan struck out seven batters in a row over three appearances on August 7, 8 and 12.

August 15 — Corey Koskie hits a two-run homer in the tenth inning to defeat the Indians 4–2 in Cleveland.

The Twins swept a three-game series from the Indians at the Metrodome on August 20, 21 and 22 to stretch their league lead from four games to seven. The Twins were never seriously threatened again and cruised to the AL Central pennant.

August 31 — Torii Hunter hits a three-run walk-off homer in the 11th inning to defeat the Rangers 8–5 at the Metrodome.

On the same day, the Twins traded B. J. Garbe to the Mariners for Pat Borders.

September 1	The Twins start a battery of 41-year-olds in pitcher Terry Mulholland and catcher Pat Borders for a game against the Rangers at the Metrodome. The Twins won 4–2 with three runs in the eighth. Making his major league debut, Terry Tiffee hit a two-run double that broke the 2–2 tie.
September 3	Johan Santana (seven innings), J. C. Romero (one inning) and Joe Nathan (one inning) combine on a two-hitter to defeat the Royals 2–0 at the Metrodome. Santana had a no-hitter in progress until Desi Relaford singled leading off the seventh. Santana also fanned 11. Romero allowed a single to David DeJesus in the eighth. The only two runs of the game scored on back-to-back homers by Torii Hunter and Justin Morneau off Darrell May in the sixth inning.

The 2002, 2003 and 2004 seasons are the only time the franchise has had three consecutive seasons of 90 or more wins since the Washington Senators did it four years in a row from 1930 through 1933.

September 4	Third baseman Terry Tiffee hits a walk-off homer in the ninth inning to defeat the Royals 4–3 at the Metrodome. It was Tiffee's first career homer, and it came in his fourth game and 13th at-bat.
September 8	The Twins score seven runs in the second inning and defeat the Orioles 9–0 in Baltimore. Johan Santana (seven innings), Juan Rincon (one inning) and J. D. Durbin (one inning) combined on the shutout. It was Durbin's major league debut.
September 14	The Twins break a scoreless tie with nine runs in the sixth inning and beat the White Sox 10–2 at the Metrodome.

The Twins finished the 2004 season leading the league in earned run average. It was the first time the franchise had accomplished the feat since 1945 when it was located in Washington.

September 19	Johan Santana strikes out 14 batters in eight innings during a 5–1 defeat of the Orioles at the Metrodome.

The success of Santana in 2004 caused another pitcher named Johan Santana to change his name. Then a pitcher in the Angels minor league system, the other Johan Santana changed his name to Erwin. Erwin Santana reached the majors in 2005.

September 20	The Twins clinch the AL Central title with an 8–2 victory over the White Sox in Chicago.

At the time, the Twins were 88–62 and had a half-game lead over the Athletics for the second best record among the three division winners, earning Minnesota home field advantage in the first round of the playoffs. The Twins lost eight of their last 12 games, however, and had to start the playoffs on the road.

September 24	Johan Santana records his 20th win of the season with an 8–2 decision over the Indians in Cleveland. It was also his 13th victory in a row.

October 2   Needing two wins in their last two games to capture home-field advantage in the first round of the playoffs, the Twins begin the second-to-last contest of the season at the Metrodome at 11:10 a.m. against the Indians to accommodate a football game between the University of Minnesota and Penn State University scheduled for 7:00 p.m. It was agreed beforehand that no inning could start after 2:30 p.m. The game was suspended after 11 innings with the score 5–5 and completed the following day.

October 3   The Twins lose home-field advantage in the first round of the playoffs on the final day of the season. The Twins kept their hopes alive by a 12-inning, 6–5 win over the Indians in the completion of the contest from the previous innings, which was stopped after 11 innings with the score 5–5. Michael Cuddyer drove in the winning run with a double. But in the regularly scheduled game, the Twins lost 5–2 to Cleveland. The defeat forced the Twins to open the playoffs on the road against the Yankees instead of at home versus the Red Sox.

> *Managed by Joe Torre, the Yankees were 101–61 in 2004. Counting the 2003 postseason, the Twins were 3–20 against the Yankees in 2002, 2003 and 2004 heading into the playoffs.*

October 5   The Twins open the Division Series by defeating the Yankees 2–0 at Yankee Stadium. Shannon Stewart drove in the first run with a single in the third inning. Jacque Jones added a solo homer in the sixth. Johan Santana, who came into the contest with a 13-game winning streak, pitched seven scoreless innings despite giving up nine hits. Juan Rincon pitched the eighth and Joe Nathan the ninth. The Twins defense bailed out the pitchers with five double plays.

> *The national television announcers were Joe Buck and Tim McCarver (game one on FOX), Jon Miller and Joe Morgan (games two and three on ESPN) and Josh Lewin and Steve Lyons (game four on FOX).*

October 6   In game two, the Twins lose 7–6 in 12 innings to the Yankees in New York. The Twins took a 3–1 lead with two runs in the second inning, but the Yanks tied the contest 3–3 in the third and added runs in the fifth and seventh to move ahead 5–3. In the eighth, the Twins added two runs to tie the game again. Torii Hunter homered in the top of the 12th to give the Twins a 6–5 lead. It was Hunter's third hit and third run scored of the game. The Twins were three outs away from taking a two-games-to-none lead in the best-of-five series with two games coming up at the Metrodome. But in the bottom of the 12th, Joe Nathan, in his third inning of work, allowed two walks and an Alex Rodriguez double to tie the score 6–6. After J. C. Romero relieved, Hideki Matsui hit a game-ending sacrifice fly.

October 8   The Yankees defeat the Twins 8–4 before 54,803 at the Metrodome to take a two-games-to-one lead. Jacque Jones homered in the first inning for a 1–0 lead, but the Yanks added three runs in the second inning on five straight singles off Carlos Silva with two out and put the game away with four in the sixth. Christian Guzman collected three hits in the losing cause.

October 9   After taking a 5–1 lead, the Twins blow the game and the series, losing 6–5 to the Yankees in 11 innings before 52,498 at the Metrodome. Minnesota took a 5–1 lead in the fifth with three runs, the first coming on a solo homer by Henry Blanco.

Johan Santana, on three days' rest, pitched five innings and allowed a run. New York scored four in the eighth off Juan Rincon to tie the score, the last three on a home run by Ruben Sierra. The Yanks scored in the 11th on a double by Alex Rodriguez, a stolen base and a wild pitch by Kyle Lohse.

The Yankees took a three-games-to-none lead over the Red Sox in the Championship Series and then lost four in a row as Boston advanced to the World Series, where they won four straight over the Cardinals for their first world championship since 1918.

NOVEMBER 16 — Two weeks after George W. Bush defeats John Kerry in the Presidential election, Christian Guzman signs as a free agent with the Nationals.

NOVEMBER 17 — Pat Borders signs as a free agent with the Brewers.

DECEMBER 14 — Corey Koskie signs as a free agent with the Blue Jays.

2005

Season in a Sentence
The Twins are favored to win their fourth straight division title but score fewer runs than any other team in the AL and finish a distant third.

Finish • Won • Lost • Pct • GB
Third 83 79 .512 16.0

In the wild card race, the Twins finished in fourth place, 12 games behind.

Manager
Ron Gardenhire

Stats	Twins •	AL •	Rank
Batting Avg:	.259	.268	13
On-Base Pct:	.323	.330	10
Slugging Pct:	.391	.424	13
Home Runs:	134		12
Stolen Bases:	102		4
ERA:	3.71	4.35	5
Errors:	102		7
Runs Scored:	688		14
Runs Allowed:	662		5

Starting Line-up
Joe Mauer, c
Justin Morneau, 1b
Nick Punto, 2b
Michael Cuddyer, 3b
Jason Bartlett, ss
Shannon Stewart, lf
Torii Hunter, cf
Jacque Jones, rf
Lew Ford, dh-cf
Matt LeCroy, dh
Juan Castro, ss

Pitchers
Johan Santana, sp
Brad Radke, sp
Carlos Silva, sp
Kyle Lohse, sp
Joe Mays, sp
Joe Nathan, rp
Jesse Crain, rp
Juan Rincon, rp
Terry Mulholland, rp
J. C. Romero, rp
Matt Guerrier, rp

Attendance
2,034,243 (ninth in AL)

Club Leaders
Batting Avg:	Joe Mauer	.294
On-Base Pct:	Joe Mauer	.372
Slugging Pct:	Jacque Jones	.438
Home Runs:	Jacque Jones	23
RBI:	Justin Morneau	79
Runs:	Jacque Jones	74
Stolen Bases:	Torii Hunter	23
Wins:	Johan Santana	16
Strikeouts:	Johan Santana	238
ERA:	Johan Santana	2.37
Saves:	Joe Nathan	43

JANUARY 19   Jose Offerman signs as a free agent with the Phillies.

MARCH 27   Twins public address announcer Bob Casey dies at the age of 79. He had been battling liver cancer and pneumonia.

Casey was the Twins announcer from the time the team moved to Minnesota in 1961 through the end of the 2004 season, a total of more than 3,000 games. He had previously worked as the announcer for the Class AAA Minneapolis Millers in the American Association for ten years. Casey also worked the games for the Minneapolis Lakers and Minnesota Vikings. Among the pallbearers at his funeral were former Twins players Tony Oliva, Kent Hrbek and Jack Morris. The home opener on April 8 was dedicated to Casey. There was an on-field tribute before the game and members of the Casey family shared PA duties during the game. The new PA announcer was Bob Kurtz, who had handled the radio play-by-play duties for the Twins from 1979 through 1986 and also did play-by-play for the Minnesota North Stars and the Minnesota Wild.

APRIL 4   The Twins open the season with a 5–1 loss to the Mariners at Safeco Field. In his debut with the Mariners, Richie Sexson hit two homers and drove in all five Seattle runs.

Brad Radke was the starting pitcher, and gave up five runs in seven innings. Radke made the Opening Day start in nine of ten seasons from 1996 through 2005, missing only in 1998 when Bob Tewksbury took the assignment.

APRIL 5   Trailing 4–0, the Twins break loose for seven runs in the fifth inning and down the Mariners 8–4 in Seattle. Seven of the first eight batters in the inning hit singles before Jacque Jones capped the rally with a two-run homer.

APRIL 8   In the home opener, the Twins lose 5–1 to the White Sox before 48,764 at the Metrodome.

APRIL 21   The Twins score a run in the ninth and another in the tenth to outlast the Royals 10–9 at the Metrodome. Joe Nathan struck out all three batters he faced in the top of the tenth.

APRIL 23   The Twins-Tigers game in Detroit is postponed by snow.

APRIL 26   The Twins and Hennepin County announce that a deal has been reached for a new stadium for the club. The Twins would pay about a third of the $375 million needed for construction, with the rest coming from a 0.15 percent county sales tax. The location for the 40,000-seat ballpark was in the Warehouse District north of downtown Minneapolis between 5th and 7th Streets near the Target Center.

There were still few hurdles before the deal was finalized. It took until June 20, 2006, for the Hennepin County Board and the Minnesota legislature to approve the plan. A dispute also arose between the County and the Burlington Northern Santa Fe Railroad, which owned the site. That was settled until May 1, 2007. Work on the ballpark began on May 21, with the official groundbreaking taking place on August 30. The groundbreaking ceremonies had been scheduled for August 2, but were delayed because of the I-35W Bridge collapse. The first concrete slab was poured on December 17. The Target Corporation acquired the naming rights to the ballpark on September 15, 2008, which opened in 2010 as Target Field.

MAY 1   Johan Santana (eight innings) and Juan Rincon (one inning) combine on a two-hitter, but the Twins lose 2–1 to the Angels at the Metrodome. Both Los Angeles hits were home runs by Jose Molina in the fourth inning and Vladimir Guerrero in the sixth. The lone Minnesota run came on a home run by Shannon Stewart in the ninth.

Santana entered the game with a 17-game winning streak over two seasons. He won his last 13 decisions in 2004 and the first four in 2005. Counting three no-decision games, Santana hadn't lost in 20 consecutive starts. He had another streak of 20 consecutive starts without a loss in 2003 and 2004, with ten wins and ten no decisions. Santana finished the season with a 16–7 record, a 2.87 ERA, and a league-leading 238 strikeouts in 231 2/3 innings. From 2003 through 2006, Santana had a won-lost record of 67–22.

MAY 5   On 5/5/05, the Twins score five runs in the fifth inning and defeat the Royals 9–0 at the Metrodome. Brad Radke pitched a three-hit shutout.

MAY 10   With no one out in the tenth inning, Jacque Jones and Shannon Stewart hit back-to-back pitches for home runs to defeat the Orioles 6–4 in Baltimore.

MAY 20   Carlos Silva throws only 74 pitches in a 7–1 complete game victory over the Brewers at the Metrodome.

Silva walked only nine batters in 188 1/3 innings in 2005. His 0.43 walks per nine innings broke the major league record among those who pitched at least 162 innings in a season since the 60 foot, six inch pitching distance was established in 1893. The previous mark was 0.62, shared by Christy Mathewson of the New York Giants in 1913 and Babe Adams of the Pittsburgh Pirates in 1920. The next best mark to Silva since 1930 is Bob Tewksbury with the Cardinals in 1992 and Greg Maddux with the Braves in 1997. Both walked 0.77 batters per nine innings. Silva had much less overall success than the four aforementioned hurlers, however. Mathewson was 25–11 with a 2.06 earned run average in 306 innings in 1913. Adams was 17–13 in 1920 and had an ERA of 2.16 in 263 innings. During the 1992 campaign, Tewksbury was 16–5 with an ERA of 2.16 in 233 innings. Maddux had an ERA of 2.20 in 1997 and a record of 19–4 in 232 2/3 innings. Silva was 9–12 in 2005 accompanied by an ERA of 3.44. The following year, he posted a record of 11–15, and his ERA skyrocketed to 5.94 when he walked 32 and gave up a league-leading 38 home runs in 180 1/3 innings.

MAY 22   The Twins score three runs in the ninth inning and one in the 11th to stun the Brewers 6–5 at the Metrodome. Jacque Jones started the ninth with a single and scored on a double from Lew Ford. After the next two hitters were retired, Shannon Stewart homered to tie the score at 5–5. Ford led off the 11th with a triple, and after two intentional walks, crossed the plate on an error. Twins pitchers combined to strike out 17 batters. Johan Santana set down 11 on strikes in seven innings with relievers Juan Rincon (two), Joe Nathan (one), J. C. Romero (one) and Jesse Crain (two) adding the remainder.

MAY 24	Justin Morneau hits a three-run double with two out in the 11th to defeat the Indians 6–3 in Cleveland.
MAY 26	Shannon Stewart homers in the 11th inning to down the Indians 3–2 in Cleveland. It was the Twins third consecutive extra-inning game, each of them against the Indians in Cleveland, and the fourth in a span of five games.
JUNE 1	Torii Hunter drives in all six Twins runs and collects five hits in five at-bats during a 6–2 triumph over the Indians at the Metrodome. The five hits were a home run, two doubles and two singles. Hunter hit a grand slam off Cliff Lee in the third inning and a two-run double with the bases loaded in the sixth while facing Rafael Betancourt.

In six games from June 1 through June 7, Hunter collected 15 hits in 26 at-bats. The 15 hits were three homers, four doubles and eight singles.

JUNE 2	Twins pitchers combine to strike out 18 batters during a 13-inning, 4–3 victory over the Indians at the Metrodome. Johan Santana fanned 14 in eight innings. Relievers Joe Nathan and Jesse Crain struck out one each, and J. C. Romero two. Jacque Jones drove in the winning run with a single.
JUNE 7	Torii Hunter collects four hits on two homers, a double and a single in five at-bats and scores four runs during a 9–8 win over the Diamondbacks in Phoenix.

On the same day, the Twins selected pitcher Matt Garza from Fresno State University in the first round of the amateur draft. Garza made his major league debut in 2006 and played two seasons with the Twins before being traded to Tampa Bay. Kevin Slowey was chosen in the second round and has become one of the team's best starting pitchers.

JUNE 8	The Twins lambaste the Diamondbacks 10–0 in Phoenix. Johan Santana pitched the shutout for his 15th consecutive victory on the road dating back to 2004.

The win represented the peak juncture of the season. The Twins were 35–22 and in second place, four games back of the White Sox. Minnesota was 48–57 the rest of the way.

JUNE 10	The Twins play the Dodgers for the first time during the regular season and lose 6–5 in Los Angeles. Terry Mulholland came in to pitch the ninth, and on his first offering allowed a walk-off homer to Hee Seop Choi. The last 21 Twins batters were retired by four Dodgers pitchers.
JUNE 12	Brad Radke gives up four solo homers, three of them to Hee Seop Choi, to lose 4–3 to the Dodgers in Los Angeles. Choi homered in the first, fourth and sixth innings. J. D. Drew also homered in the fourth.
JUNE 14	The Twins play the Giants at the Metrodome for the first time during the regular season and win 4–3 in 11 innings. Shannon Stewart drove in the winning run with a single.
JUNE 17	The Twins play the Padres for the first time during the regular season and win 5–4 in 11 innings. Glenn Williams drove in the winning run with a single, which accounted

for his first major league RBI. He entered the game in the tenth inning as a third baseman.

> *A native of Australia, Williams was originally signed by the Braves organization at the age of 16. He played 13 big league games during his career, all with the Twins in 2005 and had at least one hit in each of the 13 for a total of 17 hits in 40 at-bats for a lifetime average of .425. As a minor leaguer from 1994 through 2007, Williams hit only .245, however, which explains his short stint in the majors despite an impressive batting average.*

JULY 1 — Jesse Crain runs his season record to 8–0 and career record to 11–0 when he is the winning pitcher in a 7–4 decision over the Devil Rays at the Metrodome.

> *Crain's 11–0 record at the start of a career is the major league record for relief pitchers. On July 1, 2005, he had a 1.65 ERA in 60 games and 65⅓ innings. Crain's first loss came on July 9 when he failed to retire any of the four batters he faced in the sixth inning and the Twins lost 12–8 to the Royals in Kansas City.*

JULY 11 — The Twins purchase Bret Boone from the Mariners.

JULY 19 — The Twins score two runs with two out in the ninth inning to defeat the Orioles 4–3 at the Metrodome. Jacque Jones drove in the winning run with a single.

JULY 20 — Jacque Jones delivers a walk-off hit for the second game in a row with a home run to defeat the Orioles 3–2 at the Metrodome.

JULY 29 — Torii Hunter breaks his ankle and tears ligaments after he tries to scale the right field wall at Fenway Park during an 8–5 loss to the Red Sox. Hunter attempted to catch a drive by David Ortiz in the first inning.

> *It was a season of tough—and sometimes unusual—injuries. The most bizarre injury of the year was suffered by Jason Bartlett when he tore the nail off his left pinkie while sliding his hand under the TV set in his room at the Ritz-Carlton hotel in Detroit. Justin Morneau was in a weakened condition for much of the season after contracting chicken pox, pneumonia and having his appendix removed during the 2004–05 off-season.*

AUGUST 5 — The Twins trounce the Red Sox 12–0 at the Metrodome. Brad Radke (seven innings), Terry Mulholland (one inning) and Matt Guerrier (one inning) combined on the shutout.

AUGUST 10 — The Twins bust loose for four runs in the 14th inning to beat the Mariners 7–3 in Seattle.

AUGUST 12 — The Twins edge the Athletics 1–0 in Oakland. Johan Santana and Dan Haren each pitched complete game three-hitters. The lone run scored in the fifth inning when Lew Ford walked, stole second, and scored on a single by Michael Cuddyer.

AUGUST 16 — The Twins score five runs in the 16th inning to defeat the White Sox 9–4 in Chicago. The Twins collected 20 hits during the contest. Joe Nathan pitched the bottom of the 16th, and struck out all three batters he faced.

August 23	The Twins collect only one hit but beat the White Sox 1–0 at the Metrodome. Freddy Garcia had a no-hitter in progress until Jacque Jones led off the eighth inning with a home run. Johan Santana (eight innings) and Joe Nathan (one inning) combined on a three-hit shutout.
	Garcia and Santana are both natives of Venezuela.
August 27	The Twins score five runs in the 11th inning and beat the Rangers 7–2 in Arlington. Jacque Jones broke the 2–2 tie with a two-run homer.
August 31	Two days after Hurricane Katrina strikes the Gulf Coast, resulting in the flooding of New Orleans, the Twins collect 13 hits off three Royals pitchers but lose 1–0 in Kansas City.
September 7	After falling behind 5–0, the Twins score four runs in the fourth inning and four more in the sixth and defeat the Rangers 8–6 at the Metrodome.
September 17	Johan Santana and Joe Nathan combine for 16 strikeouts during a 5–0 victory over the White Sox at the Metrodome. Santana fanned 13 in eight innings. Nathan struck out all three batters he faced in the ninth.
September 21	Michael Cuddyer ties the Twins record for most extra-base hits in a game with four during a 10–4 triumph over the Athletics in Oakland. Cuddyer homered off Joe Kennedy in the second inning and doubled against Kennedy in the third, Juan Cruz in the fifth and Jay Witasick in the sixth. In his fifth plate appearance in the eighth, Cuddyer was given an intentional walk.
September 30	Justin Morneau hits a grand slam off Jamie Walker in the eighth inning of a 7–3 win over the Tigers at the Metrodome.
December 2	The Twins trade Scott Tyler and Travis Bowyer to the Marlins for Luis Castillo.
December 15	The Twins sign Tony Batista as a free agent.
December 22	The Twins sign Rondell White, most recently with the Tigers, as a free agent.

2006

Season in a Sentence

With the help of an MVP (Justin Morneau), a batting champion (Joe Mauer) and a Cy Young Award winner (Johan Santana), the Twins win their fourth AL Central crown in five years, overcoming a slow start (25–33) and a 12-game deficit (on July 13).

Finish • Won • Lost • Pct • GB

Finish   96   66   .593   +1.0

AL Division Series

The Twins lost to the Oakland Athletics three games to none.

Manager

Rod Gardenhire

Stats

Stats	Twins	AL	Rank
Batting Avg:	.287	.275	1
On-Base Pct:	.347	.339	5
Slugging Pct:	.425	.439	8
Home Runs:	143		13
Stolen Bases:	101		6
ERA:	3.95	4.56	2
Errors:	84		2
Runs Scored:	801		8
Runs Allowed:	683		2

Starting Line-up

Joe Mauer, c
Justin Morneau, 1b
Luis Castillo, 2b
Nick Punto, 3b
Jason Bartlett, ss
Lew Ford, lf-rf
Torii Hunter, cf
Michael Cuddyer, rf
Rondell White, dh-lf
Jason Kubel, dh-lf
Jason Tyner, lf-cf

Pitchers

Johan Santana, sp
Brad Radke, sp
Carlos Silva, sp
Francisco Liriano, sp
Boof Bonser, sp
Scott Baker, sp
Joe Nathan, rp
Jesse Crain, rp
Juan Rincon, rp
Willie Eyre, rp
Dennys Reyes, rp

Attendance

2,285.018 (ninth in AL)

Club Leaders

Batting Avg:	Joe Mauer	.347
On-Base Pct:	Joe Mauer	.429
Slugging Pct:	Justin Morneau	.559
Home Runs:	Justin Morneau	34
RBI:	Justin Morneau	130
Runs:	Michael Cuddyer	102
Stolen Bases:	Luis Castillo	25
Wins:	Johan Santana	19
Strikeouts:	Johan Santana	245
ERA:	Johan Santana	2.77
Saves:	Joe Nathan	36

January 3   Joe Mays signs with the Royals as a free agent.

January 10   Jacque Jones signs with the Cubs as a free agent.

January 12   Terry Mulholland signs with the Diamondbacks as a free agent.

January 31   The Twins sign Ruben Sierra, most recently with the Yankees, as a free agent.

February 8   Matt LeCroy signs with the Nationals as a free agent.

February 21   The Twins sign Dennys Reyes, most recently with the Padres, as a free agent.

> *Reyes came to the Twins as a 29-year-old with a 22–31 career record and a 4.80 ERA. But in 2006, he was 5–0 and had a minuscule 0.89 earned run average in 66 games and 50 2/3 innings. Reyes continued to pitch for the club as a lefty specialist in 2007 and 2008.*

MARCH 6   Kirby Puckett dies just eight days shy of his 46th birthday from complications from a stroke suffered the previous day at his home in Scottsdale, Arizona. Many, including former teammates Shane Mack and Kent Hrbek, flew to Scottsdale to be with Puckett during his final hours. At the time of his death, Puckett was engaged to Judi Olson with an expected wedding date of June 24. A private memorial service was held in the Twin Cities suburb of Wayzata on March 12, which was declared "Kirby Puckett Day" in Minneapolis. On the same day, approximately 15,000 attended a public service in honor of Puckett.

APRIL 4   The Twins open the season with a 6–3 loss to the Blue Jays in Toronto. Johan Santana was the starting pitcher and took the loss. Shannon Stewart and Tony Batista homered in the losing cause. It was Batista's first game as a member of the Twins.

APRIL 5   After falling behind 4–0 in the third inning, the Twins rout the Blue Jays 13–4 in Toronto. Torii Hunter hit a homer, a double and two singles and drove in six runs, four of them on a grand slam off Jason Frasor in the eighth.

APRIL 11   In the home opener, the Twins erase a 4–0 deficit with six runs in the third inning and defeat the Athletics 7–6 before 48,911 at the Metrodome. In his first home game with the club, Tony Batista put the Twins into the lead with a three-run homer. Justin Morneau also homered.

APRIL 15   Justin Morneau hits a two-run, walk-off single off Mariano Rivera with two out in the ninth inning to beat the Yankees 6–5 at the Metrodome.

APRIL 19   Michael Cuddyer hits a two-run, pinch-hit, walk-off homer in the tenth inning to defeat the Angels 12–10 at the Metrodome. The Angels led 9–4 in the sixth inning before the Twins rallied. The score was tied 10–10 when Lew Ford drew a walk on a 3–2 pitch from Francisco Rodriguez with the bases loaded and two out in the ninth.

APRIL 29   The Tigers clobber the Twins 18–1 during an afternoon game in Detroit. Combined with a 9–0 win the previous evening, the Tigers outscored the Twins 27–1 in a span of less than 24 hours.

MAY 6   The Twins score two runs in the ninth inning to defeat the Tigers 7–6 at the Metrodome. Shannon Stewart tripled in the tying run and scored on a walk-off single from Luis Castillo.

MAY 9   Justin Morneau drives in six runs with two homers and a single during a 15–5 thrashing of the Rangers in Arlington.

> *Morneau won the MVP award in 2006 by batting .321 with 34 homers and 130 RBIs.*

MAY 14   The Twins score seven runs in the first inning off Mark Buehrle to take a 7–3 lead, but wind up losing 9–7 to the White Sox at the Metrodome. Luis Castillo hit into a triple play in the sixth inning. With Nick Punto on second and Shannon Stewart on first, Castillo popped a bunt into the air that was caught by first baseman Paul Konerko. Moving with the pitch, Punto and Stewart were unable to return to their respective bases in time.

MAY 17   Johan Santana strikes out 12 batters in eight innings but takes a 2–0 loss against the Tigers in Detroit.

> *Santana was the unanimous choice for the Cy Young Award in 2006 by posting a 19–6 record. He led the AL in wins, ERA (2.77), games started (34), innings (233 1/3) and strikeouts (245). It was the third straight season that Santana topped the league in strikeouts. He also became the first pitcher to win the Triple Crown by leading a league in wins, strikeouts and ERA since Dwight Gooden did it with the Mets in 1985.*

MAY 19   Tony Batista hits a grand slam off Jose Capellan in the eighth inning of a 7–1 victory over the Brewers in Milwaukee.

Justin Morneau won the MVP award in 2006, when he established himself as one of the most feared power hitters in the league.

The Twins had trouble finding consistent production in left field in 2006. Rondell White was the team leader in games started at the position with 37.

MAY 20　The Twins score six runs in the first inning and outslug the Brewers 16–10 in Milwaukee.

White Sox manager Ozzie Guillen dubbed the Twins the "Little Piranhas" in reference to the many fleet-footed players who lacked power in the club's line-up in 2006. The Twins led the AL in singles (1,156) but were last in extra base hits (442). T-shirts bearing the name "Little Piranhas" were printed and marketed.

MAY 23　Joe Nathan strikes out five of the six batters he faces in a ten-inning, 6–5 win over the Indians at the Metrodome. Nathan pitched the ninth and tenth. Justin Morneau drove in the game-winner with a sacrifice fly.

Nathan was 7–0 with 36 saves and a 1.58 ERA in 64 games and 68 1/3 innings in 2006.

MAY 27　The Twins pull off a triple play in the eighth inning of a 9–5 win over the Mariners in Seattle. With the bases loaded, Juan Rincon entered the game in relief to face Kenji Johjima. On the first pitch, Johjima grounded to second baseman Luis Castillo, who tagged out Adrian Beltre and threw to first baseman Justin Morneau to retire Johjima for the second out. Morneau noticed Carl Everett leaning the wrong way off third base, and fired to third baseman Tony Batista, who tagged out Everett to complete the triple play. Richie Sexson, who started the play as the base runner on third, scored a run. It was the first Twins triple play since the club set a major league record with two in one game on July 17, 1990.

MAY 28　After fouling off four two-strike pitches from Eddie Guardado, Lew Ford hits a walk-off homer in the tenth inning to defeat the Mariners 4–3 at the Metrodome.

MAY 31　Joe Nathan strikes out all three batters he faces in the ninth inning of a 7–1 win over the Angels in Anaheim.

JUNE 2　Johan Santana (eight innings) and Joe Nathan (one inning) combine on a two-hitter to defeat the Athletics 2–1 in Oakland. The only hits off Santana were a home run by Frank Thomas and a single from Bobby Kielty, both in the second inning. Santana (19) and Nathan (3) combined to retire the final 22 A's batters.

JUNE 6　In the first round of the amateur draft, the Twins select outfielder Christopher Parmelee from Chino Hills High School in Chino Hills, California.

JUNE 7　The Twins lose 10–9 in 11 innings to the Mariners in Seattle. The Twins scored five runs in the eighth inning, the last four on a grand slam by Michael Cuddyer off Rafael Soriano, to tie the score 9–9.

With the loss, the Twins fell to 25–33 on the season. The club was in fourth place, 11 1/2 games behind the Tigers. Over the remainder of the season, the Twins posted a record of 71–33. The 96 wins were the most by a Minnesota team since 1970.

2000s

JUNE 9   Justin Morneau drives in five runs with a three-run homer in the fourth inning and a two-run walk-off homer in the 12th to lead the Twins to a 7–5 win over the Orioles at the Metrodome.

JUNE 10   Michael Cuddyer hits a grand slam off Jon Halama in the eighth inning of a 9–7 loss to the Orioles at the Metrodome. It was Cuddyer's second grand slam in four days, although both came in defeats.

> *Joe Mauer reached base four times in five consecutive games from June 6 through June 10. During that span he collected 14 hits in 20 at-bats. Including six walks, Mauer reached base in 20 of 26 plate appearances. He finished the season with a .347 batting average to become the first catcher to lead the American League in batting average. He was also the first catcher to lead the majors in batting. The only other catchers to lead a league in batting were Bubbles Hargrave of the Reds (.353 in 1926) and Ernie Lombardi, who did it with the Reds (.342 in 1938) and with the Braves (.330 in 1942). Lombardi's first title is the only one of three that would have been granted under today's rules, however. Under the rules in effect since 1957, Hargrave and Lombardi would have needed 477 plate appearances to qualify for a batting title. Hargrave had 365 in 1926, and Lombardi had 529 in 1938 and 347 in 1942. Mauer became the second catcher to win two batting titles with a .328 average in 2008 and the first to win three by hitting .365 in 2009, the latter being the highest batting average achieved by a catcher in major league history. The previous record was .362 by Mike Piazza with the Dodgers in 1997.*

JUNE 13   After the Red Sox score in the top of the 12th for a 2–1 lead, the Twins load the bases in the bottom half and Jason Kubel hits a walk-off grand slam for a 5–2 victory at the Metrodome. Johan Santana struck out 13 without walking a batter in eight innings.

JUNE 14   Justin Morneau hits a grand slam off Manny Delcarmen in the eighth inning of an 8–1 triumph over the Red Sox at the Metrodome. It was the fourth slam by a Twins player in a span of eight days.

JUNE 16   The Twins play at PNC Park in Pittsburgh for the first time and beat the Pirates 4–2.

JUNE 20   The Twins extend their winning streak to eight games with a ten-inning 6–5 win over the Astros in Houston. Justin Morneau led off the tenth with a home run to provide the margin of victory.

JUNE 22   In a starting pitching match-up between 43-year-old Roger Clemens and 22-year-old Francisco Liriano, the Twins win 4–2 in Houston. It was also the first time that Clemens pitched in 2006. He came into the contest with 341 career wins.

> *In his first full year in the majors, Liriano was 12–3 with a 2.16 ERA in 121 1/3 innings and was a member of the American League All-Star team. He made 16 starts and 12 relief appearances but developed elbow trouble late in the season. With the exception of a two-inning appearance on September 13, he didn't pitch after August 7. He would miss the entire 2007 season and didn't make a big league appearance in 2008 until August.*

June 26	The Twins play the Dodgers for the first time at the Metrodome and win 8–2.
June 27	Joe Mauer collects five hits in five at-bats during a 9–2 win over the Dodgers at the Metrodome.
June 28	Torii Hunter hits a grand slam off Odalis Perez in the first inning of a 6–3 win over the Dodgers at the Metrodome.
July 2	Francisco Liriano strikes out 12 batters in eight innings during an 8–0 win over the Brewers at the Metrodome. It was Minnesota's tenth win in a row, and the 13th straight victory at the Metrodome.
July 3	The Twins extend their winning streak to 11 games with a 6–5 decision over the Royals in Kansas City.

On July 13, the Twins had a 47–40 record and were in third place, 12 games behind the Tigers. In the wild card race, the Twins were in fourth, 9½ games behind the leading White Sox.

July 16	Both teams lead off the first inning with home runs in a 5–2 Twins victory over the Indians at the Metrodome. Grady Sizemore started the game with a homer off Carlos Silva. Luis Castillo countered by beginning the Minnesota first with a home run against Jeremy Sowers.
July 21	The Twins extend their winning streak to eight games with a 14–6 decision over the Indians in Cleveland. Eight runs scored in the fourth inning, highlighted by a three-run double from Michael Cuddyer.

Cuddyer hit .284 with 24 homers and 109 RBIs in 2006.

July 23	Five Twins pitchers combine for 17 strikeouts during a 3–1 victory over the Indians in Cleveland. The strikeouts were recorded by Francisco Liriano (ten in five innings), Pat Neshek (two in 1⅔ innings), Dennys Reyes (two in two-third of an inning), Juan Rincon (one in two-thirds of an inning) and Joe Nathan (two in one inning).

The Twins had a record of 34–8 from June 8 through July 26.

July 28	Francisco Liriano strikes out 12 batters in eight innings, but the Twins lose 3–2 in ten inning to the Tigers at the Metrodome.
July 31	Nick Punto collects four hits, including a triple, in four at-bats and scores four runs during a 15–2 pounding of the Rangers at the Metrodome.

On the same day, the Twins traded Kyle Lohse to the Reds for Zach Ward. Lohse was off to a poor start and had never shown the consistency that the team had expected after productive years in 2002 and 2003. After two mediocre years he bounced back in 2008 to win 15 games with a 3.78 ERA. Ward has never made it to the majors.

August 4	The Twins score two runs in the ninth inning and three in the tenth to defeat the Royals 8–5 in Kansas City. Joe Mauer and Michael Cuddyer began the ninth with back-to-back homers.

AUGUST 5	The Twins collect 22 hits and defeat the Royals 11–5 in Kansas City. The eighth and ninth hitters in the line-up had nine hits between them. Jason Tyner was four-for-five with four singles. Jason Bartlett had five hits, including two doubles, in five at-bats.

Tyner's middle name is Renyt, which is Tyner spelled backward.

AUGUST 9	With the Twins trailing 3–2 in the eighth inning, Justin Morneau hits his 30th homer of the season for a 4–3 win over the Tigers in Detroit.

Morneau became the first Twins batter to hit 30 homers in a season since 1987. That season, Kent Hrbek (34), Tom Brunansky (32) and Gary Gaetti (31) each reached the mark. From 1988 through 2005, every other team in the majors had at least three players with 30 or more homers. Nine teams had 20 or more 30-home run hitters.

AUGUST 31	The Twins send Adam Harbin and cash to the Cubs for Phil Nevin.
SEPTEMBER 3	During his pregame show prior to a contest against the Yankees in New York, television broadcaster Bert Blyleven twice uses an obscenity. He believed the segment was being taped and didn't realize his comments were going out on the airwaves live. Blyleven apologized in the first inning but was suspended by the network for five games.
SEPTEMBER 4	The Twins take the lead in the wild card race with a 4–1 win over the Devil Rays in St. Petersburg.
SEPTEMBER 5	Johan Santana strikes out 12 batters and allows only two hits in eight innings of an 8–0 win over the Devil Rays in St. Petersburg.
SEPTEMBER 10	The Twins rout the Tigers 12–1 at the Metrodome.

The Twins began the four-game series on September 7 four games behind the first-place Tigers. After dropping the opener, the Twins won three in a row to pull within two games of first.

SEPTEMBER 19	Justin Morneau collects five hits, including two doubles, in five at-bats during a 7–3 win over the Red Sox in Boston. The victory gave the Twins a 4½-game advantage in the wild card race with 12 left to play.
SEPTEMBER 25	The Twins clinch a playoff berth with an 8–1 win over the Royals at the Metrodome. There were six games left on the schedule, and the Twins were one game behind the Tigers in the AL Central race but were assured of at least a wild card berth.
SEPTEMBER 28	With a run in the ninth inning and another in the tenth, the Twins defeat the Royals 2–1 at the Metrodome and move into a tie for first place with the Tigers. Joe Mauer tied the score 1–1 with a home run with two out in the ninth. Jason Bartlett drove in the winning run with a single.

The win came in the 159th game of the season. It was the first time in major league history that a team took at least a share of first place for the first time that late in a season. Over the next two days, the Twins lost 4–3 and 6–3 to the White Sox at the Metrodome. Fortunately, the Tigers also lost twice to the Royals in Detroit, the first after blowing a five-run lead. Both the Twins and Tigers headed into the final game with identical records of 95–66. Since both teams had qualified for the playoffs, the Tigers would win the division championship if the two teams remained tied at the end of the regular season because of a lead in head-to-head competition (eleven wins to eight). In order to capture the AL Central crown, the Twins needed to win on October 1, the final game of the regular season and have the Tigers lose.

OCTOBER 1   The Twins beat the White Sox 5–1 at the Metrodome to clinch the AL Central title. After the game, players and fans watched the Royals-Tigers game from Detroit on the big screen at the ballpark. The Tigers held a 6–0 lead over the Royals after three innings but wound up losing 10–8 to the Royals in 12 innings.

The Twins were 12 games behind the Tigers on July 13 and were 9½ games out in the wild card race. Detroit still qualified as a wild card only three seasons after posting a record of 43–119. In the first round of the playoffs, the Tigers played the Yankees while the Twins squared off against the Athletics. Managed by Ken Macha, the A's were 93–69 in 2006.

OCTOBER 3   The Twins open the Division Series with a 3–2 loss to the Athletics before 55,542 at the Metrodome. The A's score twice off Johan Santana in the second inning, the first on a home run by Frank Thomas and held a 2–0 lead until Rondell White hit a solo homer in the seventh. Facing Jesse Crain, Thomas hit his second home run in the ninth before the Twins scored in the bottom half.

The national television announcers on ESPN were Jon Miller and Joe Morgan in game one and Dave O'Brien, Rick Sutcliffe and Eric Karros in games two and three.

OCTOBER 4   In game two, the Athletics beat the Twins 5–2 before 55,710 at the Metrodome. The only Minnesota scoring came in the sixth inning when Justin Morneau and Michael Cuddyer hit back-to-back homers that tied the score 2–2. In the seventh, Torii Hunter misplayed a drive by Mark Kotsay, and the ball went to the wall for a two-run, inside-the-park homer and a 4–2 Oakland advantage.

OCTOBER 6   The Athletics complete the sweep of the Twins with an 8–3 victory in Oakland. Justin Morneau and Torii Hunter homered, and Rondell White had three hits in the losing cause.

DECEMBER 13   The Twins sign Jeff Cirillo, most recently with the Brewers, as a free agent.

2007

Season in a Sentence
Hopes for another division title are dashed with the club's first losing season since 2000.

Finish • Won • Lost • Pct • GB
Third   79   83   .488   17.0

In the wild card race, the Twins finished in fifth place, 15 games behind.

Manager
Ron Gardenhire

Stats

Stats	Twins	AL	Rank
Batting Avg:	.264	.271	9
On-Base Pct:	.330	.338	10
Slugging Pct:	.391	.423	13
Home Runs:	118		13
Stolen Bases:	112		5
ERA:	4.15	4.50	4
Errors:	95		7
Runs Scored:	718		12
Runs Allowed:	663		5

Starting Line-up
Joe Mauer, c
Justin Morneau, 1b
Luis Castillo, 2b
Nick Punto, 3b
Jason Bartlett, ss
Jason Kubel, lf
Torii Hunter, cf
Michael Cuddyer, rf
Jeff Cirillo, dh-3b
Jason Tyner, lf-rf
Mike Redmond, c

Pitchers
Johan Santana, sp
Carlos Silva, sp
Boof Bonser, sp
Scott Baker, sp
Matt Garza, sp
Joe Nathan, rp
Matt Guerrier, rp
Pat Neshek, rp
Juan Rincon, rp

Attendance
2,296,383 (tenth in AL)

Club Leaders

Batting Avg:	Joe Mauer	.293
On-Base Pct:	Joe Mauer	.382
Slugging Pct:	Torii Hunter	.505
Home Runs:	Justin Morneau	31
RBI:	Justin Morneau	111
Runs:	Torii Hunter	94
Stolen Bases:	Jason Bartlett	23
Wins:	Johan Santana	15
Strikeouts:	Johan Santana	235
ERA:	Johan Santana	3.33
Saves:	Joe Nathan	37

JANUARY 17   The Twins sign Matt LeCroy, most recently with the Nationals, as a free agent.

FEBRUARY 8   Shannon Stewart signs with the Athletics as a free agent.

APRIL 1   Broadcaster Herb Carneal dies of heart failure at the age of 83. Carneal had been the Twins radio broadcaster since 1962 (see April 10, 1962). It was the third year in a row that a prominent figure in the Twins organization died during spring training, following Bob Casey in 2005 and Kirby Puckett in 2006.

APRIL 2   The Twins open the season with a 7–4 triumph over the Orioles before 48,711 at the Metrodome. Justin Morneau homered and collected two singles. Luis Castillo also had three hits, one of them a double. Torii Hunter had a home run and a double. Johan Santana pitched six innings for the win.

> *The victory was the 17th in a row for Santana at the Metrodome. The streak included four wins in 2005, 12 in 2006 and one in 2007. Santana also had a streak of 24 straight starts without a loss at the Metrodome, including seven no decisions. The Twins won all seven games of those games in which Santana did not figure in the decision.*

Following in the footsteps of long-time manager Tom Kelly wasn't easy, but Ron Gardenhire has made the Twins his own, continuing the team's success despite limited payrolls throughout the 2000s.

April 13   Johan Santana's streak of 24 consecutive starts without a loss at the Metrodome comes to an end with a 4–2 defeat at the hands of the Devil Rays.

Santana finished the season with a 15–13 record, a 3.33 ERA, and 235 strikeouts in 219 innings.

April 17   Torii Hunter hits a grand slam off Jeff Weaver in the third inning of an 11–2 win over the Angels in Anaheim.

April 21   Joe Nathan strikes out all three batters he faces in the ninth inning to close out a 7–5 win over the Royals in Kansas City.

Nathan had 37 saves, a 4–2 record, and a 1.88 ERA in 68 games and 71 2/3 innings in 2007.

April 26   The Twins edge the Royals 1–0 in 11 innings at the Metrodome. The lone run scored on consecutive singles in the 11th by Justin Morneau, Jason Tyner and Mike Redmond. Boof Bonser (five innings), Glen Perkins (two-thirds of an inning), Matt Guerrier (2 1/3 innings), Joe Nathan (two innings) and Juan Rincon (one inning) combined on the shutout. The quintet walked ten batters, seven of them by Bonser, but allowed only five hits.

MAY 8 Justin Morneau hits a three-run, walk-off homer in the 11th inning to defeat the White Sox 7–4 at the Metrodome.

Morneau batted .271 with 31 homers and 111 RBIs in 2007.

MAY 13 Torii Hunter drives in seven runs during a 16–4 thrashing of the Tigers at the Metrodome. Hunter belted a three-run homer in the first inning, a two-run double in the fourth, and a two-run homer in the seventh. He was lifted in the eighth for pinch-hitter Jason Tyner. Michael Cuddyer and Mike Redmond also homered. It was Redmond's first home run since 2005. The Twins had 22 hits in all.

MAY 15 The Twins collect four homers for the second game in a row but lose to the Indians 15–7 in Cleveland. Justin Morneau homered twice with Michael Cuddyer and Jason Kubel adding the other two.

The Twins had a revolving door at designated hitter again in 2007. Kubel led the club in games played at the position with only 34.

MAY 18 Torii Hunter hits a grand slam off Chris Capuano in the third inning of an 8–1 win over the Brewers in Milwaukee.

In his last season as a Twin, Hunter batted .287 with 28 home runs and 107 RBIs.

MAY 22 Twins pitchers combine for 18 strikeouts during a 7–1 win over the Rangers in Arlington. Johan Santana fanned 13 in seven innings. Pat Neshek followed with three strikeouts in the eighth. Joe Nathan struck out two in the ninth.

MAY 26 Michael Cuddyer drives in five runs with a homer and three singles, but the Twins lose 9–8 to the Blue Jays in 13 innings at the Metrodome. Toronto led 7–2 before the Twins scored two runs in the eighth inning and three in the ninth to tie the game 7–7. Both teams scored in the 11th.

MAY 27 The Twins collect only three hits, two of them by Justin Morneau, but beat the Blue Jays 4–2 at the Metrodome. With two out and the bases loaded in the third inning, Morneau hit a high chopper in front of the plate. Toronto pitcher A. J. Burnett fielded the ball and threw wildly past first, allowing two runs to score. In the sixth, Morneau hit a two-run homer.

MAY 30 After falling behind 6–1, the Twins score three runs in the third inning, two in the sixth and one in the ninth to defeat the White Sox 7–6 at the Metrodome. The winning run scored on a two-out, bases-loaded walk by David Aardsma to Torii Hunter.

JUNE 4 Jason Miller allows eight runs in only one-third of an inning while pitching the eighth inning of a 16–3 loss to the Angels in Anaheim. Among the seven hits he surrendered were two homers and three doubles. It was only Miller's fourth big league game. He was sent back to Class AAA Rochester the following day, and as of 2009, had not appeared in another game in the majors.

June 7	In the first round of the amateur draft, the Twins select outfielder Ben Revere from Lexington Catholic High School in Lexington, Kentucky.
June 8	The Twins play the Washington Nationals for the first time during the regular season and lose 8–5 at the Metrodome.
June 14	The Twins score three runs in the ninth inning to stun the Braves 3–2 at the Metrodome. Michael Cuddyer tripled in the first run and scored on an error. Mike Redmond drove home the winning tally with a single.
June 17	Justin Morneau hits a walk-off homer in the ninth inning to down the Brewers 10–9 at the Metrodome. The Twins led 9–2 after five innings before Milwaukee scored two in the sixth, three in the eighth and two in the ninth. The Brewers scored the first of the pair of runs in the ninth on an inside-the-park homer by Prince Fielder after center fielder Lew Ford lost the ball in the Metrodome's white ceiling. Ford was replaced Torii Hunter, who left in the first inning after he was hit in the hand by a pitch.
June 19	On the bus ride to Shea Stadium, Twins broadcaster Bert Blyleven tells Johan Santana he will shave his head if Santana pitches a complete game shutout. Santana went out and pitched a four-hit shutout to defeat the Mets 9–0 while uncharacteristically striking out only one batter. Santana shaved Blyleven's head the following day.
	Santana went into the game with three career shutouts, with the last one coming on August 12, 2005. He didn't shut out another opponent until August 17, 2008, when he was pitching for the Mets.
June 22	The Twins play the Marlins in Miami for the first time and lose 5–4.
June 23	The Twins trounce the Marlins 11–1 in Miami.
June 24	Johan Santana hits a triple in the second inning of a 7–4 victory over the Marlins in Miami. It was the first triple by a Twins pitcher since Jim Perry hit one in 1969.
June 26	Scott Baker (seven innings), Dennys Reyes (one-third of an inning), Pat Neshek (1 2/3 innings), Joe Nathan (two innings) and Juan Rincon (one inning) combine to allow only four hits during a 12-inning, 2–1 victory over the Blue Jays at the Metrodome. Jeff Cirillo drove in the winning run with a single.
	A left-handed specialist, Reyes appeared in 50 games in 2007 but pitched only 29 1/3 innings. In 2008, Reyes hurled 46 1/3 innings in 75 games.
June 28	Facing Carlos Silva in the first inning at the Metrodome, Frank Thomas hits his 500th career homer. The blast gave the Blue Jays a 4–0 lead, but the Twins rallied to win 8–5.
June 29	Joe Mauer hits a grand slam off Justin Verlander in the ninth inning of an 11–1 win over the Tigers in Detroit.
	Mauer hit .293 with seven home runs in 2007.

JULY 2	Pitching for the Yankees, Roger Clemens records his 350th career victory with a 5–1 decision over the Twins in New York.
JULY 6	The Twins put together an offensive display of historic proportions in defeating the White Sox 20–14 and 12–0 in a day-night doubleheader in Chicago. It was the most runs scored by a major league team in a doubleheader since 1930. The 34 runs scored in the opener were the most ever in a game involving either the Twins or the White Sox. Minnesota tallied four runs in the first inning and never trailed. The score was 5–3 at the close of the second inning, 6–4 after three, 12–4 after four, 14–7 at the end of the fifth, 14–8 after six, 18–10 after seven and 20–11 after eight. Jason Kubel drove in seven runs. The first five came on a sacrifice fly in the first inning and a grand slam in the fourth, both off Jon Garland. Kubel added another sacrifice fly in the seventh and a bases-loaded walk in the eighth. Joe Mauer had a double and three singles, scored four runs, and drove in five. Justin Morneau was three-for-five with three runs scored and three runs batted in. The Twins had 21 hits in all. In game two, Morneau belted three home runs and drove in six. He homered off Gavin Floyd in the first and third innings and against Boone Logan in the seventh. It was the first time that a Twin batter hit three home runs in a game since Tony Oliva accomplished the feat in 1973. Michael Cuddyer, Torii Hunter and Jeff Cirillo also homered giving the Twins a total of six. Matt Garza (six innings), Matt Guerrier (two innings) and Joe Nathan (one inning) combined on the shutout.
JULY 7	A day after scoring 32 runs, the Twins are shutout over the first eight innings of a 3–1 loss to the White Sox in Chicago.
JULY 10	Pitching in the seventh inning of the All-Star game, Johan Santana retires all three batters he faces, two on strikeouts. The American League won 5–4 at AT&T Park in San Francisco.
JULY 25	The Blue Jays score 11 runs in the sixth inning and beat the Twins 13–1 in Toronto.
JULY 28	Jason Tyner hits his first career homer during a 3–2 win over the Indians in Cleveland. The blow came in Tyner's 1,221st at-bat. He made his major league debut in 2000. Through 2009, Tyner had yet to hit another home run at the big league level.
JULY 30	Scott Baker (eight innings) and Joe Nathan (one inning) combine on a two-hitter to beat the Royals 3–1 at the Metrodome. The only Kansas City hits were a double by David DeJesus and a single from Mark Grudzielanek, both in the fourth inning.
	On the same day, the Twins traded Luis Castillo to the Mets for Drew Butera and Dustin Martin.
AUGUST 1	A highway bridge across the Mississippi River in Minneapolis collapses, killing 13 people and injuring 79. The eight-lane bridge on I-35W fell during the evening rush hour, dropping about 50 vehicles into or near the water. The bridge was built in 1967 and had been considered "structurally deficient" since 1990.
	The Twins were scheduled to play the Royals that night at the Metrodome and had to determine whether or not to play the game. It was decided to play because of the problems that would be caused by sending the crowd of

24,880 into the surrounding streets, which would further complicate rescue efforts. The August 2 game against the Royals was postponed until August 31. Groundbreaking ceremonies at the future site of Target Field, also scheduled for August 2, were postponed until August 30.

August 3 — The Twins sell Jeff Cirillo to the Diamondbacks.

August 5 — Scott Baker (eight innings) and Joe Nathan (one inning) combine to beat the Indians 1–0 at the Metrodome. Second baseman Alexi Casilla drove in the lone run with a double in the fifth inning.

August 15 — Torii Hunter hits a grand slam off Sean Green in the ninth inning of a 6–1 win over the Mariners in Seattle. It was Hunter's third slam of the season.

August 19 — Pitching eight innings, Johan Santana sets a club record with 17 strikeouts and allows only two hits in a 1–0 win over the Rangers at the Metrodome. Joe Nathan fanned two in the ninth to give Minnesota pitchers 19 strikeouts in the game, which set another record. Sammy Sosa had both Texas hits with a single in the fifth inning and a double in the seventh. Prior to Sosa's single, Santana retired the first 12 batters to face him and set down nine of them on strikeouts. The lone run of the game scored on a home run by Michael Cuddyer in the second inning off Kevin Millwood.

The previous franchise record for strikeouts by a pitcher in a nine-inning game was 15 by Camilo Pascual for the Senators in 1960 and the Twins in 1961, Joe Decker in 1973, Jerry Koosman in 1980 and Bert Blyleven in 1986. Walter Johnson fanned 16 in an 11-inning game for Washington in 1913.

August 22 — The Twins score seven runs in the first inning and beat the Mariners 8–4 at the Metrodome. Michael Cuddyer hit a grand slam off Miguel Batista.

August 31 — Scott Baker retires the first 24 batters to face him before settling for a one-hit, 5–0 victory over the Royals in the second game of a day-night doubleheader at the Metrodome. Two games were played because of the postponement of an August 2 game caused by the I-35W Bridge collapse. Baker entered the ninth with a perfect game intact before walking lead-off batter John Buck on a 3–1 pitch. After Esteban German grounded out, Baker gave up a single to Mike Sweeney to end the no-hit bid. Baker then retired the final two batters. Kansas City won the first game 9–4.

September 7 — The Twins collect 20 hits but lose a strange 11–10 decision to the White Sox in 13 innings at U.S. Cellular Field. The score was 4–4 after eight innings before the Twins erupted for six runs in the top of the ninth for a 10–4 lead. Rondell White capped the rally with a three-run homer. The game appeared to be in the bag, but Chicago countered with six runs in the bottom of the ninth off Julio DePaula and Joe Nathan. DePaula faced five batters and gave up five hits on three singles, a double, and a homer to Jim Thome. Nathan allowed the tying run on a walk and a double. The White Sox won the contest in the 13th on a walk-off single from A. J. Pierzynski against Juan Rincon.

September 8 — In his major league debut, catcher Jose Morales collects three hits, one of them a double, in three at-bats during an 8–7 loss to the White Sox in Chicago. Morales was lifted for a pinch-runner after his third hit.

> *Despite his impressive debut, Morales didn't play in another major league game until April 6, 2009, holding a career batting average of 1.000 for 19 months. In 2009, Morales was hitless in seven at-bats before picking up his fourth big league hit.*

SEPTEMBER 13 — Terry Ryan resigns as general manager after 12 years on the job. He guided the club to four AL Central championships in 2002, 2003, 2004 and 2006. Ryan remained with the franchise as a senior talent advisor. Bill Smith, who had been Ryan's assistant, took over as general manager. Smith was 48 at the time of his appointment.

SEPTEMBER 17 — The Twins score two runs in the ninth inning to beat the Rangers 5–4 at the Metrodome. Michael Cuddyer led off the ninth with a homer. The winning run scored on an error.

NOVEMBER 22 — Torii Hunter signs with the Angels as a free agent.

NOVEMBER 28 — The Twins trade Matt Garza, Jason Bartlett and Eduardo Morlan to the Rays for Delmon Young, Brendan Harris and Jason Pridle.

> *The full ramifications of this trade won't be known for several years. Young was the number one overall pick in the amateur draft in 2003, reached the majors in 2006 at the age of 20, and was the runner-up for the Rookie-of-the-Year Award in 2007. He had a checkered past, however, with questions about his attitude. In 2006 while playing in the minors, Young was suspended for 50 games for throwing a bat at an umpire. The bat struck the ump in the chest and arm. Young and Harris were starters for the Twins in 2009. Garza was the Twins first round draft pick in 2005. Both he and Bartlett were key members of the Rays surprising run to the World Series in 2008. Bartlett made the AL All-Star team in 2009. Garza finished the season with the Angels.*

DECEMBER 20 — Carlos Silva signs with the Mariners as a free agent.

2008

Season in a Sentence

After losing Johan Santana in a trade and Torii Hunter to free agency, the Twins miss the postseason by losing a one-game playoff against the White Sox to determine the AL Central champion.

Finish • Won • Lost • Pct • GB

Second   88   75   .540   1.0

In the wild card race, the Twins finished in third place 7½ games behind.

Manager

Ron Gardenhire

Stats   Twins • AL • Rank

Stat	Twins	AL	Rank
Batting Avg:	.279	.268	3
On-Base Pct:	.340	.336	4
Slugging Pct:	.408	.420	10
Home Runs:	111		14
Stolen Bases:	102		5
ERA:	4.16	4.35	8
Errors:	108		11
Runs Scored:	829		3
Runs Allowed:	745		8

Starting Line-up

Joe Mauer, c
Justin Morneau, 1b
Alexi Casilla, 2b
Brendan Harris, 3b-2b-ss
Nick Punto, ss
Delmon Young, lf
Chris Gomez, cf
Denard Span, rf
Jason Kubel, dh-rf
Brian Buscher, 3b
Michael Cuddyer, rf
Mike Lamb, 3b

Pitchers

Nick Blackburn, sp
Kevin Slowey, sp
Scott Baker, sp
Glen Perkins, sp
Livan Hernandez, sp
Joe Nathan, rp
Boof Bonser, rp
Matt Guerrier, rp
Jesse Crain, rp
Dennys Reyes, rp
Brian Bass, rp
Craig Breslow, rp

Attendance

2,302,431 (eighth in AL)

Club Leaders

Batting Avg:	Joe Mauer	.328
On-Base Pct:	Joe Mauer	.413
Slugging Pct:	Justin Morneau	.499
Home Runs:	Justin Morneau	23
RBI:	Justin Morneau	129
Runs:	Joe Mauer	98
Stolen Bases:	Carlos Gomez	33
Wins:	Glen Perkins	12
	Kevin Slowey	12
Strikeouts:	Scott Baker	141
ERA:	Scott Baker	3.45
Saves:	Joe Nathan	39

FEBRUARY 2   The Twins trade Johan Santana to the Mets for Carlos Gomez, Deolis Guerra, Kevin Mulvey and Philip Humber.

The Twins had been shopping Santana for months after expressing an unwillingness to sign him to an expensive long-term contract. The complete ramifications of the deal likely won't be known for a decade or more, but in the short run, it cost the Twins a spot in the postseason in 2008. Santana was 16–7 for the Mets that season and led the NL in ERA (2.53) and innings (234⅓). Of the four players acquired for Santana, only Gomez has had significant playing time for the Twins through the end of the 2009 season. While he cracked the starting line-up in center field as a 22-year-old in 2008, Gomez has put up offensive numbers well below the league average. On November 6, 2009, Gomez was traded to the Brewers for shortstop J.J. Hardy.

FEBRUARY 12	The Twins sign Livan Hernandez, most recently with the Diamondbacks, as a free agent.
MARCH 31	On Opening Night before 49,596 at the Metrodome, the Twins edge the Angels 3–2. Michael Cuddyer broke the 2–2 tie with an RBI-single in the fifth inning. Making his debut the club, Livan Hernandez was the Minnesota starting pitcher and went seven innings for the win. Outside, a snowstorm swept through downtown Minneapolis.
APRIL 9	Jason Kubel drives in six runs during a 12–5 triumph over the White Sox in Chicago. Kubel came to the plate three times with the bases loaded, and hit a sacrifice fly in the first inning, a single in the third, and a grand slam in the sixth. The slam was struck off Nick Masset.
APRIL 12	Jason Kubel scores both runs of a 2–0 victory over the Royals in Kansas City. He homered in the second inning and singled and scored in the seventh. Boof Bonser (six innings), Matt Guerrier (one inning), Pat Neshek (one inning) and Joe Nathan (one inning) combined on the shutout.
APRIL 25	Justin Morneau hits a grand slam off Kevin Millwood in the third inning for a 5–0 lead, but the Twins lose 6–5 in ten innings to the Rangers in Arlington.

> *On the same day, the Twins sent Francisco Liriano back to the minors. After posting a 12–3 record in 2006, he missed all of 2007 after undergoing Tommy John surgery. Liriano was demoted after losing his first three starts with an ERA of 11.32. At Class AAA Rochester, Liriano had a 10–2 record, but in a controversial decision, the Twins didn't recall him until August. The club was accused of keeping Liriano in the minors to delay his eligibility for arbitration by a year. During August and September, Liriano was 6–1 for the Twins.*

MAY 2	The Twins thrash the Tigers 11–1 at the Metrodome.
MAY 4	After the Tigers score six runs in the top of the first inning, the Tigers counter with one in the fourth, two in the fifth and four in the seventh to win 7–6 at the Metrodome. All four runs in the seventh scored after two were out, the last two on a single by Joe Mauer. Boof Bonser gave up the six runs in the first but pitched scoreless ball from the second through the sixth.
MAY 6	At U.S. Cellular Field, Joe Mauer doubles with one out in the ninth inning to break up the no-hit bid of White Sox pitcher Gavin Floyd. After Mauer's hit, Bobby Jenks was brought in from the bullpen to retire the final two batters and preserve a 7–1 Chicago win. The Twins scored in the fourth on a walk, an error and a sacrifice fly.

> *Mauer won his second batting title in 2008 with a .328 average. He also had nine home runs. The first batting title was in 2006.*

MAY 7	Carlos Gomez hits for the cycle in reverse order during a 13–1 win over the White Sox at the Metrodome. Gomez led off the first inning with a home run. After striking out in the third, he tripled in the fifth and doubled in the sixth. All three extra base hits came off Mark Buehrle. Gomez faced Ehran Wassermann in the ninth and completed the cycle with a single. He batted once more against Nick Masset in the six-run ninth and struck out.

> *Gomez was the third-youngest player in history to hit for the cycle. He was also the fourth player to hit for the cycle in reverse order.*

MAY 9   The Twins score two runs in the ninth inning to down the Red Sox 7–6 at the Metrodome. With two out, Delmon Young stole third. Carlos Gomez walked and swiped second. On a 1–2 pitch from Jonathan Papelpon, Mike Lamb delivered a two-run, walk-off single. Lamb entered the game as a substitute after Brendan Harris pulled a hamstring.

MAY 16   The Twins play the Rockies in Denver for the first time and win 4–2 at Coors Field.

MAY 19   Second baseman Howie Clark drives in the winning run with a walk-off double in the 12th inning to defeat the Rangers 7–6 at the Metrodome.

> *The game was the second of only four that Clark played as a member of the Twins. It was his second, and last, hit with the club and his lone RBI.*

MAY 20   The Twins score seven runs in the third inning of an 11–4 trouncing of the Rangers at the Metrodome.

MAY 24   The Tigers score 19 runs in the first five innings and rout the Twins 19–3 in Detroit.

MAY 25   Jason Kubel breaks a 1–1 tie with a grand slam off Francisco Cruceta in the eighth inning, and the Twins defeat the Tigers 6–1 in Detroit.

Since arriving in Minnesota in 2004, Joe Nathan has become one of baseball's premier closers. In 2008 he saved thirty-nine games while compiling a miniscule 1.33 ERA.

May 27	The Twins outlast the Royals to win 4–3 in 12 innings in Kansas City. The game should have been won much earlier, but with one out in the ninth, left fielder Delmon Young misplayed a fly ball by Mark Teahen, leading to a three-run, inside-the-park homer.
May 28	In a stunning rally, the Twins score five runs after two are out in the ninth inning to tie the score 8–8 and go on to beat the Royals 9–8 in the tenth in Kansas City. With two away and a runner on second in the ninth, Mike Lamb's single made the score 8–4. Singles by Carlos Gomez and Brendan Harris produced another run. Stepping to the plate as a pinch-hitter, Craig Monroe walloped a three-run homer to deadlock the contest. Justin Morneau led off the tenth with another homer for the winning run.
June 1	In the fifth inning of a 5–1 win over the Yankees in New York, pitcher Nick Blackburn is taken out of the game after being hit in the face by a line drive off the bat of Bobby Abreu. Fortunately, Blackburn wasn't seriously injured and made his next scheduled start.
June 4	Joe Mauer's hits a two-run sacrifice fly during a 7–5 win over the Orioles at the Metrodome. Carlos Gomez scored from second on the fly ball to center fielder Adam Jones in deep left-center.

After the win, the Twins lost six in a row to fall to 31–34 and six games behind the White Sox in the AL Central race.

June 5	With two selections in the amateur draft, the Twins choose outfielder Aaron Hicks from Wilson High School in Long Beach, California, and pitcher Carlos Gutierrez of the University of Miami (FL). The club received an extra pick as compensation for losing Torii Hunter to free agency.
June 14	The Twins score five runs in the 12th inning to beat the Brewers 9–4 in Milwaukee.
June 15	Scott Baker strikes out four batters in the third inning of a 4–2 loss to the Brewers in Milwaukee. The feat was accomplished because with one out Prince Fielder swung at and missed a third strike, but he reached first base when the ball sailed past catcher Mike Redmond. Baker also fanned Ryan Braun, Russell Branyan and Mike Cameron.
June 20	Joe Nathan strikes out all three batters he faces in the ninth inning to close out a 7–2 win over the Diamondbacks at the Metrodome.
June 27	The Twins extend their winning streak to ten games with a 7–6 win over the Brewers at the Metrodome.

At the end of the day, the Twins and the White Sox were tied for first place. From June 20 through the end of the season, no more than three games ever separated the two clubs.

July 1	The Twins hit into five double plays but manage to defeat the Tigers 6–4 at the Metrodome.

July 10	After falling behind 6–2, the Twins score a run in the seventh inning, another in the eighth, two in the ninth, and one in the 11th to defeat the Tigers 7–6 in 11 innings in Detroit. Justin Morneau led the comeback by reaching base six times, five of them on hits, in six plate appearances with a home run, two doubles, two singles and a walk. The home run came in the 11th to win the game.
July 14	At Yankee Stadium, Justin Morneau wins the All-Star Game Home Run Derby by beating Josh Hamilton of the Rangers 5–3 in the final round. In the first round, Hamilton struck a record 28 home runs, including 13 in a row.
July 15	Justin Morneau scores the winning run in the 15th inning to give the American League a 4–3 win in the All-Star Game at Yankee Stadium. Morneau led off the 15th with a single off Brad Lidge, advanced to third on a single by Dioner Navarro and a walk to J. D. Drew, and scored on Matt Young's sacrifice fly. Joe Nathan pitched the seventh and retired all three batters he faced.

> *Morneau finished the season with a .300 batting average, 47 doubles, 23 home runs and 129 RBIs. Nathan recorded 39 saves and a 1.33 ERA in 68 games and 67 2/3 innings.*

July 19	The Twins clobber the Rangers 14–2 at the Metrodome.
July 20	Scott Baker retires the first 17 batters to face him before giving up a home run for the lone run of a 1–0 loss to the Rangers at the Metrodome. The homer was struck by Taylor Teagarden and accounted for his first major league hit.
July 23	The Twins play at old Yankee Stadium for the last time and lose 5–1 to the Yankees.
July 31	Fans hold up play for several minutes by throwing hats and baseballs onto the field during the seventh inning of a 10–6 win over the White Sox at the Metrodome. The outburst came after Denard Span was called out on strikes. Ron Gardenhire charged onto the field and was ejected after punting his hat over the head of third base umpire Marty Foster. The barrage from the fans caused Chicago manager Ozzie Guillen to pull his players off the diamond.
August 3	In his first game since being recalled from the minors (see April 25, 2008), Francisco Liriano wins his first major league game since July 23, 2006. He pitched six shutout innings and the Twins defeated the Indians 6–2 at the Metrodome.
August 4	The Twins take a 6–0 lead over the Mariners at Safeco Field but wind up losing 11–6. The Twins still led 6–1 heading into the bottom of the seventh, but Seattle erupted for ten runs in the inning. Raul Ibanez tied an American League record (since broken by Alex Rodriguez in 2009) for most RBIs in an inning with six on a grand slam off Glen Perkins and a bases-loaded, two-run single against Matt Guerrier.
August 5	Jason Kubel hits two homers, a double and a single in five at-bats, but the Twins lose 8–7 to the Mariners in Seattle.
August 6	The Twins sell Livan Hernandez to the Rockies.

AUGUST 11	Joe Nathan strikes out all three batters he faces in the ninth inning of a 4–0 win over the Yankees at the Metrodome.
AUGUST 15	The Twins score seven runs in the fourth inning of a 9–3 victory over the Mariners at the Metrodome. Jason Kubel contributed a two-run homer and a single to the rally.
AUGUST 17	Jason Kubel collects four hits, including two doubles, and scores four runs during an 11–8 triumph over the Mariners at the Metrodome. The Twins scored twice in the fourth inning with the help of a record four wild pitches by Seattle hurler R. A. Dickey in addition to a passed ball charged to catcher Kenji Johjima on another errant pitch. Randy Ruiz singled and advanced to second on the passed ball and went to third and home on two of Dickey's wild pitches.

Ruiz played in 22 games for the Twins in 2008 after making his major league debut on August 1 at the age of 30. He played in the minors for nine different organizations before finally reaching the big leagues.

AUGUST 19	Kevin Slowey strikes out 12 batters without a walk in seven innings and the Twins trounce the Athletics 13–2 at the Metrodome.
AUGUST 21	Scott Baker (eight innings), Matt Guerrier (two innings), Jesse Crain (one inning) and Joe Nathan (one inning) combine to allow only five hits in a 12-inning, 2–1 victory over the Angels in Anaheim. Denard Span drove in the winning run with a single.
AUGUST 25	The Twins trade Mark Hamburger to the Rangers for Eddie Guardado.
AUGUST 29	Joe Mauer collects five hits, including a double, in six at-bats during a 12–2 clobbering of the Athletics in Oakland. The Twins garnered 20 hits in all.
SEPTEMBER 5	Justin Morneau hits a grand slam off Armando Galarraga in the fifth inning of a 10–2 win over the Tigers at the Metrodome. The Twins collected the ten runs on only six hits.
SEPTEMBER 12	The Twins score five runs in the ninth inning to cap a 12–2 win over the Orioles in Baltimore.
SEPTEMBER 13	The Twins score six runs in the first inning to spark a 12–6 victory over the Orioles in Baltimore.
SEPTEMBER 18	The Twins score five runs in the ninth inning to defeat the Rays 11–8 at St. Petersburg. Alexi Casilla tied the score 8–8 with a two-run homer. Doubles by Joe Mauer and Adam Everett created the go-ahead tally. Evan Longoria hit three home runs for Tampa Bay.

The Twins headed into a three-game series against the White Sox at the Metrodome on September 23 trailing by 2½ games. The Twins had six games left on the schedule, and the White Sox had seven.

SEPTEMBER 23	The Twins pull within 1½ games of first place by defeating the White Sox 9–3 at the Metrodome. Jason Kubel had two homers and a triple.

September 24 — The Twins pull to one-half game of the first-place White Sox by beating them 3–2 at the Metrodome.

September 25 — The Twins take first place by downing the White Sox 7–6 in an exciting ten-inning decision at the Metrodome. Minnesota trailed 6–1 before scoring two runs in the fourth inning, one in the sixth and two in the seventh to tie the game at 6–6. The two eight-inning runs scored on a double by Brendan Harris, a single from Carlos Gomez, and Denard Span's triple. Alexi Casilla drove in the winning run with a single off Bobby Jenks.

> *The Royals were the next team to visit Minneapolis and beat the Twins 8–1 on September 26 and 4–2 on September 27. Fortunately, the White Sox lost 11–8 and 12–6 to the Indians in Chicago on both days to allow the Twins to maintain their half-game lead. The final day of the regular season was September 28, but the White Sox had to make-up a postponed game with the Tigers if it had a bearing on the pennant race. If the Twins and White Sox were tied for first following the make-up game, scheduled for September 29, a one-game playoff to determine the AL Central champion would be played on September 30 in Chicago.*

September 28 — The Twins hold onto first place by beating the Royals 6–0 at the Metrodome. Scott Baker (seven innings), Jose Mijares (one inning) and Joe Nathan (one inning) combined on the shutout. The White Sox defeated the Indians 5–1 in Chicago to stay one-half game back of the Twins.

September 29 — The White Sox down the Tigers 8–2 in Chicago in a make-up game to force a one-game playoff against the Twins to determine the AL Central champion.

September 30 — The Twins lose the playoff game against the White Sox 1–0 at U.S. Cellular Field. Nick Blackburn allowed only two hits over the first six innings before surrendering a home run to Jim Thome leading off the seventh for the lone run of the game. John Danks (eight innings) and Bobby Jenks (one inning) combined to pitch a two-hitter for Chicago. Danks had a no-hitter in progress until Michael Cuddyer doubled in the fifth.

2009

Season in a Sentence

In the last season at the Metrodome, the Twins trail the Tigers by seven games on September 6 but win 17 of their last 21 games to take the AL Central title in a thrilling one-game playoff.

Finish • Won • Lost • Pct • GB

First   87   76   .534   +1.0

Manager

Ron Gardenhire

AL Division Series

The Twins lost three games to none to the New York Yankees.

Stats

Stats	Twins	AL	Rank
Batting Avg:	.274	.267	3
On-Base Pct:	.345	.336	4
Slugging Pct:	.429	.428	7
Home Runs:	172		9
Stolen Bases:	85		10
ERA:	4.50	4.75	11
Errors:	76		1
Runs Scored:	817		4
Runs Allowed:	765		10

Starting Line-up

Joe Mauer, c
Justin Morneau, 1b
Nick Punto, 2b-ss
Joe Crede, 3b
Brendan Harris, ss-2b
Delmon Young, lf
Denard Span, cf-lf
Michael Cuddyer, rf
Jason Kubel, dh-rf
Carlos Gomez, cf
Orlando Cabrera, ss
Alexi Casilla, 2b
Matt Tolbert, 2b-3b

Pitchers

Scott Baker, sp
Nick Blackburn, sp
Kevin Slowey, sp
Francisco Liriano, sp
Glen Perkins, sp
Joe Nathan, rp
Matt Guerrier, rp
Jose Mijares, rp
Jesse Crain, rp

Attendance

2,416,237 (fifth in AL)

Club Leaders

Batting Avg:	Joe Mauer	.365
On-Base Pct:	Joe Mauer	.444
Slugging Pct:	Joe Mauer	.587
Home Runs:	Michael Cuddyer	32
RBIs:	Jason Kubel	103
Runs:	Joe Mauer	94
Stolen Bases:	Carlos Gomez	14
Wins:	Scott Baker	15
Strikeouts:	Scott Baker	162
ERA:	Nick Blackburn	4.03
Saves:	Joe Nathan	47

JANUARY 5   Carl Pohlad dies at the age of 93. He had owned the Twins since 1984. The club won a world championship in 1987 and 1991, but Pohlad became frustrated with the inability of the state of Minnesota to finance a new stadium and tried to sell the franchise to a group from North Carolina in 1997. Then he attempted to sell the club back to Major League Baseball in 2001 when owners desired to reduce the number of teams from 30 to 28. That plan fell through, and the Twins finally received the financing needed to build a baseball-only park in 2006. Pohlad did not live long enough to see the new park, named Target Field, open in 2010. The day-to-day operation of the club passed to his 55-year-old son, Jim.

FEBRUARY 5   Two weeks after Barack Obama is inaugurated as president, Eddie Guardado signs with the Rangers as a free agent.

FEBRUARY 21   The Twins sign Joe Crede, most recently with the White Sox, as a free agent.

APRIL 6	The Twins open the season with a 6–1 loss to the Mariners before 48,514 at the Metrodome. Francisco Liriano was the starting and losing pitcher.
APRIL 7	The Twins score three runs in the ninth inning to defeat the Mariners 6–5 at the Metrodome. Seattle pitcher Brandon Morrow retired the first two Minnesota hitters in the ninth before walking Carlos Gomez, Jason Kubel and Brian Buscher. Gomez and Buscher walked on 3–2 pitches. After Miguel Batista replaced Morrow, Denard Span drove in a run with an infield single. Alexi Casilla drove in the tying and winning runs with a two-run walk-off single.
APRIL 10	The Twins score seven runs in the seventh inning to defeat the White Sox 12–5 at U.S. Cellular Field. The first eight Minnesota batters of the inning reached base on a home run (by Justin Morneau), three walks and four singles. A member of the White Sox from 2000 through 2008, Joe Crede received a standing ovation from Chicago fans when he stepped to the plate in the first inning. He then hit a home run. As he rounded the bases, he was booed.
APRIL 17	A grand slam by Jason Kubel caps a cycle and an 11–9 come-from-behind win over the Angels at the Metrodome. Kubel doubled in the first inning and singled in the third off Dustin Moseley and then he tripled in the sixth against Rafael Rodriguez. Still, the Twins trailed 9–4 heading into the bottom of the eighth. Mark Redmond singled in a run and Denard Span belted a two-run double to make the score 9–7. With two out, Justin Morneau was intentionally walked to load the bases. Kubel cleared the sacks with a grand slam off Jason Bulger, and the Twins held on for the victory.
APRIL 18	The day after hitting for the cycle, Jason Kubel collects four hits on three singles and a double in five at-bats during a 9–2 win over the Angels at the Metrodome.

Kubel hit an even .300 with 28 homers and 103 RBIs in 2009.

MAY 1	In his first plate appearance of the season, Joe Mauer hits a home run, and the Twins defeat the Royals 7–5 at the Metrodome.

Mauer began the season on the disabled list with an inflammation of the sacroiliac joint. In his first ten at-bats of the season, he collected seven hits. During the month of May, Mauer drove in 32 runs to tie a franchise record for a month, set by Harmon Killebrew as a Washington Senator in 1960. By the end of the year, Mauer led the AL in batting average (.365) for the third time in his career. In addition, he topped the circuit in on-base percentage (.444) and slugging percentage (.587). He was the first catcher in history to lead in all three categories at any point in his career, much less in a single season. Since the move of the franchise to Minnesota, the only player with a higher batting average is Rod Carew with .388 in 1977. Mauer is also second in single-season on-base percentage, behind Chuck Knoblauch's .448 in 1996, and second in slugging percentage to Harmon Killebrew (.606 in 1961). Counting the Washington years, Mauer's 2009 figures rank fourth in batting average, fifth in on-base percentage and fourth in slugging. The only player to beat him in all three categories is Hall of Famer Ed Delahanty in 1902. Mauer also hit 28 homers and drove in 96 runs in 2009.

Date	Event

MAY 3 — After holding the Royals hitless for six innings, Scott Baker gives up hits to the first seven batters he faces in the seventh. All five scored, and the Twins lost 7–5 at the Metrodome.

MAY 8 — The Twins wallop the Mariners 11–0 at the Metrodome. Scott Baker (seven innings), Jesse Crain (one inning) and Joe Nathan (one inning) combined on the shutout.

After an 0–4 start, Baker was 15–9 in 2009.

MAY 13 — Joe Crede hits a walk-off grand slam in the 13th inning off Brandon Lyon to beat the Tigers 14–10 at the Metrodome. Jason Kubel tied the score 9–9 with a two-run homer in the eighth, but the Twins fell behind 10–9 in the top of the 13th when Jesse Crain committed a balk with Curtis Granderson on third base. Matt Tolbert tied the score in the bottom half on a single and went to second on a ground out. After an intentional walk and an unintentional walk, Crede blasted the game-winner.

MAY 14 — Trailing 5–0, the Twins score six runs in the seventh inning and beat the Tigers 6–5 at the Metrodome. Four of the runs scored with two out. Joe Crede was the hero for the second game in a row with a two-run single that turned a 5–4 deficit into a 6–5 lead.

MAY 15 — The Twins play at the new Yankee Stadium for the first time and lose 5–4 when the Yanks score three runs in the ninth inning off Joe Nathan. Melky Cabrera drove in the winning runs with a two-out, two-run, walk-off single.

It was the start of a nightmare series for the Twins. Minnesota lost 6–4 in 11 innings on May 16 on a walk-off homer by Alex Rodriguez, then lost 3–2 in ten on May 17 on a walk-off homer by Johnny Damon. The Twins were 0–10 against the Yankees in 2009, counting the three-game sweep in the Division Series.

MAY 21 — The Twins stop a six-game losing streak by trouncing the White Sox 20–1 in Chicago. The Twins scored a run in the first inning, seven in the second, one in the third, one in the fourth, six in the sixth and four in the seventh. The club collected 20 hits and led 20–0 until the Sox scored in the eighth. Michael Cuddyer led the attack with four runs and four hits, including a double and a homer. Joe Mauer had a homer and two doubles and drove in six runs. His homer was a grand slam in the sixth off Jimmy Gobble.

MAY 22 — Michael Cuddyer hits for the cycle and drives in five runs during an 11–3 win over the Brewers at the Metrodome. He homered in the first inning and doubled in the third off Manny Parra. Cuddyer added a single in the seventh against Mark DiFelice and a triple in the seventh facing Jorge Julio. Cuddyer became the second Twin in 2009 to hit for the cycle and the tenth since the move to Minnesota.

Cuddyer hit .276 with 32 homers and 94 runs batted in during the 2009 season.

MAY 23 — In his major league debut, Anthony Swarzak pitches seven shutout innings and the Twins beat the Brewers 6–2 at the Metrodome.

MAY 24 — Justin Morneau hits a grand slam off Mitch Stetter in the seventh inning of a 6–3 win over the Brewers at the Metrodome.

Morneau hit .274 with 30 homers and 100 RBIs in 2009.

June 4 — Jason Kubel drives in six runs with two homers and a double during an 11–3 win over the Indians at the Metrodome.

June 9 — In the first round of the amateur draft, the Twins select pitcher Kyle Gibson from the University of Missouri.

July 3 — The Twins lose a 16-inning marathon 11–9 to the Tigers at the Metrodome. The Twins fell behind 7–1 in the fourth, but rallied to force extra innings. Both teams scored in the 14th. Detroit plated three runs in the top of the 16th and the Twins added one in the bottom half. Denard Span had five hits, including a triple, in eight at-bats.

Span led the AL in triples with ten in 2009.

July 12 — The Twins outlast the White Sox 13–7 at the Metrodome.

July 14 — Joe Mauer contributes an RBI-single and a run scored to the American League's 4–3 win in the All-Star Game in St. Louis.

July 20 — The Twins blow a ten-run lead and lose 14–13 to the Athletics in Oakland. Justin Morneau drove in seven runs on a grand slam in the second inning and a three-run homer in the third, both off Gio Gonzalez, to help Minnesota to a 12–2 lead. The Twins still led 13–7 before the A's scored seven runs in the seventh. The game ended on a bad call. With two out in the ninth, Michael Cuddyer tried to score from second base on

Another in a line of hometown heroes, St. Paul native Joe Mauer is a fan favorite—in the Twin Cities and throughout baseball. He has quickly established himself as one of the best-hitting catchers in the history of the game.

a wild pitch and was called out. Replays showed he was safe. The ten-run blown lead tied a franchise record set by the 1938 Senators in an 18–12 loss to the Tigers in Washington on June 12. The mark was tied by the 1984 Twins in an 11–10 defeat at the hands of the Indians in Cleveland on September 28.

JULY 22   The Twins suffer another embarrassing loss in Oakland, dropping a 16–1 decision to the Athletics.

JULY 28   At the Metrodome, Mark Buehrle of the White Sox makes his first start since pitching a perfect game on July 23. He came into the contest against the Twins having retired the last 28 batters to face him, over two appearances. The record was 41 set by Jim Barr of the Giants in 1972 and tied by his White Sox teammate Bobby Jenks in 2007. Buehrle set down the first 17 Minnesota batters to face him to run his streak to 45. When he retired Joe Crede on a ground out with two out in the fifth inning to break the record, Buehrle received an ovation from Twins fans. Buehrle's streak ended with a walk to Alexi Casilla with two out in the sixth. Denard Span followed with a single and Joe Mauer doubled in a run before the inning was over. In the seventh, Buehrle hit a batter and gave up three singles before being relieved. After retiring 45 batters in a row, including the first 17 in this game, the White Sox pitcher allowed seven of the next nine batters to reach base. The Twins went on to win 5–3.

JULY 31   The Twins trade Tyler Ladendorf to the Athletics for Orlando Cabrera.

AUGUST 7   The Twins acquire Carl Pavano from the Indians for Yohan Pino.

AUGUST 8   In his first start with the Twins, Carl Pavano pitches seven shutout innings and the Twins defeat the Tigers 11–0 in Detroit. Denard Span collected five hits, including a double, in five at-bats. It was his second five-hit game of the season.

AUGUST 12   Joe Nathan strikes out all three batters he faces to close out a 7–1 win over the Royals at the Metrodome.

Nathan had a 2.10 ERA and 47 saves in 70 games and 68 2/3 innings in 2009.

AUGUST 14   Scott Baker pitches a two-hitter to defeat the Indians 11–0 at the Metrodome. The only Cleveland hits were a double by Asdrubal Cabrera in the fourth inning and a single from Johnny Peralta in the seventh.

AUGUST 18   After falling behind 5–0 in the third inning, the Twins rally to beat the Rangers 9–6 in Arlington. A homer by Joe Mauer leading off the seventh tied the score 6–6. Before the inning was completed, Delmon Young broke the deadlock with a two-run homer.

AUGUST 19   After falling behind 4–0 in the fourth inning, the Twins rally to beat the Rangers 5–4 in Arlington. After scoring a run in the fifth, the Twins took the lead in the sixth with four runs.

AUGUST 23   The Twins break a 1–1 tie with eight runs in the seventh inning and beat the Royals 10–3 in Kansas City. Michael Cuddyer hit two home runs during the rally, connecting off Brian Bannister and Kyle Farnsworth. Cuddyer became the second player in franchise history to hit two home runs in an inning, and the first since the move to Minnesota. The only other individual to accomplish the feat was Jim Lemon with the Senators in 1959.

SEPTEMBER 6   The Twins lose 3–1 to the Indians in Cleveland to fall seven games behind the first-place Tigers.

>   *The Twins had a record of 68–68 at the conclusion of the game. The club lost four of their next six to fall to 70–72 on September 12 and into third place, but they gained a little ground on the slumping Tigers, narrowing the margin to 5½ games.*

SEPTEMBER 18   The Twins defeat the Tigers 3–0 at the Metrodome to pull within three games of first place. Brian Duensing, in his seventh big league start, pitched 6⅓ innings. The relievers were Jose Mijares (two-thirds of an inning), Jon Rauch (one inning) and Joe Nathan (one inning).

SEPTEMBER 26   Leadoff batter Denard Span drives in six runs with a triple and three singles to lead the Twins to an 11–6 win over the Royals in Kansas City. The win left the Twins two games back of the Tigers with eight games left to play.

SEPTEMBER 28   The first game of a four-game, pennant-showdown series against the Tigers in Detroit is postponed by rain.

SEPTEMBER 29   In a day-night doubleheader at Comerica Park, the Twins split with the Tigers, winning 3–2 in ten innings during the afternoon and losing 6–5 in the evening. The Twins scored two in the top of the tenth in the opener. Denard Span led off with a single, advanced to third on two wild pitches by Brandon Lyon, and scored on a single by Orlando Cabrera. After two walks by Lyon, one intentional, Cabrera scored on a sacrifice fly from Delmon Young. The Tigers added a run in the bottom of the tenth before Joe Nathan closed out the win.

SEPTEMBER 30   The Twins lose 7–2 to the Tigers in Detroit to fall three games behind with only four contests left on the schedule.

OCTOBER 1   The Twins stave off elimination by beating the Tigers 8–3 in Detroit to pull within two games with three left to play. There was tension late in the game when Jose Mijares inexplicably threw a pitch behind Detroit's Adam Everett. On the first pitch of the ninth, Delmon Young was hit in the knee by a pitch from Jeremy Bonderman. As he went to first base, Young glared at Mijares, who was sitting in the dugout.

OCTOBER 2   The Twins beat the Royals 10–7 at the Metrodome to remain in the pennant race. The Tigers lost 8–0 to the White Sox in Detroit to put the Twins one game back with two to play. Minnesota scored five runs in the first inning, the last four on a grand slam by Delmon Young off Lenny DiNardo, and took a 10–0 lead in the fourth. Kansas City scored seven unanswered runs, but the Twins held on to win. Starting pitcher Jeff Manship won his first major league game.

OCTOBER 3   The Twins move into a tie for first place by beating the Royals 5–4 at the Metrodome while the Tigers lose 5–1 to the White Sox in Detroit. The Twins built a 4–0 lead after six innings off Zack Greinke but allowed the Royals to tie the score. Michael Cuddyer broke the deadlock with a home run with one out in the eighth.

OCTOBER 4   In what was originally scheduled to be the last regular season game at the Metrodome, the Twins force a one-game playoff to decide the AL Central champion by beating the Royals 13–4 before a crowd of 51,155. The Tigers defeated the White Sox 5–3 in Detroit. Jason Kubel led the Minnesota attack with two homers and six RBIs. Michael Cuddyer homered twice and Delmon Young once. Before the game, dozens of former Twins players were introduced to the crowd. The club removed the curtain in right field to accommodate the largest baseball crowd at the Metrodome since 1993. Fans also received Homer Hankies, the signature souvenir from the 1987 and 1991 world championship seasons.

> *For the second year in a row, the Twins played a 163rd regular season game to decide the AL Central champion. The previous year, the club lost 1–0 to the White Sox in Chicago. In prior years, The Home Field for a playoff was decided by a coin flip. Beginning in 2009, it was decided by the head-to-head won-lost records of the two teams involved. Because of Minnesota's 12–7 record against the Tigers, the game was played at the Metrodome. Major League Baseball wanted the game to be played on Monday October 5, but the Metrodome was already booked for a game between the Vikings and the Packers. Playing his former team for the first time, Brett Favre led the Vikings to a 30–23 win.*

OCTOBER 6   The Twins win the AL Central with a thrilling 6–5 win in 12 innings over the Tigers before 54,088 at the Metrodome, the largest regular season crowd ever at the facility. Detroit took a 3–0 lead in the top of the third inning, but the Twins came back with a run in the bottom of the third, another in the sixth on a solo homer by Jason Kubel, and two more in the seventh on a home run by Orlando Cabrera. Magglio Ordonez led off the eighth with a homer, however, to tie the score 4–4. The Tigers had runners on first and third with no one out in the ninth, but Joe Nathan pitched out of the jam. Detroit scored in the top of the tenth, but the Twins came back to tie the score in the bottom half with a triple from Michael Cuddyer on a drive badly misplayed by left fielder Ryan Raburn. Brendan Harris walked with one out and was taken out for pinch-runner Alexi Casilla. Matt Tolbert singled in Cuddyer to tie the score 5–5. Casilla advanced to third on the play. Nick Punto was up next and hit a line drive to left. Casilla tried to score after the catch by Raburn but was thrown out on a perfect throw. Casilla remained in the game as the DH. The Tigers had the bases loaded with one out in the 12th but failed to break the 5–5 tie. The Twins won in the bottom half. Carlos Gomez led off with a single and moved to second on a ground out. After an intentional walk, Casilla drove in Gomez with the winning run. The Twins became the first team in major league history to trail by three games with four to play and win a pennant.

> *Casilla had been a disappointment all year, batting just .202 with no home runs in 228 at-bats. He was sent to the minors twice for a lack of production and a failure to hustle.*

> *The Twins played the Yankees in the Division Series. Managed by Joe Girardi, the Yanks were 103–59 during the regular season, including a 7–0 mark against the Twins. Since 2002, Minnesota had a record of 3–22 in New York.*

October 7   The Twins take a 2–0 lead over the Yankees in the third inning of the first game of the Division Series, but wind up losing 7–2 in New York.

The series was televised nationally over TBS with Chip Caray and Ron Darling serving as the announcers.

October 8   In game two, the Twins suffer an excruciating 11-inning, 4–3 loss to the Yankees in New York. The Twins had a 3–1 lead heading into the ninth with Joe Nathan on the mound. The usually reliable Nathan gave up a lead-off single to Mark Teixeira followed by a home run to Alex Rodridguez to tie the score 3–3. In the 11th, Teixeira hit a walk-off homer off Jose Mijares for the Yankee victory.

October 10   The Yankees complete the sweep of the Twins with a 4–1 win before 54,735 at the Metrodome. Starter Carl Pavano took a 1–0 lead into the seventh before giving up two runs on homers by Alex Rodriguez and Jorge Posada. New York added two more runs in the ninth. It was the last baseball game ever played at the Metrodome. Outside, where the Twins will begin playing in 2010 at Target Field, it was 39 degrees.